CW01208541

Rule of the Commoner

The Dravida Munnetra Kazhagam (DMK) has been singular in heralding and establishing a firm regional polity among the Indian states after the Indian Union was inaugurated as a republic. Academic scholarship has often treated the DMK as a Tamil nationalist or ethno-nationalist formation without conceptual clarity or critical insight. *Rule of the Commoner* demonstrates, with persuasive evidence, that the DMK appealed to a federalist and not nationalist imagination. The DMK's combining of the non-Brahmin Dravidian identity and allegiance to the Tamil language led to a counter-hegemonic formation of the plebs and left populism.

Drawing on Ernesto Laclau, the book argues that the DMK achieved the construction of a people as Dravidian–Tamil, with Tamil being the empty signifier of the social whole and the Brahmin versus non-Brahmin divide functioning as the internal frontier leading to the formations of the political. It elaborates the conceptual scheme under the three rubrics of ideation, imagination and mobilization.

Rajan Kurai Krishnan teaches at the School of Culture and Creative Expressions at Dr B. R. Ambedkar University, Delhi. He has been part of a multi-sited project titled 'Caste Out of Development' in which he studied Christian Dalit situations. Apart from academic writing, he regularly publishes articles in Tamil on political theory, philosophy, global affairs, climate change and film theory.

Ravindran Sriramachandran teaches sociology and anthropology at Ashoka University, Sonepat. His research interests include semiotics, environment and development, South Asian politics, and film studies. He has published both in English and Tamil.

V. M. S. Subagunarajan is an independent researcher and has been long associated with theatre and literary movements in Tamil Nadu. He has written extensively on the Dravidian movement, especially on Periyar. His book on Periyar's lectures at caste association meetings is considered a landmark in Dravidian studies. He was also the editor of Tamil film journal *Kaatchipizhai* and culture studies journal *Akam/Puram*.

METAMORPHOSES OF THE POLITICAL: MULTIDISCIPLINARY APPROACHES

The Series is a publishing collaboration of Cambridge University Press with The M. S. Merian–R. Tagore International Centre of Advanced Studies 'Metamorphoses of the Political' (ICAS:MP). It seeks to publish new books that both expand and de-centre current perspectives on politics and the 'political' in the contemporary world. It examines, from a wide array of disciplinary and methodological approaches, how the 'political' has been conceptualized, articulated and transformed in specific arenas of contestation during the 'long twentieth century'. Though primarily located in India and the Global South, the Series seeks to interrogate and contribute to wider debates about global processes and politics. It is in this sense that the Series is imagined as one that is regionally focused but globally engaged, providing a context for interrogations of universalized theories of self, society and politics.

Series Editors:

- Niraja Gopal Jayal, King's College, London
- Shail Mayaram, formerly at Centre for the Study of Developing Societies, Delhi
- Samita Sen, University of Cambridge, Cambridge
- Awadhendra Sharan, Centre for the Study of Developing Societies, Delhi
- Sanjay Srivastava, SOAS, University of London, London
- Ravi Vasudevan, Centre for the Study of Developing Societies, Delhi
- Sebastian Vollmer, University of Göttingen, Germany

ICAS:MP is an Indo-German research collaboration of six Indian and German institutions funded by the German Federal Ministry of Education and Research (BMBF). It combines the benefits of an open, interdisciplinary forum for intellectual exchange with the advantages of a cutting-edge research centre. Located in New Delhi, ICAS:MP critically intervenes in global debates in the social sciences and humanities.

Books in the Series

1. *The Secret Life of an Other Indian Nationalism: Transitions from the Pax Britannica to the Pax Americana* – Shail Mayaram
2. *Properties of Rent: Community, Capital and Politics in Globalising Delhi* – Sushmita Pati
3. *Debt, Trust, and Reputation: Extra-legal Finance in Northern India* – Sebastian Schwecke
4. *Saffron Republic: Hindu Nationalism and State Power in India* – Edited by Thomas Blom Hansen and Srirupa Roy
5. *Women, Gender and Religious Nationalism* – Edited by Amrita Basu and Tanika Sarkar

Rule of the Commoner

DMK and the Formations of the Political in Tamil Nadu, 1949–1967

Rajan Kurai Krishnan
Ravindran Sriramachandran
V. M. S. Subagunarajan

Metamorphoses of the Political
Merian Tagore International Centre of Advanced Studies

CAMBRIDGE
UNIVERSITY PRESS

CAMBRIDGE
UNIVERSITY PRESS

University Printing House, Cambridge CB2 8BS, United Kingdom

One Liberty Plaza, 20th Floor, New York, NY 10006, USA

477 Williamstown Road, Port Melbourne, vic 3207, Australia

314 to 321, 3rd Floor, Plot No.3, Splendor Forum, Jasola District Centre, New Delhi 110025, India

103 Penang Road, #05–06/07, Visioncrest Commercial, Singapore 238467

Cambridge University Press is part of the University of Cambridge.

It furthers the University's mission by disseminating knowledge in the pursuit of education, learning and research at the highest international levels of excellence.

www.cambridge.org
Information on this title: www.cambridge.org/9781009197175

First published 2022

Printed in India by Avantika Printers Pvt. Ltd.

A catalogue record for this publication is available from the British Library

ISBN 978-1-009-19717-5 Hardback

to the millions of party cadres

the site of historical transformation

Great popular movements are not mere accidents of history. They are the outcome of the urge of the people for an assertion of the true nature of their corporate personality. Often humble and obscure at their source, they swell into oceanic proportions on their march towards their destination. Generally, these movements are noticed only when they reach their final crescendo. We then work back laboriously to trace their beginning.

—S. Vedaratnam, *A Plea for Understanding: A Reply to the Critics of the Dravidian Progressive Federation* (a pamphlet in English released during the first state conference of the DMK, 1951)

Contents

List of Illustrations ix
Acknowledgments xi
Note on Transliteration xv
Illustrations xvii

Introduction: Two Scenes of Departure 1

Ideation 17

1. Construction of "Dravidian–Tamil" People 19
2. The Uses of Language 40
3. Human Immanence 63
4. Left Populism 85

Imagination 103

5. The Play Is the Thing 105
6. Critical Hermeneutics 123
7. Counter-Narratives 141
8. Power of Fiction 159

Mobilization 175

9. The Grassroots 177
10. The Waves 201
11. The Eruption 217
12. The Climb 239

Conclusion: Formations of the Political 258

Bibliography 277
Index 288

Illustrations

C. N. Annadurai and Periyar E. V. Ramasamy xvii

Source: R. Kannan, "EVR and Anna: A Look Back at the Guru-Disciple Relationship over the Years," *News Minute*, September 15, 2020, https://www.thenewsminute.com/article/evr-and-anna-look-back-guru-disciple-relationship-overyears-133080 (accessed March 3, 2022).

C. N. Annadurai xvii

Source: M. Niaz Ahmed, *BBC Tamil*, September 15, 2018, https://www.bbc.com/tamil/india-45532503 (accessed March 3, 2022).

M. Karunanidhi and C. N. Annadurai xvii

Source: "Kalaignar Karunanidhi: The Dravidian Sun Has Set over Tamil Nadu," *HW News*, August 8, 2018, https://hwnews.in/news/opinion/kalaignar-karunanidhitamil-nadu/52279?infinitescroll=1 (accessed March 3, 2022).

Acknowledgments

All three of us grew up in Tamil Nadu in the 1960s and 1970s, separated by a few years, immersed in the social that was stirred and shaken by the Dravida Munnetra Kazhagam (DMK). V. M. S. Subagunarajan was already in school at the time of the anti-Hindi agitation in 1965. Rajan Kurai Krishnan and Ravindran Sriramachandran vividly remember the public outburst of grief on the demise of Annadurai in 1969. We gratefully recall our families, relatives and neighbors, classmates and teachers for filling our political commonsense. Interestingly, all three of us, though in different social and geographical locations, charted a similar path in our adult life; we studied English literature in our undergraduate and postgraduate programs, picked up our acquaintance with Tamil modernist literature first and literary circles identified as the little magazine subculture later that included film societies and experimental theater groups. Our critical sense, largely influenced by Marxist, neo-Marxist, and post-Marxist thoughts that wafted from the West, kept us reevaluating our lifelong engagement with Dravidian politics. We recall with gratitude the countless number of writers, activists, and thinkers in the adult phase of our life who immensely added to our reflective processes. We don't have the space even to produce a selective list here as we are indebted to so many. Rajan Kurai Krishnan and Ravindran Sriramachandran had a late, mid-life entry into the world of academics when they enrolled in the graduate program in the anthropology department at Columbia University, New York. The present work owes much to the rigorous conceptual training that was made possible by the program. While again the list of names to whom they are indebted would be too long, it is necessary to acknowledge a few for the crucial insights and mentorship they provided: Partha Chatterjee, Valentine Daniel, Nicholas Dirks, Rosalind Morris, David Scott, and Gayathri Spivak contributed to their education immensely. The companionship and conversations with Nauman Naqvi and Milind Wakankar were an indispensable part of learning.

There are a few signpost events that incrementally prepared us for writing this book. V. M. S. Subagunarajan organized a three-day seminar on the Dravidian movement at Madurai in 1997, which gathered many important scholars and thinkers writing in Tamil to reflect on the historical phenomenon. Though the papers presented could not be compiled, the event inaugurated a strong impetus for further research. Similarly, the five-day workshop on Tamil cinema organized by M. S. S. Pandian through MIDS, Chennai, in 1997 also honed our engagement with history, particularly through our encounter with the inimitable collection of material at RMRL, Chennai. Finally, we could organize an international seminar in Delhi to mark the historical signpost of 100 years of Dravidian movement and 50 years of Dravidian rule in January 2018, jointly sponsored by Ambedkar University, Delhi, and Ashoka University. V. M. S. Subagunarajan organized a Tamil version of the conference in Chennai later that year. We thank all the individuals who made organizing these events possible and scholars who participated in them. By then, the three of us were already into preparing to write the book.

Even though we had undertaken several exercises of field immersion on various occasions for research engagements, election time participant observation traveling across the state, we decided to plan some fieldwork anew for the book jointly and severally. Such invaluable exercises were made possible by the kindness and generosity of many individuals. We thank Ramasamy, Coimbatore; A. B. Shanmugasundaram, ex-MLA, Devanurpudur; Chinna K. R., Lakshmapuram; Rajasekhar, Pethampalayam; Sundarrajan, Pudukkottai; Marimuthu, Pudukkottai; Senthalai Gowthaman and friends, Sulur; Mannavan, Sulur; Sivasenathipathy and Karthikeya Sivasenathipathy, Kuttapalayam; Singaravel and Govindarajan, Coimbatore; Ezhirko Pamaran, Coimbatore; Maran, Trichy; Mahadhevan and Kuppulakshmi for their hospitality at Trichy; R. Govindaraj and N. Sriram, Trichy; Anush and Srinivisan of Ethir Veliyeedu, Pollachi; Manoharan, Mahalingam, and Prakash, Pollachi; S. N. Subramaniam, Raveendran alias Vamanan, M. Vijayaraghavan, Manimozhi, Pollachi; Rathinakumar, Madurai; R. Natarajan, Bodinayakanur; Muthu, Nagu, Vetri Arasan, Allinagaram, Theni; Mohan Kumaramangalam, Theni; M. Paranthaman, K. R. Ganesan, Periya Mayan, Mokkaraju, Gudalur; M. S. Prabhakar, K. M. Lawrence, Rayappanpatti; Hebeeb Mohammed alias Saketha, Uthamapalayam; Kumarandass, Sami Dravidamani, Arangasamy, Kaivalyam, Kalavathi, Puluvar Pazham Nee, Karaikudi; Kalai Kamal and Mohammed Safi, Cumbum; Nagappan, Thamparam; Ravi Karthikeyan, Villupuram; Srinivasan, Ira.Ilakkumanan, Ramanathan, Imayam Annamalai, Virudhachalam. We have included only the key interlocuters in all these locations, leaving out a host of others who had something to say in response to our queries.

The support of staff members in various archives was inestimable. We thank Vibha. S. at the *Hindu* archives, Kannan and Thangapandi at G. D. Naidu Memorial Library in Coimbatore, and Sundar Ganesan and his staff at Roja Muthiah Research Library, Chennai, for their assistance. Kamaraj Karuppannan and Praveen Chandrasekharan, both research scholars at Madras University, functioned as research assistants to gather and sift through the print literature connected to the DMK. We cannot thank them adequately for their involvement, enthusiasm, and insightful collaboration.

We thank Gilles Verniers and Mohit Kumar of Trivedi Centre for Political Data, Ashoka University, for their help with the map of Tamil Nadu. Ravindran Sriramachandran would like to thank Ashoka University for a semester of sabbatical and other institutional assistance provided. Rajan Kurai Krishnan would like to acknowledge Ambedkar University, Delhi, for the stimulating intellectual atmosphere and various forms of support provided.

We were encouraged by a set of senior scholars and activists in undertaking this project. We would like to particularly thank S. V. Rajadurai for being warm and generous in our meeting with him at the beginning of the project. His essay with rich personal anecdotes published in the Tamil journal *Uyir Ezhuthu* on the occasion of the demise of M. Karunanidhi was a real source of inspiration for us. We thank Thirunavukkarasu, whose three-volume history of the DMK and numerous other publications served as necessary resource material, for his words of encouragement. We thank Viduthalai Rajendran for his advice and counsel. Senthalai Gowthaman and friends stand as proud specimens of the values inspired by the DMK. It was inspiring to meet them. Our long-time interlocutors V. Arasu and Sundar Kali have contributed in ways too many that are hard to recall. We are grateful to the collegiality and encouragement provided by A. R. Venkatachalapathy, S. Anandhi, M. Vijayabaskar, and A. Kalaiyarasan at MIDS, Chennai, and for their sustained research engagement with Dravidian movement. We particularly thank S. Anandhi for many helpful leads, most particularly for pointing to the work of Charles Ryerson. We dearly miss M. S. S. Pandian whose name was metonymic with MIDS for us in the mid-1990s. In a sense, Pandian pioneered our research interests.

We drew much strength during the writing of the book from our interactions with Dr J. Jeyaranjan, whose enthusiasm for research and reflection was infectious. We were also stimulated by interactions with A. S. Panneerselvam, who was completing a biography of Karunanidhi simultaneously.

Partha Chatterjee, Arjun Appadurai, Milind Wakankar, and Santhosh Sadanandan were extremely generous to find the time to read the manuscript and offer their comments. Without their critical remarks, encouragement, and advice we would not have had the confidence to take the manuscript for publication. Salil Misra of Ambedkar University read the chapter on the "Uses of Language" and offered helpful comments. We cannot adequately express our indebtedness to all of them. However, we authors are responsible for all the shortfalls that may still remain.

We finally need to acknowledge the inner circle members of the authorial group. Srikumar Kannan is almost part of our team and always ready to help with any material required for consultation and bounce off ideas. We thank R. V. Bhavani and Srikumar for their generous hospitality whenever we gathered in Chennai. Our consultative meetings at Kodaikanal were enriched by the care and attention bestowed by Dr Suthanthira Devi. Likewise, Dr Suthanthira Devi, Rochana Mitra, Nandhini Venkatachalam, and Jayashree Venkatadurai alias Monikhaa took care of our base camps called home, allowing us to focus on research and writing. Without their constant support we could not have accomplished the task.

We cannot adequately thank Debjani Majumdar of ICAS for her interest and support in guiding us towards publication. We thank Qudsiya Ahmed and Anwesha Rana of Cambridge University Press for mentoring the process of publication with patience and attention. We thank Priya Das for the care with which the manuscript has been edited and many helpful suggestions. We are grateful to the two anonymous readers for their generous appreciation, comments, and provocations.

We still feel we may have left out someone. The feeling is not only generated by the inexhaustible list of empirical individuals who we encountered but also the overwhelming recognition of the abstract presence of millions of grassroots workers who made history and hence this book possible. In all humility imposed by the momentousness of the transformative process, we dedicate our tiny conceptual analysis of that history to them.

Note on Transliteration

A book of this kind inevitably has a considerable number of transliterated words. We have chosen to use diacritical marks for book titles, names of authors, and direct quotations, wherever needed. Diacritics are also used wherever there is a gloss of a particular word or where the word itself is used for its significance and wherever it is crucial to retain the metrical composition. Elsewhere we have kept them to a minimum so as not to distract the reader. We have followed the transliteration scheme of the Tamil lexicon published by Madras University.

C. N. Annadurai and Periyar E. V. Ramasamy

C. N. Annadurai

M. Karunanidhi and C. N. Annadurai

Introduction

Two Scenes of Departure

> I claim Sir, to come from a country, a part in India now, but which I think is of a different stock, not necessarily antagonistic. I belong to the Dravidian stock. I am proud to call myself a Dravidian. That does not mean that I am against a Bengali or a Maharashtrian or a Gujarati. As Robert Burns has stated, "A man is a man for all that." I say that I belong to the Dravidian stock and that is only because I consider that the Dravidians have got something concrete, something distinct, something different to offer to the nation at large. Therefore it is that we want self-determination.
>
> —C. N. Annadurai, in his maiden address to Rajya Sabha, April 1962[1]

It rained that evening, September 18, 1949, at Robinson Park, Royapuram, Chennai, where the public meeting to announce the founding of the Dravida Munnetra Kazhagam (DMK) was held. People never fail to mention the rain whenever the legendary first public meeting is remembered. The rain has many valences in a narrative; it is primarily a cathartic device that epitomizes the emotional surge of a moment. It is hard to imagine a greater moment of a mix of intense emotions for the people gathered there than that evening. They were sad, bitter, despondent, angry, hopeful, euphoric, and happy all at the same time. They had parted company with the father figure, the inimitable Periyar E. V. Ramasamy (1879–1973), who had adamantly refused to listen to their plea for negotiation over the future of the organization, the five-year-old Dravidar Kazhagam (DK), molded in 1944 from the fragments of the Justice Party, also known as the South Indian Liberal Federation (founded in 1917), and the vibrant group of activists gathered in the Self-Respect Movement nurtured by Periyar (since 1925).

Tear Drops

The public meeting at Robinson Park was the culmination of the deliberations held on September 17 and 18 in several rounds. The decision to launch a new party was first taken by a smaller group of those who were holding offices in the DK closeted in a room and was announced to all those gathered outside. The name of the party and a provisional design of the party flag were decided (the provisional design of the two-color flag, black strip on top and red strip at bottom, was later confirmed as the party flag). The general council, with 133 members, with several subcommittees were formed and office bearers were selected on the 17th. The modus operandi of the new party was discussed. Following these discussions, the public meeting was held on the 18th in the evening (Tirunāvukkaracu 2017, 325–332).

There were about twenty-six speakers on the dais to address the gathering of several thousand people, presided over by Pethampalayam Palanichamy. However, only about nine of them could actually speak due to the rain. The final declamation lasting one and a half hours, on the rationale on which the party was founded, setting out the goals and aspirations was delivered in the pouring rain by the General Secretary Conjeevaram Natarajan Annadurai, commonly referred to as Anna, to be pronounced with stress on the second syllable, *un-nnaa*. "Anna" is the kinship term for elder brother. Annadurai characterized himself as the foster son of Periyar Ramasamy who was often referred to as *thanthai*—the father. Hence, the kinship metaphor of the parting was obvious. The father had thrown the son out of the house and family, disinheriting him. The reason was, it appeared, sufficiently personal: the remarriage of the father, which Anna and the other foster sons objected to. Periyar Ramasamy, at the ripe old age of seventy years, married Maniammai, aged thirty, the daughter of a party worker who had become his personal attendant some years back. In the era in which the joint family structure was beginning to break up with sons setting up separate households, known as *thanikudithanam*, a word that signified familial discord, this moment of parting was suffused with anguish and sorrow, of having to leave the father figure. Since Annadurai listed the names of the party members who did not approve of the late marriage of Periyar as "tear drops" (*kanneer thuligal*) in the journal *Dravida Naadu*, Periyar started derisively referring to their new party, the DMK, as the "Tear Drop party" (Kanneer Thuli Katchi).

The family allegory and the emotional underpinnings should not be allowed to cloud our critical appreciation of the nature of the political departure. There can be no doubt that the marriage precipitated the issue. We need to basically consider why a personal event like the leader's remarriage, however unseemly in terms of the age gap between the partners might be, should cause such devoted followers to rebel. In personal terms, Periyar did reason out the marriage well; he felt that marriage was the most honorable form of relationship that would recognize the intimacy needed for nursing him placed on the loving attendant on a day-to-day basis. The choice could have been regarded as less scandalous than the Brahmacharya experiments of Gandhi a couple of years before, where physical intimacy without sexual desire was being forged. As Periyar had consistently opposed the ascetic image, it was only natural for him to disambiguate intimacy as conjugal through a marriage, even if the purpose was not a conjugal relationship. This should hardly have been a concern for Annadurai and his followers. What really mattered, however, was Periyar's claim that he resorted to marriage also in order to find a trustworthy successor to manage the affairs of the organization or movement. Periyar had formed a trust combining his personal wealth and the funds raised for the organization, which he thought would sustain the movement. It is in terms of access to this trust-held property that Periyar claimed to seek a trustworthy successor. This, Annadurai and his followers felt, was a deliberate insult. While Periyar's lack of trust in Annadurai, the most obvious political successor, cast personal aspersions on the latter, again, this is more a political discord than anything actually personal.

There had been several moments when differences between Annadurai and Periyar had surfaced since 1944, the most widely known among them being the dispute over the organizational response to Indian independence. Periyar announced that the Independence Day, August 15, 1947, was to be treated as a day of mourning—*thukka nal*—as it affirmed north Indian suzerainty over south India, also known as the Dravidian country. Annadurai publicly disagreed, calling for celebrations to mark the end of colonial rule.[2] While instances such as these were certainly indicative, the actual problem was far deeper in terms of how political activity was conceived by them, to which we will return to several times in the course of our reflections. However, we need to take a brief note, at the outset, of what was the common Dravidian formation of the political and how Periyar and Annadurai differed in their modus operandi. What was the common or shared political aim of the Dravidianists was to fight Brahmin, casteist hegemony to instill political aspiration in those disempowered by the practices of caste hierarchy. It was feared that such a Brahminic–Hindu hegemony would be strengthened through the rule of the nationalist power elite combining a Sanskritic past and the Anglicized present.[3] The power elite, it was widely felt, would best serve the interests of the north, as Hindi was being Sanskritized to make for the national language on a majoritarian premise. In the period of anti-colonial struggle, the Congress had sufficiently manifested such tendencies to consolidate a power elite that perhaps lead the subaltern to realize the need for strengthening the political through the languages of India, which in the case of Tamil Nadu, then part of the Madras Presidency, was Tamil. The language of the people was the necessary site of development of the political. These processes crystallized in the demand for Dravida Nadu, an independent Dravidian republic. We will consistently translate the Tamil phrase "Dravida Nadu" as Dravidian republic and not as Dravidian nation, the import of which will become clearer as we proceed.[4] While this shared understanding was the bedrock of the political, Periyar was focused on promoting a political culture of agonism as a way of strengthening the republican spirit, the basis of a new political order. Annadurai, however, was intent on constructing a people aspiring for democratic self-governance. The crucial manifestation of this difference is with regard to the formalization of organizational structure and functioning, possible electoral participation, and taking up governance. Periyar preferred to remain a force outside of any ruling formation and electoral fray so that there was no constraint placed on the propagation of critical and agonistic formulations by the need for evolving consensus. Annadurai felt that without building consensus and capacity for democratic self-governance through which political power could be harnessed, a mere capacity for agonistic thinking would not help in contesting the power consolidation at the national level by the nationalist elite with the deeply entrenched shades of Brahmin hegemony. The parallel this difference between Periyar and Annadurai holds with the difference between Gandhi and Nehru is unmistakable in their variated approach towards social transformation and governance. Gandhi and Periyar aspired to work for political awakening, both of them self-styled, popular pedagogues with a historical mission who were never keen on or even abhorred offices. While Gandhi strategically maintained an "official" distance from the Indian National Congress as a political party, Periyar had no interest in building a political party as an organization, which Annadurai had already begun to undertake with the formation of DK in marked contrast to Periyar's style of functioning as a tenuously networked movement.

We should conclude by noting that though the parting was inevitable, Annadurai could hardly match Periyar in terms of resources, political experience, clout, and the support of the wealthy. The 133 members of the first general council of the DMK, formed on that day prior to the rain-drenched meeting in the evening, were all mostly from a lower-middle-class background with no significant property holdings to speak of. Furthermore, they were mostly young, who could treat the forty-year-old Annadurai as an elder brother. For example, Karunanidhi, who was to become the fulcrum of political mobilization and subsequently the leader of the party succeeding Annadurai, was only twenty-five years old; E. V. K. Sampath, who would be the agent of a major split in 1961, was only twenty-three; Nedunchezhian, who was billed as an ideologue, was twenty-nine, and so on. During the course of the day of founding the party, reference to paucity of funds came up several times. Annadurai could only bank on his skills for propagation. He and his followers appear to have felt, however vaguely, that the winds of history would set them sail.

Ocean of Sorrow

Almost twenty years later, on February 3, 1969, the whole state of Tamil Nadu came to a standstill. In fact, while normal life came to a halt, there was an unprecedented surge of masses in the magnitude of several millions towards Madras. Every moving vehicle was loaded with people filled with grief, who were going to participate in the funeral procession of their leader, Annadurai. The cry "Anna ..." rented the air everywhere. The upsurge was such that it could be claimed that a staggering number of 15 million people attended the funeral, though estimates varied. The term "massive" manifested its full meaning. The entire phenomenon was spontaneous, as testified by several eyewitnesses. Many died on the way, while many others were grievously hurt. Nothing could contain the bursting of welling emotions. It was indeed an ocean of sorrow (*thuyarak kadal*).[5] The DMK had come to power with a thumping majority exactly two years before, in 1967, when Annadurai assumed the office of chief minister. His premature death at the age of sixty just two years after taking the DMK to power grieved the whole state beyond measure. The spontaneous mass gathering confirmed what election results announced two years earlier: *a* people, Tamils as Dravidians, *had* been constructed as the work of formation of the political executed by the DMK.

Earlier, at the moment of their electoral victory, Annadurai and other leaders of the DMK surprised everyone by going to Trichy, 200 kilometers away from Madras, the capital city, to meet the long-estranged Periyar before assuming office. The old man was overwhelmed; he had opposed the DMK the whole of eighteen years, never sparing a moment to take a jibe at the "tear drops." He campaigned for the Congress and its leader Kamaraj in the elections. But Annadurai and the DMK maintained their claim that Periyar was indeed their estranged leader by leaving the position of the president of the party unoccupied for him to grace whenever he chose. Hence, they went to dedicate the electoral victory to him, to seek his endorsement, before assuming office. For the next final six years of his life, Periyar made good on his estrangement from the party by his steadfast support to the DMK rule. He of course had many reasons to do so. To begin with, the entire ministry took an oath swearing on their conscience and not on the divine, allegedly for the first time anywhere in India. Periyar beamed with pride and all acrimony of intervening years was forgotten. When Annadurai died soon after, Periyar mourned the premature demise of his foster son.

The DMK had accomplished many things in the elections apart from just coming to power. They were in alliance with both the liberal and left extremes of the political spectrum. The Swatantra Party headed by C. Rajagopalachari (1878–1972), better known as Rajaji, and the Communist Party of India (Marxist), or CPI(M), headed by P. Ramamurthy (1808–1987) in the state were aligned with the DMK.[6] Rajaji had many a historical role to play as the friend and foe of the Dravidian formations. It was he who inducted Periyar into the Congress in 1919; he provided causes for the grist of political opposition through imposition of Hindi in schools in 1938 as the premier of the Madras Presidency under dyarchy, and a family-centered vocational stream in primary education in 1953 as chief minister of Madras State in free India. He had finally broken his ties with the Indian National Congress in 1956, launching the Swatantra Party, campaigning for a free market economy in opposition to the socialist creed of Nehru. But neither he nor the CPI(M) had any problem in becoming minor partners in the alliance led by the DMK, along with parties like the Praja Socialist Party. The DMK lead the coalition, contesting in 174 seats and winning 137 of them. The Swatantra Party contested 27, winning 20; the CPI(M) won 11 out of 22 contested; the Praja Socialist Party of Jayaprakash Narayan and J. B. Kriplani won all 4 out of 4 contested; the Indian Union Muslim League won 3 out of 3; the Sanghata Socialist Party 2 out of 3, and the DMK-backed independents won 2 out of 2 seats. The coalition could win 179 seats in the 234-member assembly, conceding only 51 seats to the Indian National Congress, which contested in 232 constituencies all by itself. The broad electoral alliance against the Congress, which the DMK forged, and the massive funeral procession of Anna clearly demonstrated that the DMK had managed to evolve a broad consensus on the nature of political goals in the state which it represented.

The assumption of power by the DMK was not just a one-time electoral victory. The Indian National Congress has never managed to come to power in the state after that. Half a century later, it appears more unlikely than ever that a national party can come to power in Tamil Nadu. It can be said that in a federal vision, Tamils have become a self-governing component of the Indian nation. The power sharing between the state and the Union government is still a fraught question with the Center accumulating powers all through the decades. The fact that the DMK and other regional parties often become part of the coalition government at the Center does not result in decentralization of powers, which allows for the countervailing tendency of homogeneous and centralized nationalist power consolidation by the Hindutva forces. However, the fact that the political is being increasingly localized in the states betokens the eventual need for the rise of the truly federal governance of the nation. The DMK is the exemplar for the nation in locating the post-independent political history in the state of Tamil Nadu.

The eighteen years between 1949, in which the DMK was founded, and 1967, in which the DMK came to power in the state, present a unique history of formation of the political in which the political mobilization and propagation of political ideas by the DMK played a pivotal role. The intent of the book is to provide a synoptic overview of the key aspects of this history.

The DMK and History

We do not intend to write the empirical history of the DMK, though it provides the necessary template for our conceptual analyses. We are rather interested in posing the question of what the political process initiated by the DMK in the eighteen years of our study means for our understanding of history as such. Is construction of a people a historical process if they do not aspire for or achieve a sovereign nation state? Is "becoming sovereign" the only axis of history? Can "becoming a people" replace "becoming sovereign" as the axis of history? We posit that this opens up the question of the distinction between self-governance and sovereignty. Since freedom is conceptually associated with sovereignty, constructing a people without making them a sovereign nation state, as the uncritical common sense feels and historiography succumbs to agree, appears to make their history incomplete, a sort of miscarriage.[7] We believe "becoming a people" as an axis of history relates to immanent transformation of the social through infusion of the political, a form of content of the political, while "becoming sovereign" as an axis of history relates to transcendental claims of a collective, a form of expression of the political. The distinction we make between "becoming a people" and "becoming sovereign", "immanence" and "transcendental," as well as between "form of content" and "form of expression" calls for elaboration, which we will undertake iteratively throughout the book. However, it might still be useful to offer an outline of our conceptual scheme at the outset. We take political to mean, as Schmitt (2008) suggested, "pure" friend–enemy antagonisms emanating from the social. In populist reason, as theorized by Laclau (2005), these antagonisms transcend the social antagonisms predefined in the order of the social through forging a transcendental schema of internal frontier contextually inscribed between the segment standing in for plebs and the segment standing in for power elite (non-Brahmin vs Brahmin in the case of the DMK). This internal frontier will be notional and not rigidly identarian since the frontier inscribed is internal to the imaginary whole proposed by the plebeian aspiration, which also posits an empty signifier (Tamil in the case of the DMK). The positing of a putative unity by the plebeian aspiration through the empty signifier constructs a people; this will retain democratic and socialist potential only when accompanied by the inscription of internal frontier alongside, since it is the plebs who imagine the whole, which will mobilize and realign the socially nuclear friend–enemy dyads into political formations. The shifting electoral alliances formed by various political parties and outfits will offer a good demonstration of what we suggest here. We call such formation of the political to take place on the axis of "re-formation" and "becoming a people." The DMK, in our analysis, provides a good example for this process of forging left populism. In contrast, if the internal frontier is de-emphasized by hegemonic groups in favor of a totalizing empty signifier through locating the enemy "externally" in the axis of "becoming sovereign," the result would be a fascist consolidation through popular sovereignty. The politics of Hindutva offers a ready example for such a process. Even as both processes could be incomplete, as captured in the insightful title of Partha Chatterjee's second book on Indian nationalism, *Nation and Its Fragments*, we would urge that the former process of becoming a people be accorded greater attention, loosening the fixation with the latter, with the materialization of sovereign nation state as the only locus of history.

We contend that there is a serious disciplinary problem in taking India, the name of the nation-state, as the location of history. The singular historiographic construction of India impedes the federal imagination of the nation. It will not be wrong to say that the major political problem of contemporary India is such a historiographic practice. The understanding of the political process initiated by the founding of the DMK, its organizational growth, mobilization of popular support, and the electoral victory depends much on our appreciation of historical unfolding of formations of the political. We find the existing literature on the political party in English language lacking in that respect due both to traditions of historiography and historical methods employed or, as it often happened, the additional buttress through anthropological accounts of the "ethnic" politics as against the politics of the imagined cosmopolis of the nation.

The first conceptual problem is the distinction made between the nation and its region. Whatever processes that constitute the politics of the nation and its state formation is taken as historical. Whatever processes that constitute politics in the region is considered external or at best supplementary to the history of the nation. Such an approach becomes pre-selective in so far only such of the elite formations that have national provenance and circulation will be deemed to be part of history. We find this attitude making a crippling impact on the literature on post-colonial political history of India. We can find many books on Indian politics where states like Tamil Nadu are hardly paid any attention to or given cursory attention. Those who write on Tamil Nadu tend to see it as a deviation from the mainstream of national history. Terms such as "ethnic" as descriptive appellate to the so-called regional identity deny historical validity to the construction of the people as formation of the political.

The second conceptual problem is understanding the role of language. A term like "vernacular" inaugurates the problem here. What does it mean to call Tamil a vernacular language? What distinction is introduced by such an adjective? Tamil is certainly one of the oldest languages of the world; it is also a classical language in terms of possessing literary texts of antiquity, many parts of which can still be read contemporaneously without the aid of lexicons and commentaries. It is a language spoken by about 800 million people in Tamil Nadu. In writing the history of Tamil-speaking people, if one refers to Tamil language sources, it is to be deemed as referring to vernacular language sources, whereas English-language sources are not deemed as vernacular sources. It is unclear what kind of hierarchy is assumed between "vernacular" and "non-vernacular" sources, but it can be shown that many of the works on Dravidian movement written by Euro-American scholars have not found it necessary to access vernacular language sources, that is, what is available in Tamil language, since the business of scholarship and the business of the lay people are known to be conducted in two different languages: that of the court on the one hand and that of the people on the other hand. Hence, we suspect that efforts to write about a political party such as the DMK suffer from a certain lack of universal attributes which get marked by qualifiers such as regional and vernacular. Such a lack is in marked contrast to the self-perception of the DMK, which assigned itself the task of mobilizing Tamil people to participate in the world historical processes mankind was going through as they were unfolding in most nations after the Second World War, in realizing democratic self-governance marked by liberty and equality, in short, human emancipation. The DMK, in the footsteps of the previous iterations of Dravidianism, the Justice Party, the Self-Respect Movement, and the DK, obviously felt that the Indian National Congress, which was controlled by Hindi-speaking north Indians or Brahmins, was not capable of being agents of such history since the Congress cannot lay claim to the cultural historical distinction of Tamil people, which the party would erase in favor of a composite Indian identity. What we hope to narrate is how the DMK applied itself to such a historical task that it had undertaken to construct a people towards democratic self-governance.

Such a task for the DMK was set by history through the founding of the Indian republic and the inception of electoral democracy with universal adult franchise. It was like a blank cheque issued by history to the people that needed to be encashed by a fast-tracked spread of political awareness and the desire for empowerment in terms of individual freedom which was enshrined in the secret ballot. The vast swathe of the people was still locked in agrarian hinterlands in various kinds of bondage to landlords; the small towns and urban centers were still being formed with nascent industries sprouting here and there. The literacy rate among the people was about 20 percent, which meant that the people were still largely uneducated about the kind of political modernity they had been ushered into.

The Indian National Congress trained in anti-colonial nationalist discourse could not immediately grasp and come to terms with the internal contradictions that should animate the political in the free country. The Communist Party was well aware of the inequal power structures but, constrained by the doctrine of class antagonism leading to class essentialism, could not find ways of constructing a people as a necessary process for the formation of the political through electoral democracy in Tamil Nadu. This has been the problem of the Communist Party in most parts of the country, with the exception of Kerala, the state adjacent to Tamil Nadu, and later West Bengal. We propose that the DMK stepped into the fissure where it could forge a discourse of emancipation that could become popular and allow for people to be politicized in the process of metaphoric encashment of the blank cheque issued by history. What we seek to do through an account of such unfolding of history in Tamil Nadu via the formation of the political lead by the DMK is also to help understand what preceded half a century of Dravidian rule in the state, its achievements, and shortcomings. We are aware that any critical evaluation of the period we study is now clouded by the half-a-century rule of the Dravidian parties and many discontents, actual and perceived, in its wake. This requires that we remark on what we deem to be certain uncritical dispositions about the party and also certain frames of polemical and critical engagements. Our purpose is not to take sides in the polemics or refute critical engagements. We state them as pointers to future reflections on the basis of a new framework of analysis we develop, which aspires to moderate such uncritical dispositions and polemical frameworks. The analysis rests on a critical appreciation of the party as an exemplar of populist mobilization that has produced a historical outcome that we describe as the twin enterprise of "construction of a people" and "formations of the political" as outlined above. It is our surmise that the conjoining of two enterprises has allowed for continued rearticulations of injuries suffered by various constituencies within a well-energized democratic contestatory field.

Uncritical Dispositions

There is a mute pervasive sense of opprobrium, which sometimes turns vocal, in English-language writing and also elite writing in Tamil in explaining how a political party started by people of inadequate financial means and social status, the commoners or *samanyargal,* could defeat the Indian National Congress of pan-Indian provenance, backed by the rich and mighty, in the electoral turf in such a short span of time, eighteen years to count. There are many significant reasons for such an opprobrium. First of all, the DMK's opposition to pan-Indian nationalism was perceived to be ill-informed, since the nationalist elite had already posited the unified civilizational history of India, however plural it might be, informed by Brahminic Hinduism as its political unconscious. It was feared that to speak of a distinct Dravidian–Tamil cultural history made for a divisive politics, often denounced as fissiparous tendency, that would weaken the new nation that had heroically thrown off the colonial yoke. Further, it was feared a mobilization based on caste, particularly non-Brahmin, would ruin governance with the ascent of the "uneducated" and "uncultured" to ruling positions. We will be citing some such expressions of uncritical dispositions in the chapters that follow.

Second, while the DMK adopted rhetorical strategies that would appeal to the masses, the same were seen by the elite as empty of true political content, banking merely on affective potential and emotional appeal, often stooping to "rabble-rousing" tendencies. The alliterative and rhyming phrases and sentences coined by the DMK speakers and their attention to sound patterns in language earned them much criticism for lacking in real political content. Such a word play, *varthai jalam,* was accused of both conceit and deceit.

Third, such perceptions were further aided by the use of theater by the DMK leaders to popularize their ideas. They wrote plays and acted in them at every party conference. These were seen to be the means of seduction of the masses. Further, the DMK leaders famously got involved in the film world. Popular Tamil cinema was considered to be low-brow entertainment aimed at uneducated lower classes. The DMK's involvement in the medium added immensely to the opprobrium. All these elements added together combined to produce a perception of inauthenticity to the political awareness that the DMK claimed to build.

This is not to say that there was no appreciation of the political will and sagacity of the party. All that could be said positively for the political work of the party was overshadowed by the sense of inauthenticity ascribed to its methods, which still hampers a gainful evaluation of the democratic process.

Polemical Frames and Critical Perceptions

One of the enduring criticisms of the party and a ready-to-hand polemic relates to its non-adherence to Marxist thought. The DMK is seen to have assigned a misguided priority to caste inequality, which distracted the party from focusing on class contradiction and class-based mobilization. The DMK did not manage to represent the interests of the working class or economically weaker sections; its brand of populist politics has clouded and impeded the growth of class consciousness and the understanding of class contradiction as the fulcrum of history. This has made the party compromise with the interests of the nascent-indigenous and the global capitalist class and the exploitative relationships of production. This strand of critical perception aligns well with the elite misconception that the party fashioned a rhetoric that is empty of authentic political discourse and historically grounded meaning. This is not much unlike the criticism the Indian National Congress has faced from the same vantage point; we find the work of Shashi Joshi and Bhagwan Josh, *Struggle for Hegemony in India*,[9] very relevant in this context. One familiar question in this polemic has been whether a democratic revolution should precede the formation of socialist state and if so, what exactly is the means of achieving that. For our own work, we have found the exposition on the political society by Partha Chatterjee in *The Politics of the Governed* (2006) and the treatise on populist reason by Ernesto Laclau in his work *On Populist Reason* (2005) crucial to developing a more nuanced paradigm for understanding the possibilities opened up by the electoral democracy in India with universal adult franchise.

The second and more virulent critical perception and a highly charged polemic is that of the various strands of Tamil nationalists particularly within Tamil Nadu. Their charge is that the party betrayed the cause of sovereign Tamil nation by first displacing it to the impossible goal of a Dravidian republic known as Dravida Nadu spread over all of South India, later giving up even that demand and subsequently aligning actively with the Union government, going to the extent of being part of coalition governments at the Center. This charge has been exacerbated by the genocidal end to the civil war in the neighboring island nation of Sri Lanka in 2009, where the Tamil-speaking minority in the northern and eastern part of the island sought an independent Tamil Eelam for which an armed struggle was waged for nearly three decades. The DMK has been both criticized for its support to the struggle or even accused of abetting terrorism by some and at the same time for its alleged indifference to and betrayal of the Eelam struggle by others. This critical perception is now a major impediment to the appreciation of the political process initiated by the DMK in the period of our study, which is from 1949 to 1967. One particular condensation of this criticism is the charge of willful catachresis deployed by the party in calling the possible Tamil nation Dravidian. This is captured by the famous adage *tirāviṭattāl vīḻntōm* (we fell because of Dravidianism) (Guna 2019). In the gloss that we have developed, we find that such dual coding for the construction of the people as both Dravidian and Tamil has helped the political process to escape the clutches of obsession with sovereignty, a banal preoccupation with personal identity, allowing a healthy focus on self-governance, a political option that has scarcely invited attention and appreciation. There has been no serious analysis of the actual benefits, possibilities, and limits of being a sovereign nation-state in the age of the global capital, which, as argued by Hardt and Negri, has inaugurated a new form of "empire," which is global and immanent.[10] If the substantial meaning of nation-state is self-governance, sovereignty becomes a costly and ungainly supplement, a form of expression divorced from the form of content which is the actual formation of the political that we will return to discuss in the conclusion.

The third critical perception, an increasingly vibrant field of polemic, is the view that the DMK mobilization and the rule of the Dravidian parties served only the interests of the backward castes vis-à-vis Brahmins or forward castes and not that of Dalits, also known as Scheduled Castes and Tribes. This perspective posits a three-tier social hierarchy of "upper castes," "middle castes," and "Dalits" and seeks to argue that the Dravidian movement, in all its iterations—the Justice Party, Self-Respect Movement, DK, DMK and All India Anna DMK (AIADMK)—helped the so-called "middle castes" to consolidate into power bastions excluding Dalits. A more extreme version of this criticism goes to the extent of claiming that this has exacerbated the suppression of Dalits, while a moderate version claims that the Dalits have been excluded from the process of political emancipation since the Brahmin-centric approach to the caste question has allowed for the widespread discrimination against Dalits by the land-owning backward castes to escape the historical and discursive scanner. While such a criticism is necessary to highlight the continued caste oppression widely faced by Dalit communities, there is a conceptual risk in isolating the DMK mobilization and its ideational force as primarily responsible for this. This criticism assumes, rather arbitrarily, that the processes of social transformation in their entirety is controlled and driven by the political processes instead of seeing the formation of the political as a mitigating influence on the violent processes of capital accumulation that exacerbate inequal power structures. At an empirical level, it remains a challenge to fully evaluate the participation of Dalits in the DMK mobilization, since no elaborate research into actual processes of mobilization, as permeation of the social with the political, have been conducted so far even as we can readily take note of many activists and leaders of the party hailing from Dalit communities; at the conceptual level, one should not fail to distinguish between the struggle against Brahminic and casteist hegemony in the political sphere and the actual dynamics of social transformation, which is premised on the transition from agrarian to capitalist economy. While we recognize Chatterjee's concern about populism succumbing to the passive revolution of capital, we seek to remain open to the historical possibilities of the formations of the political, while continuing to forge a critical lens, which we will discuss in the conclusion.[11]

Three Aspects of the Mobilization by the DMK

Given such a background, we propose to approach the eighteen years of political mobilization by the DMK in post-Independence India under three rubrics. In the first section, we will discuss what we call ideation; we intend to carefully sift through the political discourse and rhetoric of the party to glean what kinds of political ideations it conceived and propagated. We prefer the term ideation to ideology, to indicate the diffuse spirit of egalitarianism and democratic self-governance that the party articulated. There are four distinct aspects to the ideation: construction of a people as Dravidian–Tamil, the resistance to Hindi imposition through the steadfast articulation of allegiance to Tamil language, a view of human immanence that challenged Brahminical Hinduism, and finally a strong orientation to socialist goals and an awareness of state–capital nexus or the ideological ground of economy.

The second rubric is the domain of imagination. The leaders wrote and produced plays that articulated the ideational underpinnings of the party. It also famously made critical and oppositional readings of Brahminical Puranic texts. It promoted counter-narratives to Puranic stories. Finally, many leaders of the party wrote fictional narratives that created the social and historical worlding in which the ideational moorings of the party were exemplified. The party made extensive use of Tamil classical literature to sketch the glorious Tamil past to serve as the bedrock of imagination. The involvement of the party in the film world is but an extension of all these, which, being a widely known and an overrated phenomenon, we have chosen to exclude from our narration in this book except for occasional references. It deserves a separate book-length critical assessment.[12]

The third rubric is the most crucial account of mobilization. The party was built meticulously as a grassroots organization forming innumerous branches and district committees. Such a party organization was kept fully engaged through various activities, struggles, and mobilizational programs ably supported by a slew of magazines and print literature. The opposition to Hindi galvanized the growth of the party alongside the estrangement of the people from the Congress. The electoral participation of the party was envisaged early on for which the party prepared itself in a systematic manner. Hence this section will focus on four major dimensions: the building of party organization, protests and propaganda activities, the anti-Hindi agitation of 1965, and finally the history of electoral participation and eventual ascension to power in 1967.

It is through synoptic and selective narrations in these three rubrics that we hope to capture what we consider as the historical unfolding of the construction of a people as Dravidian–Tamil through participation in electoral democracy by the political party, the DMK, under the leadership of C. N. Annadurai between the years 1949–1967. What the party demonstrated in the process is that grassroots mobilization and channeling of subaltern energy could lead to a lasting formation of the political that would help democracy to prioritize the welfare of the people against the inexorable propulsion of capital accumulation, ensuring some measures of redistribution through governance.[13] A fair assessment of the social indicators of economic development of the state in comparison to many other parts of India bear testimony to the main characteristic of the rule of Dravidian political formations in the last fifty years, which was enabled by the mobilization that preceded it in the period of our study when the party famously called its aspiration as the rule of the commoner, *saamaniyarkalin aatchi*.

Notes

1. Annadurai (1975, 8).
2. For a detailed account of the debate, please see Es.Vi.Rājaturai (1998b). The book contains, apart from the full statements of Periyar and Annadurai, an intervention by an activist of the Self-Respect Movement and the Justice Party, Kesari alias Thirumalaisami, and a long editorial note by S. V. Rajadurai, which proposes that this discord reveals the fundamental reason for the split between Annadurai and Periyar. For more on Periyar's disposition towards Indian independence, also see Es.Vi.Rājaturai (1998a).
3. For a good example of what we mean here, please see a discussion of the life of P. S. Sivaswamy Iyer (1864–1946) in Pandian (2002).
4. Our use of the expression "Dravidian Republic" to characterize the demand for Dravida Nadu in Tamil is because "Nadu" does not translate as *desam* or *desh*, which is used as equivalent to nation. "Nadu" is equivalent to the expression "country." There is no mention of Dravidian nation in the discourse of the party. Written in English, the pamphlet of S. Vedaratnam, published during the first state conference of the DMK in 1951, calls it a Dravidian state. This, however, will create ambiguity with the present usage of the term "state" to refer to regional governments in India, of which Tamil Nadu is one. Hence, we would resort to the expression "Dravidian Republic" as the goal of the DMK, which it coined as "Dravida Nadu" in Tamil.
5. Please see Ramakrishnan (2018) for a later day recapitulation of the event. Also see Guinness World Records (n.d.).

6. It should be noted that both Rajaji and P. Ramamurthy were Brahmins. Those who subscribe to hearsays of "Brahmin-hatred" abetted by the DMK or have concerns over nurturing of ressentiment need to think of the implications of such alliances and political formations.
7. In pursuing a similar question, Prasenjit Duara sees history and history writing as a series of multiple, often conflicting narratives produced simultaneously at national, local, and transnational levels. Focusing primarily on China and including discussion of India, Duara argues that many historians of post-colonial nation-states have adopted a linear, evolutionary history of the Enlightenment–colonial model. As a result, they have written repressive, exclusionary, and incomplete histories. See Duara (1997).
8. For example, Robert L. Hardgrave's book *The Dravidian Movement* does not contain a single Tamil language source in its bibliography. See Hardgrave (1965). Obviously, there are a few exceptions to this, but even those scholars who have made use of Tamil sources have used them in an extremely limited way and their reading of these texts leaves much to be desired.
9. *Struggle for Hegemony in India* is the common title of the three volumes on the history of Indian communists written by Shashi Joshi and Bhagwan Josh. It elaborately documents how the nascent communist movement failed to come to terms with the historical relevance of the mass movement lead by the Congress. They basically assert that hegemonic politics cannot be practiced by a class party. See Joshi and Josh (2011).
10. Even as one may not agree to the whole set of propositions in their work, Michael Hardt and Antonio Negri do show that the configurations of sovereignty have changed. See Hardt and Negri (2016).
11. For a reflective and cautionary note on the claims of popular sovereignty and populism, see Chatterjee (2020).
12. For an outline of the argument relating to the role of film-making practices in the formations of the political, see Krishnan (2004).
13. The recent publication of *The Dravidian Model: Interpreting the Political Economy of Tamil Nadu* (Kalaiyarasan and Vijayabaskar 2021) provides ample and elaborate testimony to the beneficial effects of Dravidian rule since 1967 almost in tandem with the conceptual scheme we develop here on the construction of the people and formations of the political.

IDEATION

1 Construction of "Dravidian–Tamil" People

... the political operation par excellence is always going to be the construction of a "people."

—Ernesto Laclau, *On Populist Reason*

The political vigor and success of the Dravida Munnetra Kazhagam (DMK), a particular political vehicle of the diffuse ideation of Dravidianism, rests on the metaphoric hyphen that both brings together and separates the twin political identities of Dravidian and Tamil. The Dravidian aspiration was anchored in the demand for an independent, sovereign, socialist south Indian federation of states that the party declared as its goal at the moment of its inception in 1949 and held until 1963, when it was officially given up due to a constitutional amendment by the Indian government that proscribed "secessionism."[1] Such a political aspiration was made possible by Tamil language as the source of the cultural distinction, which enabled the DMK to articulate the demand for a Dravidian republic. Since the party primarily operated within the precincts of the linguistic state of Tamil Nadu, its goal to form a federation of the four south Indian linguistic states without such an aspiration being expressed by political organizations in the other states made it a case of a part standing for the whole. While critics have called it a weakness, detractors a joke, and scholars have found it difficult to parse, we seek to posit it as the gift of history that enabled the party to succeed so well in the basic act of the construction of a people through the formation of the political. We argue that the anchorage of Dravidian identity in the apparently distant demand for a south Indian republic instead of a nation of Tamil-speaking people helped to lay emphasis on the internal antagonism between Brahminical social order and the underprivileged plebeian stock who sought empowerment. Since much of our analysis of the various attributes of the political mobilization of the party rests on this basic hypothesis, we would like to pay close attention to this unique combination of the two identities, Dravidian and Tamil, with a hyphen of simultaneous conjunction and separation.

We also need to spell out how this pairing of Dravidian and Tamil was key to the processes we call "construction of a people" and the "formations of the political." If constructing a people can be taken as demographic delimitation of the site of the political, the formation of the political as the accompanying act needs to set the stage for the play of agonism that Laclau calls internal frontier. Our understanding draws extensively from the exposition of populist reason by Laclau. In his scheme, the internal structuration of the people, the inbuilt antagonism of the aggrieved constituencies with the forces of domination and hegemony produces an equivalential chain of demands that results in defining an internal frontier, which, in the case of the DMK, was signified by the Brahmin–non-Brahmin or Aryan–Dravidian divide. Hence, the term "Dravidian" emphasizes the internal frontier. However, in the formulation of Laclau, populism has to posit a mythical totality in which the part, plebs, stand for the whole, the Populus. Hence, while the concept, the rule of the commoner or plebs, is signified by the term "Dravidian," the name of the mythical whole, the empty signifier, and the name of the people is Tamil.[2]

Interestingly, in the case of populism of the DMK, the efficacy of the Dravidian–Tamil pair is that both can become the subset of the other as it will become evident through this chapter.

Tamil, as a language, can be a subset of Dravidian languages, while Dravidian as a racial entity can be a subset of Tamil people too, since "Aryan" Brahmins not only speak Tamil but have also deeply imbued the language with Brahminic ideas. This goes a long way in preserving the constitutive heterogeneity through the combined operation of the floating signifier that defines a people and the shifting frontier that contingently defines the political, as elaborated by Laclau. While we just flag this critical assessment here, we will return to discuss the same in the concluding section of the book. However, we need to articulate, at the outset, why this is different from a mere nationalist aspiration.

What makes the populist mobilization different from nationalist mobilization is the emphasis on the internal frontier as against a mere externalization of enemy. Constructing a people through a mere externalization of the enemy would only lead to fascism; it is only when the struggle for liberation is set against an internal condition does populism succeed as a meaningful and historical formation of the political. It is also our conviction that such a historical process in Tamil Nadu has also, subsequently, set an example for reimagining India as a substantial federal entity by locating the political in the aspiration for autonomy of self-governing states as an extension of the internal frontier created earlier. The hyphen that separates and conjoins Dravidian and Tamil managed all this with a rare efficacy that has not been sufficiently appreciated. As Tamil identity can readily be construed as relating to speakers of the Tamil language, it is the Dravidian identity that needs some parsing.

What Does "Dravidian" Stand For?

Dravidian refers to three classificatory groups, mostly overlapping but significantly distinct, in the discourses of the party and elsewhere: non-Aryan "original" or earlier inhabitants of the Indian subcontinent (racial entity), the speakers of the Dravidian languages (linguistic identity), and finally the inhabitants of the peninsular south India (territorial identity). We need to quickly recapture how these conceptual fields emerged and produced valences in orientalist knowledge production and colonial governance before understanding the political use of the sign "Dravidian" in mid-twentieth century and later.

Scholarship of the nineteenth century and the early twentieth century firmly attested that Aryans migrated from central Asia to the Gangetic plains. It was also believed that they were pastoral tribes and Sanskrit was their language. When excavations in Mohenjadaro and Harappa took place, it was felt that the traces of urban civilization excavated there could not have been that of the Aryans. The non-Aryan inhabitants of the Indian subcontinent, at least a section of them, who pre-existed the Aryans began to be thought of as Dravidians. While it was believed that south India was home of the Dravidians for long, it was also postulated that the Dravidians migrated from the north to the south after Aryan incursions.[3] While most tended to concur that the races mixed easily, the original distinction between the Aryans and Dravidians was also believed to have left civilizational vestiges, the most significant of which was the Dravidian group of languages largely housed in southern India. European scholars like F. W. Ellis of the Madras School of Orientalism and Bishop Caldwell argued for the distinct origin of Dravidian languages from that of Sanskrit, even if most would agree that there were mutual influences between them.[4]

Brahmin scholars, mutt heads, and lay people were happy to accept the Aryan tag primarily as purveyors of Vedic texts, Dharma Shastras, and Puranas in Sanskrit.[5] The orientalist scholarship that placed Sanskrit as a member of Indo-European languages made the nationalist elite feel equal to the colonizers. The constitution of Hindu personal laws on the basis of Dharma Shastras by the British, a crucial part of the discursive construction of a unified Hinduism with the Vedic corpus as sacred texts, centralizing Brahmins and Sanskrit was accompanied by the rise of Brahmins in various nodes of power in the colonial dispensation of the Madras Presidency. Brahmins, who held education as their preserve in the caste hierarchy, were quick to learn English to be able to fill various positions in colonial administration, the most significant of the emergent professions being the legal profession, thus having a predominant presence in the formation of civil society.[6] This resulted in non-Brahmin caste groups in Tamil Nadu, who felt marginalized, identifying with Dravidian origins, in opposition to the alleged Aryan origins of Brahmins, harking back to a Dravidian civilization as encapsulated by Dravidian languages, with Tamil occupying a privileged position as the oldest of the languages. Importantly, the Tamil corpus of devotional doctrinal texts of both Shaivite and Vaishnavite religious groups proved powerful markers of Tamil difference in the discursive construction of unified Hinduism. The Bhakti movement in south India and various sects founded by saints left a strong non-Brahmin, anti-orthodoxy imprint on the sociology of piety.

On another significant plane, the enumeration of castes through the census instituted by the British gave rise to caste associations as civil society formations, appealing for higher social status and redressal of injuries caused by discrimination, prepared the ground for non-Brahmin consolidation since Brahmin-instituted *sastras* formed the basis of caste hierarchy.[7] While there could be conflicts around their hierarchical superiority among non-Brahmin castes, the status of Brahmins as lawgivers of both ancient and modern regimes provided the possibility of non-Brahmin consolidation against Brahminical caste order and hegemony. It is against this backdrop that the Brahmin identification with the Aryan tag resulted in non-Brahmin identification with the Dravidian tag.

Oblivious of the extent to which non-Brahmin discontent could grow, the Indian National Congress was obsessed with a national language that could replace the colonizer's English as the language of governance and communication among Indian regions. As we shall see in Chapter 11, Hindustani or Hindi was seen to be the obvious choice. When the Congress formed the government in the Madras Presidency under dyarchy in 1937, it decided to introduce Hindi in schools. This brought a range of social constituencies oriented to non-Brahmin and Tamil identity together in opposition to Hindi. The agitation against Hindi, the language of the "north," placed emphasis on the meaning of Dravidian identity as south Indian. When a large section of the Justice Party, ousted from power by the Congress in 1937, and the Self-Respect Movement merged to form a new political vehicle in 1944, it was named Dravidar Kazhagam (DK), hoping to demand a south Indian republic consisting of the regions speaking the four Dravidian languages: Tamil, Telugu, Malayalam, and Kannada. As we will soon note, there was a certain oscillation initially as to whether to demand a separate nation for Tamils or a Dravidian federation. Both Periyar and Annadurai opted for the identity of Dravidar since their politics was anchored on non-Brahmin consolidation; a mere Tamil identity might not sufficiently connote the counter hegemonic struggle against Brahminism and caste hierarchy.

This was the moment, the decision of Periyar and Annadurai to call the new party Dravidar Kazhagam in 1944, that instituted the populist logic with the identities of Tamil and Dravidian taking the place of empty signifier denoting the social whole as Tamil and the internal frontier of Brahmin–non-Brahmin respectively. In what follows, we will study how the DMK articulated this complex ideation at the time of its inception. We will first take note of the difference signified in the name of the new party when it branched from the parent body, the DK, from a person-centric definition to a territorial definition. We will then examine two significant tracts, both authored by Annadurai, that were in circulation at the time of the founding of the party: *Aryan Allure* and *The History of the Political Goal.*

"Dravidar" versus "Dravida": From Person Centric to the Territorial Entity

When the need to break away from the DK, lead with an iron grip on the organization by Periyar, became a historical necessity, Annadurai made use of the moment to produce a distinction that speaks volumes to the altered political vision and purpose of the party. In Tamil language, the suffix "r" is the plural or honorific suffix that stands for personhood. Hence, "Dravidar Kazhagam" meant the "Forum of the Dravidian People." If the new party merely wanted to add the notion of historical progression as a marker, the name should have been "Dravidar Munnetra Kazhagam," which would have meant "the Progressive Forum of Dravidian People." However, Annadurai chose to drop the suffix "r," calling it "*Dravida* Munnetra Kazhagam," an adjective that refers both to the land and the people, to make it a territorial entity that could still include the people of the land since political action and historical progression always referred to the people. It is important that now the *people* are defined as inhabitants of the territory who chose to subscribe to the ideals of Dravidianism. This was an extremely significant move from the racially derived person-centric formulation to the territorially derived formulation. In fact, the change made possible for an inclusive politics with regard to empirical Brahmins while retaining the conceptual egalitarian non-Brahmin ideal as the core tenet. The Brahmin could be included in the Dravidian fold if he gave up the supremacist claim and the desire for social and political domination.

Periyar would choose to continue with the person-centric name of "Dravidar Kazhagam" since he had no intention of ever giving a structure to the party organization, mobilize membership, and finally constitute a self-governing people. His vision consisted of a relentless propaganda as catalyst action until the hegemonic structures crumbled, paving the way to reimagine a different kind of polity and governance. As a purely counter hegemonic agonist movement not interested in state power, Periyar could and needed to isolate the figure of the Brahmin both in hegemonic and empirical terms to effect distribution of power. Hence, it did not matter that he continued to intone a sectarian approach in the name of the organization, keeping it person centric, as he intended to keep opposing the Brahminic Hindu–north Indian hegemony. Annadurai, however, was keen on forging a party structure and effect grassroots mobilization to constitute a self-governing people. The variation in approach resulted in the shift to a territorial understanding of Dravidian identity rather than a person-centric approach.

It is instructive to read an anecdotal narrative about how the name of the party was coined. It is largely indicative of the ways in which the party functionaries lived and acted at that time. The anecdote is from the narration of Rama Arangannal, a party functionary and a sub-editor in the weekly *Dravida Nadu*, which was edited and published by Annadurai. Arangannal would go on to be a minister in the DMK cabinet.

One late evening, in the days following the controversial marriage of Periyar and the failure of all subsequent negotiations, July–August 1949, Arangannal and a couple of others gathered in the terrace of the building where the office of the *Dravida Nadu* magazine was functioning. K. A. Mathiazhagan, a young lieutenant of Annadurai who was to become a prominent leader of the party, joined them. They were tensed and unhappy about the volatile situation. Dravida Nadu had been carrying the names of those who disagreed with the marriage as the list of "tear drops." Annadurai was pouring metaphors and allusions in the emotionally charged essays in the party vehicle *Malai Mani*. It was not clear what the future course of action would be for all those who felt estranged from Periyar. The small gathering on the terrace was speculating that Annadurai would launch a party and they wanted him to do so earlier than later. Annadurai, who happened to drop by, stopped at the staircase to overhear their discussion for a while before appearing in front of them. On his prompt, they put forth their anxieties and viewpoints to him. In the course of the conversation, Annadurai said, "Well, if you want a party, then bring a pad, let us coin a name for the party." When one of them suggested Tamil Socialist Forum, Annadurai quipped the word "Dravidian" was mandatory in the name. Several names were proposed in Tamil and in English. Finally, "Dravidian Progressive Federation," suggested by Anna, sounded appropriate. When rendering it in Tamil, Annadurai first said "Dravidar Munnetra Kazhagam." All agreed that the name sounded good. Then he asked them to consider making it "Dravida Munnetra Kazhagam." He prompted them to think whether it should be Dravidar or Dravida. Mathiazhagan said, "Yes; Dravidar is restrictive. We are all rationalists. All those who endorse rationalist principles should be able to join our party. We should clearly pronounce our difference with Ayya (Periyar E. V. Ramasamy) on this score. Let us indicate the territory by using the term *Dravida*." Then the name of the party was first written in the notepad there as "Dravida Munnetra Kazhagam" (Tirunāvukkaracu 2017, 332–335). As this anecdote clearly indicates, in the urge to be inclusive by shifting the emphasis from the racial to territorial meaning of the term "Dravidian," the party could immediately indicate its aspiration for constructing a people historically and form the political. The goal and purpose of the DMK, in that sense, was at once different from that of the DK, though Dravidianism as a diffuse idea of difference with the Brahminic Hindu North provided the raison d'etre for both organizations. While both parties were aware that the majority of north Indians were also non-Brahmins, the political template of pan-Indian nationalism remained

Brahminical and hence the identification of Brahmin with north was essential to lessen the grip of the Brahmin hegemony. Moreover, both these organizations were keen on reaching out to the people to build awareness rather than building elite consensus, pressure groups, or vanguard organizations for achieving a separate Dravidian republic. Periyar was keen on building critical awareness as a prelude to political articulation and the DMK sought to construct a people in the political sense through organization building. With this understanding, we should now proceed to parse two significant texts written by Annadurai that were widely in circulation at the time of the founding of the party, almost functioning like manifestos. One was *Aryan Allure* (*Āriya Māyai* or *Arya Mayai*) (Aṟiñar Aṇṇā 2008a), published in 1943, and the other was *The History of the Political Goal* (*Ilaṭciya Varalāṟu*) (Aṟiñar Aṇṇā 2010b, 605–662) published in June 1947. This will help us to see how the present understanding of the political core of the DMK, articulated above, has been expressed in these two key texts.

Aryan Allure

When Anna wrote the tract *Arya Mayai* (*Aryan Allure*) in 1943, the immediate provocation, as inscribed in the text, was a conference held at Madurai by the Hindu Mahasabha of B. S. Moonje and V. D. Savarkar, which was being spearheaded in Tamil Nadu by Varadharajulu Naidu, an erstwhile friend of Periyar in the Congress non-Brahmin league between the years 1919–1925. The tract, as the name suggests, offers a comprehensive picture of what the Aryan–Dravidian antagonism implied. A careful reading of the text reveals the layers of significance that accrued to the opposition. The importance of the text for understanding various facets of Dravidianism cannot be overemphasized. If there is one text that encompasses the entire gamut of issues that underpin Dravidianism as a conceptual field, that would indeed be *Aryan Allure*. It is based on an extensive reading of literature in English and Tamil on both Aryans and Dravidians. It needs to be noted that the text was written for the lay reader, hence laying emphasis on rhetorical and emotional appeal. A scholarly reader today might find such a style clouding or compromising the rigorous reasoning implicitly expounded. This is perhaps why, in spite of the considerable amount of academic literature on the Dravidian movement in English, we are unable to come across any close reading of the text that serves as crucial a role as M. K. Gandhi's *Hind Swaraj* (1910) for understanding the larger historical processes initiated by such a textual composition.[8]

We should pause to note that for whatever reason, the newborn Indian state initiated much belated legal proceedings against *Aryan Allure* in 1948, a good five years after its publication. On September 18, 1950, Annadurai was sentenced to serve imprisonment for six months or pay 700 rupees as penalty for writing the tract. Annadurai gladly chose the prison term (Tirunāvukkaracu 2017, 408–410).

He was, however, released on bail after ten days, allegedly owing to public unrest; a subpoena was issued to collect the money from him. The tract technically stood banned. However, since it was already available with the party cadre, they held events in which the book was read in public—an activity we will discuss in the section on mobilization. No action was taken against the people organizing such readings of the banned tract. Obviously, the state was unsure how far should it exercise its muscle power to extinguish the tract that had been in circulation for seven years.

The tract invokes the presidential lecture of one Diwan Bahadur Ramasami Sastri delivered in the Hindu Mahasabha meeting held at Madurai and the various articulations of Savarkar and Varadharajulu Naidu that were in tune with the lecture; Moonje is also cited as Naidu's advisor. The "allure" referred to in the title can hence be construed primarily as the putative Hindu nationalism sought to be emphasized by the Hindu Mahasabha and its mobilization. In the course of the text, Annadurai pointedly asks: "If the Hindus want to construct Hindustan why should they cry hoarse on the banks of Vaigai? What have the Hindus got to do with the Dravida country?"(Aṟiñar Aṇṇā 2010b, 1:246).

If this radical question in the text appears odd to the present-day understanding of Hinduism, which includes a vast number of people of Tamil Nadu, the whole text in some ways aspires to substantiate the question by equating the Hindu of the Hindu Mahasabha with the Aryan Brahmin and Brahminic Hinduism. As a historical eye-opener, a pivotal section in the *Arya Mayai* relates to a Madras High Court verdict delivered in 1941, which categorically declared that a Brahmin cannot take a "Sudra" wife as per law. The plaintiff in the case was a non-Brahmin, that is, a "Sudra" woman who a Brahmin lawyer took as a consort, only to leave her stranded on his death with his offspring. She requested alimony from the properties of the lawyer, which was bequeathed to his Brahmin wife and children. The lower court sanctioned 20 rupees a month to the "Sudra" woman as alimony. The Brahmin wife appealed to the high court against the grant of alimony.[9]

The high court had to adjudicate on two issues: whether a marriage actually took place between the "Sudra" woman and the deceased Brahmin advocate and, if so, whether the "Sudra" woman and her child were eligible for alimony. One of the judges gave the verdict in the negative for both the questions. The other judge affirmed the marriage in response to the first question but decreed that such a marriage, even if performed, cannot be held valid and the children born of the wedlock cannot be deemed as legal heirs as per Hindu law based on the injunctions of the Dharma Shastras. The judgement elaborately discusses the Sanskrit commentaries and their English translations to ascertain whether *anuloma* marriages, that is, a person of higher caste taking a wife from a lower caste, was still envisaged in the current age, or Kali Yuga, and whether such marriages are recognized for the purposes of inheritance. Rajamannar, a lawyer who appeared for the "Sudra" woman, appears to have based his arguments as well on the right interpretation of the related texts. The judges, however, on a detailed reasoned interpretation of the portions of the texts, which gave rise to ambiguity, affirmed that such marriages could not be recognized for purposes of inheritance and could not have any legal validity. They overturned the lower court order granting alimony to the non-Brahmin woman. This judgement was delivered according to Hindu Law as extracted and codified from the Dharma Shastras.

Anna uses the "case in point" to show that Sanskritic *sastras* differentiate between Brahmins and Shudras in such absolute terms that they cannot be married. This was not any ancient practice but contemporary legal system. Anna cites several scholars and texts to argue that the cultural turf of Brahmins and non-Brahmins, coded as Aryans and Dravidians, were absolutely distinct. He points out that this was true of religious life and worship since Brahmins did not go to non-Brahmin temples. Even in Shaivite temples that have come under the sway of Brahmins, the worship in Sanskrit and worship in Tamil were done separately. Thevaram (Tēvāram), the Tamil panegyric (the collection of Tamil hymns), is sung after the Brahmins left. If we want to abstract the arguments of the text *Aryan Allure* that connect the verdict in the court case to the question of what Hindus have to do with the Dravidian land, they would appear like this:

1. The Hindu is a person who adheres to Sanatana Dharma.
   Anna cites the above definition provided in the *Gem Dictionary*, edited by T. A. Saminatha Iyer. He even mentions the page number as 467, though the details of publication of the edition he consulted are not provided. He mentions *Chambers Dictionary* and also prompts those interested to consult the encyclopedias.
2. The Sanatana Dharma are codes and precepts developed in Sanskrit, an Aryan language, which is learned and purveyed by Brahmins.
3. Hence, a Hindu is one who follows such of the tenets as propounded by Aryan Brahmins.
4. Dravidians have cultural and religious mores that are sharply distinct from that of the Aryan Brahmins.
5. There was no Aryan invasion or conquest since the indigenous Dravidians were a developed civilization; there was only a migration and social infusion, first in the north and then in the south.
6. Though Aryan Brahmins spread to south India and were able to win the patronage of Tamil kings, who used them to hone support for their kingship and statecraft, the Brahmins could never fully integrate with the Dravidian way of life.
7. The fact that Brahmins and Dravidian non-Brahmins, called Shudras by the Brahmins, live totally separated in their belief systems, norms, and world views demonstrates that Dravidians are not Hindus.

This is an issue that is elaborated at length in the text of *Arya Mayai*. We can say the core value of the protestation rests on the factum of residual Dravidian difference in spite of the substantial inroading of Aryan ideas.

8. Hindustan, the land where Hindus live, has been identified as north India. Anna mentions the cartographic practices in which India was divided into different regions, each colored distinctly, having separate colors for the region of Hindustan and the region marked as Dravidian. He refers to the atlas produced by the Constable company in this context.
9. The lands to the south of the Vindhyas, peninsular south India, is a distinct region that never came under the rule of any of the empires of the north like those of the Guptas, Harshavardhana, Kanishka, and so on.
10. Indian nationalism does not sufficiently address this historically derived distinction of the Dravidian south India.
11. Since the Dravidian south had always been distinct, southern peninsular India with the four major linguistic communities of the Dravidian language group should become an independent republic, a federation of four distinct linguistic states, to be called as Dravida Nadu. The Hindu Mahasabha is being deliberately erroneous by asking south India to be a part of their imagination of Hindustan, a nation with a religious identity.

In the argument of *Arya Mayai*, the mid-twentieth century Brahmin adherence to Sanskrit texts, *smriti*s and *sastras* in legal affairs, and Vedas and Puranas in religious affairs, clearly situate them in the realm of historical Aryanism, which is resoundingly distinct from Dravidian cultural mores. The linguistic distinction sought for the Dravidian language group from the Indo-European language group is not merely about language in the sense of grammar or etymology. It is the cultural semantics that is innate to the function of grammar, which is crucial to linguistic difference.

As an example, Annadurai points to the fact that material objects are gendered in Sanskritic languages but not in Tamil. The reason is that only *uyartiṇai*, a higher category of beings, could be gendered and not those that lack *thinai* (*tiṇai*), that is, *al-thinai* or *aḵriṇai*. In Tamil, the concept of *thinai* refers to an ordering of life, a compendium of cultural mores, emotional states integrated with different kinds of natural habitat.[10] It is only because human beings are capable of producing such order in life that they belong to the higher form of *thinai*.

What is even more crucial is how Anna distinguishes between different glosses produced for this categorical distinction. The actual Tamil distinction based on human capacity for ethics is outlined in *Tolkāppiyam*, the quintessential text of Tamil grammar. Unmindful of the same, one contemporary Tamil scholar, Mu. Ragavaiangar, had suggested human capacity for linguistic expression as the source of distinction. Anna disapproves, saying that even ants could communicate—we might not hear the sound due to variation in the frequency. He takes a serious objection to another definition found in Nannool that says "Makkal, Thevar, Naragar" belong to the class of *uyartiṇai*. These terms refer to humanity, gods, and demons in the Puranic imagination. Anna claims that whoever that be, if a person does not show a capacity for restraint and ethical action, displaying *thinmai*—as in, resolve—cannot belong to *uyartiṇai*. He speculates that *thinmai* has been elided as *thinai*. The Tamil distinction for gender could only be applied to a species that has evolved restraint in action as a form of resolve. If a human being fails to produce the resolve, he or she too will be treated on par with mere sensory beings and the inanimate as one lacking in resolve or *thinai*, belonging to the grammatical category of *aḵriṇai*. Hence, a mere belonging to a species is not adequate to be qualified as *uyartiṇai*. Anna is making an important intervention here since in contemporary Tamil even newborn babies are referred to in *aḵriṇai* as they are not yet capable of restraint and ethical judgement; when one says "The baby cried" in Tamil, one cannot use gender or honorific *uyartiṇai* suffixes *āṉ*, *āḷ*, or *ār* to the verb *azhu*. Only the *aḵriṇai* suffix *atu* can be used—*kuzhanthai azhuthathu*. The association of gender distinction with *uyartiṇai*, which is exclusively based on human capacity for ethical action, which Sanskrit-based languages do not practice, is a distinct feature of Tamil civilization.

Annadurai however does not fail to note that in spite of this crucial difference, Tamil poetics had, due to the infiltration of Aryan scholars as Tamil exponents, accommodated in its prosody the key feature of Aryanism: caste hierarchy. He mentions a twelfth-century text called *Vachananthi Malai (Vaccaṇanti Mālai)*. In the text, Tamil letters as well as prosody were classified on the basis of the Varna system. A type of verse called *Veṇpā* is reserved as ideal for depicting Brahmins: *Āciriyappā* for Kings, *Kalippā* for Vaisyas, and *Vañcippā* for Shudras. Annadurai laments this inroading of the Varna system into Tamil prosody. His analyses stress both the aspects of Dravidian difference that still persist and the aspects that have come under the sway of Aryanism, which needed to be weeded out.

It will be difficult to expand on all such references and pointers of the densely argued tract here, since it calls for a monograph-length exposition. Suffice it to say that Anna challenges his detractors to consult a substantial bibliographic compilation in support of his reading of Dravidian distinction from the Aryans. He provides this list in the middle of the text in a polemical gesture. The names of authors and Tamil translation of the titles are given without other publication details. The following list will be a reconstruction with the possible titles in English to get an idea of the range of books he referred to in consolidating his view: E. B. Havell (*The History of Aryan Rule in India*); Romesh Chunder Dutt (*A History of Civilization in Ancient India*); Ramesh Chandra Mazumdar (*The History and Culture of Indian People*); Swami Vivekananda (a lecture titled "Ramayana"); *Cambridge History of Ancient India* (E. J. Rapson [ed.]); Radha Kumudh Mukherjee (*Hindu Civilization*—section on the Rig Veda); James Murray (*Oxford English Dictionary*); R. G. Bhandarkar (*Collected Works of Sir R. G. Bhandarkar*); Krishnaswamy Iyengar (*Some Contributions of South India to*

Indian Culture); P. T. Srinivasa Iyengar (*Advanced History of India*); Jagdish Chandra Dutt and A. C. Das (*The Rig Vedic India*); C. S. Srinivasachariar (*Indian History, Hindu India*); H. G. Wells (*A Short History of the World*); *New Age Encyclopedia*; C. J. Varkey (*An Analytical History of India*); Henry Beveridge (*A Comprehensive History of India*); H. G. Rawlinson (*History of India*); Nagendranath Gosh (*Indo Aryan Literature and Culture Origins*); Vincent A. Smith (*The Oxford History of India*); William Wilson Hunter (*Imperial Indian Gazette*; *A Brief History of the Indian Peoples*); and Ragozin (*Vedic India*). Anna made it resoundingly clear that the proposition that the Dravidians were the original inhabitants of India and the Aryans came as migrants was a widely held scholarly opinion of the times. This had to be added to the issue of distinctness of the Dravidian languages, with Tamil being the oldest.

Anna takes note of those who claim that while this racial distinction in ancient history might be true, the races have fully integrated by now, making it hard to say who would be Aryan and who Dravidian in contemporary society. It is in this context that Anna points out to the aforementioned Madras High Court judgment annulling a Brahmin's marriage with a Shudra woman. He elaborately shows how the Brahmins are markedly distinct from others in their cultural mores. Since they were the custodians of Sanskrit *shastras*, which the British have made the common law of Hindus, Anna was able to derive that such laws inimical to the interests of Dravidians cannot be called their own. Hence, Dravidians are not Hindus as it meant accepting Brahminical social order in which an inferior status of being is imposed on them. It will be worth concluding our discussion of the text with a quote that clinches the issue:

> When we begged with folded hands "Am I not a Hindu too? Why do you humiliate me? Why do you call me as belonging to an inferior caste?"—they would never show empathy. We then needed to think. How come such a miniscule group could make us all subjugated? We then found the answer. They are Aryans and we Dravidians ... we do not however wish to expatriate Aryans as is alleged; we only wish to wipe out Aryanism. (Aṟiñar Aṇṇā 2010b, 1:274)

The distinction made here between the empirical Aryan Brahmin and the ideology of Brahminism as a hegemonic scheme is crucial to the politics of the DMK since an acknowledgement of the fact that non-Brahmin castes too were casteist is implicit in this understanding. By forging an internal frontier, the concept developed by Laclau as fundamental to populist reason, between Dravidian non-Brahmins and Aryan Brahmins, the Dravidian movement created the most crucial tool for fighting casteism and founding an egalitarian society; as the plebs stand for Populus, the Dravidian stand for the whole people who, within the precincts of Tamil Nadu, would bear the name Tamil. The *Aryan Allure* then is quintessentially the seductive structure of caste hierarchy that is couched as Hindu dharma, which is the core of Hindu nationalism of the Hindu Mahasabha, that needs to be repudiated in categorical terms.

The History of the Political Goal

We now need to look at another pamphlet called *Ilaṭciya Varalāṟu* that would translate as the "History of the (Political) Goal." Why was it necessary to set a political goal such as calling for a separate Dravidian republic, a federation of the four southern states, if wiping out Aryanism without expatriating Aryans is the political aim? Annadurai had already accepted the deep permeation of Aryanism in the Tamil language. It follows that other Dravidian languages would be more permeated with Aryanism than Tamil since Tamil had been celebrated as the most resilient to Aryan influence.[11] What use would be a federation of southern states if they had already been permeated with Aryanism?

The answer rests with, again, a certain understanding of hegemony that would undergird the Indian state. Indian nationalism had been so celebrative of the orientalist scholarship that held Vedic civilization as the core of India, which position the Brahmins and various Dharma Shastras that validate caste hierarchy as pivotal to social life, a case brought out with great efficacy in the tract *Aryan Allure*. The deep apprehension of the non-Brahmin Dravidianists was how much of power would be concentrated at the Union Government of India, which will be held by the Indian National Congress, the protagonist of the national movement that was not sufficiently critical of Brahmin hegemony. This crystallized as Dravidian separatism at the time of imposition of Hindi-language learning in schools in Tamil Nadu by the provincial Congress government in 1938. *Ilaṭciya Varalāṟu* captures this historical trajectory in all its conflictual nature.

Written in mid-1947, a couple of months before Indian independence, as a prelude to the celebration of the first of July as the day of putative Dravidian liberation, the text presents at least three different goals but presents them as one—a free Dravidian land. However, what this "freedom" meant is not clear from the fragmentary nature of the text—which perhaps best betokens the fragmentary nature of the concept of sovereignty when the political replaces war as a collective expression. The first and primary goal is freedom of the Shudras from Aryanism, the ideational complex promoted by Brahmins, a struggle for hegemony; the second is the Dravidian–Tamil aspiration for sovereignty; the third is the self-rule of Dravidian people as part of any political federation.

The first section of the pamphlet contains an essay by Periyar, the leader of the movement, with whom the author of the text, Annadurai, had already developed considerable tension. The short essay by Periyar strangely and categorically asserts that democracy with universal adult franchise would substantially liberate the vast majority of non-Brahmin masses from Brahmin dominance as they would be able to elect the rulers and frame the laws of the land. Hence, it was not necessary for the movement to aspire to form the government or insist on a separate sovereign state to achieve the final aim of freedom from Shudra status, an ignominious inferior social entity imposed by the Brahmins. Anna offers no comment on this essay but proceeds to narrate how the demand for a separate nation evolved. It appears Dravidian–Tamil sovereignty itself is supplementary to the basic political liberation from Shudra status, but it is a necessary supplement that would frame the process of such a liberation. In Periyar's words,

> The removal of ignominy imposed on us, the removal of blockades to our progress, freedom from Aryanism and superstitions, becoming a rational and dignified society—these being the kind of work we want to do, we need to work with common folk, which is like playing with fire. We have to win their confidence to reform the society. We need substantial propaganda, unity of purpose and cooperation. Our situation is such that, we need to rally the highly fragmented and subjugated people for a cause. That we shall no longer live as Shudras is the ultimate expression of our aspiration, our political breath. (Aṟiñar Aṇṇā 2010b, 1:606)

The rest of the pamphlet written by Annadurai then elaborates on how the demand for a Dravidian republic has always been a desire of the subjugated Dravidian, that is, Shudra people, but found political articulation in a gradual unfolding.

Annadurai mentions several conferences where the political resolve was firming up. As already seen, in his view the dormant idea of a separate Dravidian republic, expressed by a few leaders like Nadesan of the South Indian Liberal Federation, which was informed by the Aryan Brahmin, Dravidian non-Brahmin, and the Aryan–Dravidian languages' distinction, found its crystallization with the anti-Hindi uprisings of 1938. Annadurai lists a few conferences from 1938 as specific markers. It will be good to tabulate these historical stepping-stones as recapitulated by him, also noting the initial oscillation between Tamil Nadu and Dravida Nadu (see Table 1.1).

As an appendix to the listing of this timeline, Annadurai offers two quotes from the year 1940, a good seven years before the pamphlet was written, regarding the formation of Pakistan. The first quote from *Viduthalai* (*Viṭutalai*), the party organ, dated December 16, 1940, states that the Muslims had pitched for Pakistan and "they were not unloaded guns"; the other quote, a statement by Nehru from October 1940 (source not given) condemns the idea of Pakistan as mischievous, vulgar, and unworthy of attention from the Congress. The appendix closes with a short question and response following these two articulations from seven years before: "What then happened? Pakistan has become a reality" (Aṟiñar Aṇṇā 2010b, 1:612).

Table 1.1 Timeline of events showing the evolution of Dravida Nadu demand

S. No.	Date	Event	Description
1	September 11, 1938	-	We raised the slogan "Tamil Nadu for Tamils"
2	December 27, 1938	Vellore Conference of Tamils	The future of the Tamil people was discussed
3	December 29, 1938	Justice Party Regional Conference	The idea of Tamil Nadu as an independent nation was emphasized
4	December 10, 1939	Commemorative meeting	Public dissemination of the concept of "Tamil Nadu for Tamils"
5	July 2, 1940	Kancheepuram conference for the partition of Dravida Nadu	Formation of a committee to formalize the demand for a separate Dravidian republic
6	August 24–25, 1940	Thiruvarur State Conference	Dravida Nadu as an independent republic becomes a resolution
7	August 20, 1944	Salem Conference	Amalgamation of the Self-Respect Movement and sections of the Justice Party into the DK. A separate Dravidian republic becomes the basic program of the party.
8	September 29, 1945	Trichy State Level Conference of Dravidar Kazhagam	The demand for separate Dravida Nadu as sovereign republic was reemphasized
9	July 1, 1947	-	Celebration of the day as Independence Day of Dravida Nadu—the occasion for which the pamphlet was being written

Source: C. N. Annadurai, *Ilaṭciya Varalāṟu.*

The reference to Pakistan at the end of the timeline serves many purposes. In this pamphlet and elsewhere, Annadurai was keen to dispel the myth that the demand for Dravidian republic is a historical corollary to the demand for Pakistan. The idea of a separate Dravidian republic was mooted much before the crystallization of the demand for Pakistan; the demand for a Dravidian republic found a clear articulation after the anti-Hindi uprising in 1938. He wished to remind the Congress how dismissive it was about the demand for Pakistan initially, thereby pointing out that such a dismissive attitude towards the demand for the Dravidian republic might also fetch a similar result. He also repeatedly points out that the Dravidian republic located in peninsular India, separated from the northern plains by the Vindhya mountains, has a greater geopolitical integrity than a Pakistan carved out in two separate geographical stretches. Hence, historically, culturally, and geographically, the Dravidian claim for difference is far more entrenched than that of the demand for Pakistan based on religious identity.

Having outlined the evolution of the concept of the Dravidian republic thus, Annadurai points to the Congress prevarications about regional autonomy. If Nehru had spoken of a federation of regions with the right to self-determination, the Tamil Nadu Congress leaders were also anxious about the powers to be concentrated at the Center. They still did not want to speak of a separate republic but insisted that they should be part of the federal India as independent political units. Anna pointed to a statement from Kamaraj where he had said that Andhra, Tamil Nadu, and Kerala should become part of the Indian federation as "independent units." Annadurai said that there should be no problem in becoming part of the Indian federation, or an Asian federation that Nehru had suggested, or a world federation Wendell Willkie, the American presidential aspirant, had suggested, but what was crucial was to define what this "independence" of the given political unit substantially meant. All that the Dravidianists demanded was that the Dravidian republic should be an independent federation with rights to self-determination of the constituent parts, which then can be amalgamated with any other federal entity. He drew attention to the Indian constitution that was being drafted, in which the powers were being accumulated at the Center, which was in the grips of north India. He was certain that such a political arrangement would gradually pave the way for the evolution of Dravidian consciousness for independence.

Ilaṭciya Varalāṟu details the conferences in which the resolve for a separate republic was further nurtured by the spontaneous outpouring of emotions by the cadres of the movement. It is a narrative of the growth and strengthening of the aspiration. Having taken note of the contents of both the *Aryan Allure* (*Arya Mayai*) and *The History of the Political Goal* (*Ilaṭciya Varalāṟu*), we should now proceed to understand what actually the political consequences of these proclamatory statements were once the DMK was founded in 1949.

Enigma of Sovereignty

There are three charges that were laid against the DMK by the lay people and the learned, which were based on the DMK's demand for a sovereign republic of Dravidians that appeared facetious. The first criticism was laid against the DK, the parent body of which Annadurai was the general secretary, which never took to oppositional politics like strikes and civil noncooperation, and so on to insist on an independent Dravidian republic. They appeared to pay mere "lip service" to the cause. Secondly, in the case of the DMK, which as a political party opted for a democratic path to attain independence by rallying peoples' support in the electoral fora, there was a gradual decline of emphasis on a separate republic, which was finally given up in 1963. The charge was that the party used the demand for a separate nation merely as an emotive issue to garner support of the people in the elections. The third, a much more persistent charge is the insistence on the Dravidian nation instead of a Tamil nation, knowing fully well that the political mobilization done by the DK and the DMK was in the Tamil-speaking region, using and articulating in the Tamil language. We need to look at all these charges in detail to understand the precise nature of the aspiration for sovereignty. We will largely follow Annadurai's narration and gloss related to these phases in *Ilaṭciya Varalāṟu* discussed above, of course, as abstracted and interpreted by us for this synoptic recapture.

Dravidar Kazhagam, 1944–1949

The DK was born out of the merger of the Self-Respect Movement of Periyar and the Justice Party in the Salem conference, listed as S. No. 7 in Table 1.1. It is necessary to understand the circumstances in which this merger happened and the significance of the naming of the party if we are to make sense of the historical timeline provided above.

Of the two strands that merged, the Justice Party was older and was formed in 1917 as the South Indian Liberal Federation. Many of the leaders of the Justice Party were not keen on opposition to Brahmins in the cultural sphere nor did they have any quarrel with Brahmin hegemony. Their objection, barring a few exceptions, was only to the garnering of positions by Brahmins in the government machinery and the emergent professional and educational avenues that constituted civil society, where they wanted a fair representation of the non-Brahmin elite. The notable exception was C. Nadesa Mudaliar (1875–1937), a key actor in the formation of the South Indian Liberal Federation. Annadurai claims that Nadesa Mudaliar, who met with an early death, felt betrayed by party leaders who were just keen on offices, titles, and privileges. He mentions J. N. Ramanathan, Kannappar, and T. V. Subramanian as the other few who were keen to work among the people to enlighten them about the detrimental role of Brahmin dominance or hegemony. We should keep in mind that the electoral college was restricted to taxpayers and graduates in the colonial times. Hence, reaching out to the people who had no franchise would be redundant for those interested in finding a berth in governance. Interestingly, it could be argued while the franchise was restricted, the opinions that molded the mindset of society, consisting of those with suffrage and those without, were undivided. The Congress that had successfully created the ethos of freedom struggle from foreign rule could easily dethrone the Justice Party once it decided to participate in dyarchy in 1937. The Justice Party, on the other hand, had not reached out to the people with the larger significance of the non-Brahmin movement.

The Self-Respect Movement stood as the exact antithesis of the Justice Party. Lead by the exemplary figure of Periyar E. V. Ramasamy, who abhorred offices and participation in governance, the Self-Respect Movement focused fully on the cultural mores of Brahminism as pivotal to caste hierarchy, to which it forged a strident opposition. Periyar's experience in the Congress between the years 1919–1925 had convinced him that the party was deeply embedded in Brahmin, casteist hegemony. The ultimate flashpoint was the Congress' refusal to endorse the call for proportional representation of all castes in education and services. It then became Periyar's purpose to question the foundations of casteist hegemony in religious culture and belief system through the Self-Respect Movement. Annadurai had a brief stint in the Justice Party before joining Periyar's self-respect brigade in 1935 (Kannan 2010, 37).

The anti-Hindi agitations of 1938 brought various oppositional groups to Brahmin–Sanskrit–Hindi north India together. The Tamil purists, proponents of Tamil Shaivism, and sections of the Justice Party that were aligned to elite Tamil non-Brahmin groups all joined the Self-Respect Movement in opposing Hindi. Periyar's seniority, stature, and capacity for mobilization gave him the unofficial leadership of the anti-Hindi struggles of the final years of the 1930s. The movement was successful in having the provincial government retreat in their attempt to impose Hindi learning. This moderate success in combining disparate forces opposed to the Congress enabled the formation of the DK in 1944.

In the next few crucial years leading to Indian independence, Periyar was not in a position to insist with the British to consider the demand for the Dravidian republic. He loathed insurrectionary politics and so would never call for 'direct action', irrespective of the question whether such a call might have worked as effectively as it worked for Jinnah. Further, Periyar, in spite of a ceaseless propagation of his critical idiom, did not nurture a strong organizational base even to launch a successful nonviolent civil disobedience movement à la Gandhi. He was not backed by the elite in the demand for a separate nation. He had styled himself way too radical for any elite endorsement of the demand for the Dravidian republic. His radicalism in matters of culture with his strident anti-caste and iconoclastic atheist positioning was not to the liking of Shaivite and Vaishnavite non-Brahmin elite. As a result, Periyar could only entreat Jinnah to add the call for a Dravidian nation to his demand for Pakistan. Jinnah politely replied that it was for the people of south India to work for this demand.[12] In spite of the rigorous conceptual basis on which the demand for an independent Dravidian republic was raised and the critique of Indian nationalism was launched, the DK had no means to make an actual political intervention, either through elite lobbying or a mass movement, for the separatist cause. Obviously, the British had no interest in adding to the troubles they already had in withdrawing from India. Annadurai wrote another brilliant tract explaining the reason for the British withdrawal, saying that direct rule in India was no longer profitable to them, while installing a government friendly to their economic interests could be more profitable.[13] However, the DK was not in a position to force a negotiation with the British. It is believed by the old guard of Dravidianism, that if Sir A. T. Panneerselvam, a prominent Justice Party leader, had taken his position as secretary to the Indian minister in the British government without getting killed in a plane crash en route to London on his appointment, it might have become possible to influence British opinion in favor of a Dravidian republic.[14] This however is a moot point now. What is pertinent for our purposes is to realize that during the years 1944–1947, the DK did not have the organizational strength to compel the British to discuss a separate Dravidian republic in addition to Pakistan.

From 1949 Onwards

The DMK did succeed in building a mass organization throughout the state within a decade of its founding in 1949. However, its strength was in the realm of the subaltern, with no critical endorsement from the rich and the elite for the cause of Dravidian republic. The only path left open to the party was to contest elections and get into governance so that its demands could be consolidated. The overturning of the Indian nationalist Brahmin hegemony appeared to need a lot more time, given the economically weak support base of the party. The DMK, like the DK of Periyar, did not believe in insurrectionary politics, though they were militant in their agonistic articulations and nonviolent protest action. Annadurai then opted for the parliamentary path and actually tried to convince the Indian parliament, when he became a Rajya Sabha member in 1962, of the fairness of the demand for a separate Dravidian republic. The Congress government responded by outlawing such separatist demands through a constitutional amendment that required the elected representatives to abide by the sovereignty and integrity of the Indian Union, as stated earlier. The choice then became one between insurrectionary politics for a sovereign state or the possibility of democratic self-governance at the state level within the Indian union. The DMK, in near unanimity, opted for democratic self-governance since what had always been of greater import was to fight on the hegemonic turf. Annadurai categorically said that the demand for a separate Dravidian republic was being given up only under duress and not because it lost its validity (Kannan 2010, 269). However, in consonance with his earlier reflections on the issue discussed above, being part of a federation with sufficient powers for self-rule was as good as a separate sovereign state. If the sovereign republic was the form of expression of the Dravidian aspiration, democratic self-governance was the form of content. It was an act of political sagacity that the DMK chose to lay emphasis on the latter.

Since then, various fringe Tamil nationalist groups that keep getting formed under varied circumstances have always felt that the DMK betrayed the cause of the sovereign nation-state for Tamils. They fault the DMK for keeping to the implausible Dravidian tag and for giving up on the separatist demand. As we have seen, the insistence on the Dravidian tag was crucial for the internal frontier of the populist reason forged by the DMK in naming the hegemonic opposition to Aryan Brahminism. Second, the blind insistence on the sovereign nation state as a form of expression of the construction of a people completely fails to understand the substantial gains in opting for democratic self-rule as the form of content of Dravidian difference. The seemingly casual mention of Wendel Wilkie and the world federation by Annadurai in *Ilaṭciya Varalāṟu* written in 1947, when he seeks to know what notion of independence the Congress proposes for the regions, should alert us to the depth of political vision he was capable of in terms of the political goal of Dravidianism.

That said, the question as to why the DMK then waxed eloquent on allegiance to Tamil, in the much-glorified attribute of Tamil *patru* (attachment to Tamil) needs to be addressed separately. We will begin with a careful reading of historian Sumathi Ramasamy's account in her monograph, *Passions of the Tongue.*

Notes

1. The 16th amendment to the Constitution via the Committee on National Integration and Regionalism appointed by the National Integration Council recommended that article 19 of the Constitution be so amended that adequate powers become available for the preservation and maintenance of the integrity and sovereignty of the Union. This implied that elected representatives should swear an oath to uphold the sovereignty and integrity of India, which effectively proscribed any advocacy of right to 'self-determination' of any region in any form. For more on this, see "The Constitution (Sixteenth Amendment) Act, 1963," National Portal of India, https://www.india.gov.in/my-government/constitution-india/amendments/constitution-india-sixteenth-amendment-act-1963 (accessed June 3, 2020).
2. This can be read through Laclau's pairing of "Concept" and the "Name" as well as "Populus" and the "Pleb" (the hegemonic claim of a part as the whole) or even the much broader grid of "Universal" and the "Particular." Please see the subsection "The Internal Structuration of the People" in, Laclau (2005, 93–100).
3. The recent elaborate statement of this argument is that of Balakrishnan (2019). It draws on researchers like Asko Parpola. Also see Mahadevan (2002).
4. Recently, Trautman has called Ellis and his group that ran College of Fort St George as Madras School of Orientalism. Please see Trautmann (2009). However, a text that had much influence on nineteenth-century Tamil scholars was that of Robert Caldwell. See Caldwell (2012).
5. For a good instance of the happy Brahmin appropriation of the Aryan tag for both Brahminical Hinduism or Indian nationalism, see the discussion of G. Subramania Iyer's *Arya Jana Ikium Alladhu Congress Mahasabhai* (Unity of the Aryan People or the Congress Party) published in 1888 in Pandian (2007).

6. Brahmins who constituted 3.2 percent of the total male population in 1912 held 53 percent of deputy collector positions, 71.4 percent of the sub judge positions, and 66.4 percent of district munsiff positions. See Nambi Arooran (1980, 37–38).
7. For more on this, see the works of Bernard Cohn (1968, 1996) and Nick Dirks (2002). Cohn's work has made clear how constitutive the history of colonial knowledge in general and the census in particular has been for modern understandings of caste. Dirks, while discussing the census, says,

> District level manuals and gazetteers began to devote whole chapters to the ethnography of caste and custom; imperial surveys made caste into a central object of investigation; and by the time of the first decennial census of 1872, caste had become the primary subject of social classification and knowledge. Although the village continued to be seen as the dominant site of Indian social life, it became understood as more a setting for caste relations than the primary building block of Indian society. By 1901, when the census commissioner H. H. Risley announced his ambition for an ethnographic survey of India, it was clear that caste had attained its colonial apotheosis. (Dirks 2002, 15)

8. Apart from the comparability in terms of the significance of the text for the respective political movements, what is striking is the emphasis on fighting against an internalization of alien norms that is found detrimental rather than a mere identarian antagonism. For Gandhi, the goal was to exorcise British modes of governing life rather than a racial antagonism with the British. Similarly, for Annadurai the goal was to exorcise Aryan cultural mores rather than a racial antagonism with Aryans or Brahmins. See Gandhi (1938).
9. Justice Pandrang Row and Justice Somayya, *Swayampakula Subbarammaya and Ors vs Swayampakula Venkatasubbamma*, Indian Law reports Madras Series (Madras High Court 1941).
10. For more on the concept of *thinai*, see Ramanujan (1994) and Shulman (2016).
11. Robert Caldwell says, "Tamil however the most highly cultivated *ab intra* of all Dravidian idioms can dispense with its Sanskrit altogether, if need be, and not only stand alone but flourish without its aid, and by dispensing with it rises to a purer and more refined style...." For more on this, see Kailasapathy (1979).
12. For a perceptive discussion of the situation in which Periyar wrote to Jinnah, see Tirunāvukkaracu (2019, 28, 29).
13. This essay, titled "1858–1948," was written on March 2, 1947, trying to make sense of and historically interpret the British withdrawal from India and the difficulties faced by the Congress in working out a smooth transition of power. See Aṟiñar Aṇṇā (2010b, 1:519–577).
14. For example, see the musings of Thirunavukkarasu in his history of the DMK. Tirunāvukkaracu (2017, 194).

2 The Uses of Language

தமிழன் என்றோர் இனமுண்டு;
தனியே அவற்கொரு குணமுண்டு;
அமிழ்தம் அவனுடைய வழியாகும்;
அன்பே அவனுடை மொழியாகும்.

There is a race known as Tamilian
They do possess a singular character
Their ways are sweet as nectar
Love is the language they speak

—Namakkal Ramalingam[1]
(poet, congressman and Indian nationalist)

The political rise of the Dravida Munnetra Kazhagam (DMK) was intimately connected to the use of the Tamil language, the recovery and circulation of its literary corpus of the last two millennia, and a celebration of Tamil difference, its past, its civilization, and its glory. However, officially, and for all intents and purposes, the DMK aspired to work for an independent federation of the south Indian states speaking four languages, to be called Dravida Nadu. This was the only form of secession it articulated from 1949 to 1963. It never demanded the secession of the state of Tamil Nadu alone. Hence, whether one likes it or not, the DMK was not a Tamil nationalist party. This disambiguation is necessary if we are to understand how exactly the relationship between Tamil, as a signifier that can stand for not only the language but also a people and a land, and the politics of the DMK are intimately connected. It will be rewarding to begin with a text that best betokens the ambiguity surrounding this issue.

Sumathi Ramaswamy's *Passions of the Tongue* (hereafter *PoT*)[2] opens with the dramatic scene of Chinnasamy, a well-known martyr for the Tamil cause and a DMK cadre, walking out of his house early in the morning on January 25, 1964, with a fuel can in his hand to douse and set himself on fire. His death cry "Inti oḻika! Tamiḻ vāḻka!" (Death to Hindi! May Tamil flourish!), launches the train of reflection for the book. In other words, in a semiotic sense, Chinnasamy's self-immolation provides the token for the whole enquiry; assuming that he belonged to the type called Tamil devotee, the enquiry turns out to be about the passion invoked by language.[3] The book *PoT* is a history of Tamiḻ *paṟṟu*, a composite of terms "Tamiḻ" and "paṟṟu"—the latter standing for attachment or allegiance—the act of holding on to something, which *PoT* glosses as Tamil-language devotion. We will stay with devotion as the meaning of *paṟṟu* as suggested by *PoT* when we discuss the text. Elsewhere, we would prefer allegiance, the reason for which will become clear towards the end of this chapter and also through an extensive discussion of *paṟṟu* in the next chapter.

The desired critical yield of the book is best stated when following Prasenjit Duara's work *Rescuing History from Nation*, Sumathi Ramasamy avers:

> In this book, I hope to "rescue history from the nation" by displacing the latter as the locus of this particular history I write, and by refusing to subordinate, all too quickly, the sentiments and notions of all those who lived and died for Tamil under the rubric of "nationalism." Which is why I propose a new analytic to theorize the discourses of love, labour, and life that have coalesced around Tamil in this century, discourses which can only be partially contained within a metanarrative of nationalism, or even a singular conception of the nation, as we will see. (Ramaswamy 1997, 5)

This impossibility of containment of Tamil devotion within a singular conception of the nation is primarily because both Indianism and Dravidianism could lay claim to Tamil difference and devotion, a point that is well elaborated in *PoT*, its important critical yield. By coining this oppositional pair of Indianism and Dravidianism, abstracted from Indian nationalism and Dravidian republicanism, in the scheme of its analysis, *PoT* demonstrates the interpenetrating ideational force of India and Dravidam (the substantive noun in Tamil) as pivotal concepts that constituted political life in colonial Tamil Nadu.

However, this promising trajectory of displacing the nation and finding other meanings for the passions of the tongue appears to give away all too quickly in spite of the desire not to do so. This is because we find, right in the beginning, the admission:

> How then do I write differently the (hi)stories of Chinnasamy and his fellow speakers who claimed a willingness to die for Tamil? Although Chinnasamy's self-immolation by itself is a spectacularly singular act, defying easy translation into universal categories, the attitudes that produced it could be conveniently assimilated into the metanarrative of nationalism, as yet another instance of "linguistic nationalism." (Ramaswamy 1997, 4)

It is after this admission that allegiance to Tamil could be conveniently assimilated into the metanarrative of nationalism that *PoT* goes on undertake the task of rescuing history from the nation. In other words, the history of Tamil passion is perhaps rescued from the history of the Indian nation only to be ensnared by the Tamil nation. Hence, the task of attempted rescue is plagued by doubt, since the metanarrative of nationalism is seen to be so powerful that these activities of linguistic devotion are sort of colonial mimicry, which merely have to intone that they are different. That is, in order to be mimicry, they should mark the difference with the original. Hence, the question: "But how do we narrate the lives of those who lived in the colony so as to keep alive this ambivalence of mimicry, this tension between the 'almost the same' but the 'not quite,' which dismembers European norms and forms, as Bhabha reminds us?" (Ramaswamy 1997, 5).

If the doubt is marked right at the beginning, by the time we reach the conclusion there is a near capitulation to the metanarrative of nationalism:

> Which is why this history of Tamil devotion is almost the same even when it is not quite, to paraphrase Homi Bhabha: in the process of talking and writing eloquently about their love and devotion for their language, Tamil's devotees, who were colonial subjects after all, began to subscribe to the reigning certitudes of linguistic nationalism. In their narratives, as in those of Herder or Fichte, the state of the language mirrors the state of its speakers; language is the essence of their culture, the bearer of their traditions, and the vehicle of their thoughts from time immemorial. (Ramaswamy 1997, 244)

It is indeed curious that the constant oppositional pairing of Indianism and Dravidianism in the analysis of the book that divides the passion for Tamil suddenly transforms into "linguistic nationalism" mimicking Johann Gottfried Herder and Johann Gottlieb Fichte. When we look closely, we find a giveaway moment that explains this shift. In the middle of the narration, we are told:

> And indeed, as the Dravidian movement itself split, when Annadurai parted company with Ramasamy and his DK in 1949 to found his own party, the Tirāviṭa Munnetra Kalakam or "Dravidian Progress Association" (DMK), the inherent tensions between the alternate conceptions of the "Dravidian" and "Tamil" nation came to the fore. By the late 1950s, as the DMK entered the domain of electoral politics, its agenda was primarily formulated in terms of a Tamil nation (albeit one often referred to as "Dravidian"), confined to the territorial space of a Tamil speaking area, rather than coeval with the more ambitious nation that Ramasamy envisaged comprising the speakers of all Dravidian languages. (Ramaswamy 1997, 64)

This statement, an unfortunate conceptual mishap unsupported by evidence in the narrative of *PoT*, results in the basic confusion that runs through *PoT* as to what exactly the political aspirations of the DMK were. Elsewhere, we find another statement: "For Dravidianism, at least until the early 1960's, the state renaming was linked to a separatist project for creating an independent Tamil nation" (Ramaswamy 1997, 155). There is no citation given to this alarming claim. There is a reference to the autobiography of Karunanidhi, which of course never says anything to the effect of "abandoning the dream of multilingual Dravidian nation." There appears to be a grave misunderstanding of sorts that gets articulated in *PoT*, which becomes arbitrary and misleading in its imputations.[4]

In his maiden speech in the Rajya Sabha on May 1, 1962, Annadurai clearly stated that the DMK demanded a separate south Indian republic to be known as Dravidastan (Annadurai 1975). When Joseph Mathen, a member from Kerala, asked what the language of the south Indian republic would be, Annadurai quipped that those details would be worked out in the constituent assembly of the new state. One of the features he specifically mentioned in the speech was the geographical contiguity of peninsular south India, which would not make partition a messy affair like Pakistan. Subsequently, when the Government of India proposed the sixteenth amendment to the Constitution which required all the elected members to swear that they would abide by the sovereignty and integrity of India, thereby making it difficult to advocate secession in a parliamentary debate, on January 25, 1963, Annadurai again unambiguously mentions that it was the independence of the south India that was sought. After the passing of the amendment, since the DMK was keen on electoral participation and forming a government in Tamil Nadu, no advocacy of secession was undertaken. Hence, it can be seen beyond doubt that the DMK never demanded a separate Tamil nation-state and has nothing whatsoever to do with linguistic nationalism, as Ramaswamy misconstrues. It was Periyar, who lead the Dravidar Kazhagam (DK) in the 1960s, who had conceptually articulated that the Dravidian nation can just as well be the Madras State. Ramaswamy elsewhere attests Periyar was far from championing Tamil devotion or linguistic nationalism. He was just pragmatically redefining the territorial spread of the Dravidian nation, albeit in the company of fringe groups like the "We Tamils" movement of Adithanar.[5] The DMK never ever endorsed his idea.

The DMK's valorization of Tamil devotion then was clearly not aligned to linguistic nationalism but the political task of construction of the Dravidian–Tamil people on the primary plank of non-Brahminism. *PoT*, in spite of the desire to wrench Tamil devotion free from the clutches of nationalism to grant autonomy to its regimes of articulation, misses the opportunity to come up with a different theoretical premise other than the idea of mimicry of linguistic nationalism that it attributes to the DMK, a typical conceptual error shared by many others. The reasons are not far to seek since it is in the basic outline of the text considered as a project, which drifts away from the pivotal concerns of non-Brahminism. Let us stay a while to see how this happens. The text, *PoT*, proposes four distinct regimes of Tamil devotion with a certain implicit chronology or the order of appearance, which is not fully asserted since these also overlap. The four regimes are neo-Shaivism, Classicism, Indianism, and Dravidianism.

Neo-Shaivism, as it is referred to in *PoT* and elsewhere, is the name given to the rearticulation of Shaivism as it was practiced in Tamil Nadu by the non-Brahmins as a distinct Tamil philosophical and religious system that found itself in a tense and ambiguous relationship to the Brahmin- and Vedic-derivative Shaivism in the nineteenth century. It is a response to the oriental scholarship in the eighteenth and early nineteenth century that singularized Aryan Sanskritic Vedic civilization as the source of all Indian languages and cultures; most particularly, the south Indian languages, religion, and civilization were also seen as derived from and shaped by Aryan origins. In the mid-nineteenth century, the distinctiveness of, and a possible independent origin of, Dravidian languages, cultures, and civilization began to be posited by colonial officials and missionary scholars like F. W. Ellis and Robert Caldwell (Caldwell 2012). Thomas R. Trautman (2006) has recently written extensively of the Madras school of orientalism, which differed with the Calcutta-centered oriental scholarship. Encouraged by the observations of the Madras school of orientalism, the Shaivites of Tamil Nadu, many of whom hailed from the powerful non-Brahmin Vellala land-owning community, formed the neo-Shaivite movement, which claimed a Shaivism distinct from and predating Aryan influence.[6] Shaiva Siddhanta is the philosophy of this religion. In the gloss offered in *PoT*, this was indeed the quintessential non-Brahmin moment in the history of Tamil devotion.

This gave way to competing claims about the comparative classical status of Sanskrit and Tamil. It is explained by *PoT* that two distinct trends emerged in this turf of civilization and the classical status of the languages. One was compensatory classicism, which tried to say that both Sanskrit and Tamil were classical languages of independent origin that came together in a mutually beneficial interaction; the other was contestatory classicism that held Tamil language and civilization far superior to Sanskrit and Aryan civilization. In the era of nationalist political mobilization, these gave rise to Indianism and Dravidianism respectively. Indianism tried to hold both India and Tamil as equal in terms of claims of belonging. Dravidianism claimed primary or exclusive loyalty to Tamil. The gendered images of Bharata Mata and Tamil Thai (Mother India and Mother Tamil) became competing figures. *PoT* mobilizes a whole range of articulations in which some try to combine these loyalties and those who make it a bitter rivalry by demanding a complete surrender to Tamil Thai. However, the contestatory classicists and Dravidianists are no longer seen to belong to the genealogy of non-Brahminism. As the Hindi language policy of the Indian National Congress queers the pitch, the Dravidianist adherents of Tamil devotion swell in numbers, gradually drawing neo-Shaivites and Indianists as well into their fold.[7]

Nevertheless, this is not a story of success for Dravidianism in the gloss offered by *PoT*. Because the DMK, the political expression of Dravidianism that could come to power in the state, was constrained to make allowances to Indianism due to both legal and political compulsions. Their "reluctant" abolishing of Hindi education in government schools comes with a cost for those dependent on government education in being deprived of skills in the putative official language of India. These distortive attributes of failure listed by *PoT* pale in insignificance compared to the posthumous fate of the Tamil devotee, like the one provided by the token of analysis, the self-immolating martyr, Chinnasamy, whose volition is negated and political articulation muted. *PoT* laments that in the populist phase of Tamil devotion, it was enough to acquire the negative attribute of opposition to Hindi to serve Tamil. The anti-Hindi Tamil devotee is not graced by the earlier positive attributes of love, labor, and life devoted to and inspired by Tamil. Hence, it is a case of mere subjection to linguistic passion that explains the martyrdom of Chinnasamy, even if the passion is part of the genealogical strand of Tamil devotion that we extracted above from the text of *PoT*.

What makes the narration in *PoT* run aground so badly in doing justice to the figure of Chinnasamy is segregating the genealogy of non-Brahmin politics and its thrust against casteist hegemony from the genealogy of Tamil devotion beyond the first regime of neo-Shaivism. The compensatory and contestatory classicism are not linked to Brahmin and non-Brahmin interests and hence the later opposition between Indianism and Dravidianism also becomes a discourse about language and not about caste. Political formations like the Justice Party, the Self-Respect Movement of Periyar, their 1944 merger into the DK, and the DMK are all mobilized as part of the mise-en-scène for the drama of Tamil devotion, which unfolds in a dialectic internally set by discourses, metaphors, and imageries produced by the devotees of the four regimes. The later typologies offered by the text for various kinds of devotion to the trope of the feminine mother Tamil and of the devotee figures pay nominal attention to the Brahmin–non-Brahmin divide and its link to the competing nationalist visions of India and Dravidam as intrinsic to the contours of Tamil devotion. For example, an extremely significant manifesto-like text, *Arya Mayai* of Annadurai, which we discussed in the previous chapter, is just mentioned once in passing for the sake of the title, with no attention paid to the analytical structure of the text. Hence, the possibility that Chinnasamy's act of self-immolation, albeit reprehensible, could as well be an expression of his assertive self-respect as a member of a subordinate caste, in refusing to get once again subjugated to the rule of another alien tongue, Hindi, and the demand to learn it, is eschewed by this singular narration of language devotion, as if language in and by itself mattered so much. Instead of rescuing history from the nation, the text makes passions of the tongue an atavistic force unhinged from political history.

It will be critically rewarding to read, alongside *PoT*, a much shorter and less noticed text written by a Delhi-based Tamil journalist, Mohan Ram, soon after the victory of the DMK in 1967. The title of the book is a sure winner: *Hindi against India: The Meaning of the DMK*, which seems to have escaped the attention of Ramaswamy (Mohan Ram 1968). Instead of historicizing Tamil devotion, Mohan Ram speculates on the telos of the desire for a national language that Indian nationalism developed. It should at the outset be said that Mohan Ram was no supporter of the DMK. In fact, with his book not being an academic work, Mohan Ram was free to express his elitist scorn for the populism of the DMK, which he thought lacked any credible ideological premise. The DMK, to push his argument a little further, is rather one of the adverse consequences of the most unreasonable folly of insisting on Hindi being the national or the sole official language. We will briefly summarize the outline of his argument in the book.

Mohan Ram borrows the central idea of his book from Ram Manohar Lohia, which is the crucial contradiction between "midlanders" and "coastlanders" in India. Lohia wrote of this contradiction out of his dismay about the economic backwardness of midland regions since he thought the British impact on the three presidencies, Calcutta, Madras, and Bombay, helped the coastland to develop its economy. He further thought the princely states and miniscule affluent sections that formed the political class of the midland had hidden the acute poverty of the people from consideration. Mohan Ram points out how this idea of Lohia has been vulgarized by his followers like Vinayak Purohit in marking this distinction as between Hindi-speaking midlanders and others. In Purohit's view, the midland Hindi speakers naturally identify with the Indian nation; the Gujarat capital needs them and hence supports the nation; a group of other regions feeling reluctantly nationalist like Bengal, Kerala, and so on with a few regions like Andhra, Tamil Nadu, Karnataka, and Maharashtra harboring anti-national tendencies.

Mohan Ram alters Purohit's formulation even as he chastises Purohit for his misreading. He finds the cultural backwardness of midlanders more threatening. He too finds Gujarat underwriting the backward Hindi nationalism for the sake of the operations of its capital. However, he notes that Maharashtra makes its own contribution from the vestiges of the Maratha rule: the reactionary Hindu nationalism in the form of the Hindu Mahasabha and the RSS. Barring these two coastal aberrations, the rest of the coastlanders appear to be capable of a progressive democratic politics, which the midlanders abhor. The question of Hindi as the national language, link language, or official language is all about establishing the hegemony of the culturally backward Hindu hegemony forged by the midlanders. The sections on cow protection and Jan Sangh clearly show the links between the communal agenda and the promotion of Hindi. It is to the strength of this short book to have shown that this aspiration of the midland Hindi–Hindu backward hegemony cut across party lines in the sense many in the Congress too joined in making several of these demands, though Mohan Ram singles out the Jan Sangh as the most virulent expression.

As a journalist, Mohan Ram makes brief and emphatic statements. The very opening lines of the book read:

> A bizarre permutation of Hindu middle-class ethos and the political, economic and cultural backwardness of India's Hindi-speaking midland threatens the country's disintegration in the coming decade or two. No people would accept the status of a second language for their mother tongue. But India's Constitution expects 70 per cent of the people to accept Hindi, the language of 30 per cent, as the sole official language of the country. Those who do not speak Hindi are second class and third-class citizens. (Mohan Ram 1968, 13)

The statements in the concluding section are equally emphatic: "If India is not going to be held together as a voluntary union with a minimal centre, the only alternative would be a strong Centre with fascist tendencies, looking to the army for help in imposing unity on all the ethnic and national minorities" (Mohan Ram 1968, 143).

Mohan Ram's analysis of the DMK is important in the context of much of his observations about Hindi since, as the title suggests, in his view, the party had no other positive meaning than this. Like the anti-Hindi Tamil devotee of *PoT* without positive attributes, the politics of the DMK, in the view of Mohan Ram, had no positive attribute either. We should sample one of his descriptions of the class base of the DMK:

> In its formative years the DMK was essentially a petty bourgeois party of the educated and semi-educated urban classes, petty traders and unemployed youth. It was at best a party articulating middle class frustration and the political charlatan was coming into his own in the form of the small time DMK demagogue. (Mohan Ram 1968, 94)

On its ideological premise:

> The DMK tried to fill the vacuum, with its incoherent talk of socialism, communism, revolution, and social reform, all without an ideology. The DMK leaders claimed to be the disciples of all the great thinkers of all times. Its soap box Demostheneses kept up a spate of tub-thumping oratory from a thousand street corner meetings, quoting practically every thinker from Socrates and Plato through Machiavelli and Ingersoll to Lenin and Hitler in the same breath.... It had a vague goal—a sovereign Dravida Nadu—but no ideology or a programme to give its political goal a content. (Mohan Ram 1968, 94–95)

More precisely, "minus its secessionist plank, the DMK had no political purpose" (Mohan Ram 1968, 108).

If these were the characteristics of the party in its early stages, after the journey through the electoral successes, giving up the secessionist demand, softening of the anti-Brahmin angularities (read alliance with the Swatantra Party lead by Rajaji), widening of the Tamilian's identity horizon, and finally being in power in Tamil Nadu, Mohan Ram has this update as he finished writing the book in 1968, which is full of instructive coinages of phrases:

> An assessment of the DMK is difficult even at this stage. It cannot be dismissed as the party of the Tamil bourgeoisie or of the vested interests. Nor can it be called a leftist force. It has no definable class base. Ideologically, it still defies classification. It has no ideological inhibitions even as it professes an amorphous populist radicalism and calls itself socialist. But the DMK has helped traditionalize the political processes in Tamilnad through its appeal to Tamil nationalism. It is a well-organized party with an extremely maneuverable machinery, drawing its support from the small trader, the urban and rural intelligentsia, the uncommitted working class, and the exploited farm laborer. The DMK did operate in terms of caste identification in the past but its mass base should have legitimately belonged to the Communists had they discovered the Tamil idiom in politics in time. (Mohan Ram 1968, 123)

What is pertinent to our analysis is the unavoidable appearance of appeal to "Tamil nationalism" in the middle of an otherwise consistent account, which ends with the lament that the Communists failed to discover the "Tamil idiom" in time. Is this Tamil idiom the same as Tamil nationalism? Why was the party insisting on a Dravidian republic if it was a Tamil nationalist party? Since at any rate Mohan Ram was intent on showing the pivotal role played by Hindi imposition, he had no investment in raising this question for all the baffling amorphousness of populism, which obviously exasperated his apparently Marxist perspective.

Reading Mohan Ram and Ramaswamy together, it is not difficult to see that every Indian region responded to colonial difference by delving into its own pasts through cultural memories archived in the language of the region. The popular base of political awakening could only be formed through the languages spoken by people in various regions, while as a civil society formation the official leadership vehicle of the Indian National Congress transacted business in English. It is the Congress leadership that unimaginatively mimicked the European brand of linguistic nationalism in trying to fashion Hindi as a national language through the construction and extension of a Hindi public sphere to spread over the nation. Ignoring this well-known history documented earlier by many, including Mohan Ram discussed above, *PoT* lays the blame of imitative linguistic nationalism on the doors of Tamil devotion. In doing so, like in other instances, the book primarily misses out on two crucial dimensions: (*a*) the Dravidian republic covering the whole of south India was the alternative proposed to the Indian nation by the DMK, the most populist of the political movements to have been associated with Tamil devotion; (*b*) Dravidianism primarily drew its strength from opposition to Brahmin hegemony and not from Tamil devotion. The oversight in excluding these crucial dimensions that accompanied the historical construction of Tamil *paṟṟu* as part of the populist politics of the DMK leads to a misreading of the historical outcome of the evolution of Tamil *paṟṟu*, as we observed above in the case of *PoT*'s analysis of the token of Tamil devotion, martyr Chinnasamy who belonged to the DMK.

If Mohan Ram and Ramaswamy complement each other in excluding the history of Tamil or Hindi devotion, both eschew the genealogy of non-Brahmin politics and counter hegemonic thrust which was central to the advent of the DMK. This was amply compensated by a later day treatise by M. S. S. Pandian, aptly titled *Brahmin and Non-Brahmin: Genealogies of Tamil Political Present* (2007). In his scheme, the orientalist extolling of the Brahmin figure as Aryan as the harbinger of Indian civilization created other contestatory claims of Brahmin-like superiority for other communities. The Congress was fully accommodating Brahmin exclusivism and hence the genesis of the Justice Party, which tried to open up the political space for others. It was, however, with Periyar that the Brahmin was finally challenged in full measure with the idea of a non-Brahmin ideal. Pandian manages to show how deeply the emergent civic culture and ethos of governance were centered around the Brahmin that the political necessarily took the form of non-Brahminism. While such discursive production of the Brahmin and the non-Brahmin is convincingly mapped by Pandian, his book does not bring the DMK into discussion and hence does not fully engage with the language question in spite of the insightful conceptualization of Brahmin–Sanskrit–north India as a transitive category.[8]

Nambi Arooran's book preceding Ramaswamy's *PoT*, *Tamil Renaissance and Dravidian Nationalism*, does a fine job of weaving both the threads of development of the Tamil language and identity and the development of non-Brahmin, Dravidian identity together. However, this book too does not fully address how these threads contributed to the rise of the DMK since the period covered ends with the birth of the DK and the demand for Dravida Nadu in 1944 (Nambi Arooran 1980). The concluding sentence of the book is a strange abdication of the very framework the title suggests: "The Non-Brahmin Movement not only provided the catalyst to a new cultural awakening among the Tamils but also brought a new sense of Dravidian consciousness and cultural pride, which led to the rise of linguistic sub-nationalism in Tamil Nadu" (Nambi Arooran 1980, 267). The sudden transformation of the non-Brahmin movement-inspired Dravidian consciousness into "linguistic sub nationalism" is unanticipated in the narration of the book until the very last sentence. The difficulty obviously appears to be a certain use and celebration of Tamil by the DMK, which make all commentators assume that it was a Tamil nationalist party or promoted linguistic nationalism, neither of which is factually correct. It then becomes necessary to understand the role of Tamil in the DMK mobilization.

Tamil as Empty Signifier

Let us recall that in the previous chapter we noted that the inscription of the Brahmin–non-Brahmin divide was central to the marking of the internal frontier suggested by Laclau that would set the ground for populist mobilization. If the agonism was set as internal, then there should be an empty signifier that can traverse the internal frontier to signify the totality of the *Populus* (Laclau 2005, 107). The signifier is deemed empty in the sense that one could read different meanings into it. When we suggest that Tamil functioned as such an empty signifier, it may appear strange at the outset since Tamil refers to the language that has a material praxis and is the very turf of political expression and consciousness. It is legitimate to object how this could be empty. But if we pause for a moment to consider all the passionate articulations of the Tamil devotees listed in *PoT* that "Tamil is my body," "Tamil is my breath," "Tamil is my life," and so on, it is obvious that the denotative range of the term far exceeds the instrumental purposes of language. Laclau offers the most persuasive gloss on this.

The initial discursive shift occurs when a literal term takes a rhetorical displacement as a figural term. For example, when the term "leg" is displaced as "leg of a chair." In classical rhetoric, says Laclau, when the figural term which cannot be substituted by the literal term is used, the operation is called *catachresis* (2005, 71). Tamil in the figural sense, Tamil that becomes one's body, one's breath, one's life, and so on is not the literal Tamil that denotes a language. This catachrestic movement, the rhetorical device, Laclau finds crucial for the formation of both an empty signifier and hegemony. In that sense, Laclau concludes, "the political construction of the people is, for that reason, essentially catachrestical" (2005, 72). Again, there can arise a legitimate objection to this since constructing people as Tamil could simply mean those who speak the language. The enigma of Dravidianism is that this is not exactly the case.

We know the term "Dravidian" stands in opposition to "Aryan." These are the racial discursive markers for non-Brahmins standing in opposition to Brahmins. If this is the case, the most crucial question is, can non-Brahmins constitute a people? It is in response to this that we find Laclau's core insight helpful. We know Brahmin is a *varna*. Interestingly, though Brahmin castes, like Iyers and Iyengars and numerous subdivisions thereof in Tamil Nadu, are intensely differentiated with bitterly competing claims for higher echelons in caste hierarchy, the *varna* exclusivity and privileges make the social group immediately cohesive for anyone outside the group. In other words, attempts of Brahmin castes—now bearing the strange label of subcastes—at competitive hierarchization, for example, between a Vadama and a Brahacharanam Iyer or Vadakalai and Thengalai Iyengar in Tamil Nadu, does not prevail upon the social injunctions related to purity and pollution placed on others in treating them. Hence, the Brahmin *varna* easily slides into a caste identity. However, the non-Brahmin category cannot achieve such cohesiveness since the innumerable castes have been hierarchized fully, though there has been certain mobility of caste groups in the hierarchical scales, like in the case of Nadars. The cultivating landowning caste of Vellalas did not want to be classified as Shudras along with others and hence came to be billed as Sat-Shudras. Obviously, the descriptive appellate non-Brahmin does not sufficiently free the identity of social location from caste since it is based on caste difference. Even if the racial marker "Dravidian" is used, it was already in practice to call a certain section of the Dalit people as "Adi Dravida," thus rendering Dravidian identity divisible. Hence, another signifier, sufficiently empty of the caste marker, is required for the construction of a people. We need to see how this requirement arises in the scheme of Laclau.

We need to note that Laclau theorizes by abstracting political processes in general. We find his gloss connecting perfectly with the populist mobilization in Tamil Nadu, which needs some parsing. The most crucial section in his treatise *On Populist Reason* is titled "'The 'People' and the Discursive Production of Emptiness" (Laclau 2005, 67–128). In order to sum it up briefly, at the cost of missing out on the theoretical elaborations and historical nuances, let us list the arguments that build the framework. We have taken the liberty of interpreting and extending his gloss for our purposes.

1. Populism cannot be the expression of an already pre-existing social group, since it will not enable the emergence of a collective political entity in the act of constructing a people for political purposes. This, we may add, is the crucial difference between nationalism and populism. Nationalism posits a pre-given collective, the people of a nation opposed to an external entity, while populism constructs "a people" through a process in which a dominant group within a totality is sought to be opposed to reform the totality in a political act. It is quintessentially the *plebs* standing for the *Populus*. We may even go further to say that nationalism will have to work on the axis of sovereignty while populism will work on the axis of self-governance or, even more precisely, a hegemonic inversion. Hence, populism cannot begin with a pre-given totality of the idea of a people, as Laclau demonstrates through the example of the experience of the Ataturk.
2. Hence, we need to begin with the smallest social unit possible that can be rearticulated for the purposes of political relationship. Laclau calls this unit as something formed out of a "demand." For example, emigrant settlers demand civic amenities in their dwelling. This demand constitutes them as a political unit.
3. The demand of one political unit will be different from the other. However, when these demands are not met by those holding power, they develop an equivalential chain or relationship in their collective opposition to such an enclosure of power, which will be marked as the internal frontier.

4. Now, the units forming the equivalential chain cannot erase or submerge the differences between the demands that constitute them. At the same time, they would find themselves on one side of the internal frontier. Hence, in order to discursively hold them together above this conflict between equivalence and difference, they need to invent an empty signifier that would hold these together. This is the discursive production of emptiness that brings forth the empty signifier.
5. Finally, the dividing function of the internal frontier and the unifying glue of the empty signifier together constitute the mythic totality of the Populus that is central to populist reason.

We should, for a moment, take a detour to note that M. K. Gandhi in *Hind Swaraj* displaces the question of "opposition to foreign rule as a sovereign aspiration" with the larger question of "civilizational difference" by saying that the British can remain and rule as long as they allow Indians to live the way they had lived before. It is pertinent to recall that it is in a similar note that Annadurai describes the *Aryan Allure* as Brahmin social order having been internalized by Tamil polities, stating categorically that it is more important to return to pre-Aryan values than thinking of driving the Aryans out. These gestures pave the way to a populist mobilization as against a mere nationalist mobilization since the "enemy" is internalized. It is because the thrust of the work becomes counter-hegemonic against the internally located enemy that the state and sovereignty are sidelined in populist reason, giving priority to self-governance.

For the DMK, even when it appeared on the political scene, the internal frontier dividing the Brahmin and non-Brahmin was well entrenched due to the work of Periyar and the DK. What was needed to construct a people was the empty signifier that would help the equivalential chain to hold in spite of the stark play of differences. Let us explain. All the caste groups that were not Brahmins would readily see their inferior status in relationship to the Brahmin whose scriptural authority was responsible for assigning such inferior status. However, the differences among the non-Brahmin castes were too stark to be neutralized by the common cause against the Brahmins. The exploitation of untouchables by landed castes and the dominant relationship trading castes had with laboring castes were all well forged into a highly naturalized system. While every caste demanded equality, they would only be too anxious not to grant it to those below them in the hierarchy before those above them accorded equal status to them since they would only slide down further if they equated themselves with the lower ranks without the higher ranks coming down to their level first. Hence, the differences among the social units as castes were too stark to have the equivalence work effectively.

When the first wave of anti-Hindi agitations in 1938–1939 brought neo-Shaivites, Self-Respecters who were turning atheists, Dalits, and people of several castes finding a common cause against Hindi imposition, it foretold the possibility of Tamil becoming the signifier that united everyone. Tamil was already undergoing a shift from its literal meaning as a language to a figural meaning that stood for the demands of respectability and well-being of its speakers. The sacred image of mother Tamil, the civilizational antiquity of Tamil, and so on at once helped various caste groups to feel equal to the British, who were empowered by the language of governance, English, and to the Brahmins who valorized Sanskrit as the language of gods. As a result, adherence to the Tamil identity suddenly appeared to free everyone from their binding to the caste identity.

While this proved to have a rare efficacy in rallying people, the risk of the dominant groups like Vellala Shaivites holding on to their hegemony through masquerading common Tamil identity was also stark. Even Brahmins themselves had a huge stake in the Tamil language in the sphere of religious life of both Shaivites and Vaishnavites due to the wealth of Tamil devotional literature of the Bhakti movement that lasted from the seventh to thirteenth centuries. Brahmins were also active Tamil devotees as scholars, poets, writers, and publicists, as Ramaswamy points out. If the Tamil identity united the non-Brahmins of various caste denominations, it also extended to the Brahmins on the other side of the internal frontier. This implied that the Dravidian identity should necessarily accompany the Tamil identity if equivalence among the non-Brahmin castes vis-à-vis the Brahmin injunctions had to be highlighted and the recalcitrant differences that perpetually metamorphized into hierarchy among non-Brahmins had to be mitigated. This resulted in a certain discursive conflation of non-Brahmin identity and Tamil identity, which became inseparable, confounding scholars and lay people alike.

In fact, the period between 1938 and 1944 is crucial to understanding how when the threat of Hindi imposition pushed the Dravidianists to demand a separate nation, the question of whether the nation should be Tamil Nadu or Dravida Nadu became a difficult historical choice. As we noted in discussing the recapitulation of the events of the period in Annadurai's *Ilaṭciya Varalāṟu*, or *The History of our Political Goal*, in the first post-anti-Hindi agitation conference of Tamils in 1938 and later in the Justice Party conference, there did arise the slogan "Tamil Nadu for Tamils" (the first four events listed in the table [Table 1.1] provided by *Ilaṭciya Varalāṟu* contain this slogan). It was after Periyar was released from prison, in 1940, that the idea of a separate nation was articulated as "Dravida Nadu for Dravidians." In the course of the next few years, the insistence on a Dravidian identity became far stronger, resulting in the new political vehicle formed in 1944 getting named as Dravidar Kazhagam. Annadurai was a key player in the formation of this new political vehicle under the leadership of Periyar. He had, in the interregnum, launched a periodical called *Tirāviṭa Nāṭu* in 1942, written the celebrated tract *Arya Mayai*, and also turned a playwright with *Cantramōhaṉ* or *Civāji Kaṇṭa Intu Cāmrājyam*, which we will discuss in detail in Chapter 5. All these works point to the priority Annadurai assigned to fighting Brahmin, casteist hegemony over a mere nationalist discourse.

Name of the People

The biggest challenge in the whole issue of understanding "Dravidian–Tamil" construction of the people is what could be the name of the people. While we could coin the phrase "Dravidian–Tamil" for analytical purposes, populism cannot have such combinations. It should either be this or that. The name of the people cannot be Dravidian for many reasons. The obvious and practical reason is that Dravidian as the name of the people far exceeds the territory of Tamil Nadu where the DMK was doing the mobilization. Conceptually, according to the line of argument we are pursuing, it can only mark the internal frontier and will not find it possible to stand for the equivalential chain of various social units, which for the moment we take as caste groups. Hence, the name of the people has to be necessarily Tamil.

As a corollary, if populism is not merely to replicate nationalism to do its work on constructing the people as a political act, the claim for national difference cannot be based on Tamil. It will have to intone the counter-hegemonic politics and hence can only be based on Dravidam. It is in realization of this compulsion that the DMK obstinately insisted on the federation of four south Indian states as an independent republic called Dravida Nadu. This made Tamil Nadu standing in for all of south India, in so far it spoke for the collective aspiration of all the four states, a synecdoche. Conversely, the Dravidian people who would be constructed as Tamil is an operation that is an intentional catachresis, since this naming of Tamil people is not descriptive, referring only to those who spoke Tamil. The two rhetorical operations of synecdoche and catachresis, as detailed above, inform the foundation of the Dravidian–Tamil polity. The naming of the people as Tamil, since it is not descriptive in this sense, refers to other non-Brahmin Dravidians speaking Telugu, Kannada, or Malayalam, not to mention other possible languages. It is only when the non-Brahmin or Dravidian subset consisting of heterogenous social units posits itself as Tamil people, claiming a totality for itself, thereby freeing the signifier Tamil from the signified who are the actual speakers of Tamil, can the act of naming construct a people as a political act. This is what we began to parse when we noted the populist dictum proposed by Laclau "the political construction of the people is, for that reason, essentially catachrestical." It will be useful to see how Laclau demonstrates this point through the division of plebs and Populus.

The original constitutive order imagines a Populus, a totality of social relationships. This can take the universal form of the state. The particular instances of civil society are deemed to be subsumed in it. This does not acknowledge the persistence of unfulfilled demands of those whom we may call plebs who feel excluded from the totality. Hence the totality presupposed is false. Conversely, the plebs who form an equivalential chain through the various particular demands seek to constitute the new Populus. They necessarily claim to be the totality. Laclau finds Hegel upholding the state at the cost of civil society, while he finds Marx upholding civil society while positing the withering away of the state. Laclau finds that it is with Antonio Gramsci

> that the articulation of both these instances becomes thinkable: for him there is a particularity—a plebs—which claims hegemonically to constitute a Populus, while the Populus (the abstract universality) can exist only as embodied in the plebs. When we reach that point, we are close to the "people" of populism. (Laclau 2005, 107)

We discussed in the last chapter how Annadurai found Tamil to be infused by Aryanism or Brahmin hegemony. Ramaswamy elaborately attests to the Indianist claims on Tamil. For the DMK, this pre-given totality of Tamil people is false. It is the plebs like the Dravidian non-Brahmin that now can lay claim to the totality of the Tamil people. It is in this necessary reversal that the signifier Tamil ceases to be merely descriptive, where it narrowly designates the signified as only those who speak Tamil, freeing and emptying itself of such a signification, expanding to refer to all the groups that develop equivalential demand for self-respect and dignified treatment on par with others. Thus, Tamil becomes the new name of the people who are non-Brahmin and Dravidian. It is only by endorsing Dravidian ideals that even the Brahmin can be readmitted to the totality of the Tamil people, an ideal now embodied in the Dravidian. In the words of Laclau,

> This is the same as saying that any hegemonic displacement should be conceived as a change in the configuration of the state, provided that the latter is conceived, not in a restrictive juridical sense, as the public sphere, but in an enlarged, Gramscian sense, as the ethico-political moment of the community. (Laclau 2005, 121)

When Ramaswamy asks the question "And why is it that one of the chief government buildings in Madras city carries the message, boldly emblazoned across its facade, 'Declare yourself a Tamilian! Stand proudly, your head held high!'? What is at stake in making such a claim?" and proceeds to answer with "My attempt to answer this question begins with the proposition that as the language they speak becomes subject to the discourse(s) of Tamilparru, its speakers become subjects of Tamil, their state of subjection reflected in the terms Tamil-an, 'Tamilian' (literally, 'he-of-Tamil'), or familiar, 'Tamilians' (literally, 'they-of-Tamil')," [9] we see an exact antithesis of what we are proposing. This is predictable since she thinks the signifier Tamil descriptively refers to the language and Tamilian descriptively refers to the one who speaks the language. In our understanding, following Laclau, Tamil now has become an empty signifier that can glide over various demands of heterogenous social units and Tamil people or Tamilians refer to the non-Brahmin Dravidian claiming to stand for the Populus of Tamil speakers. The exhortation *to stand proudly with the head held high declaring oneself as Tamilian* intones this claim of the pleb as Populus, the Dravidian as Tamil. This is not subjection to the language that is spoken of but taking possession of the language as the "ethico-political moment of the community."

One of the welcome consequences of this dual rhetorical operation of synecdochic nationalism and catachrestic construction of the people is that the social groups and castes that speak other languages at home like Telugu or Kannada but have been domiciled in what is now Tamil Nadu could join Tamil politics wholeheartedly. Tamil language for them is a public language, one that articulates the political aspirations of all the social units forming the equivalential chain. It is amazing how seamlessly and un-self-reflexively these linguistic groups take on the Tamil identity, as we will have occasions to narrate in the section on mobilization. In fact, one of the popular chief ministers of the Dravidianist era, M. G. Ramachandran, is well known to be a Malayalee. Though political rivals did talk about the leaders belonging to linguistic groups other than Tamil as a "lack," it never amounted to a serious challenge, unlike the Bharatiya Janata Party's campaign against Sonia Gandhi's Italian origin, which apparently stopped her from assuming the office of prime minister. After all, many a virulent Tamil nationalist of different political movements hailed from Telugu-speaking communities.

Radical Investment, Affect, and Performativity

It is well known that caste differences are not exactly like the differences among social units constituted retroactively by demands in the gloss of Laclau. They have a greater ontological validity due to the well-entrenched, nearly naturalized caste system than the emergent social units based on demands even when we grant the historical transformation that seek to reposition the caste groups with different sets of demands in the political arena (like, for instance, communal representation or reservation). The import of this factor of caste ontology is that the efficacy of the empty signifier in Laclau's schema can only work with far greater intensity in three of its accompanying features listed by him: radical investment, affect, and performativity. It is exactly the workings of these that are documented as the manifestations of passion by Ramaswamy. The usefulness of *PoT* vastly increases when it is reread through the analytical lens provided by Laclau, jettisoning the ill-fitting idea of colonial mimicry of linguistic nationalism à la Herder and Fichte, which act of mimicry is rather assumed and posited without fathoming the actual links to their work in the articulations of Tamil passion. It becomes necessary for us then to show how exactly we can claim to read passion for Tamil through the lens borrowed from Laclau.

The crucial task is to analytically segregate and see how the genealogy of non-Brahminism and the genealogy of Tamil investment had a tenuous and uncertain connection up until 1938 so that we can pry out the moment of the radical investment in Tamil as a populist moment. We need to begin with the fact that there were many contestations around the figure of the Brahmin in early twentieth-century Tamil

Nadu. The neo-Shaivites had a conflict with them in terms of the distinction of Tamil Shaivism, which they claimed to have independent origin from the Vedic religion. Though neo-Shaivites also championed Tamil antiquity vis-à-vis Sanskrit, this cannot be said to exceed the confines of the Shaivite Vellala–Brahmin conflict. Iyothee Dass, as Pandian showed, also had contestatory claims with regard to Brahmins on behalf of Adi Dravidas who he deemed as Buddhists, who were the "original" Brahmins (Pandian 2007, 112–115). Dass also had an investment in the Tamil identity and language. The Justice Party was founded by non-Brahmin elite to contest Brahmin domination in the government service, the emergent professions, and education constituting civil society. The Self-Respect Movement led by Periyar negated the whole system of caste hierarchy, which, it believed, is propagated and sustained through Brahmin hegemony. Periyar had no investment in the Tamil language, which he critiqued as imbued with reactionary values. The genealogy of non-Brahmin politics or Dravidianism and the genealogy of investment in Tamil were not always welded together or synchronized. Further, that the people of various castes spoke Tamil hardly helped mitigate the antagonisms of caste hierarchy.

It was the imposition of Hindi in 1938 that brought many caste groups and the genealogical strands of non-Brahmin Dravidianism together. It was at this moment that a new radical investment in Tamil came about as the name of the people. People belonging to different castes who always spoke Tamil suddenly realized that they were Tamil people. Phrases such as Tamiḻ *iṉam* (Tamil race), Tamiḻ *camūkam* (Tamil society), and Tamiḻarkaḷ (Tamilians) all came into vogue as a new rhetorical possibility of constructing a people. Tamil glided from its literal meaning as a language to mark a civilization, a culture, a land, and a people. Hence, the investment various scholars of Tamil renaissance, neo-Shaivites, and creative writers had in Tamil is vastly different from the radical investment that Dravidianism forged as the name of a people since 1938. Instead of seeing such a people constructed under the orbit of the "signifier Tamil," becoming subjects of history, enunciatory and agentive in their political assertion, Ramaswamy characterizes them as becoming subjected to the dictates of a now discursively inflated "Tamil," abdicating their selves in the service of and sacrifice for Tamil. The fact that the subaltern energy required such a construction of a people to address a range of grievances and subjugation is what came to be demonstrated by the widespread participation and martyrdom of commoners in the anti-Hindi struggle. It was also the secret of the phenomenal growth of the DMK, a manifestation and vindication of populist reason singular in its emergence under the sign Tamil.

In Laclau's gloss, the radical investment in the name of the people will not work without an affective relationship that provides the glue or link. It is customary for the Indianists, elites, and Congressites, from C. Rajagopalachari to contemporary scholars, to ridicule the emotional attachment of the uneducated, illiterate people to the Tamil language. Laclau is precise in saying

> affect is not something which exists on its own, independently of language; it constitutes itself only through the differential cathexes of a signifying chain. This is exactly what "investment" means. The conclusion is clear: the complexes which we call "discursive or hegemonic formations," which articulate differential and equivalential logics, would be unintelligible without the affective component. (This is further proof—where one still needed—of the inanity of dismissing emotional populist attachments in the name of an uncontaminable rationality.) (Laclau 2005, 111)

We can only add that the more recalcitrant the differential logic is for easy accommodation in the equivalential chain, the greater will have to be the affective charge of the radical investment in the name of the people, if the name is to do its function in the struggle for hegemony. Though all politics and social units formed by various demands cannot be reduced to caste groups, the salience of the dialectic of caste as differential logic and Tamil as the equivalential logic in the populist reason of Tamil Nadu in which the non-Brahmin plebs aspire to attain the mythical fullness of the Populus cannot be overemphasized.

We will not be able to understand the affective potential of the radical investment in the name of the people as Tamil without paying attention to the performativity of the language use fashioned by the DMK leaders, led by the personal example of Annadurai. His success as a publicist, as an orator, as a dramatist, and as a script and dialogue writer in films all depended on his innovative style of language use, which consisted of free use of rhyme and alliteration, and a close attention to cadence produced when read aloud or listened to. In being so performed, the signifier Tamil attained a greater degree of freedom for political purposes in its figural meaning as against the language of everyday use.

Performing Tamil: The "I" of the *Medai* Tamil

The most popular form in which the *adukku mozhi* (literally, "structured language") or ornamental language was used was of course in public speaking called *medai peccu* (stage talk) in Tamil. Bernard Bate (2011) has elaborated on this phenomenon in his work *Tamil Oratory and the Dravidian Aesthetic: Democratic Practice in South India*. Before we discuss this work to elaborate on our own understanding of the democratic practice, let us note that the feature known as *aṭukku moḻi* was common to print literature, fiction, dialogues in drama, and cinema that the DMK produced. As already stated, it was Annadurai who lead the way in fashioning such usage in all these forms. It will be useful to consider a sample from a sentence written in his magazine *Dravida Nadu*. We will first give the passage in Tamil, then in English transliteration and finally an approximate translation. This is necessary to understand the use of sound patterns and the resultant rhetorical structuration of the argument.

> மணம் வீசும் மல்லிகைத் தோட்டம் மாற்றானுடையது என்று தெரிந்ததால் உண்டான மன எரிச்சலைப் போக்கிக் கொள்ள மன்னார்சாமி ஒருவன், மலக்குவியலை கண்டுபிடித்து, வாரி வாரி வீசினானாம் மல்லிகைத் தோட்டத்தில், மணம் கெடும் என்று. ஆனால் வீசப்பட்டது உரமாகிவிட்டது தோட்டத்துக்கு. அது போல வசைமாரி பொழிந்து வருகிறார்கள்.

> ***ma***ṇam vīcum ***ma***llikait tōṭṭam ***mā***ṟṟāṉuṭaiyatu eṉṟu terintatāl uṇṭāṉa ***ma***ṉa ericcalaip pōkkik koḷḷa ***ma***ṉṉārcāmi oruvaṉ, ***ma***lakkuviyalaik kaṇṭupiṭittu, vāri vāri vīciṉāṉām ***ma***llikait tōṭṭattilē, ***ma***ṇam keṭum eṉṟu. āṉāl vīcappaṭṭatu ura***mā***kiviṭṭatu tōṭṭattukku. atupōla vacai***mā***ri poḻintu varukiṟārkaḷ.

> On finding, that the garden of fragrant jasmine belongs to the other person, one Mannarsamy, in order to heal his heartburn, found a pile of feces and threw that in the garden, thinking the fragrance would fade. However, what was thrown became fertilizer to the garden. Likewise, abuses are being showered (on us—by the Congress).

While the use of the "ma" sound in ten places, eight of them being the first syllable of the words, makes the sentence rhyme fully, there are many other repetitive sounds that add to it like the *vicum, vicinanam, vicappattatu, vacaimari* sequence. With all these repetitive sounds the sentence acquires a cadence, which makes the sentence appealing to the ears when read aloud. A shorter phrase extracted from the sentence, *māṟṟāṉ tōṭṭattu mallikaiyum maṇakkum* (the jasmine in the other man's garden is also fragrant), became a standard allusion for appreciating anything said or done by members of other political formations or opposing political formations in the spirit of bipartisanship.

This ornamental mode of speaking, the use of such sound patterns, is not common to everyday speech, particularly since most of the suffixes indicating the tense, gender, and honor are elided in common speech. If these are pronounced fully and properly, the language sounds like written grammatical Tamil and not speech. When such a grammatically perfect language is used in oration, added with a whole range of rhyming and alliterative sound patterns, it performs Tamil language as a distinct signifier of political communication and mediation. As everyday speech is marked by tonal inflections that are specific to caste groups and regions, this new ornamental or structured speech, *aṭukku moḻi*, helped to mark a new political subjectivity of the speaker. In a different context, discussing the emergence of the lingua franca Melayu, in Indonesia, anthropologist James Siegel proposed that the use of lingua franca constituted a new political subjectivity that was poised between the speaker and the listener, the "I" of the lingua franca, which marked their new relationship.

> The lingua franca was exterior to all speakers in that no one thought it originated with them, it existed merely, as it were, between them. Of course, all languages mediate. But the lingua franca is always, by definition, a language in some way foreign to both the speaker and his interlocutor. It contains the possibility, therefore, of changing the "I" of the original language into a second— "I", an "I" incipient in dual form in the other as well as myself. Once it becomes the medium that generally pertained between the groups of a plural society and once it was "activated" in the way that we have suggested, other languages, and even other forms of mediation, take on heightened powers of transmission as well. (Siegel 1997, 32)

The *medai* Tamil was certainly not lingua franca. As Bate has elaborately shown, this belonged only to the DMK speakers of a given era. The elder politicians spoke in everyday language or some in a scholarly Tamil, the language of the pundits. The Congress leaders, particularly Brahmins, spoke a heavily Sanskritized Tamil. For example, they would address the people as *mahajanangale*, meaning "a congregation of people." It was routine in the DMK stage to begin with *periyorgale, thaimarkale*, which is akin to "ladies and gentlemen," but literally "elders and mothers." Bate has analyzed in detail the structure of the speech by a female party worker in the 1980s in Madurai. In his own description, in the "Afterword," Bate has this to say in brief about the use of this new language:

> What we have called the centamil revolution embodied a "proper" distinction between leaders and the people, a political distinction between the DMK and the Congress Party, and a civilizational distinction between the Dravidian and the Indo-Aryan civilizations. A new, archaic, feminized, literary, and therefore "proper" mode of speech was markedly different from the ordinary speech of people in their everyday lives. It was distinguished from the plain speech of a previous generation of Congressmen and people like Periyar E. V. Ramasamy of the DK (who was decisively not engaging in party politics). And Dravidianist orators became avatars of Tamil itself, of its purity, its virginity and its antiquity. As far as the vast majority of Tamilians were concerned, the Dravidianist paradigm embodied a Tamil tradition, and in so doing invented it. (Bate 2011, 183)

While this description of the language is helpful, there is one distinction that is mentioned, that "between the leaders and the people" is not necessarily correct. Many of the speakers of the DMK, like the example of Kavitha in Bate's work, hailed from among common people to train themselves in the political articulation through *centamil* or *medai* Tamil. More than that, instead of creating a hiatus between the leaders and the followers, as Siegel has suggested, this new mediality, through difference of the ornamental Tamil, in fact forged a new relationship between the speaker and interlocutor that was the work of empty signifier in naming a people.

Bate is accurate in his identification of the nature of the political mobilization effected by the speech.

> In the case of the Tamils (and much of South India generally), the struggle took the form of lower caste/class groups challenging the hierarchical paradigms of the highest caste/class, Brahmins. Contrary to the situation in North India, which saw a "vertical" mobilization of castes and classes in the Indian independence movement, Dravidian nationalist politics was characterized by a "horizontal" mobilization of the lower classes and castes vis-a-vis the Brahmin-controlled Congress. (Bate 2011, 184)

Thus, the name of the people, Tamil, generating a new radical investment, affective bonding, and performative dalliance, came to function as the empty signifier that accompanied the internal frontier set between Brahmin and non-Brahmin in the effort to dismantle casteist hegemony to found an egalitarian space for the conduct of democratic politics.

Notes

1. Namakkal Ramalingam (1888–1972) was active in the Congress in the early decades of the twentieth century. After independence, he was recognized as a state poet by the Tamil Nadu government; he also served two terms as a member of the Madras legislative council between 1957 and 1967. We will see more of him in Chapter 8.
2. See Ramaswamy (1997).
3. The relationship proposed between token and type in semeiotic is fraught. In the case of Chinnasamy, if he is taken to be token that belonged to the type of subaltern pleb, asserting his self-respect and dignity in seeking to construct a new Populus under the sign Tamil, the trajectory of analyses will have to be entirely different than that is pursued in *PoT*. The book does not even gesture in this direction. In simple terms, the first part of Chinnasamay's cry "Hindi oliga!" is subsumed under the second part of the cry, "Tamil valga!" It could have been the other way around.
4. If nothing else, any acquaintance with the debates in the wake of the party split engineered by Sampath, who called his party Tamil Desiya Katchi (Tamil Nationalist Party) should have alerted one to the fact that the DMK held on to the idea of the south Indian multilingual Dravidian republic. The manifesto of the DMK released for the 1962 elections after Sampath split categorically reiterated the goal of the Dravidian republic comprising four major linguistic regions.
5. For Periyar's disquiet about Tamil nation as a derivative of Tamil past, see Pandian (1993).
6. We will be discussing the take of Ravi Vaitheespara on the crucial role of neo-Shaivism in the next chapter. For an intensive case study of the life and career of Maraimalai Adigal, arguably the most celebrated exponent of neo-Shaivism and Shaiva Siddhanta in early twentieth-century Tamil Nadu, who forged a distinct ideological projection of

a Tamil nation in contradistinction to an Aryan Brahmanical nation, even as he recast Shaivism and Shaiva Siddhanta as an exclusively Tamil religion, see Vaitheespara (2015).

7. For tracking the relationship neo-Shaivites forged with the Self-Respecters, see Venkatachalapathy (1995).
8. See Pandian (2007). We find his framework relevant for the politics of the DMK as well, though his book does not extensively deal with it. However, in an earlier essay published in 1989, it appears that Pandian too had thought that the DMK subscribed to Tamil nationalism, that too a regressive one, though by 2007 he does not appear to reiterate the idea. See Pandian (2019, 22–29).
9. Ramaswamy (1997, 250). The phrase is a translation of a line from a poem titled "Tamiḻaṉ" by Namakkal Ramalingam Pillai, whose another verse we have given as epigraph of the chapter: "Thamizhan enru sollada! Thalai nimirnthu nillada!"

3 Human Immanence

> Rather the question is what sources can support our far-reaching moral commitments to benevolence and justice.
>
> —Charles Taylor, *Sources of the Self: The Making of the Modern Identity*

We have postulated, through the first two chapters, that the populist logic that informed the DMK is the hegemonic assertion of non-Brahmin–Dravidian (the pleb) as Tamil (the populous) through dismantling the Aryan–Brahmin hegemony established in Tamil Nadu. If the name of the people, Tamil, the empty signifier, is not to eclipse the internal frontier necessary for the counter-hegemonic assertion, the catachrestic naming of the non-Brahmin Dravidian as Tamil is to be complemented by the synecdochic claim of Tamil Nadu to aspire for a Dravidian republic that spread all over peninsular India. What we need to consider is that while this can be the populist logic, whether such counter-hegemonic assertion can be made without recourse to certain appeal to a historical sense of change, which came to be known as "modernity" or "modernization." The populist logic will not work effectively if it does not involve what Charles Taylor has called the forging of a new social imaginary which is involved in the making of a modern identity through locating a range of sources of the self in tradition.[1] Our postulate in that regard in this chapter is that the DMK managed to make connections, imaginatively and creatively, to sources in Shaivite metaphysic without having to yield to the Tamil nationalist prodding of neo-Shaivites of the nineteenth and early twentieth centuries, as argued by some.

We need to recognize that in the Tamil instance, the creation of modern social imaginary with appeals to traditional sources of the self was fraught with innumerable conundrums because the core of the imaginary consisted of removing caste from the public sphere by either sequestering it to the private lives or annihilating it fully to fashion a caste neutral self. This entailed a need to repudiate, challenge, or at least critically interrogate traditional Brahminical mores enmeshed with practices of rituals and piety. This placed a huge demand on political actors of all kinds to make a statement on where they stood in terms faith, belief, customs on the one hand, and humanist credo and scientific rationality on the other. Periyar created a unique space for political mobilization with his unrestrained agonism, which called every aspect of the belief system and cultural practices into question, opening up the possibilities of newer modes of associational life and collective action. He was unencumbered by the need to evolve consensus, either to build a party organization or enter the electoral fray towards participation in democratic self-governance. The DMK, which by definition wanted to seek empowerment through the exercise of universal adult franchise the new Indian republic offered, necessarily needed to invent other ways of combining modern social imaginary and traditional sources of the self. This predictably led to charges of compromise from the vantage point of pursuers of radical change.

In what follows, we will take note of the role of neo-Shaivites in making headways in the direction of fashioning a new selfhood for modern polity in the Tamil region. We will then study the work of Charles Ryerson, who analyzed the Dravidian movement and particularly the DMK in the prism of social change or modernization in tandem with neo-Shaivism. Following the exercise, we will try to connect with the thoughts of Taylor through a reading of the conceptual developments of the Dravidian movement. We will read a seminal essay by C. N. Annadurai on the question of moral allegiance in the light of latter-day postulates of Taylor. We will then return to consider certain claims related to the DMK being an extension of nationalist thought made possible by neo-Shaivism in an essay by Ravi Vaitheespara. It is through a critical engagement with such a proposition that we hope to show a far more refined genealogical connection the DMK made with Shaivite metaphysic as sources of the self rather than being inheritors of nascent articulations of Tamil nationalism by neo-Shaivites. This continues our argument in the second chapter that the DMK is a populist party appealing to republican spirit and democratic practice, and not a Tamil nationalist party.

Modernity of Caste, Tradition of Anti-Caste Piety

The caste system backed by religious injunctions became all the more refined through colonial modernity via census and with the Dharma Shastras being accommodated in colonial jurisprudence, as we discussed earlier in the first chapter through a reading of Annadurai's *Aryan Allure*. In fact, it has been argued by Nicholas Dirks that caste as we know it in contemporary society was invented by the colonial rule (Dirks 2002). In addition to such an imputation of "modernity of caste" or the invented tradition of caste as part of modernity, there were of course several movements in the history of religious practices, based on the devotees' direct appeal to God known as Bhakti, circumventing the priest and the temple, that had defied caste hierarchy. They may remind us of the idea of *communitas* that Victor Turner developed with Francis of Assisi as the prime example, a social group moving outside the social structure under the influence of a direct appeal to God led by a saint (Turner 1995). In India, such movements initially posed a challenge to the caste order only to later become *societas* finding a niche in the same order, as Turner noted in his theorization. It is possible that in the process some social groups climbed up the ladder in caste hierarchy. A good example could be the low-caste converts to Vaishnavism during the twelfth century under the influence of saint-philosopher Ramanuja, who probably turned into Brahmin sects in due course.[2] The implication of this phenomenon for our analysis is that there were indigenous sources of defiance to the authority of the Brahmin and his caste injunctions. There have also been notably non-Brahmin sects and practices that were later taken as an integral part of Hinduism like Shaivism in Tamil Nadu and Karnataka.

If we take caste as an invention of tradition and anti-caste spirit as a part of the actual tradition, "a traditionalization of change," invented or otherwise, there is an explanation of modernization in Tamil Nadu that can be read as continuity of tradition rather than rupture in terms of religion. Understandably, various theories of Tamil or Indian modernity have been put forth by political actors, Indian and Western scholars, historians, anthropologists, religionists, and so on, in which the rupture and continuity models, welcome or deleterious influences of the West, and colonialism have all been variously stated. For our purposes of understanding the structures of ideation that accompanied the political mobilization of the DMK, we need to primarily consider both the genealogies of non-Brahmin and Tamil identity that had the religious imprint to see how exactly the DMK could mark its position in the matrix to carry out the task of constructing a people, the Dravidian–Tamil people, with a social imaginary based on the indigenous sources of moral conduct of the self.

Neo-Shaivism as the Template of Regionalism

We encounter a daring thesis in the work of Ryerson (1988) who suggested that "regional Hinduism" is the primary template on which regionalism is forged. With some hand wringing as to whether the regional variations are little traditions apropos the great tradition of Sanskritic Hinduism or sometimes as in Tamil Nadu, there are independent great traditions involved and so on, Ryerson feels that while something like a Great Tradition, a highly reflective religious school, might have prevailed in the region of Tamil Nadu, it was not entirely independent of the pan-Indian great tradition. The case in point of course is neo-Shaivism, with which we are already familiar. Neo-Shaivism first posited both non-Brahmin Dravidian as well as the Tamil identity, say like in the work of Manonmaniam Sundaram Pillai,[3] whose verse has been adapted as the state anthem, which is a benediction for Tamil Thai. Hence, neo-Shaivism is seen to be the genealogical fountainhead for the later movements or the later phases of the Dravidian movement, in singular. We need to consider the claim a little elaborately to understand the specific historical formation of the DMK.

The general problem of the extant literature on the DMK is to treat it as a part of, or rather a particular phase of, the homogenous Dravidian movement, which assumption fails to grasp the absolute distinction and novelty of what we outlined above as the populist logic of DMK politics. We need to distinguish the DMK from all previous articulations of both Dravidian and Tamil identity. Until the birth of the South Indian Liberal Federation (the Justice Party), all articulations were in the nature of public sphere debates and formation of sectarian associations. The Justice Party gave non-Brahmin interests a definite liberal political plane in which it could address the state for redressal as part of the emerging political modernity. However, as already noted through Annadurai's recounting in the first chapter, it remained restricted to civil society liberalism to the extent the colonial state would be supportive. The Justice Party did not mobilize people at large. It did not appear to be preoccupied with what we posit as Brahmin hegemony and the task of dismantling the same. In total contrast, the Self-Respect Movement of Periyar (1925–1944) fully focused on the counter-hegemonic struggle with an avowed distance from electoral politics and governance. When both these streams merged to form the Dravidar Kazhagam (DK) in 1944, Annadurai was a key player who tried to combine both the liberal structure of a political organization, mass mobilization, and the counter-hegemonic thrust against Brahmin dominance. As Periyar was not amenable to building an organizational structure, opting for a free-flowing range of agonistic interventions and to act as a pressure group in the political scene, Annadurai had to leave the DK. Hence, it was only with the birth of the DMK that the truly populist phase of the Dravidian movement, which combined the task of building an organization, mobilizing the people, and effecting a hegemonic assertion, emerged. It was through the DMK mobilization that non-Brahminism and the Tamil identity came to reinforce each other as the internal frontier and empty signifier respectively as the building blocks of populist reason, which should mark its absolute distinction when we discuss modernization of the polity.

It became the historical task of the DMK to forge a new social imaginary and find alternative sources of the self to build a modern identity and politics. In the widespread commonsensical recounting among the people of Tamil Nadu, the DMK "compromised" on the ideological purity of Periyar's atheism to articulate an inchoate accommodation of belief, which is deemed to signpost its desire for power at the cost of ideological integrity. While, of course, the supporters of the party call it a necessary liberal rearticulation of the radical position, the charges of dilution are all too frequent. Everyone repeats the catch phrase "Oṉṟē kulam Oruvaṉē Tēvaṉ," which we would translate as "Singular is the race, Singular the Lord"—a line Annadurai approvingly adapted from *Tirumantiram*, a twelfth-century Shaiva Siddhanta text by the mystic Tirumūlar, a Siddha, as the DMK's alleged official position on religion (Tirumular 1991). Ryerson reports asking Periyar about this slogan of Annadurai only to fetch a dismissive response calling it an electoral compulsion (Ryerson 1988, 136). Of course, it appears a whole deal is involved in the shift from a strident "there is no God" position to the admission of an unnamed singular Lord. Was it conceding too much of a ground to the religionists? Does it compromise secular politics? By the way, what does it mean to speak of a singular Lord without naming him? Is it just cleverness? We need to approach the question a little elaborately to see what is at stake for the DMK in this reformulation. In a sense, to boldly abbreviate the elaborate meditations of Taylor, the fundamental challenge is the question of whether it is possible to have a conception of the Good, without a conception of God or a hyper good that helps to order the multiplicity of Goods. In Taylor's conclusion, we see this as the necessary dilemma in the project of modernity. Periyar did not have to face the challenge since he was not in the act of constructing a people; he was only dismantling a prior construction: caste hierarchy. The DMK was founded to construct a people as a formal requisite for the hegemonic assertion of non-Brahminic, egalitarian social imaginary. Having taken note of the particularity of the populist reason that the DMK forged, let us return to Ryerson to see how he frames the DMK in a scheme of modernization.

Religion and Themes of Modernization—I: Charles Ryerson

It is more or less the period of our study that Charles Ryerson covers. He finds Tamil renaissance having its "Golden Years" between 1949 and 1972. The year 1972 marks the split in the DMK with M. G. Ramachandran founding the Anna DMK, later to be known as All-India Anna DMK. Ryerson credits the DMK as the primary vehicle of Tamil people through which they forged a new identity, albeit with firm links with the past. He opts to work on history backwards from the present that Clifford Geertz suggested based on an observation by Søren Kierkegaard. In addition to his indebtedness to Geertz, Ryerson develops much of his framework from a succinct essay of Robert Bellah that summarizes the problematic of modernization (Bellah 1968).

The basic outline of Bellah's summary goes like this: The stability of identity of both the individual and society was being provided by religion. Modernity, which is fundamentally a new mentality, a welcome attitude to change to be directed and controlled by reason, produces tension with the stability of identity that continuity of tradition ensures. In its political form, secular liberalism is the mainstay of modernization. One of the mitigating interregnums between the traditional religious society and secular liberalism of modernity could be religious reform that prepares the ground for modernization, like the much-celebrated example of protestant Christianity. It also appears implicit to Bellah's analysis that civic culture, certain individualism, brought about by economic, scientific, and political activities is of course key to such a change. If there has been some traditionalization of change in resident cultures, that also would sure be of help. When these helpful conditions are not fully present, Bellah suggests, certain primordial identities of language, ethnic origin, and religion are mobilized to produce romantic nationalism that could produce solidarity to contain the tensions of modernization brought about by the "psycho-sociological revolution." The other alternative is radical socialism that aspires to negate any and all of the unequal conditions of the traditional society by forging new unity. In fact, it is various combinations of romantic nationalism and radical socialism that could ameliorate the conflictual conditions of modernization. It should be noted that Bellah proposes romantic nationalism based on primordial identities as distinct from civic nationalism of the Anglo-French thought. Bellah passingly mentions India in the essay as using religion as the resource to encounter the "impinging modernity" that may be read as colonial inauguration of modernity. Interestingly, he does not appear to think of India as a site of religious conflict but as a candidate for romantic nationalism based on a unitary religion. The essay first appeared in 1968 and it is certainly not clear how this reading of India came to pass in spite of the famed inculcation of Nehruvian socialist, secularist ethos in popular politics lead by the Congress.

Ryerson, in trying to understand the modernization of Tamil Nadu, prefers to use Geertzian terminology of "primordial sentiment" in the place of "primordial identity." He does not take time to explain why Indian or Tamil nationalism cannot be considered "civil nationalism." At any rate, Ryerson is genuinely fascinated by what he considers as the rich amalgam of tradition and modernity in Tamil Nadu. His introductory chapter lists three personal experiences that had an affective bearing on him: one was finding a lonely singer in an ancient temple singing a hymn written a thousand years ago; the other was the sighting of a rocket launched for atmospheric testing in the evening sky of Kanyakumari, which interestingly he remarks as the demonstration of the "onrush of modernity" like something that happened in thirteenth-century Europe, the generous separation in the world historical timescale being remarkable; the third is his watching a film in which a dark-skinned woman protagonist sings to Lord Krishna, the dark-skinned god, about how his skin tone is revered while hers is reviled. Of course, all these benign signs of synthesis of the past and present stand against the tumult of violent caste conflicts, which is caused by and further strengthen the resolve of the outcastes in refusing to endure indignity anymore. It is through these juxtapositions that Ryerson is fascinated by the rise of modern Tamil identity at the behest of the DMK. Hence, primordiality is the bedrock of this modernization. Language, ethnic origin, and religion, all three primordial ties listed by Bellah have a role to play since the DMK appealed to Tamil language and identity, Dravidian race as the origin of the people, and of course the very instrument of caste, which is embedded in religion.

Given this framework, Ryerson conveniently places Periyar E. V. Ramasamy as standing for radical socialism and Annadurai for romantic nationalism. In a fusion of sorts, he names M. Karunanidhi as standing for resurgent regionalism since the chapter on him covers the period from 1969 to 1972, in which Karunanidhi manages to consolidate the DMK with a thumping electoral victory in 1971. Among these, what is most pertinent for our analysis is the description of Annadurai as standing for romantic nationalism. The primordial sentiment with regard to the Tamil language, the passion for the tongue we discussed in the previous chapter, gets exemplified in this account as well. As for continuing with the "racial" Dravidian identity, of course the case is obvious. Ryerson's discomfort is regarding DMK's sentiment about religion. He is able to show easily that Annadurai and the DMK did not endorse atheism in so far as they did not seem to dismiss the idea of God totally. What proves elusive, however, is what they mean by God, since it always appears to be displaced into some kind of secular ideal like servicing the poor and holding on to duty and so on. Ryerson notes that Annadurai categorically denounced Shaivism with regard to the stories of its saints, Nayanmars, and its gods. Still Anna had taken his one-line policy statement on religion, the quizzical "Oṉṟē kulam Oruvaṉē Tēvaṉ" (Singular is the race, Singular the Lord) from a Shaivite text. For all his interest in religion and modernity, Ryerson leaves this extraordinary appropriation of a phrase from a text on metaphysics as the core principle of a modern-day political party without much explanation.

In fact, Ryerson's book begins with a chapter on the history of Tamil Nadu, early renaissance during the nineteenth century, figures of saint poets in the Shaivite tradition, the reformist figure of Ramalinga Adigalar, and then the Indianists and Compensatory Classicists we encountered in Sumathi Ramaswamy's account, Maramalai Adigal, Thiru Vi. Kalyanasundaranar, Subramanya Bharathi, and finally, Bharathi Dasan, to name a few. It is in this backdrop that the radical socialism of Periyar and romantic nationalism of Annadurai are placed. In effect, Ryerson invests so much energy on continuity and primordial sentiments and links to the past that he hardly grapples with the newness of the political situation in any substantial sense. He reports on political developments in summary fashion and offers sociological or anthropological gloss à la Bellah and Geertz. The radical socialism of Periyar is easily accommodated as "religion like anti-religion" and as one that does not entirely refuse to engage with religion. In such an analytical lens, though Periyar's atheist credentials are good, the effect of his work is evaluated more like religious reform than that of abolishing it. If that is the case with Periyar, it is not very hard to show that the DMK had no intention whatsoever of abolishing religion. Though the primordial sentiment related to religion is certainly not as strong as that of those about language and ethnic origins, it can be deemed to make itself present as some kind of ideational complex involved with the other two since there was no particular aspiration to "abolish" religion. The contemporary "human metaphors" Ryerson picks up, from public sphere figures like Kundrakudi Adigalar and Kirubanandha Variar to the anthropological sample of one unmarked citizen named Chidambaram, show a healthy amalgamation of political interests in Tamil identity, regionalism, and religious life of various kinds. As a result of all this, Ryerson thinks by and large what enabled the formation of modern identity in and through Dravidianism is the particularly distinct form of Hinduism that developed in Tamil Nadu in contradistinction to the Great Tradition of Sanskritic Hinduism. Ultimately, Ryerson, for all his admiration for the Dravidian movement, does not identify and demonstrate any innovative contribution made by the DMK to the paradoxical process of modernization.

Nevertheless, there are crucial unexplored indicators in Ryerson's work. For example, he introduces Annadurai with these remarks:

> There is no greater embodiment of Tamil primordial sentiments than he, but he also represented a "civilizing" of the sentiments, accommodating them to the civil politics of India, and to a lesser degree, to the Sanskritizing process of Hinduism. In so doing, he articulated a regional Hinduism more than a new religion or an atheistic stance. (Ryerson 1988, 109)

It is not clear what contributes to this perception of the agonistic binding of primordial solidarity and civil politics. Generally, as we saw with Bellah, who classified India as taking recourse to religion for its nationalist politics vis-à-vis Anglo-French civil nationalism, there is a general confusion about secular liberalism and civil nationalism outside Europe since many scholars of Western academia are unable to recognize different forms of civil nationalism for which apparently the West owns the sole model or prototype.[4] A far more confusing assertion is the claim about Annadurai contributing to the Sanskritization of Hinduism, while articulating "regional Hinduism" (with the underlying formula Tamilization = Sanskritization = absorption into Great Tradition). The general source of trouble appears to be a lack of theoretical understanding about populism, which alone can bring about liberalism and civil nationalism in a country that has not gone through industrialization and a substantial spread of print culture due to widespread illiteracy. This becomes clear when Ryerson throws in another summing up evaluation of Annadurai: "He articulated this powerful combination of radical socialism and romantic nationalism in a unique and compelling way. To continue with Bellah's terminology, Annadurai infused the potentially disruptive mixture with a large dose of liberalism. In so doing, he provided a framework of meaning for large numbers of Tamils" (Ryerson 1988, 109). What Ryerson leaves without explaining is the meaning of the "large dose of liberalism" much akin to the earlier task achieved by Annadurai described as "civilizing primordial sentiments."

Even as Ryerson, in spite of his many insightful observations and admiring remarks, does not come up with a sufficient distinction between the primordial sentiments and civil nationalism or liberalism in the making of the politics of the DMK, the claim on behalf of neo-Shaivism that it was the precursor of "Dravidian and Tamil national politics" continues to have certain salience. For Ravi Vaitheespara once again lays claim that it was the group of neo-Shaivite proponents inspired by Ramalinga Adigalar and were English educated such as Manonmaniam Sundaram Pillai (1855–1897), Nallaswamy Pillai (1864–1920), and Maraimalai Atikal (1876–1950), most particularly the third, who instantiated a "grammar of critical practice" that laid the groundwork for later phases of the Dravidian movement, including Periyar's Self-Respect Movement (Vaitheespara 2012).

Ravi Vaitheespara states in the abstract that they deployed Shaivism for "Dravidian and Non-Brahmin Tamil nationalist project." The title of the essay makes a bolder suggestion: "Re-inscribing Religion as Nation." The primary analytical axis of the essay rests in mapping the adversarial debate between Naveener Shaivite (Tamil term for neo-Shaivite; literally, "modern Shaivite") and other contemporary Shaivite scholars, the orthodox mutts and so on, who were opposed to the contamination of the religion with political claims for the language and anti-caste sentiments. Vaitheespara is unhappy with Pandian's characterization of both neo-Buddhism of Iyothee Dass and neo-Shaivism of Maramalai Atikal for taking the Brahmin ideal as the model to which claims are made on behalf of certain pasts of Adi Dravida or Poorva Buddhists and Shaivite Vellala culture. In Pandian's gloss, these early formulations had an appeal limited to the respective groups so posited, to which these scholars belonged, though Tamil as a signifier and Dravidian racial identity were invoked. Pandian distinguishes it from the liberal political articulation of the Justice Party and the popular counter-hegemonic Self-Respect Movement, which fostered a certain "universal" idiom of non-Brahminism (Pandian 2007, 111–142). Vaitheespara protests that such an easy dismissal of the neo-Shaivite critical idiom does not do justice to a possible continuity in the intellectual history of non-Brahminism. Vaitheespara also expresses a similar dissatisfaction with the detailed historical account of the much-troubled actual relationship between neo-Shaivite Vellala scholars and the Self-Respecters sketched by A. R. Venkatachalapathy, with attendant trifold classification of Shaivite world. We can see that a certain abstraction like "grammar of critical practice" helps Vaitheespara to remain dissatisfied with the actual historical narration etched by A. R. Venkatachalapathy both in English and Tamil (Venkatachalapathy 1995; Ā.Irā.Vēṅkaṭācalapati 2020) as to the adversarial distance that existed between the Shaivite scholars and the Self-Respect Movement, in spite of the historical conjunctions that brought them together.

In our analysis, the problem with Ryerson's speculations about regional Hinduism and the claims of "grammar of critical practice" made by Vaitheespara, or any such claim made for other religious and intellectual practice, does not lie in adjudicating how exactly they may have aided the discursive formation of Dravidianism. Instead, what calls for critical attention is how, after the anti-Hindi agitation of 1938, Periyar and Annadurai with extraordinary acuity, deliberately and willfully disinvested themselves of the primordial sentiments about language and religion to make the synecdochic claim for a Dravidian country comprising all the four linguistic states of south India, a purely putative political identity. We find most of the existing scholarship and debates appearing so uncomfortable with this stunning act of rendering the national aspiration putative and the accompanying catachrestic naming of the Tamil people as Dravidian that they generally chose to treat the resultant politics as Tamil nationalist politics in disguise.

Vaitheespara repeatedly mentions Tamil nationalism in his essay, though the abstract coins the elaborately descriptive "Dravidian and Non-Brahmin Tamil Nationalist project," thus ordering the adjectives hierarchically through closeness to the substantive noun phrase "nationalist project." First, Tamil; second, non-Brahmin; third, Dravidian. As fact would have it, in the stormy years in which the post-colonial Indian nation was being shaped, the claim made by Periyar and Annadurai was for a republic comprising the whole of south India for which they had not mobilized elite consensus or popular support. This should have completely marginalized them as some political pressure group falling between two historically realizable nation-states: India and Tamil Nadu. It is the ingenuity of Annadurai that found a space for populist reason and a historic construction of a people as the cornerstone of democratic politics in the emerging global context instead of opting for a prototypical nation-state. Of course, Periyar had a similar intellectual distance from aspirations to sovereignty. Hence, both were able to desist the temptation to demand a Tamil nation. It is not difficult to speculate that their reason for such a political decision was not only the Brahmin hegemony that they sought to displace onto the pan-Indian nationalist project but also the equally casteist Shaivite hegemony waiting in the wings for a Tamil nationalist project to emerge. For tactical reasons, we presume, they were unable to articulate this key reason for disavowal of Tamil nationalism in such clear terms in the turbulent years between 1938 and 1944.[5] This is why perhaps, much later in the late 1950s, Periyar felt closer to the Tamil nation sponsored by emergent Nadars vis-à-vis the long entrenched, hegemonic, and landed Vellala-sponsored Tamil nationalism of the early 1940s. Our hypothesis would be that such intrinsic concern for the subaltern assertion in democratic politics is what has given salient energy to the populist politics of the DMK, which opted for the primary act of constructing a people over any elite-sponsored nationalist project. It is necessary to conceive the act of construction of a people as a continuous deferral and a multi-directional displacement of fragmented sovereignty to which concept we would return in the Conclusion.

Religion and Themes of Modernization—II: Charles Taylor

The political evolution of the DMK is eminently suited to the discussion of the problem of modernity as outlined by Taylor in both *Sources of the Self: The Making of the Modern Identity* and *Modern Social Imaginaries* (Taylor 1992; 2007). The reason is not hard to seek if we fully grasp the lineaments of Tamil society when the party was founded, about which we have already made some remarks in the previous chapters. Tamil Nadu, as any of the religionists would attest, is literally flooded with temples, shrines, and deities with attendant rituals of a breathtaking variety. The website of the government department in charge of temple administration, Hindu Religious and Charitable Endowments Board (HR&CE), mentions that there are 44,121 temples under its control.[6] This obviously does not include a vast number of village and roadside shrines that are privately managed by individuals or communities, which may often lack elaborate temple structures and other criteria to come under the management of HR&CE. In the widespread common sense of the people, moral rectitude is inalienably linked to the fear of God (not faith or belief since such dispositions do not arise distinctively in the ontic pre-supposition of God).[7] It is common to see the adjective "god fearing" qualifying the bride or bridegroom in matrimonial columns even today. In other words, the predominant understanding of the essence of being in Tamil Nadu, all through the twentieth century until this day, has been theistic and onto-theological. It should also be noted that it is a culture that is resoundingly polytheistic with an inherent resistance to monotheism. The seemingly widespread provenance of Jainism and Buddhism in the early centuries of Common Era gave way to the unrestrained proliferation of gods and shrines now clubbed as Hindu. Except for a few anglicized, urban enclaves and individuals, disenchantment, in the Weberian sense, has hardly been an experience of the people even as the state could deploy instrumental reasoning aligned to capitalist thrust.[8] When people are invited into the production consumption cycle of economic life in the lure of development before the maturation of modern social imaginary, a widespread schizophrenia results in further proliferation of godmen and modern-day temples. It is against this backdrop of uneven social transformation that the political work of Dravidianism in general and the DMK in particular has to be studied.

Periyar turned increasingly atheist in his articulations against the bulwark of this common sense, to remain an agonist par excellence in order to mitigate the superstitious acceptance of the exploitative ways of the priestly class and the surrendering of human reason and agency. He particularly targeted the Great Tradition with occasional jibes at little tradition. He articulated a conception of radical immanence, which only a person who had no investment in political mobilization could. In a certain sense, it was absolutely necessary to create a space for "disengaged reason" in the terminology of Taylor so that the primary modern social imaginary of self-rule could be launched (Taylor 1992, 331). However, for the DMK, which sought to mobilize the masses, it was neither possible to persist with theistic orientation to the world nor propagate atheism as a precondition for social change. They could only perform modes of disengaged reason, displacing the perception of the Supreme Good from God to human values of community enterprise. If it were to succeed as a political creed, a strong endorsement of moral values derived and rearticulated from the values of selfless surrender to God, to be replaced as a perception of Good, was absolutely necessary. In fact, Taylor's recurrent reference to self-immolation as the extreme possible outcome of pursuing the Good is pertinent in the context of our discussion of Chinnasamy as a token in the previous chapter.[9] In the slogan, "Uṭal maṇṇukku uyir tamiḻukku" (Body to the soil, life given to the cause of Tamil), we do see Tamil taking the place of Supreme Good like God, and hence the characterization of the relationship as "devotion" in Ramaswamy.

What often gets ignored in the disparate prisms of analysis is that the DMK was keenly aware of the multiplicity of Good. While the party used Tamil as the empty signifier that would unite various constituencies, it never denied the multiplicity of Good or sought their subsumption in the cause of Tamil devotion. In the tumultuous year 1965, when anti-Hindi agitations raged in Tamil Nadu, Annadurai wrote a two-part essay on *paṟṟu*, which we noted as something approximating the term "affinity" or "allegiance," while Ramaswamy glossed it as devotion in the case of Tamiḻ *paṟṟu*. In pursuing the idea of affinity, in the light of our engagement with Taylor, we would like to think of it as the moral affinity a being develops with a conception of Good. Literally, *paṟṟu* is to hold on to something, a form of allegiance. Taylor remarks on the theme of his analysis: "… notion of good as the object of our love or allegiance or, as Iris Murdoch portrayed in her work, as the privileged focus of attention or will" (Taylor 1992, 3).

Moral Allegiance: Annadurai's Thesis on *Paṟṟu*

Interestingly, the idea of Good that calls for the allegiance of being is significantly displaced in the discussion of *paṟṟu* by Annadurai, in which allegiance-in-itself or capacity therefor is the Good. It prioritizes the middle ground of the act of "holding onto" over the being that does the holding and the Good held onto. In fact, it is the act of allegiance that defines both the being and the Good. In that sense, Annadurai's discussion of *paṟṟu* is similar to yet distinct from the discussion of Good in Taylor. However, they are together in placing this as moral choices of being. We will refer to *paṟṟu* as allegiance in the following discussion of Annadurai's text. This two-part essay was published in his journal *Kanchi* in October 1965 (Pēraṟiñar Aṇṇāturai 2002, 6:170–190). They are written in an epistolary form of address to "Thambi," the younger brother who is the party worker. Earlier that year, in the month of

February, Tamil Nadu had witnessed the most singular eruption of subaltern energy in the anti-Hindi agitations, resulting in loss of life and property in many places and the many instances of self-immolations by party cadres. Though the DMK played the role of spreading awareness about the impending consequences of Hindi becoming the sole official language of the Indian state since 1963, the eruption of mass action in February 1965 was neither instigated nor anticipated by the party, as could be gathered from many witnesses and records. We will return to this "event" in Chapter 11. The purpose of bringing this up is only to understand the historical context of the somber reflections of Annadurai on the question of *paṟṟu*, which obviously includes Tamiḻ *paṟṟu*, the center piece of analysis for Ramaswamy.

Annadurai begins by postulating that before we declare our allegiance to something, that is deciding what is the object of *paṟṟu* or rather towards which is our *paṟṟu* is directed, we need to understand what *paṟṟu* is. He explains that the meaning of the noun *paṟṟu*, a sort of binding or care, is derived from the verb *paṟṟu*, which is to hold on to something. He notes the religious advice to hold on to the one who does not hold on to anything, the Lord: "Paṟṟuka Patrilanai." It is the allegiance to the self-substantiating absolute that can secure our being fully. Annadurai does not seek to dispute this religious idea, except for noting the interesting circularity in the notion that the absolute is said to have an investment in the salvation of the souls that hold on to it, thus compromising its absolute lack of allegiance; that is, in inviting the allegiance of souls of the mortals to it, the absolute is placed in reciprocal allegiance to the souls. Annadurai then proceeds to distinguish allegiance from desire. Desires, whether seemingly gratified, fulfilled or otherwise, wither away; moral allegiance, in contrast, provides the ground for the being. This is particularly exemplified in the word *paṟṟu* standing for both the temperament and action, that is, the sense of allegiance and the act of holding on to. Hence, it is a much more intense form of desire, which cannot easily be given up or traded. Annadurai makes a brief mention of the Shaiva Siddhanta triad, Pasu–Pathi–Pasam, which only explains the beings' allegiance to the Greater Being or God before he moves on to the domain of the social.

Some form of allegiance is a necessary condition of being. All those who access a sensorium are bound to forge a bonding to a matter or a concept or a way of life. The bonding is not merely generated through feelings; this becomes an inalienable source of feelings. The bonding originates in taste or usefulness but leads on to a dependency. A fear or insecurity develops that the sense of happiness and gratification afforded by the bonding should last. This leads to a resolve to secure the object of bonding against alienation or destruction. This takes the form of allegiance, or *paṟṟu*. Annadurai offers a naturalistic metaphor in the seed and soil holding on to each other to enable the tree to grow. Such a bonding is contingent on propriety of what is being held by whom and the sense of purpose. If one is frivolous in forging a bonding, it obviously would not last. Annadurai once again distinguishes the transient forms of desire and a lasting sense of bonding. A child may desire to hold a butterfly; it may indeed catch one and keep it for a while. After a few such acts, the interest in butterflies would recede in favor of others; however, for one who desires to study the biological phenomenon of the life of the butterflies, the bonding with the species will take a lasting form. Annadurai appears to suggest that the bonding is stronger at the conceptual level or when the multitude is abstracted to unity. Both desires and allegiances can be many. While desires are transient and exchangeable, allegiance is formed by lasting commitment. It becomes a comportment of being. Allegiance merges with the person.

Annadurai then introduces a much more substantial difference between desire and allegiance. One who desires something is not keen on inculcating the desire in others. Merchants may want to inculcate the desire for their merchandise in others. But a normal person may recommend, say, a particular item of food to another. He may describe it persuasively but will not expend too much effort to make the other person desire the same thing. Whereas, in the case of allegiance, it is almost necessary for a person to seek to inculcate similar allegiance in others. People go to any extent to instill the form of allegiance in others. In short, desire is personal; allegiance is collective. The Good is implicit in allegiance only because it is collective. Allegiance emanates from a collective sentiment. People sacrificed a great deal to inculcate such feelings among others to foster common allegiance. Annadurai then lists four major forms of collective allegiances: to country (patriotism), to religion, to language, to ethnicity. He adds that one may whisper "to family."

The analysis then moves on to more complicated issues or moral predicaments. There are situations in which one may have to choose one form of allegiance over the other. When threatened with the life of someone held dear, one may compromise on a principle held dear. One may give up allegiance to one entity for the sake of allegiance to another entity. It all depends on those who are faced with such moral dilemmas, their temperament, character, and situations and how they chose to act when such conflicts arise. Not only are allegiances many but people do prioritize them in accordance with their own aims and character. It is not possible to fix the relative values of allegiances like the value of material goods. When even material may acquire fetish value, it is indeed difficult to fix the value of one allegiance in comparison to another. However, it may be agreed that there is a consensus about the beneficial yield of the four commonly held allegiances: to country, religion, language, and ethnicity. If any of these four develop a conflict with another one of the four, much turmoil is likely to ensue in the society.

Another common problem would be the horizontal conflict among the same kind of allegiance to different entities. Allegiance to one country conflicts with allegiance to another country, resulting in wars. Annadurai once again mentions Wendel Wilkie's internationalist suggestion about the global state, reminding readers of the famous Tamil maxim "All places are one's own to belong, all humans are related to each other,"[10] the opening line of a celebrated Sangam poem circa second century BCE. The problem, from Annadurai's perspective, arises when allegiance to one country, instead of producing the labor to make it rich, decides to conquer another country to enslave and appropriate the wealth of the conquered country. This leads to the desire to bring all other countries under the rule of one country, making a global empire built on violence and conquest.

Annadurai reasons that the amount of labor by generations of people invested to make a territory a country is what underlies the allegiance to the country so created. However, for such allegiance to be productive and good, the country cannot have a political dispensation that allows the ruling elite to appropriate the wealth of the nation while most of the toiling masses live in poverty. Such disparities, dictatorships, despotic regimes will not inspire much allegiance to the country from people. If there is a democratic dispensation in which people can voice their grievances and participate in governance, the allegiance will get strengthened. The idea of self-rule will make the allegiance powerful. If people form a bad or ineffective government, they should have an opportunity to change the government. It is such procedures that nurture allegiance to the nation in the modern world.

While this is a legitimate sense of allegiance of the inhabitants of the territory, an excess of self-glorification results in two negative consequences. One is the desire to conquer other countries as we saw above; the second, more sinister desire is to negate all other allegiances in favor of this single allegiance. It is possible people may have allegiance to a city, a village, an area, a religion, an ethnic group, and so on. To demand that a people of a country should follow only one religion, speak only a single language, should have no other identity than that of the nation is also detrimental to the very nature of allegiance. There are countries where many religions prevail; conversely, there are many countries that follow a single religion. When such is the case, it is absurd to think that allegiance to religion and country should be merged. Only those who do not have any basic understanding of politics would think of such impossible propositions. Annadurai mentions when Jesus was asked about allegiance to the Roman Empire, he said to give unto Caesar is his due, that the kingdom of God is not territorially bound. Religion is a phenomenon of the mind that does not depend on spatial location. There is no guarantee that nations that follow the same religion would not war with each other. Annadurai cites the conflict between Malaysia and Indonesia despite both of their allegiance to Islam; he also mentions the conflict between North and South Vietnam.

It will be similarly disastrous to insist on a single language as the official language in a country where many languages prevail. Allegiance to different languages will never come in the way of allegiance to the country. It is only some aggressive people who develop such sinister thoughts that there should only be one religion or one language in a country to ensure allegiance to the country. An allegiance has a purity of purpose as allegiance to a Good, which will be destroyed if it is used to harass people in the name of it. If one allegiance tries to erase other allegiances, it would soon face its own destruction. Hitler provided the most powerful example of how much evil can come out of the seemingly pure allegiance to the nation if it is not carefully moderated.

Annadurai then goes on to discuss how allegiances cannot come in the way of allegiances to certain values like justice, fairness, honesty, and such. If a judge in a court belongs to the same religion as the convict, could he allow his allegiance to the religion come in the way of giving fair judgement? Hence, we need to deploy our reason in every instance to moderate our sense of allegiance since there will always be people who would seek to exploit us through the promotion of blind allegiance.

Further, it is necessary to think of allegiances as functional in the collective sense. If there is a congregation of medical practitioners to discuss health, doctors belonging to many countries, many religions, many a system of medicine may all participate. If the practitioners of one system of medicine gather, like Ayurveda, the nature of discussion would be different. Each form of allegiance would bring forth its own advantages in terms of the collective deliberation and action. Having said that, Annadurai reaches for a far more nuanced proposition. While allegiances can make any kind of associational group, it would generally be beneficial to have as large a number of people as possible to share the allegiance, cutting across differences in other vectors of allegiances, if it is to produce greater good. In offering an imaginary example of "Young Progressive Thondai Mandala (region) Thuluva Vellala (caste) Writers Conference," Anna asks, would not the number of people who assemble be too few to be of any help? If various allegiances are brought together in a subtractive mode, it will hardly be useful as allegiance to a Good. Instead, only when the allegiance brings together a large number of people will it have better capacity to function as an allegiance to a Good.

Finally, allegiance cannot be for self-promotion, indulgence, and domination, in which case it would not produce any good. By its very definition, allegiance should be for a principle, ideal, and a beneficial system. Even such allegiances cannot blind us in our actions; it should always be accompanied by a clarity of purpose, increased awareness, enlightened thought, and energy, which would result in the augmentation of the well-being of society. Annadurai wraps up the letter by asking the cadres to think whether their allegiance to the DMK is for narrow goals or for the betterment of society.

Annadurai's analysis, we seek to posit, has strong resonances with Taylor's reflections two decades later. Let us point out a few important links even if we cannot do justice to the most elaborate and complex reasoning of Taylor within the space our discussion here. Taylor's one major concern is what he calls the objections that the positing of "hyper good" has encountered in contemporary times. The "hyper good" is such that all other Goods one may find in life is expected to be sacrificed or negated for the sake of the "hyper good." The basic understandable suspicion is that such a positing of hyper good would run against individual freedom and liberty. Taylor finds three explorative frontiers in which the positing of a hyper good in some amenable form in consonance with other Goods may still be undertaken: one is the old theistic frontier; the second is dignity of human life as expressed through disengaged reason (Descartes, enlightenment, instrumental reasoning, and so on); and the third one is the expressive human self that is the work of nature (Romanticism, Modernism, Nietzsche, and so on). In a pithy expression that is quick to grasp, Taylor states: "The nagging question for modern theism is simply: Is there really a God? The threat at the margin of modern non-theistic humanism is: So what?" (Taylor 1992, 317). If theism can be challenged on the basis of it not being true, both disengaged reason and goodness of nature suffer from inadequacy of purpose. Therefore, the need to posit hyper good based on which humans can develop a sense of priority is in crisis.

Annadurai's reflections differ from Taylor in one significant aspect. Instead of discussing the Goods to which one may find allegiance, Anna discusses allegiance itself as a necessary condition of being. This gives his approach a far greater existential dimension than a mere discussion on Goods. He is able to gently disengage from the horizon of theism since it is only one of the forms of allegiance. Even when it was the reigning hyper good, humans have always fallen for several other Goods of ordinary life, a source of much lamentation. As a result, without having to posit atheism, Annadurai can produce a list of "hyper goods" as they are available for a person in the form of allegiance to country, religion, language, and ethnicity. All these are *paṟṟu*. Of course, these hyper goods are always in supersession of a plethora of Goods like family, ties of kinship, love, associative life of various kinds, persuasions, artistic expressions, and so on. Then there are the general problems of hierarchy of allegiances to the hyper goods and also the negative animus among allegiances of the same kind to hyper goods like enmity among countries, religions, cultures, and languages deprecating other entities and seeking to dominate them that Annadurai discusses.

There are three things that are implicit in Annadurai's discussion that are significant for a reader of Taylor or such allied persuasions.

1. Annadurai is not afraid of or does not feel negative about the demands of sacrifice or mutilation demanded by allegiance to hyper goods.
2. He finds disengaged reason a necessary force of mitigation through a critical evaluation of the demands of hyper goods since they can easily mask schemes of domination.
3. While he notes harmony of nature playing a crucial role, he is aware that it still does not preclude difference or even violence. In an insightful moment, he makes a passing reference to the Tamil word *isai*, which means music as a noun and the act of assent or compliance as a verb, suggesting a natural harmony to human collectives but notes that there are many kinds of music.

For the purposes of our discussion, what this remarkable text of Annadurai reveals is a grasp of the plane of human immanence that takes both theistic and non-theistic allegiances as possibilities of human life. It notes the conventional wisdom of ascetic distance or detachment as a cure to the passions of allegiance but gently replaces it with the spirit of disengaged reason, which can launch a critical appraisal of the demands of hyper good at each moment, thus opening up a vast scope for conscientious moral action in the contemporary world. The references to Shaivite sources in this text and elsewhere needs to be acknowledged. However, to suggest a seamless continuity of tradition on the basis of those references, apart from being totally untenable in the light of a comprehensive evaluation, also does injustice to the innovative thrust of humanism that can accommodate theological dispositions within a larger frame of moral foundations for an equitable society. In other words, the hyper good of equitable society and the rule of the commoner can contain within it allegiances to gods and religions without calling for an atheistic repudiation as a necessary precondition for the work of humanism. In order to understand the innovative nature of the move, we need to consider a contemporary response from a communist leader.

Singular is the Race, Singular the Lord

One of the most popular leaders of the Communist Party in Tamil Nadu was Pā Jīvāṉantam (1907–1963). He was closely associated with both the Congress and the Self-Respect Movement before emerging as a socialist and communist leader in the late 1930s. He was elected to the Madras Assembly in 1952. In the ensuing years, the Communist Party developed an intense conflict of interest with the DMK in winning over the allegiance of the masses. We should recall the pithy statement of the journalist Mohan Ram that we noted earlier that the Communist Party failed to find the "Tamil idiom" soon enough to prevent the rise of the DMK on the electoral turf in spite of powerful orators in Tamil like Jīvāṉantam. However, the conflict was not merely restricted to whatever was the historical magic wand of the Tamil idiom. The political stance regarding religion and God also became a crucial site of contestation. Jīvāṉantam wrote a tract titled *Matamum Māṉiṭa Vāḻvum* (Religion and Human Life), in which he countered the challenge posed by the DMK cadres as to why the Communists were soft pedaling the issues of religious adherence and belief in God (Pa.Jīvāṉantam 2005). If they were materialists, as they claimed, why would they not be in the forefront of denouncing religious superstitions and obscurantist practices?

In responding to such charges from the DMK cadres, with ample citations from Lenin, Engels, and Marx, Jīvāṉantam explains that the doctrine of "dialectical materialism" considers religion to be the outcome of the exploitative conditions prevailing in feudal society and among the unorganized labor of a capitalist system. While at the dawn of civilization human beings would have invented God out of fear of the forces of nature, in the later epochs faith in God and the religious systems became an expression of the subjugation of the toiling people to the exploitative powers, since those who suffered needed recourse to God to endure their suffering, and the exploiters needed the religious order, priests, and the like to perpetuate the exploitative order. Hence, it is only through the revolutionary action when the working class overthrows the exploiters that the basis of adherence to God and religion would disappear. A premature campaign against God and religion without the maturing of class struggle is mere bourgeois radicalism or adventurism. Initially, class unity should be forged without religious faith or lack of it coming in the way; in the transformative process of class struggle, the liberated working class would emerge with a scientific approach towards the question of faith and religion. This is the essence of tactics.

To this familiar line of argument, Jīvāṉantam adds two more caveats. The first caveat is that in a socialist state only the state would be secular, leaving it for individuals to freely pursue their religious calling as their conscience demands as a purely private affair. Soviet Russia supplies the prime example of such a wonderful state of affairs. The second caveat is the Communist Party, which is ideologically opposed to the idea of God and religion. All this together does present a somewhat complicated picture of a three-tier approach, making it ambiguous where the communists stand with regard to God and religion. The first tier is the tactical abstaining of the party from interference in the religious pursuits and faith in God of the working class that it seeks to mobilize. The second tier is the ideology of the Communist Party, which of course scientifically knows that God and religion are the superstructure of exploitative feudal order, which it repudiates. The third tier is the socialist state achieved by the Communist Party, which is tolerant to religious practice as a private affair. Jīvāṉantam pleads for an understanding of the ingenuity of dialectical materialism thus explained, which he claims is devoid of any self-contradiction. He also confesses that he is personally an atheist, which implies that it is not the official position of the party.

As opposed to such "clarity," Jīvāṉantam finds Periyar Ramasamy's propagation of atheism and iconoclasm a brand of vulgar materialism. Like Eugen Dühring and Ludwig Feuerbach, whose inadequacy of thought were explained by Marx and Engels, Periyar Ramasamy lacked a clear understanding of dialectical materialism. His rants against belief in God are hence purely adventurist. In the case of the DMK, Jīvāṉantam finds adaptation of the cryptic slogan from Shaivite text *Tirumantiram* "Singular is the Race, Singular the Lord" as the stated position of the DMK party cunning and deceitful. He claims that the idea "Singular is the Race" denies class contradiction and the idea "Singular is the Lord" would pave way for all the evils of obscurantist belief systems. At one moment in the tract, Jīvāṉantam emphatically asks what the philosophical basis of the DMK was and whether they have any philosophical system like "dialectical materialism" to back their ideology.

The DMK of course expressed certain affinity to enlightenment rationalism and humanism, particularly as expressed by figures like Jean-Jacques Rousseau. The party had a high priority assigned to challenging Brahminic Hinduism, its Puranic tales, gods, and ritual practices, all of which coded caste inequality. It is in this necessary task of opposing Brahmin supremacy and hegemony that the DMK found the need to challenge religious order, which they thought the communists totally missed out in seeking mindlessly to replicate the European sources of Marxism. The DMK had to find its own indigenous sources as the philosophical premise to counter Brahminic ritualism. It is in such context that Annadurai appears to have taken recourse to a recondite text like *Tirumantiram* for ideas. The conceptual abstraction of the human race as singular and the spirit as singular in the slogan "Oṉṟē Kulam Oruvaṉē Tēvaṉ" (Singular is the Race, Singular the Lord) should be read in the context of other such aphorisms like "Uṭampai Vaḷarttōm Uyir Vaḷarttōmē," which translates to "When we nurture the body, we nurture the soul." There are repeated suggestions in Shaivite discourse that the human body and material universe are the manifestations of the spirit. Annadurai and his colleagues apparently found such notions of spirituality embedded in human immanence far more appealing in contradistinction to the endless agonizing over the alienation from the Lord in the Bhakti tradition and the myriad ritual formations around a plethora of deities in popular practice. Another popular slogan of the party "Eezhayin Sirippil Iravainaik Kanbom" (We see God manifest in the smiles of the poor) can also be traced back to *Tirumantiram*, which claims that nurturing the moving temples that are the bodies of the people would be the actual manifestation of piety rather than nurturing the lifeless structures of the temples.[11] The DMK does not appear to borrow from neo-Shaivism of Maraimalai Adigal et al. and their investment in the religious order or Vellala civilization, but directly from the conceptual premise of Shaiva Siddhanta, most particularly the enigmatic text of *Tirumantiram* as a source of imagination.

It appears that the DMK leaders believed such abstraction and unification of the spirit as manifest in the human universe, as a kind of transcendental immanence, is not radically opposed to atheism. Ryerson recounts a popular episode that when Karunanidhi, successor to Annadurai as chief minister and the leader of the DMK, suggested in the presence of Periyar that their idea of "Singular is the Lord" is not much removed from the "No God" position of atheism, Periyar rushed to register his disagreement, breaking the protocol of not responding to the concluding remarks of the chief minister (Ryerson 1988, 191). What the episode shows is that the DMK's understanding of the immanence of the spirit in the human materialist praxis allowed them to imagine a closer tie to atheism than to the traditions of Bhakti, in which the transient soul of the devotee stood alienated from the intransient Great Soul or the transcendental God, mandating the devotee to constantly seek redemption through reunion. While the DMK did not elaborate on such a philosophical premise of human immanence, content to draw from several of the non-Brahmin and anti-caste articulations of the Tamil past, the general reflective stream of Tamil writing has often noted the strong resonances the anti-caste, anti-deification articulations of the Siddha tradition had with the articulations of the Dravidian movement. To speak of such resonances is not to claim some authentic rootedness in tradition but to pay attention to the underlying philosophical current of human immanence that informs such egalitarian aspirations against caste hierarchy and Brahmin hegemony in different epochs. The missing out of the Tamil idiom by communists appears to also mean missing out on the abundant wealth of the sources of the self that could trigger a modern social imaginary. It is surprising a person who had a great deal of personal investment in Tamil literature like Jīvāṉantam could not appreciate the ability of the DMK to mobilize such indigenous sources of the self. He was perhaps restrained by adherence to doctrinaire positions espoused by the communists like the ill-defined catch phrase, dialectical materialism.[12] This naturally requires that we proceed to consider the difference between the DMK's left populism and the class essentialism that inhibited the Communist Party in the period of our study in Tamil Nadu.

Notes

1. We draw arguments from Taylor (2007). We also connect them to his other seminal work *Sources of the Self: The Making of Modern Identity* (1992).
2. Karunanidhi, who lead the DMK for nearly half a century, in the final years of life wrote a script for a television serial based on the life of Ramanuja as a challenge to political mobilization of Hindu identity through reiterating the question of caste hierarchy. For more details on Ramanuja and his life, see Seshadri (1996).
3. Manonmaniam Sundaram Pillai (1855–1897), academic, historian, poet, and dramatist, was a Tamil scholar who penned the poem used as the Tamil Nadu state anthem. He was a well-known Shaivite scholar and professor of Philosophy at Maharaja's College, Trivandrum.
4. Among the literature on anti-colonial and post-colonial nationalism, we are inspired most by the work of Partha Chatterjee in critiquing this assumption.
5. In a personal interview given to Rajan Kurai Krishnan and friends in 1993, K. A. P. Viswanatham (1899–1994), one-time general secretary of the Justice Party and a Shaivite scholar, regretted in very strong terms the refusal of Periyar and Annadurai to name the party Tamilar Kazhagam, opting for the Dravidian tag at the pivotal moment in 1944 in spite of his fervent appeals and protests.
6. "Government of Tamil Nadu—Hindu Religious & Charitable Endowments Department," (n.d.), https://hrce.tn.gov.in/hrcehome/hrce_portalpolicy.php?searchcase=termsofuse (accessed August 8, 2021).
7. For a helpful discussion of the difference between ontic presupposition of God and the god of the religions based on faith or belief, see Daniel (2001, 83–102).
8. Such "hybrid" forms consciousness has been studied in multiple contexts. One example, in the context of the working class, will be Dipesh Chakrabarty's discussion of jute mill

workers in Calcutta (Chakrabarty 1989). In fact, there are many such instances in the essays of the Subaltern Studies Collective.

9. See, for example, in the concluding chapter titled "Conflicts of Modernity in Charles Taylor" (1992, 518–521). The basic argument is such acts of self-destruction or mutilation should not make us think of the Good itself as invalid, since the absence of Good can also lead to mutilations in so far as it impoverishes capacity for conceiving ideals collectively. "The dilemma of mutilation is in a sense our greatest spiritual challenge, not an iron fate."
10. "Yātum Ūrē Yāvarum Kēḷir," a poem from *Purananuru,* written by Kanian Poonkundran. For a translation of the poem, see Ramanujan and Tolkāppiyar (2011).
11. We thank K. Kamaraj, research scholar, Madras University, for bringing this to our attention.
12. For a succinct critique of the inadequacy of the coinage "dialectical materialism," see the entry by Roy Bhaskar in *A Dictionary of Marxist Thought* (Bottomore 2006). For a fuller exposition of dialectics on similar lines, see Bhaskar (2008).

4 Left Populism

> … the central axis of the political conflict will be between right-wing populism and left-wing populism … it is through the construction of a people, a collective will that results from the mobilization of affects in defense of equality and social justice, that it will be possible to combat the xenophobic policies promoted by right wing populism.
>
> —Chantal Mouffe, *For A Left Populism*

Philip Spratt, aged twenty-four, arrived in India in December 1926. He was a member of the British Communist Party sent to India by the Comintern (the Communist International) to found and guide the activities of the Communist Party in India. He was instrumental in founding the front organization Workers and Peasants Party (WPP) and was guiding the activities of the party and trade unions. He was arrested in 1929 and subsequently convicted in what came to be known as the Meerut conspiracy case.[1] His twelve-year sentence was later reduced to two years and he was released in 1934. By that time, he had turned very critical of the Comintern, which dictated the activities in India without a proper appreciation of ground realities. He became disillusioned with communism, moving gradually to support market economy and liberal democracy. He recorded his experiences in 1955 in a book with the tell-tale title *Blowing Up India: Reminiscences and Reflections of a Former Comintern Emissary* (Spratt 1955). However, what interests us here is his last book published in 1970, a year before his death, succinctly titled *The DMK in Power* (Spratt 1970).

Spratt developed a Tamil Nadu connection in the 1930s when he married the grandniece of Malayapuram Singaravelu Chettiar, popularly called Singaravelar (1860–1946), one of the founding figures of the communist movement from Tamil Nadu, who was also a close associate of Periyar in the 1930s. Spratt initially moved to Bangalore, where he became the editor of *Mysindia*, a pro-American journal. He later moved to Chennai and became the editor of *Swarajya*, a magazine run by C. Rajagopalachari, who was heading the Swatantra Party, which was extremely critical of the Congress brand of socialism and state control. It should be borne in mind that Rajagopalachari was in support of the DMK since the late 1950s in its opposition to the Congress in Tamil Nadu. In 1967, both the Swatantra Party and the Communist Party of India (Marxist), were in an electoral alliance with the DMK, as we already noted. Under these circumstances, it is not clear what prompted Spratt to write a book on the DMK in power. It appears he could not but be impressed by the huge support of the people the DMK drew, though Spratt was not sure how to interpret it.

For our purposes, we need to note the reiteration of some of the well-known prejudices in Spratt's book. In the very opening lines, Spratt betrays his prejudices against the DMK.

> The victory of the Dravida Munnetra Kazhagam over the apparently well entrenched Congress party in the Madras state was the greatest surprise of the 1967 general election. To many who remembered what the DMK had said and done in the past it was also alarming. The party had long demanded the secession of Madras from the Indian Union and in internal affairs it had been guilty of threatening to persecute Brahmins and of disorderly methods of agitation. (Spratt 1970, 5)

The apparent purpose of Spratt is to take stock of how the DMK has ruled in the first fifteen months in office (and another nine months in postscript). He feels the record is mixed; though by and large "disappointing," he also appears to have some hopes that the party may be able to bring real benefits to Madras and India if the shrewd leaders could "discipline" their followers. His rather "neutral" reportage of the events, good and bad from his point of view, of the initial two years of the DMK rule is however marked by two streaks of deep-seated paranoia. One is the "unruly," "disorderly" side of the DMK party members and supporters, and the other is the persistence of manipulative powers of international communism. Here's a sample of the first streak of paranoia from the postscript:

> Mr. Karunanidhi has given the impression that he is a man who cannot be trifled with; on the other hand, he and his ministers have shown no sign of abandoning the civilized standards with which Annadurai came to be identified. *The fears that the wild men in the party would come to the fore have hitherto been entirely belied.* (Spratt 1970, 157; emphasis is ours)

However, the stranger paranoia is that of the international communist takeover:

> ... big changes are taking place in the Congress party and the Union government and it is considered possible that a coalition government including one or both of the communist parties may come to power before the general election in 1972. This will be taken as a major victory for Russia and China cannot be expected to tolerate it. With America's impending withdrawal from Asia, China

> is free to undertake a strong guerrilla offensive, for which in fact she has already made extensive preparations. Thus, a likely outcome of the present changes is a civil war, reminiscent of that in the eighteenth century, in which the ultimate victor will be Russia or China; or they may partition India between them. (Spratt 1970, 158)

Spratt appears to be worried about the meaning of the DMK in such a context since, while having popular support, the leaders seem not to comprehend such a larger picture. He felt that they didn't understand communism and were not interested in learning what happens outside Tamil Nadu. Spratt repeats the oft-stated truism that the "the ideological attitude of the DMK remains an enigma" and states, for example, "there is no great change in the DMK from Annadurai's non-ideological, sentimental yet opportunistic inclination to the left." In spite of such apprehensions, Spratt feels "the political understanding and inclinations of the firmly established government of Tamil Nadu and a strong contingent of the DMK members in Parliament can be of great importance" if only they can realize what is at stake. In short, Spratt feels that despite the DMK leaders not appearing to deserve the mandate they have secured, their rather quick adaptation to civilized ways of ruling shows that they may still play a role in the gloomy prospects of the takeover by the Russian or Chinese communists if only they can get educated ideologically to become aware of the larger picture on the one hand, and also can hold their "wild" party men in control on the other. It is such a vision of the precarious situation of democracy in Tamil Nadu and India that perhaps had prompted Spratt to write this short book. Central to the problematic is the vague and enigmatic gesture to the left that the DMK was making, which worries the former Comintern emissary-turned-paranoid supporter of capitalism and free enterprise. We have now clearly seen that for the right and the left, the ideology of the DMK appeared ambiguous, enigmatic, opportunistic, and contingent. We however propose that the DMK provided an early example of what Chantal Mouffe has recently described as left populism.

DMK and Left Populism

Chantal Mouffe has summed up in great brevity and clarity the lineaments of left populism in a short book titled *For a Left Populism* (Mouffe 2019). Mouffe's context of analysis is what is known as the post-democratic West of the contemporary times. However, there are significant issues that relate to the "pre-democratic" Tamil Nadu as well in terms of the constitutive features of populism. Hence, we feel entitled to freely draw from her analysis if not from her examples. In fact, so many of the postulations in the work appear to fit admirably to the formation of the political through the advent of the DMK. For the sake of brevity, we need to focus on two key questions to get a clear idea of why the ideology of the DMK is seen as an enigma, a puzzle, inconsistent, and so on. The first is the communist obsession with the category of class and the engine of class contradiction as the driving force of history. The second problem is the paradox of democracy, which is formed by the constitutive agonism of constitutionalism and popular sovereignty.

In recounting the process that lead to the writing of the path-breaking work she authored with Ernesto Laclau (Laclau and Mouffe 1985), Mouffe says,

> We soon realized that the obstacles to be overcome came from the essentialist perspective dominant in left thinking. According to this perspective, that we called "class essentialism," political identities were the expression of the position of the social agents in the relations of production and their interests were defined by this position. It was no surprise that such a perspective was unable to understand demands that were not based on "class." (Mouffe 2019, 2)

This best captures the problem the DMK faced. The party was keenly aware that the Brahmin castiest hegemony was totally antithetical to the spirit of democracy since it forecloses the possibility of free association of individuals, the very cornerstone of the modern social imaginary that we call democracy. The internal frontier it forged, as between Brahmins and non-Brahmins, was crucial for the counter-hegemonic assertion of the "non-Brahmins" as the conceptual totality of society, which would free the same of the implications of caste hierarchy since the hierarchy as a hegemonic scheme rested on Brahminical texts and injunctions. This was the position available to the party in the final years of colonial regime that had given legal status to the orientalist construction of the Brahminized society, as we learned through Annadurai's *Aryan Allure*. This operation was not necessarily antithetical to the securing of equitable distribution in terms of economy. The communist blind spot of class essentialism could not recognize the priority assigned to the counter-hegemonic struggle. Assuming they were armed with a far more "scientific" notion of class antagonism as the base structure of society, they kept looking for the familiar terms of "ideology" in the DMK which was organically responding to the oppressive social structure the people found themselves in.

In fact, populist politics exceeds the prescriptions of an ideology as it is understood in the Marxist lexicon. In the precise summation of Mouffe, we read:

> Laclau defines populism as a discursive strategy of constructing a political frontier dividing society into two camps and calling for the mobilization of the "underdog" against "those in power." It is not an ideology and cannot be attributed a specific programmatic content. Nor is it a political regime. It is a way of doing politics that can take various ideological forms according to both time and place, and is compatible with a variety of institutional frameworks. (Mouffe 2019, 10–11)

If this is not a flattering description for the conventionally minded, it is necessary to understand the possible outcome of such a politics. Mouffe continues:

> As a result, the historical bloc that provides the social basis of a hegemonic formation is being disarticulated and the possibility arises of constructing a new subject of collective action—the people—capable of reconfiguring a social order experienced as unjust. (Mouffe 2019, 10–11)

As already stated, the theorization of Laclau and Mouffe applies to the so-called neo-liberal post-democratic, post-ideological; one may wish to add a range of "post" prefixed substantial nouns here to indicate a certain stasis in the formations of the political. The reason why such theorization serves best as the explanatory framework to the politics of the DMK in the early years of vibrantly political post-independent Tamil Nadu is not far to seek. It lies in the phrase "social basis of hegemonic formation," that is, politics being an affair of the closed elites, which freezes the possibility of both liberal politics essentializing the right-based individual's civil society activism and the class essentialism of the communists. In both these formations, the unclassifiable multitude of the plebs, the underdogs, the commoner, or *samaniyan* in the DMK vocabulary, is left out of political action. Our leftist journalist Mohan Ram's "charlatans," "soap box Demosthenes," and Spratt's "wild men" who constituted the DMK were the people written off as possible agents of history. The need and necessity of left populism arises in recognition of what Partha Chatterjee has called the "political society" whose only recourse to justice is the myriad formations of political energy in popular democracy underwritten by the elections with universal adult franchise.

Once populism is seen to be rooted in some form of radicalization of democracy, that is, taking agency to the grassroots mobilization of the people of all descriptions, the inherent agonism in democracy between oligarchic formations, the interest in the protection of their privileges, and the endless array of demands of the various underprivileged sections come to the fore. This takes the form of the conflict between constitutionalism and popular sovereignty. In the words of Mouffe:

> In all cases what is in question is a political regime characterized by the articulation of two different traditions. On the one hand, the traditions of political liberalism: the rule of law, the separation of powers and the defense of individual freedom; on the other hand, the democratic tradition, whose central ideas are equality and popular sovereignty. There is no necessary relationship between these two traditions but only a contingent historical articulation that, as C. B. Macpherson has shown took place through the joint struggles of the liberals and democrats against absolutist regimes. (Mouffe 2019, 14)

The trouble is while subaltern political energies are mobilized in various struggles and uprisings, the governance eventually becomes the privilege of the elite circles of civil society. In electoral democracies like India, reaching out to the commoner for votes places the political parties and leaders in the need to appeal to popular sovereignty as against the rule of political liberalism. The grassroots mobilization of the DMK was made possible only in the backdrop of universal adult franchise that was introduced by the Indian Constitution after independence, even if it had to skip the first general elections in terms of direct participation for various reasons.

One of the key aspects that will separate right populism and left populism, if we chose to name them so, will be the aspiration with respect to the unity and totality of society. The right populism of the nationalist and xenophobic varieties externalizes the enemy in seeking to construct a social totality. As we noted in our reading of *Aryan Allure*, Annadurai's context of writing the pamphlet was opposition to the call for a Hindu nation that encompasses the whole of India. Instead, left populism identifies an internal frontier, refuses to totalize society, seeing conflictual nature of social relationships and the struggle for hegemony. Mouffe summarizes:

> There are two ways to envisage the domain of the political. The associative view sees it as the field of liberty and of acting in concert. Alternatively, dissociative one conceives it as the field of conflict and antagonism … two key concepts are needed to address the question of the political: 'antagonism' and 'hegemony'.… This impedes the full totalization of society and forecloses the possibility of a society beyond division and power. (Mouffe 2019, 87)

It is significant that the castiest society the DMK was seeking to dismantle was not a totality but was already full of divisions and power variations. Where the innovation took place, instead of just presenting a new unifying identity that would totalize society, the DMK could use the Brahmin–non-Brahmin divide to bring social antagonism into play. This, however, did not prevent the DMK from paying attention to economic disparity, poverty, and deprivation. Unfortunately for the Communist Party, seeped in class essentialism, it was hard to come to terms with the hegemonic struggle the DMK launched through active mobilization of the people with Tamil as the empty signifier and the Brahmin–non-Brahmin divide as the internal frontier. This is not different from the difficulties faced by communists at the national level in coming to terms with the anti-colonial struggle launched by the Congress.

In recounting the history of Indian communism, Sashi Joshi points to the problems class essentialism led the Indian Communist Party to face:

> We have found Gramsci's concept of hegemony very useful towards understanding how states, classes, and mass movements are realized. However, the experience of the Gandhi-led movements and Gandhian strategy in India shows that Gramsci's conception of building counter-hegemony cannot be performed by a Communist Party as Gramsci continued to believe. The Indian experience makes it quite clear that hegemonic politics cannot be practiced by a class party. (Joshi and Josh 2011, 1:392)

The economism inherent in class essentialism prevented a true integration with the larger political process based on hegemonic assertion and popular mobilization. It does not help when the Communist Party merely becomes an electoral vehicle in spite of the Kerala and Bengal experiments. "… Communists of India have fallen between the two stools. Over the years, what has emerged is a party which is neither 'Communist' nor 'Socialist'." The class essentialism prevents it from mass mobilization by adopting a populist reason, while the electoral path has compelled the party to jettison insurrectionary politics" (Joshi and Josh 2011, 1:392).

It is enough to read a text like *The Freedom Struggle and Dravidian Movement*, written by the eminent leader of the Communist Party in Tamil Nadu, P. Ramamurthy (1908–1987), to understand the insurmountable difficulty the Communist Party faced even to engage with the DMK in a critical and analytical lens (Ramamurthy 1987). While the title of the book is chosen from the cliched critique of the Justice Party and the Periyar-led Dravidian movement having been "collaborators" of the British, the later section of the book is devoted to engaging with Annadurai's seminal texts like *Aryan Allure*. What is pertinent to our discussion of left populism here is a text by Annadurai called *The Garden of Money—Panathottam* (Aṟiñar Aṇṇā 2010b, 1:437–505) and the way Ramamurthy engages with it. *Panam* in Tamil refers to money. For some reason, Ramamurthy translates this as "Garden of Wealth," thus inaugurating his misinterpretation right with the title. We need to apprise ourselves of this unique text by Annadurai, an essay in popular pedagogy of economics, before engaging with Ramamurthy's misplaced critical assessment based on class essentialism.

Garden of Money

Annadurai uses the biological metaphor of a seed yielding several more seeds through the life of a plant to the capitalist activity of multiplying money when used as capital, which we can paraphrase by recalling the formulaic expressions of Marx as Commodity–Money–Commodity becoming Money–Commodity–Money (M-C-M) and therefrom Money–More Money (M-M'). Hence, capitalism is the garden of money where it grows and spreads. Annadurai's major concern in the text is the centering of capital accumulation in the north, particularly in Bombay. The resulting unevenness of development in comparison to the south worries Annadurai. He is both concerned about trade and industry in Tamil Nadu being run by north Indian capital and the concentration of industrial development in the north, most particularly Bombay. He finds the comparative accumulation of capital very weak in the south, most particularly in Tamil Nadu. He complains that the Madras government does not seem worried about the imbalance due to the nationalist sentiments that blinds it to the aggressive thrust of north Indian capital.

Annadurai does not raise these concerns on behalf of the Tamil bourgeoisie. His concern is that lack of capital accumulation would lead to lack of industrial development on a footing compared to the north, which would reduce Tamil people to the status of laboring class in continuation of the immediate past of a large number of Tamils emigrating as indentured laborers to Sri Lanka, Fiji, Malaysia, and South Africa to work in plantations and mines. He suggests state initiatives to found industries as a public enterprise to initiate comparable development with the north.[2]

Annadurai's immediate provocations to write the text in 1946, three years before launching the DMK, appear to be three. The primary provocation was the policy initiative of the state government to promote hand-spun khadi, a Gandhian program in a determined preference to the promotion of the mills in Coimbatore and other places. Annadurai asks if emerging Baniya capitalists and the likes of G. D. Birla are all in support of the Congress, why do they promote the mills in Bombay instead of hand-spun khadi? He mentions the massive new initiative to produce rayon through the National Rayon Corporation founded with a capital of 10 crore rupees in 1946 by nine of the Bombay capitalists and one from Ahmedabad. Annadurai lists their names. When such industrial initiatives were made in Bombay, the Madras chief minister was proposing to give a spinning wheel to every household to promote hand-spun khadi.

The next provocation was the permission granted to Birla to produce Vanaspati (a thick vegetable oil) in Madras State. This was another way of allowing north Indian capital to control industries in Madras State. Chief Minister Tanguturi Prakasam Pantulu and Industries Minister V. V. Giri claimed that the permission had been granted by the Union government. Annadurai questions them as to why they did not lodge a protest with the Union government. He provides the long list of north Indian companies operating in Tamil Nadu in shipping and trading.

The third provocation was the railway strike and other such labor disputes. Annadurai points to the language of the state and the press in calling such labor protests as intimidation and violence. He explains that since the profit of the capitalist and the wages of the worker come from the people who buy their produce, people should have a say as to how the money they pay for the goods should be apportioned. Annadurai clearly sympathizes with the labor who are exploited. However, he sees labor as the aggrieved party, capitalists as the contested party, and the state keen on imposing law and order cannot find a resolution without people understanding the plight of the labor, which is where he proposes that a movement like the Dravidar Kazhagam (DK) had a role to play. In other words, he believes the ultimate resolution rested with popular sovereignty. He also discusses the formation of Industrial Finance Corporation by the Union government, which he says was founded with the sole purpose of supporting the survival of capitalism and capitalists as the government knew fully well that there would be crisis brewing in the capitalist order. He points the contradiction that while Jawaharlal Nehru professes socialism, right under his nose the state is working to safeguard the interests of capitalists through such initiatives to secure financial support. While this is a polemical taunt,

Annadurai is really asking why the state could not let the public sector undertake industrialization, aviation, and so on instead of promoting the interests of private capital. Annadurai's focus here is trained on the collusion between political power or the state and the capitalists, which gets missed by those totally invested in the hope of labor power to overcome capitalist order.

It will be useful here to see a relevant passage from Giovanni Arrighi's treatise *The Long Twentieth Century: Money, Power and the Origins of Our Times*. The book owes its premise to Fernand Braudel (1902–1985), the French historian famous for the long-durée analysis of the world system. The passage points out that while Marx sought to find the secret of the capital accumulation in the hidden abode of labor extraction, Braudel asked one to look at another secret abode of the state system and collusion between political power and capital. It will be useful to read the passage in full:

> Marx invited us to "take leave for a time of [the] noisy sphere [of circulation], where everything takes place on the surface and in view of all men, and follow [the possessor of money and the possessor of labor-power] into the hidden abode of production, on whose threshold there stares us in the face 'No admittance except on business'." Here, he promised, "[w]e shall at last force the secret of profit making." Braudel also invited us to take leave for a time of the noisy and transparent sphere of the market economy, and follow the possessor of money into another hidden abode, where admittance is only on business but which is one floor above, rather than one floor below the marketplace. Here, the possessor of money meets the possessor, not of labor-power, but of political power. And here, promised Braudel, we shall force the secret of making those large and regular profits that has enabled capitalism to prosper and expand "endlessly" over the last five to six hundred years, before and after its ventures into the hidden abodes of production. (Arrighi 2010, 25)

It is not only that Annadurai's analytical lens is focused on the connection between north Indian hegemony in political terms and the connection it bears with the capital accumulation of the Baniya and Parsi communities but he is also aware of the separation that exists between the everyday material world of the worker and peasant and the spheres of political nexus with capital. He says:

> ... the peasant on banks of the fields does not know that he is a Dravidian, he only knows that he is poor. But we know that he is both. The worker in the factory would find the Aryan–Dravidian conflict a meaningless clatter; he knows only his everyday difficulties. We know both. It is no surprise that they would ignore us. But it will be unpardonable for us to ignore them. They may not know us. But we know them and hence also that we need to serve their interests. (Aṟiñar Aṇṇā 2010b, 495)

In Annadurai's vision, the political party connects all of what Arrighi following Braudel describes as the three-tier system of capital: the base tier of material life and labor; the middle tier of market, distribution, and consumption; and the top tier of political powers and the "the freely roaming predators of capital accumulation." Hence, *The Garden of Money* is a reiteration of the need for south India to aspire for popular sovereignty to save itself from the clutches of the Bombay capital, which Annadurai metaphorically calls the "money bomb" that may be dropped on the unsuspecting southerners. Ramamurthy completely misses the point since he assumes that Annadurai, not being a Marxist, is not a true socialist. He denounces the text as totally inadequate in terms of scientific analysis. There are a few key misinterpretations that lead him to these conclusions. He takes Annadurai's concerns about capital accumulation in the north and its nexus with political power as a mere comparison of relative state of industrial development. He claims that industries can only be founded where there is raw material and other related resources. He faults Annadurai for not noticing south Indian industries wherever there are facilities. He then charges Annadurai for covering up for the south Indian rich, chiefly moneylenders who want to have it easy without taking risks as industrial entrepreneurs. If they lack the vision that Tata had, who was to blame? Finally, Ramamurthy's major objection lies in Annadurai's idea that people could adjudicate between workers and capitalists. Naturally, it appears to deny and foreclose the historical possibility of workers owning the means of production. When such a dialectical overcoming is denied then Annadurai appears to seek to perpetuate class society and, at best, turns out to be a class collaborationist.

Ramamurthy writes this book well after the demise of Annadurai. His reading of Annadurai's *The Garden of Money* is the best instance of demonstration of the conceptual hiatus between class essentialism and popular sovereignty. As we noted above, this led communists to lose the ground of democratic politics to the DMK. Ramamurthy was an alliance partner with the DMK in 1967, when he was elected to the parliament from Madurai even as he knew that the Swatantra Party of Rajaji was also an alliance partner. This tendency of the communists to treat elections as merely instrumental for their political survival as a party of trade union interests not only rendered their larger political aspiration a distant idea but also the possibility of forging greater integration of political vision and programs on the ground with the DMK.

Enigma of the Shared Ground

A male child was born to the young and aspiring leader of the DMK, Muthuvelar Karunanidhi, on March 1, 1953. A few days later, Josef Stalin of Russia died. The child was named Stalin. It had its costs. A prestigious school in Chennai refused to admit the boy years later due to the name. He was asked to give another name for official records; the father refused. Today, if some young student outside Tamil Nadu or India Googles the name Stalin, she would be confused to find links to media reports on Tamil Nadu appearing among many links related to the Russian leader. Thousands of children might have been named Stalin, but the only person to have a mass political following is the present leader of the DMK, and the chief minister of the state of Tamil Nadu, son of Muthuvelar Karunanithi, M. K. Stalin.

The naming of the child was neither incidental nor serendipitous. The DMK did believe that it shared the ideological space with the communist parties, while the latter was generally incensed by such claims. In the early years of grassroots mobilization, the DMK and the communists shared the oppositional space to the Indian National Congress. The DMK mobilized various strata of organized and unorganized working class, traders, and the rural peasantry, including the economically and socially vulnerable sections. Though they aspired for equity leading to equality, the opposition was to Brahmin and north Indian hegemony, which was also entwined with the powers of the rich. The communists focused on building trade unions among the organized working class, using class antagonism as the primary principle, and refused to identify with the opposition to Brahmin and north Indian hegemony.

In a sense, the DMK was countering the Indianist populism of the Congress with the Dravidianist populism. Further, the DMK characterized their populism as left oriented, as opposed to the Congress populism which the DMK characterized as operating under Brahmin–Baniya hegemony. The Communist Party abided by the unity of India but was unsuccessful in aligning with the socialist sections in the Congress or winning them over at the time of independence. In Tamil Nadu, the communists were aligned with the socialist orientation of the DMK and its mobilizational base but could not successfully gain on them due to their indifference to the Dravidianist cause. It is possible to say that the DMK displaced the Congress in Tamil Nadu, filling the role of the successful populist party in electoral democracy. The communists repeated the history of their alienation at the national level all anew in Tamil Nadu. If they were alienated from the Congress populism at the all-India level during the 1930s and 1940s at the behest of international communism, later, in post-independent Tamil Nadu, they were alienated from the DMK at the behest of Indian nationalism. This needs some parsing to understand the significance of the idea of left populism in the case of the DMK.

In a close analysis of the early years of the formations of the Communist Party with front organizations like the WPP and as part of the Congress socialist wing, Sushil Joshi demonstrates how the Comintern failed to recognize the importance of anti-colonial nationalism. In her gloss, the colonial state was forging a hegemonic hold on the emerging Indian civil society, which the Congress, under the leadership of Gandhi, was seeking to displace through both constitutional methods and mass mobilization through *satyagraha*. The communists under the guidance of the

Comintern however believed in insurrectionary methods that would pave the way for the rule of the working class. This led to a constant prevarication about how to align with the Congress-led movements on the part of the communists. They cite a key passage from Shripad Dange written in 1931.

> If you accept Marxism thoroughly, you have to logically accept Leninism, the Party and Comintern. We stand for complete application of Leninism to the Indian conditions, unequivocal adherence to Marxism–Leninism by everyone who is a Communist and further, complete adherence to the Comintern. If you deny the Comintern, you then naturally deny the Party.... Attempts of pseudo socialists to separate Marxism from Leninism and contrapose them is an attempt to introduce opportunism into the Indian Communist movement. For us there can be no such thing as an independent attitude.... For us Moscow is all truth.... (Joshi and Josh 2011, 1:124)

Such an unquestioned adherence to the Russian model of revolution in the colonial world, according to Joshi, made the party fail to recognize the possibility of aligning with Gandhi's war of positions against the colonial government, in which he sought to withdraw the consent of the ruled to be governed through mass mobilization. This is due to the party's indifference to the hegemonic aspect of the struggle and its obsession with war of maneuver. In Joshi's analysis, the communist movement would have gained much ground by joining the Congress-led anti-colonial struggle and pushing for a socialist agenda as part of it. Though the formation of the socialist wing in Congress tried this, the Communist Party never managed to integrate itself fully due to the towing of Comintern instructions. As we noted in the opening of the chapter, sending a twenty-four-year-old Philip Spratt as Comintern emissary to "blow-up" India offers ample proof of the level of their understanding of the Indian conditions.

If this was the situation with regard to the possibilities of aligning with the Congress, the Communist Party in Tamil Nadu exactly repeated the same set of mistakes in understanding the vitality of the Dravidianist political movements, particularly the DMK, thereby once again missing on the possibility of gaining a popular base for the combined socialist aspirations after independence. Once again, the DMK's thrust, in extension of what was forged by the DK, was to oppose the consolidation of the Brahmin hegemony as Brahmin–Baniya north Indian hegemony through the Congress in Tamil Nadu. This came to assume a gravity, as we have already seen, with the imposition of Hindi learning in 1938 by the Congress government led by Rajagopalachari. In the early 1930s, Periyar had taken a serious interest in communist principles; he famously travelled to Russia in 1932 and on return vowed to bring together the twin causes of self-respect and equality as *Suyamariyathai–Samatharmam*.[3] The Erode declaration of 1934 brought leaders like Jeevanantham and Periyar together. However, when the colonial government showed that it would not brook propagation of communist ideals by arresting Periyar, he decided that it was more important to continue work on the anti-caste front than become constrained by adherence to communism, which anyway he thought should be preceded by abolition of caste inequity. This made Jeevanantham leave Periyar's fold to join the Congress socialists initially than later the Communist Party. Both Periyar and Annadurai, however, were still invested in socialism since their larger goal was the empowerment of the commoner.

The DMK was keen on winning over the communists for the Dravidianist cause. In the first state-level conference of the DMK held in the city of Madras in 1951, a momentous occasion for the new political vehicle, Annadurai in his address made a passionate plea to Jeevanantham, the communist leader present on the dais.

> I recall our leader Periyar on this occasion. Our comrade Jeeva is present on this stage. Three of us are functioning in different political movements now. But I have the faith that time will create an opportunity for all three of us, Periyar, Jeevanantham and I, to function from the same location in future. I don't run a counter in the bazaar bartering principles. So are the other two. As much as I will not give up on my principles they too would not. They should not. However, there will be a united front one day. Let that be a communist front; may that be called a *samadharma* front. I have no worries. But it should be qualified as a Dravidian front. You say Dravidian Communist party, I will be the first member in the party. Call it Dravida *samadharma* party—I will rush to join it as the first member. Dravidian Extremist League—so be it. Dravidian Revolutionary Movement—no objection. I will still be the first member. However, if the appellate Dravidian is eschewed, I will not be part of the movement. (Tirunāvukkaracu 2017, 1:332–335)

Annadurai reiterated on the need for a territorial boundary for the nation practicing communism. He proposed to let Dravidian land be the territory. He insisted on the necessity of prioritizing the call for a separate Dravidian republic through referendum, which is the prerequisite for a communist republic. He further insisted that the DMK was the correct, genuine communist party within the Dravidian context. He proposed that the modus operandi for securing a Dravidian country would be a combination of electoral participation and governance combined with mass mobilization and peaceful struggles to gain greater autonomy till such time that independence is achieved. This appears to be an exact repetition of what the Congress approach to the colonial state was. In a sense, Annadurai perceived it as a relay of sorts when he disagreed with Periyar on marking the day of Indian independence as a "Day of Mourning." His angle was that the success of the anti-colonial struggle should be seen as one step towards the realization of a Dravidian republic since it too had been colonized by the British as well as the emerging north Indian suzerainty. He had a keen awareness that sufficient popular mobilization had not taken place to secure a Dravidian republic alongside the Indian nation like in the case of Pakistan, which we already noted earlier.

The Communist Party persisted with the same approach it had forged with regard to the Congress in the case of the DMK as well. A good example would be a document written for inner party circulation by six members of the Communist Party in Tamil Nadu dated December 16, 1952, placing certain requests to the Union and state committee for further reflection, study, and action, including circulating the document to all the party members in Tamil Nadu.[4] The document's conclusive statement is that Nehru represents the interests of the Baniya–Parsi capital while Rajaji and Periyar represent the interests of the Chettiar capital. It warns that as the party suffered considerably due to the mischief perpetrated by the diversionary tactics of the Congress socialists like Nehru and Bose a decade ago, similar false endorsements of socialism by the likes of Periyar and Rajaji are bound to hurt the party once again. It treats the DMK to be an extension of Periyar's services to Chettiar interests; the Congress party in Tamil Nadu is alleged to serve the interests of Brahmin capital in the state. In a nutshell, we can surmise from the document that all political mobilization that does not take the contradiction between the working class and capital as the primary site of politics, which speak in terms of general welfare of the people, regional interests, and so on, are seen to be working at the behest of the vested interests of one capitalist group or the other. It is not necessary for us today to engage with such reductionist readings and fathom the litany of unanswered question such formulations lead us to.

In spite of this typically reductionist perspective, the document is intriguing in many respects. While the struggle against Brahmin hegemony and Hindu nationalism as articulated by Annadurai's *Aryan Allure* is totally ignored, the document has no hesitation in combining caste identity with capital formation to speak of Chettiar and Brahmin capital, not to mention Baniya and Parsi capital all within the emerging Indian nation. The document doesn't even make an attempt to explain how these capitalist groups are pitted against each other in concrete terms, except for the vague assumption that any competition among the entrepreneurial class implies contradiction among the capitalists through a listing of various investment profiles. This needs to be compared with Annadurai's studied concerns about unevenness of capital formation and complementary state support for industries in the north and the south, as articulated in his pamphlet, *The Garden of Money*, to understand how the DMK could think of itself as the communist party of Dravidian politics. However, the chief aporia of the said document prepared by Communist Party members lies in its apprehensions about the deleterious effect of the diversionary tactics of the populist parties getting combined with its larger goal to build a popular united front to carry out the task of forming a people's democratic government. While the ultimate aim is to overcome the imperialist and feudalist forces, the immediate task is to wrench governance from those interests to form a people's government. In choosing the parliamentary path, this can be achieved only through forming, under the leadership of the workers, a united front with the peasants, petty bourgeoisie, and the national bourgeoise. If the strategy was to form such a united front, then how could the successful and progressive mobilization of the DK and the DMK be ignored? The problem, on the one hand, appears to be that the DK and the DMK not accepting the so-called "working class" leadership, which is the Communist Party; on the other hand, there is a larger problem of deciding who the "national" bourgeoise is. If, as the document alleges, the Chettiar capital of Tamil Nadu is in a conflict of interest with the Baniya capital of the north, should not the Communist Party be concerned about how to use it to forge a united front? Should they not then accept the need for the Dravidianist plank to exploit the contradiction? Why would the party then abide by the Indian nation? The lack of a clear answer to the question is again the reason why the DMK could think of itself as the right kind of communist party.

In 1961, when some of the DMK functionaries lead by E. V. K. Sampath split the party to form Tamil Desiya Katchi (Tamil Nationalist Party), claiming that the demand for a Dravidian republic has no basis in reality since the demand is made only in Tamil Nadu, the Communist Party published a pamphlet titled *India? Dravidam? Tamizhagam?* (A. Balasubramaniam 1961). The pamphlet holds that both India and Tamil Nadu have legitimate basis to be taken as collective identity and candidates for nation-states. Since India was realized through anti-colonial nationalism as part of the world historical processes of capitalist development and formations of the nation-states, the Indian nation has materialized itself as an entity that people affectively and emotionally identify with. The Tamil identity is surely a distinct but composite part of Indian identity, the welfare of which needs to be foregrounded by a regional party like the DMK without negating the Indian identity. However, the Dravidian identity has no basis in reality but is a complete misnomer. How can the identification of Brahmins as Aryan lead to holding the whole of north India, including non-Brahmins, as opposed to the interests of south India? Hence, Balasubramaniam pleads with both the DMK and the newly formed Tamil Desiya Katchi to give up on secessionist demands and rally with the Communist Party in opposing the pro-rich Congress government.

This line of argument again fails to take into account the hegemonic aspects of Brahminism, which underwrites pan-Indian nationalism often as Hindu nationalism. The DMK was fully conscious of the underlying template of Brahminical Hinduism in the making of Indian nationalism to which the Communist Party chooses to turn a blind eye. The opposition to "Brahmin hegemony which turns into North Indian hegemony" can be understood by reading *Aryan Allure* alongside *The Garden of Money*. These tracts clearly argue how Brahminical hegemony and the north Indian capitalist hegemony reinforce each other to the detriment of the south. Thus, for the DMK populism, the internal frontier with Brahmins as indicated by appellate

Dravidian is as important as the empty signifier Tamil. Nevertheless, since the DMK has spoken of the concrete territory of south India as the spread of Dravidian republic, it was hard put to justify the feasibility of it in the absence of the idea taking root in other states. However, after considerable electoral success in 1962 and the subsequent official withdrawal of the secessionist demand owing to the constitutional amendment, it became obvious that the retention of the Dravidian appellate purely as standing for the non-Brahmin identity deferring the possibility of confederation of south Indian states to an uncertain future. As we shall see, the combination of Dravidian and Tamil identity continued to help the party in its mobilization in more ways than one.

The decline of the Communist Party became imminent due its self-imposed class isolationism. Hence, its own existence became predicated on the left populism articulated by the DMK, particularly by what signified the internal frontier between the underdogs and the power elite, the appellate Dravidian. The Communist Party stood to gain from what they dismissed as unscientific and had no basis in reality. If only the DMK had opted for the Tamil identity as the sole plank of political mobilization, the progressive intonation of the anti-caste and hence the politics of the commoner might have been lost in the Tamil nationalist drift. However, the politics of the commoner that the DMK articulated continued to place it on the ground shared with the communists. There was an incessant polemic in the party journals and among the party organs as to which party represented best the interests of the poor, underprivileged, and the commoner. When the debates forged local idioms, it is said that the DMK would taunt the communists as to what mattered most: “Sora, Manama?” (Food or Honor). It is alleged that the communists, in order to maintain a materialist outlook, used to respond that food was the fundamental necessity, thereby falling into the trap of crassness lacking in human dignity. One DMK journal ran a serialized polemical column titled “Moscow or Kanchipuram?” (Ka. Appadurai 1954). The DMK journal *Manram* published an essay in 1953, claiming that henceforth the DMK would not work for joint programs or action with the Communist Party since the latter had a Leninist vision in which it sought to weaken allies in order to become the sole representative of the people (Neṭuñceḻiyaṉ 1953, 3). The essay invoked a classical Tamil expression, *nodumalan*, which meant neither a foe nor a friend, to describe its attitude to communists. Since, on the one hand, they shared similar aspirations to secure justice for the poor and the underdog, they ought not be foes. On the other hand, as the communists were for weakening an ally programmatically to grow at its cost, they can’t be friends either. Further, as Annadurai emphasized in his address at the first state-level conference of the party, allegiance to communist principles was different from what relationships might obtain with the Communist Party. The bold and indigenous adaptation of socialist ideals by the DMK was completely lost to the anglicized elite and those blindfolded by class essentialism, thus leading to the failure to identify and theorize the growth of the DMK as the growth of left populist aspirations.

Notes

1. For a discussion of the historical context of the case and the role of Spratt, see Joshi and Josh (2011).
2. In fact, he was only articulating concerns that Buddhadeb Bhattacharya, the Marxist chief minister of West Bengal, was to articulate fifty years later. For example, Buddhadeb said, "Without industry how do you progress? This is the general trend of all civilisation—from village to city, from agriculture to industry. You cannot stop it, you should not stop it. And for that you need private industry, private capital, you need big business. We need multinationals—the only reservation is that we won't let them enter the retail sector." See his interview in *Hindustan Times* for this quote and more such thoughts of his, which he said the left was having difficulties in coming to terms with ideologically (Kalbag 2007).
3. The work on Periyar written in Tamil by V. Geetha and S. V. Rajadurai bears this as its title (Kītā and Rājaturai 2018).
4. We'd like to thank Dr Arasu, former chair, the Department of Modern Tamil, Madras University, for providing us with a copy of this document.

IMAGINATION

5 The Play Is the Thing

I'll have grounds
More relative than this—the play's the thing
Wherein I'll catch the conscience of the King.
—William Shakespeare, *Hamlet*

The Dravidianist journey in the terrain of arts and literature that we call the domain of imagination preceded and substantially contributed to the founding of the DMK. Of the many key interventions Annadurai made in the mid-1940s writing plays for the stage assumes a unique significance since imagination takes the form of the performative and the theatrical in a highly potent combination. We have already discussed *Aryan Allure*, the seminal treatise he wrote in 1944, which was to function as a kind of manifesto for the party that he would launch a few years later in 1949. We will be discussing the intervention in literary criticism, or rather a challenge to canon formation in Tamil that he made with regard to the twelfth-century rendition of Ramayana in Tamil by Kamban in the next chapter. We will also be discussing the writing of prose fiction that he popularized among the party men in Chapter 8. Of all these, there is a reason to feel that the stage played the most crucial role. Given the fact of lack of literary training of the subaltern populace when they were barely literate, not to speak of the bulk of illiterate people, theater or plays had the unique facility to combine refined expression in language with melodramatic imagination through which a certain political sensibility could be cultivated. The language used in the play synchronized with the mode of public address that the DMK leaders cultivated in terms of its rhetorical flourish. Such discursive synergy was further enhanced by the fact that the DMK leaders themselves acted in these plays which they wrote. In fact, perhaps it was the turn to imagination that created the ground for a new party, the DMK, to be headed by Annadurai, who lead Dravidianists in this new battlefront, recruiting able lieutenants like Karunanidhi to wage the culture war on the turf of imagination. The foray of the DMK leaders into cinema, enabled by the relative newness of that cultural form that catered to the whole of society than any other form that catered to selective audiences, has been much overemphasized. This, however, needs to be seen as part of a much larger political investment on the widespread tropes and modes of imagination, a nurturing of Dravidian ethos as opposed to the Brahminical Hindu ethos. It is riding on the waves of such initiatives in the domain of imagination by the DMK leaders and cadres that M. G. Ramachandran, the film actor, could become a leader of the masses after 1972, claiming to be the true heir of Anna, who pioneered the initiative in the mid-1940s.

Annadurai appears to have developed a keen interest in arts and literature from a young age. He was publishing short stories from the early 1930s. Anna was also given to wide reading in English and Tamil, as can be evinced by the stupendous amount of writing which are being compiled now into a set of 120 volumes with copious references to literature both Tamil and global. He naturally earned the encomium "Aṟiñar" from adoring party cadres, which denotes a person of scholarly accomplishment and learning. This does not appear to be superficial praise when his oeuvre, as indicated above, is considered. He realized that he needed more space for his writing than *Kudi Arasu* (Republic) or *Viduthalai* (Freedom), the two newspapers Periyar ran, could afford. Hence, he decided to launch his flagship weekly newsletter in 1942. In hindsight, this can be seen as a clear indication that his political aspiration and imagination considerably differed from Periyar. Periyar was a passionate and incessant critique of human weakness in succumbing to dogma. His investment was in forging an agonistic and critical discourse, a mode of Socratic practice in the public sphere. Even when he endorsed many positive ideas like a separate Dravidian republic, he could not channelize his critical energy to the task of a positive discursive construction of an entity like that even when he could write a powerful pamphlet titled *Is India a Nation?* (V. Anaimuthu 1974, 2:649–654). Hence what is more significant than Annadurai having to launch his own newsletter was that he named it *Dravida Nadu*, the putative country that they hoped to strive for and his authorial stance in positing the same.

It should not be surprising then that Annadurai would use his creative abilities to sustain the magazine. It is in order to buy the printing equipment needed for the newsletter *Dravida Nadu* that he wrote his first play *Cantirōtayam*, which was staged in Erode in 1943. Annadurai himself acted as the protagonist in the play. The play was about a corrupt godman, a mutt head, and the many intrigues through which the hero impersonating as the godman exposes the frauds. The play not only helped to raise sufficient funds for buying the printing machine but also launched Annadurai as a playwright and an actor. Legendary professional drama artist T. K. Shanmugam approved Annadurai's talent in both capacities.[1] However, it was the subsequent plays written by Annadurai that became far more successful than the first attempt. As the initial plays were overtly propagandist, on being prompted by professional drama companies, Annadurai went on to write two more plays for the general audience with subtler political and reformist themes. Both of them, *Ōr Iravu* (A Single Night) and *Vēlaikkāri* (The Servant Maid) went on to become huge hits onstage and later as films, thus heralding the era of social themes on drama stage and cinema screen, which were until then saturated with Hindu mythological stories, devotionals, and folktales replete with supernatural elements.

It was widely acknowledged that the plays of Annadurai ushered in a whiff of fresh air, though there were social themes on stage and screen before; Annadurai could give the socials a tone and diction that freed itself of caste-specific articulations, which also heralded the virtual domain of a new public. The most widely recounted statement of recognition of Annadurai's achievement came from the other side of the cultural divide, from a nationalist Brahmin. Kalki Krishnamurthy, pioneering fiction writer, journalist, and a standard bearer of emerging Tamil modernity and public sphere, a Congressman and a close acolyte of Rajagopalachari, famously celebrated in his review of the play *Ōr Iravu* that Tamil Nadu had found its Bernard Shaw, Ibsen, and Galsworthy in Annadurai (Tirunāvukkaracu 2017, 1:133). The reason this statement is oft recounted is that Kalki could not be accused of partisanship in praising Annadurai since they belonged to rival formations not only in politics but the attendant cultural politics as well. After his debut play *Cantirōtayam*, Annadurai wrote the play we will focus on in this chapter, *Cantramōhaṉ* or *Civāji Kaṇṭa Intu Cāmrājyam* (Chandramohan, or The Hindu Empire Shivaji Founded) (Aṟiñar Aṇṇā 2018). The play, though staged first in 1945, is indistinguishable from the DMK since the party conferences in the initial years invariably staged the play in the late evenings after the conference proceedings during the day, as if it contained all that the party was trying to stand for or represent.

The ingenuity of Annadurai lies in having picked the historical event of the coronation of Shivaji, who founded the Maratha kingdom that was to become the last exercise in empire building in precolonial India, as the theme of the play. It was Jadunath Sarkar's historical account *Shivaji and His Times* (Sarkar 1920) that inspired Anna to think of the play.[2] He found the need for Shivaji to invite the renowned Brahmin scholar Gaga Bhatta from Varanasi to officiate in his coronation and bestow the status of Kshatriya on him—a revealing instance from recent history that demonstrated the hegemonic role played by Brahmins and their casteist ordering of society. As we saw in Chapter 1, Annadurai had already explained his nuanced understanding of how the non-Brahmin Tamil kings found it expedient to lean on the casteist hegemony forged by Brahmins to build stable polities and social order at the cost of acceding superior status to Brahmins over themselves. Hence, the title of his track *Aryan Allure*. Instead of merely villainizing the "wily Brahmin," Annadurai also strove to question the complicity of the rulers of yesteryears in leaning on Brahmin scriptural, priestly, and epistemological authority for the propagation of their rule. He sought to balance the distribution of responsibility between the self-perpetuation of Brahmin authority and the dependency of the warrior kings on the scholarship and law-making skills of the Brahmins for purposes of ruling. Since the complexity of such a nuanced understanding might be lost on the readers of the tract, the play on Shivaji's coronation came in handy to illustrate the issue much more powerfully. It is of considerable significance that Annadurai decided to act as Gaga Bhattar instead of playing the titular role of Shivaji or the protagonist of the play, the fictional brave soldier Chandramohan. It is in the subtle etching of the scheming and wily character of Gaga Bhattar on stage through his histrionic potential that Anna hoped to illustrate the cunning of the Brahmin. One can read the synopsis of the play in a couple of brief paragraphs from Sarkar's book.

> Shivaji and his ministers had long felt the practical disadvantage of his not being a crowned king. True, he had conquered many lands and gathered much wealth: he had a strong army and navy and exercised powers of life and death over men, like an independent sovereign. But in theory his position was that of a subject.... He could not claim equality of political status with any king. Then again, so long as he was a mere private subject, he could not, with all his real power, claim the loyalty and devotion of the people over whom he ruled.... The territories conquered by his sword could not become his lawful property, however undisturbed his possession over them might be in practice.... The higher minds of Maharashtra ... longed for the Hindu Swaraj, and that implied a Hindu Chhatrapati.
>
> But there was one curious hindrance to the realization of this ideal. According to the ancient Hindu scriptures, only a member of Kshatriya caste can be legally crowned as king and claim the homage of Hindu subjects. The Bhonsles were popularly known to be neither Kshatriyas nor of any other twice-born castes, but were tillers of the soil, as Shivaji's great-grandfather was still remembered to have been. How could an upstart sprung from such a Shudra (plebeian) stock aspire to the rights and honours due to Kshatriya? The Brahmans of all parts of India would attend and bless the coronation of Shivaji only if he could be authoritatively declared a Kshatriya.
>
> It was then, necessary first to secure the support of a pundit, whose reputation for scholarship would silence all opposition to the views he might propound. Such a man was found in Vishweshwar, nicknamed Gaga Bhatta, of Benares, the greatest Sanskrit theologian and controversialist then alive, a master of the four Vedas, the six philosophies and all the scriptures of the Hindus, and popularly known as the Brahma-deva and Vyas of the modern age. After holding out for some time, he became compliant ... and declared that the Rajah was a Kshatriya of the purest breed.... (Jadunath Sarkar 1920, 238–241)

It can be readily imagined how this passage should have excited Annadurai's imagination as the most potent thrust of Shudra politics against Brahmin hegemony.

Since it was the general practice during the phase of the emergence of nationalist thought to overlook the not-so-savory side of the kings and emperors of the past, at least through the lens of a contemporary democrat, but to hail them as icons of the nation, as Christopher Bayly has argued for rather sympathetically (Bayly 2005), Anna could not be faulted for overlooking the unflattering descriptions of Shivaji's plunders and raids, which included northern parts of Tamil Nadu in Sarkar's book. All that mattered was that here was the person whose sheer valor, strategic acumen, and swordsmanship created the possibility of a birth of kingdom and empire, most generously a "patria" in Bayly's terms (Bayly 2005, 42), but still he had to find a Brahmin pundit and his sophistry to have him recognized as king. The ways of Brahminical social order in determining the source of power through hegemony could never reveal itself more transparently than in this instance of Shivaji, ironically, having to become a "Hindu sovereign," even as the same Hindu tenets demeaned him as a person of lowly Shudra birth. All that Anna had to do was to package the historical anecdote in a dramatic sequence for the people to understand the irony of Hindu identity as determined by the self-serving Brahmin.

Before we get to see how Anna structured the play in a thoughtful weaving of thematic concerns, it may be worth noting a minor episode in casting for the play that was to assume many valences much later. A professional actor D. V. Narayanasamy, an admirer of Annadurai, was to introduce an upcoming actor to Annadurai to be cast in the role of Shivaji. He was the young M. G. Ramachandran, who had played minor roles in many films, waiting for a break. Annadurai decided to give the role to the charismatic young man. Apparently, even the costume was stitched to his measurements; his name appeared in the initial advertisements for the play. There are many accounts as to why M. G. R. withdrew from playing the role at the last moment. As per M. G. R's own account, he had the temerity to ask Annadurai to let him, as Shivaji, address the audience at the close of the play instead of asking Chandramohan, the protagonist, to do the propagation.

It is not clear from his account whether this led to his estrangement from the assignment. There are many who allege that the real reason was that he could not manage the dialogues Anna wrote, since emotive dialogue delivery, particularly the long ornamental ones, was to elude him all through his career.[3] His strength on-screen was in playing the swashbuckler. Whatever be the actual reason, M. G. R. dropped out of playing the role. Incidentally, the last-minute replacement found was V. C. Ganesan, who was famous for donning women characters on stage but had a sterling capacity for instantly memorizing the dialogues and delivering them with panache. The young Ganesan, thrilled by the opportunity, etched an impressive performance in the inaugural show. It is widely held that Periyar E. V. Ramasamy, who was present to preside over the show, suggested that he be known as Sivaji Ganesan henceforth in appreciation of his performance.

Sivaji Ganesan, later to be known just as Sivaji, debuted as a hero in cinema in the legendary, quintessential DMK film *Parasakthi* (1952), speaking the evergreen dialogues written by Karunanidhi.[4] However, in the meantime, M. G. R. had befriended Karunanidhi, and was launched to stardom through the films scripted by the latter. M. G. R. and Sivaji, men of crossed destinies, both made famous through the scripts and dialogues of Karunanidhi, were to dominate the Tamil film world with a significant role in the formations of the political, the charting of which deserves a book-length study.[5] M. G. R. became an icon of the DMK, later successfully founding his own party, the All India Anna DMK (AIADMK), to oppose his one-time mentor Karunanidhi after Anna's demise. Sivaji, strangely, charted a miserably failed political career as the mascot of the Indian National Congress. It is however pertinent to note that V. C. Ganesan is known to the masses only as Sivaji all through his life, and posthumously as well, due to his playing the role on the inaugural day of the play. When the DMK was launched in 1949, there were several other young leaders who would compete to play the role, while some professional actors stepped in as well. Sivaji Ganesan never seems to have played the role in the party fora in spite of having taken the name of the character in real life.

We should conclude this detour once again by clarifying that certain expression of the political as faciality machine by the M. G. R.–Sivaji combination is one possible outcome of the successful mobilization of the DMK and its forays in the domain of imagination (Krishnan 2018). The commonsensical misattribution of the DMK's success in the electoral turf to the later-day popularity of M. G. R. is erroneous since it was the DMK that helped M. G. R. to become popular in the first place as any close study of historical material would demonstrate. Hence, our attempt in this section of the book is to capture in detail the role of imagination in the DMK politics as a broad-spectrum cultural intervention.

Like his first play *Cantirōtayam* that had its inaugural performance in Erode in the presence of Periyar, Annadurai was keen to have the inaugural performance of *Civāji Kaṇṭa Intu Cāmrājyam* too only in the presence of his leader. The Self-Respect conference in Chennai on April 29, 1945, appeared to be the appropriate occasion. Periyar of course was happy with the purposive nature of the play. He conceded that Anna had imparted ideas in the play that would take ten conferences for him to convey. However, his apparent disquiet about Annadurai's close association with the acting fraternity continued, which also could have contributed to the widening gulf between the two leaders, as can be evinced in some of the allegorical fictional writings of Annadurai during the period of gradual estrangement. A novella known as *Rajapart Rangadurai*, in particular, made many suggestive references to the newfound vocation of Annadurai, causing heartburn or misapprehension on the part of Periyar, which was actively fanned by inimical interests within the organization.[6] With this background in mind, we should now proceed to understand the emplotment of the play *Cantramōhaṉ* or *Civāji Kaṇṭa Intu Cāmrājyam* to appreciate how the play contributed to the ideological messaging of the DMK.

Ascription of Maratha or Indian Nationalism as Setting for the Play

Annadurai had a voice-over providing the historical context of the play before the stage was lit. This contextualization described Shivaji as the liberator of a subjugated India, hailing from Maratha land, freeing it (Maratha land as a metonymic substitution of India) from the clutches of occupying forces. Obviously, if Shivaji was portrayed as an ambitious chieftain who aspired to become a king or monarch in the quest of power, the story of his submission to the Brahminical authority for getting recognized as a sovereign would not convey the political import, that of the aporia inherent in founding a Hindu kingdom as per Brahmin tenets. After all, someone guided by personal ambition would always make compromises required to achieve what they desired. Hence, certain ascriptions of a putative nationalism to the Maratha clans that rallied behind Shivaji were necessary to illustrate how the military success was inadequate for assertion of sovereignty as Brahmins had the hegemonic sway over the constituencies of the putative Hindu kingdom.

Annadurai surely latches on to the observation found in Jadunath Sarkar, cited above, about the desire of Maratha elite ("higher minds") to found a Hindu kingdom. He uses it as the ironic title of the play *Civāji Kaṇṭa Intu Cāmrājyam* (The Hindu Empire Shivaji Founded). The irony is because of the inherent disqualification Shivaji's Shudra birth had bequeathed on him, as only a Kshatriya could become a sovereign, even when it was Shivaji who could lead the military campaigns to carve out the Hindu kingdom. There are three conditions operating simultaneously that create the irony, the constitutive tension of the putative Hindu kingdom. The first condition is that while one could win territories by war, but to rule them productively consensus of the people is needed. The second condition is that in producing the consensus for the rule, the support of the priestly class of Brahmins was mandatory since they had successfully made their *shastras* binding on influential sections of the society. The third condition is that while the Brahmins wanted a Hindu kingdom to perpetuate their own hegemonic position, the shastric injunctions would not accept a Shudra as the king, thus rendering Shivaji unfit to rule. As a result, it is only by acceding to the notion of the illegitimacy of his sovereign aspiration and by bribing Brahmins to condone the same could Shivaji finally found the Hindu kingdom against its own normative prescriptions. While condoning the Shudra status of Shivaji compromises the Brahmin, the *shastras* as well as Shivaji, only the Brahmins could come up winners since they have made their consent more powerful than the military might of Shivaji, which anyway is the very purpose of the *shastras*. Hence, the Hindu kingdom is only a euphemism for Brahmin rule, making the sovereignty of Shivaji lack true substance. Overthrowing foreign rule amounts to nothing for the non-Brahmin masses, since they are anyway enslaved to Brahmin *shastras*. The true liberation is only the liberation from Brahmins; to achieve that one has to wage a struggle for hegemony in which Brahminical *shastras* are challenged and overthrown.

In order to make Shivaji's predicament in seventeenth-century Maharashtra speak to the Dravidianist radical distancing with the Congress aspiration for freedom from the alien rule of the British without a thorough repudiation of Brahminical caste order, Annadurai coded Shivaji's military expeditions as a war of liberation against foreign powers. All the same, while he relished the irony of calling the putative kingdom "Hindu," which demeans its own rightful sovereign, he was careful never to name the foreign rule Muslim or Moghul. While the independent kingdom sought to be created is ironically coded Hindu in order to connect it to the contemporary schism foreshadowing Indian independence, the oppressive foreigner from whom the liberation is sought remained nameless. After all, for the non-Brahmins, the only liberation that was acutely needed was from the tyranny of Brahminical caste order. This is the fact that intimately connects the disability imposed by Shivaji's Shudra birth to the politics of the DMK that the play tried to dramatize. It manages to do so by three key typological figures that constitute the play: the Brahmin, the sovereign, and the soldier. Apart from the characters who belong to these three types that are central to the play, there are also a few other complimentary characters that support the essential contradiction that is played out between these three.

The Brahmin

The play opens with two Brahmins Keshava Bhattar and Balachandra Bhattar on the street. They beat up Pacchai, an untouchable *panchama*, with canes since he had polluted a pond considered sacred by rinsing his body in it after the day's work in a neighboring field. As he begs to be let off, bleeding profusely, they warn him never to do it again. As he runs off, the Brahmins lament the possible disorderliness into which the world would sink if people started transgressing boundaries like Pacchai. In the next scene, we see Pacchai being accosted by Aandi, who fumes against the gross injustice. Though in pain, Pacchai blames himself for stepping into the pond, while Aandi feels that the Brahmin order should be opposed. At this moment, a member of a devotional cult, a religious mendicant, a *sadhu*, comes that way. He empathizes with both and affirms that all are equal in the eyes of God. But Aandi contests him saying what is the use of all the devotional lyrics if such caste atrocities continue. He says that even God is not able to overrule the boundaries created by Brahmins. The gods are subservient to Brahmins. The *sadhu* says that these are false claims made by oppressors and a day will come in Maharashtra when the truth of equality would shine forth by the grace of God. Aandi speaks to him at length about the futility of such faith and devotion, which does not show the way in which such social hierarchy and oppression could be ended.

Pacchai represents the type who are resigned to their fate; Aandi represents the birth of consciousness about the unjust order and oppression. The *sadhu*, while offering a counterpoint within religion to the Brahmin theocracy, is articulating the problem only in terms of moral refinement and not as a political program. We will encounter the *sadhu* a few more times in the play.

Keshava Bhattar and Balachandra Bhattar are the typical Brahmins who subsist by officiating in various life cycle rituals of the people. While both are extremely conscious of the need to defend the social order that has placed them at the apex, Balachandra Bhattar is a more cunning schemer than Keshava Bhattar, who lacks in political acumen. When news reaches them about the impending coronation of Shivaji, both feel very agitated by the transgression in which a Shudra is trying to become a sovereign. Keshava Bhattar is disturbed that the Brahmin prime minister, or *peshwa*, of Shivaji, Moropant, is consenting to this transgression. Balachandra Bhattar tells him that Moropant would never agree to the proposed coronation. At that moment, Moropant himself appears and it turns out that he is against the violation of the *shastras*, as predicted by Balachandra Bhattar. He in fact beckons the two to spread word among the Brahmins about the need to stand united against such a violation of the *shastras* involved in Shivaji's coronation. We can deduct in their conversation a certain insecurity they have of non-Brahmin devotional cults that preach equality. They also fear that if Shivaji is allowed to become sovereign, Brahmin interests could seriously get compromised. Hence, there are two sides to the objection. One is Shivaji, a Shudra ascending the throne is in itself a violation; the second is the fear of how Brahmin interests could get compromised in his rule.

When Chitnis (the official title of the head of government bureaucracy) gets wind of the Brahmin discontent, he accosts Keshava Bhattar, who pleads that this objection is nothing personal but is raised purely on the basis of shastric injunctions. He further assures Chitnis that Brahmins bear no personal grudge against Shivaji, a great warrior. If only, he further suggests, anyone who commands considerable authority in the *shastras* would endorse Shivaji's coronation, people like him would not stand in the way. When prompted by Chitnis who this person could be, Keshava Bhattar suggests the name of Gaga Bhattar of Varanasi. Chitnis then asks him to go as an emissary with one or two other Brahmin pundits to seek the endorsement of Gaga Bhattar by explaining the many virtues of Shivaji to him. When Keshava Bhattar asks why him, Chitnis says if he does not go as emissary, it would mean that he bears a grudge against Shivaji. Then Keshava Bhattar decides to go with his friend Balachandra Bhattar. Balachandra Bhattar, true to his cunning ways, decides to advise Gaga Bhattar against issuing any approval to Shivaji's coronation. When Chitnis receives the reply in the negative from Gaga Bhattar, he understands the villainy of the two Brahmins. He then sends his own emissary to whom Gaga Bhattar gives assent not only to the coronation but also to come in person to officiate it.

When Gaga Bhattar comes in person to a royal reception, he is accosted first by Shivaji, who wants to know why a Shudra could not ascend the throne. After a fiery exchange, Shivaji yields to the proposals of Gaga Bhattar to undergo rituals to compensate for his Shudra birth and be ordained as a Kshatriya. He further concedes that he would atone for his sins in the battlefield through generous gifts to the Brahmins as prescribed by Gaga Bhattar. After this encounter, Gaga Bhattar is accosted by Moropant, who entreats Gaga Bhattar not to agree to the coronation as it would turn out not to be in the interests of Brahmins in Maharashtra. Gaga Bhattar vacillates and tries to tempt Chitnis that being a Kayasth, a twice-born caste, he should ascend the throne on behalf of Shivaji. When a dejected Chitnis sternly rebuffs the suggestion, Gaga Bhattar, weighing the pros and cons, finally swings in favor of going ahead with the coronation.

Gaga Bhattar does not merely oscillate. He has two major concerns. On the one hand, he does not want to do anything against the wishes of the local Brahmins in Maharashtra; after all their interests need be protected and their support to his decision is necessary. Hence, when first Balachandra Bhattar and subsequently Moropant request him not to consent to the coronation, he immediately accedes to their request. However, he also has a larger consideration, or rather the larger picture, in mind. In the political climate prevailing in the subcontinent, it is rather prudent to demonstrate the power of the Brahmins and their *shastras* to create and sustain a sovereign head who has the potential to expand his reign through military might. While the fears of Maharashtrian Brahmins about a possible decline in their status by bowing to the Shudra king is true, they might also gain more by having him depend on them for recognition and for the perpetuation of the rule.

In essence, if Brahmin power could be demonstrated by refusing to recognize Shivaji's ascension to the throne, it could as well be demonstrated by creating legitimacy to the same. In the final count, what should be carefully considered is which of the two strategies is more pragmatic and more beneficial to Brahmins. The local Maharashtrian Brahmins take the position that a Shivaji without legal authority would depend more on them for the sake of governance. Gaga Bhattar envisions the possibility that a Shivaji empowered by Brahmins would have to retain their support for governance. In the second case, greater power to Shivaji might mean greater power to Brahmins. It is in delineating the win-win situation of the Brahmins through many dialogues between Gaga Bhattar and his disciple Ranga Bhattar that Annadurai brings out the nature of Brahmin exceptionalism to the fore. For example, when Ranga Bhattar regrets that the kings wallow in luxury while a learned man like Gaga Batter languishes in austerity, Gaga Bhattar reminds him that the powers of the kings are temporally limited while the powers enjoyed by him transcend temporal power. He says, "When a king goes to war, he would seek our blessings. He will perish in the battle. However, the victor will come and bow to us before ascending the throne. Such is the nature of the power we have" (Aṟiñar Aṇṇā 2018, 75). As makers and interpreters of law, they are bound by law but are also above it, like in the case of sovereign exception; their powers of sanction are drawn from the gods, who in fact are their own creations. The play also points to the spiritual and lay authority held by them through Gaga Bhattar and other priestly Brahmins on the one hand, and Moropant, the *peshwa*, on the other. It is perhaps this combination that makes them a necessary component of state formation of any kind.

The Sovereign

There cannot be a more perfect demonstration, as the dialogues of the play beautifully reveal, of the dual function or double articulation of sovereignty than the case of Shivaji. He was the perfect war machine who could create a territorial authority and guard it against any other possible invader; he could, as was the nature of such enterprise, expand the territory in his possession to the extent possible and raid further territories to gather ransom. However, having a demarcated territorial possession needs to be accompanied by a self-constitutive governance of the people who live in it. The de facto control of the territory needs to become de jure sovereign possession. This involves the recognition of the people within the territory, which will then lead to the recognition of other sovereigns in varying measures, since there could always be disputes about the extent of territorial possessions.

It is in Scene 8 of the play that we are introduced to the problem; in fact, the problem unfolds before Shivaji appears onstage. It opens with Chitnis welcoming the *sardars*, the military commanders, into a bouquet hall on behalf of Shivaji, who hosts the dinner. The *sardars* see two rows of chairs and a single chair at the head of the table on a raised platform. When they are told it is meant for Shivaji who is to preside over the occasion, they rise in rebellion. The confused Chitnis ask them whether they were not willing to fight under his command during the wars and raids. They say warfare is different from civil life; in the sphere of civil life, they, who were born in respectable clans and caste denominations, cannot accept Shivaji from a humble Shudra peasant stock presiding over the dinner in which all of them partake. Protesting thus, they leave a frustrated Chitnis who is the accosted by Shivaji, who had overheard the heated exchange. It is then that Chitnis proposes that Shivaji be enthroned as emperor, which will then give him Kshatriya status. Shivaji consents.

While the primary cause of sovereignty could be the war machine, the assertion of ability to be a free actor, it is only the recognition of the subjects that can constitute the sovereign as a legal authority. In the scheme of "double articulation," we borrow from Gilles Deleuze, the war machine is the form of expression of sovereignty, and the ordination of subject populace, at least the stakeholders in power, is the form of content.[7] In other words, the war machine is a proposition that needs to be validated by a consensual and contractual binding of the populace. If a word is proposed by someone, it can only survive if more and more people agree to the union of the signifier and signified so proposed. As is the case of meaning proposed by a word, so is the case of the power proposed by a sword. The mere existential force should transform into a transcendental and relational symbol. The word should enter the dictionary, the power should crystalize as sovereignty in the comity of such legally valid entities. In the context of Shivaji, it is possible that such a need was further accentuated by the presence of the British trading posts in the vicinity that was perhaps consolidating early modern polity.

The historical question then, in the case of Shivaji, was that whether he should remain a warlord enjoying his possessions as long as his war machine remained strong enough or should he assume the sanctity of a legal authority, which will give his deeds a transcendental validity beyond the existence and efficacy of his war machine. We can understand that the *jaghirdar*s and chieftains deriving their tenuous authority from Deccan sultanates should have been hesitant about the transformation of one of them into a new sovereign authority, even if they could not challenge the war machine he had assembled. It is then in the turf of producing consensus around the new legally validated authority that the Hindu identity and shastric injunctions of Brahmins come into play. Those who are opposed to Shivaji's symbolic assertion of sovereignty through coronation point to his Shudra birth, which disqualifies him from being the sovereign that is only reserved for a Kshatriya; however, the power to recognize who is a Kshatriya is in the hands of the Brahmins, who created and continued to interpret the *shastras*. Hence, the need to placate Gaga Bhattar of Varanasi; satiate him and other Brahmins with generous gifts and feasts.

We don't know whether Shivaji or any of his Shudra soldiers felt humiliated by either the *shastras* disqualifying him or having to succumb to the ruse of Gaga Bhattar coming to their aid in bestowing recognition on Shivaji in consideration of lavish amounts of *dakshina*, or ritual offerings, made. However, 300 years later, the Shudras were unwilling to accept any discrimination based on birth. They were also acquiring a new index of power: the ballot in the hands of the commoner that would express their consensus over who should rule. This profound transformation in the existential axis to power naturally changed the symbolic nature of sovereignty as well, which has now taken the shape of an abstract state constituted and bound by secular law, making the exercise of sovereignty juridical in a large measure as expressed by the commonplace maxim, the rule of law. We should remember when both *Aryan Allure* and *Cantramōhaṉ* were written, the colonial governance still had Brahminical *shastras* ruling over the life of all those deemed Hindus, the majority of them Shudras. We also discussed a reference in *Aryan Allure* to the adjudication in a case seeking alimony to the non-Brahmin wife of a deceased Brahmin lawyer in which the court declared, in 1942, such inter-caste marriage null and void as per the *shastras*. Hence, the attribution of anger and a sense of humiliation to Shivaji was a necessary contemporary imagination.

In a crucial scene after Gaga Bhattar reaches the Maratha capital, Shivaji calls on him. Shivaji reveals that the soldiers are unhappy and agitated that he is seeking a Brahmin exoneration from the lowly status of Shudra. Gaga Bhattar tells him that soldiers are unaware of the intricacies of the *shastras*. Shivaji then directly demands to be explained why Shudras are not qualified to become kings. Gaga Bhattar lays out the origin myth of the four *varnas*, having come forth from different parts of the body of Brahma. Shivaji still persists, asking why penalize Shudras for having originated from the feet. Gaga Bhattar declares that it is blasphemous to question the *shastras*. When Shivaji talks of the many ordeals that he underwent to conquer the territory under his command, Gaga Bhattar tells him that it is in recognition of that that he is being considered for conferment of Kshatriya status. Gaga explains further that such a Brahmin endorsement would earn him recognition in many parts of the subcontinent as they are widely networked. On observing Shivaji still being restless, Gaga admonishes him not to waste his time if Shivaji was not willing to agree to the ritual process. The ensuing exchange between them has a great economy of expression but reveals the underlying dynamics of power.

> Shivaji: What if I refuse to accept your suggestion?
> Gaga: Not a suggestion but an instruction.
> Shivaji: Who can dare issue instructions to Shivaji?
> Gaga: Aryans could. They are Gods on earth.
> Shivaji: I can refuse to abide by the instructions.
> Gaga: You cannot. You will not be crowned if you refuse.
> Shivaji: Cannot? I cannot? Oh, Gaga Bhattar, behold who you are talking to.
> Gaga: You are the bravest of the brave. So what? You need to yield to the *shastras*.
> Shivaji: What will you do if I say no?
> Gaga: Me? What will I do? I will simply leave. However, you will stand accursed for refusing to abide by my words.
> Shivaji: I cannot be intimidated. I am free to act as I please in my kingdom.
> Gaga: Sure. Of course, you have the power to even kill me. Try.
> Shivaji: Gaga Bhattar, Shivaji's determination knows no wavering. Whatever will happen if I do kill you?
> Gaga: What will happen. I will just lose my life. However, before my body is cremated, your kingdom will be destroyed.
> Shivaji: What arrogance!
> Gaga: Whose?
> *(prolonged silence)*
> Shivaji: Well, what are the rituals that should take place?
> (Aṟiñar Aṇṇā 2018, 125–126)

As this acerbic exchange and the tame ending indicates, there was not much to do than to accede to Gaga Bhattar's rather helpful compromise solution and play by it. The enormously costly ritual process of coronation, while being an extravaganza and a compromise of sorts with Brahmin authority, would indeed help culminate an aspiration for sovereignty. Coercive measures can propose the same but only consensus generation would consolidate it then as ever.

The Soldier

Cantramōhaṉ (Chandramohan), the protagonist of the play is the quintessential "ideal soldier." While he is absolutely devoted to his commander, the mighty leader Shivaji, his commitment to the founding of a kingdom that enshrines the best values of freedom is larger than that. It is only in the hope that Shivaji is fighting to found a new kingdom with a noble vision that the soldier had put his life on the line. In one of the scenes, Chandramohan says that he does not take to war as a profession or privilege but for achieving an ideal Maratha polity that is free and independent. Chandramohan faces two challenges in the initial scenes in which he is introduced. The first comes from Shantaji, the father of his beloved, and the second from an anti-caste devotional mendicant, a *sadhu*, who we have already met in the opening scene.

Chandramohan and Indumathi are in love. Indhumathi's father Shantaji is a rich man who likes Chandramohan a lot but does not approve of his choice to wield the sword. His love for his daughter's well-being makes him adamant that her spouse should not be risking his life in the battlefield. It is hinted that Chandramohan is also from a family of considerable means, probably related to Indhumathi's family. As a soldier, he heads the group that ensures the personal safety of Shivaji and hence has a direct access to the de facto king. In spite of the honor and prestige that accrues through Chandramohan's accomplishment in the battlefield, Shantaji is unwilling to give his daughter in marriage in view of the risk involved. Indumathi is certainly in too intense a love with Chandramohan to care about the risk or annoy Chandramohan by asking him to go against his ideals, but she would nevertheless prefer if Chandramohan would voluntarily quit being a soldier as per her father's wishes since it is in the interest of the longevity of their married life.

Caught between the father and her beloved, Indumathi agrees at one point to be part of the ploy the father devises to apply pressure on Chandramohan. The ploy is to have one Bahadur, a dunce and a coward, to propose to Indumathi so that Chandramohan, not wanting to lose Indumathi, would accede to adopt a civilian life. The ploy backfires when Chandramohan resolutely makes a choice to pursue his ideal even at the cost of losing Indumathi. Having realized the mistake of her complicity in the ploy to apply pressure on Chandramohan, Indumathi is distraught. We can thus say the first challenge Chandramohan faces is from the civilian vision of life that abhors the risk involved in war and strife.

The second challenge comes from a reformist *sadhu*, a religious mendicant of the Bhakti tradition with a strong anti-caste appeal. Chandramohan encounters him on the street when the mendicant is singing a devotional lyric that envisions a new ideal society for all. When Chandramohan appreciates the song, the *sadhu* is happy but notes that being a soldier, Chandramohan might not be able to guarantee the flowering of such a society or nation. Chandramohan protests, saying that he and Shivaji are not fighting merely for the sake of power. The *sadhu* says once anyone, even Chandramohan, ascends the throne (a suggestion that momentarily shakes Chandramohan), the person is likely to be immersed in the privileges and pleasures of royalty, which would make one forget the widespread inequality in the society. The *sadhu* says the soldier's life calls for such recompense. He also points out that in order to rule, the king would have to yield to the order that exists. As Chandramohan firmly disagrees that would hardly be the case in the new Maratha kingdom they create, the *sadhu* beckons him goodbye with deep sarcasm, foretelling the eventual compromise.

We find that Chandramohan is not part of the machinations of Chitnis, who finds it necessary to have Shivaji coronated to win the continued subordination of various chieftains in peacetime, even as they were ready to fight under his command during the war. The manipulations, as we noted, involved the Brahmins and Gaga Bhattar. It is only later that we find Chandramohan to be present when the news of Gaga Bhattar's acceptance to accord Kshatriya status to Shivaji and officiate his coronation reaches Shivaji. Chandramohan immediately protests that Shivaji did not need any recognition from Brahmins for his rightful authority won by valor. He further points out exonerating Shivaji alone would mean that his clan would still suffer the indignity of being Shudra.

A highly disheartened and conflicted Shivaji asks to be spared of further disputations. Finally, when Chandramohan finds Shivaji bowing to Gaga Bhattar, accepting the superior powers of the Brahmin to cleanse him of the sins of his birth and deeds, he mounts a direct challenge to Gaga Bhattar's authority. Shivaji, who has to save the occasion for the coronation to be completed, summarily dismisses Chandramohan from military service, banishing him from the capital forever. Interestingly, when the anti-caste *sadhu* encounters the euphoric disciple of Gaga Bhattar in the following penultimate scene, he tells the Brahmin that the seeming banishment of Chandramohan is actually an assignment of a new mission to him, that of spreading awareness of the unjust Brahminical order among the masses. In the final scene, Chandramohan, no longer a soldier, finds the obstacle to marry Indumathi removed as a consolation. As they prepare to marry, Shivaji himself meets with Chandramohan, confirming what the *sadhu* surmised. Shivaji apologizes to the soldier for having had to betray him, requesting him to take up the mission of raising people's consciousness. Only an intellectual awakening of the people that make them throw off the shackles of Brahminic injunctions can make the sovereign free in a substantial sense. A mere capacity to win wars is not adequate for founding and ruling a just nation. The nature of war itself should change as one that is waged over the general ideology, a struggle for hegemony.

The transformation of the selfless, valorous soldier into a public intellectual, a social reformer, can be seen as the main thrust of the play. While this performs the displacement of goals in a typical valorous soldier, what is imagined is also a historical transformation of the goal of the political. The enemy now is a more abstract scheme of social structure rather than an identifiable outsider. In an interesting moment in the play, Shivaji asks who objects to the coronation; Is it the Badshah in Delhi? The answer is that the Moghuls are not averse to it, but rather his own minister Moropant, whose objection allegedly is not personal but based on shastric injunctions. These are the injunctions that work against all those common men who are deemed to be of low-caste birth, as we saw in the very first scene. In a more profound sense, the locus of freedom shifts to the common man who should be freed of all oppressive structures of exploitation. That was the desire of the self-conscious untouchable Aandi, whose voice finds resonance in Chandramohan in the end. Such a transformation of the soldier into a propagandist invokes the distinction made by Gramsci between war of maneuver and war of position. While Gramsci used it in the context of the class war, the exploitative social hierarchy will surely qualify as a good historical candidate as well for the need to undertake the war of position. Instead of a miniscule foreign power occupying a large populace by force, it is a miniscule community of Brahmins holding a large populace under the grip of caste ideology. That the form of opposition to such hegemonic formation can certainly not be a war of maneuver is made explicit in the case of Shivaji, where the sword is purely helpless against the laws of the Brahmin, who, as the play repeatedly states, has only the dry grass used in rituals as his weapon. In other words, the soldier who is the body of the sovereign should displace the Brahmin as the head of the sovereign.

The debate within the Indian National Congress between those who insisted on social reform and political evolution and those who urged insurrectionary methods against the foreign rule is well known. In fact, Gandhi offered to strike a middle path through his methods of *satyagraha*, which could distribute the fight both against internal as well as external forces of domination since the recourse to the path of Satya (Truth) will require infinite self-correction. It is well known that Gramsci cited Gandhi as one involved in war of positions. It is important to see how any war of positions will have only a relative value with reference to a possible war of maneuvers against a foreign body. We have already noted this complementarity in our discussion of Laclau's scheme of the complementarity of "internal frontier" with "empty signifier." Hence, Gandhi's efforts at national awakening through a war of positions would make sense only against the possible, albeit muted, war of maneuvers against foreign rule as the work of empty signifier like *Hind Swaraj*.

Likewise, in the case of the DMK, the war of positions to dismantle Brahmin casteist hegemony needed to call for an independent *Dravida Nadu* against the dominance of Hindi-speaking north India, even if the later call is all but an inscription of an empty signifier, housed in the idea of "Tamil," as we elaborately discussed in Chapter 2. In the imagination of the play, the combination of "Maratha" identity as empty signifier and the internal frontier between the Maratha non-Brahmin and Maratha Brahmin is but a precursor to Tamil identity as empty signifier and Dravidian non-Brahmin pitted against Aryan Brahmin as the internal frontier. It is as if Chandramohan time traveled at the end of the play to become the DMK party activist at the behest of Shivaji to fight against the still-prevailing Brahmin hegemony.

In the Footsteps of Annadurai

The success of Annadurai on the drama stage inspired many in the Dravidian movement to follow suit. Of course, within the DMK party fora, Karunanidhi took over from Annadurai to write plays to raise funds and supplement party conferences, leaving more time for Annadurai to focus on more ideational writings after the mid-1950s. Karunanidhi's stupendous success in cinema as a screenplay and dialogue writer from 1948 to 1954 helped him in gaining the requisite popularity to make his plays successful fundraisers for the party and enthuse cadres. Further, the play-writing activity became far more widespread with innumerous local practitioners springing up in many parts of the state, increasingly forming amateur theater groups as against the earlier professional theater groups. The themes, plots, and style of dialogue delivery invented by the plays of Annadurai and Karunanidhi became a prototype of the socially conscious plays.

We should conclude with one important example. Sometime in 1950, Pavalar Balasundaram, a firebrand activist and orator who stayed with Periyar's Dravidar Kazhagam, wrote a play that found considerable success in the professional theater circuit. Learning of the appeal to the audiences the play had, S. A. Perumal, a Dravidianist himself who ventured into the cinema world, wanted to produce it as a film. He spoke to A. V. Meiyyappa Chettiar, a leading film producer and the owner of AVM studios who was willing to partner with Perumal. They decided to hire the upcoming and trailblazing script and dialogue writer, the young Karunanidhi, to convert the play into a film script and write dialogues. The title given to the film was *Parasakthi*. Though this fact is not unknown, the writer of the play has largely faded in popular memory now. Conversely, not all the successful plays were successful on screen. Karunanidhi's own *Manimagudam*, a fundraiser play for the 1957 election, is hardly remembered as a film. Unfortunately, in popular memory the history of cinema more or less eclipsed the history of the drama stage in the middle decades of the twentieth century, perhaps owing to attenuation of the professional drama circuit in the 1960s caused by a variety of social factors, the enumeration of which would far exceed the brief of this chapter. Against such general amnesia, the invariable staging of a play in every district conference of the party till it came to power is a phenomenon that should never be overlooked for a proper understanding of the DMK mobilization. Of course, in the later years, the decade between 1957 and 1967, the participation of film stars like M. G. Ramachandran and S. S. Rajendran in the plays staged in party conferences definitely added much attraction to the event. Perhaps the whole phenomenon is today best encapsulated in the oft-repeated disparaging comment of Kamaraj that the DMK was after all a party of "Koothadikal," that is, performance artists.

Notes

1. On seeing Anna's play *Chandrodayam* in November 1943, T. K. Shanmugam told Periyar, "If Anna were to continue acting like he did he would surpass us, the traditional actors" (R. Kannan 2017, 97).
2. The review of the play in *Kudi Arasu* clearly mentions that Anna was inspired by Sarkar's book.
3. Arurdoss, a well-known Tamil film scriptwriter, says that M. G. R. was

   > overwhelmed by the dialogues and that he would take at least three to four days just to memorize. More importantly MGR's elder brother, M.G. Chakrapani, had advised against MGR acting in the play as he would be branded as a DMK man and risked losing opportunities. (Kannan 2017, 94–98)

   Also see Tirunāvukkaracu (2017, 1:118).
4. For more on this, see Pandian (1991).
5. For a preliminary sketch, see Krishnan (2004).
6. For a synopsis of the novella and the historical context, see Kannan (2017, 107).
7. For more on the idea of double articulation of sovereignty, see Krishnan (2018). For greater delineation of form of expression and form of content pair, see Deleuze and Guattari (1988).
8. Gramsci famously gave the example of Gandhi for both passive revolution and war of positions. See Gramsci, Buttigieg, and Callari (2011, 1:218–219).

6 Critical Hermeneutics

If every key text authored by Annadurai in the 1940s that functioned as ammunition for the ideological propagation of the DMK at its inception was controversial in some sense, there is one text that particularly makes even his supporters feel awkward to speak about. In drawing-room conversations in middle-class, educated households, the text is whispered as Annadurai's all-time low. His detractors always lay it against him as an exhibition of bad taste. This text, *Kamparacam* (Aṟiñar Aṇṇā 2008b), is a critical albeit selective reading of *Kamparāmāyaṇam*. Kamban is the twelfth-century Tamil poet who rendered Valmiki's Ramayana in Tamil as *Irāmavatāram* (The Rama Incarnation). The text however is popularly known as *Kamparāmāyaṇam*. Annadurai's *Kamparacam* is a close reading of some of the verses of the text with explicit and "inappropriate sexual references" that a common reader feels embarrassed to speak about. However, it is really surprising that in the seventy-five years since Annadurai wrote the text, no critical tradition has developed in Tamil scholarship to actually study what Annadurai tried to do as critical hermeneutics and how far his work could be validated.

For the limited purposes of this chapter, we would like to contextualize the work and a pamphlet that preceded it known as *Tī Paravaṭṭum* (Let the Fire Spread), a compilation of debates that Annadurai had with scholars on the question of whether *Kamparāmāyaṇam* should be burnt along with another twelfth-century Shaivite classic *Periya Purāṇam* as a program of spreading awareness among the people against Brahminical Hinduism (Annadurai 1995). The call to burn these two texts was given by the Self-Respect Movement. Since Tamil scholars had come to be aligned to the Self-Respect Movement from the days of the first wave of anti-Hindi agitations in 1938–1939, their objections to the burning of the two literary texts were engaged with in the mode of public debates, a significant gesture in the still-emerging public sphere. Though there were two texts to be consigned to flames, what wholly preoccupied the debates was *Kamparāmāyaṇam*, which excited a sharp conflict in views particularly because of the high literary value the text was accorded.

It will be beyond the scope of this chapter to provide the outlines of the many controversies about *Many Rāmāyanas*, as made famous by A. K. Ramanujan and the edited volume derived from his insight by Paula Richman (Richman 1997). It is however necessary to note that in terms of how ancient epics or narratives can have pivotal consequences for contemporary politics, the Ramayana and Indian politics would stand a good contest with any other candidate in the world including the founding of Israel, the Jewish nation-state, on the basis of biblical references, with unending misery heaped upon the Palestinian population rendered homeless, secondary citizens, their territory occupied, and people terrorized by the Israeli state. Nevertheless, many a great mind, including that of a visionary like M. K. Gandhi, have made a highly beneficial reading of the Ramayana, taking Rama, the prince-king of Ayodhya as *maryadha purushottam*, an ideal and virtuous being, capable of expressing infinite kindness, *karuna murthy* or *shanta murthy*, whose example should have an ennobling effect on people. Such an embodiment of moral axiom, to abstract an argument of Milind Wakankar,[1] is unvarying whatever be the variations in the narrative making the idea of the Ramayana singular in all its pluralized narratives. In a sharp contrast to such beneficial readings of the Ramayana story, Indian politics was later seized with a hyper masculine, conquistador Rama,[2] who has been brought into being through the incessant machinations of the Rashtriya Swayamsevak Sangh (RSS) and allied Hindutva organizations, one of which is the political party the Bharatiya Janata Party (BJP).

A crucial part of this machination began in 1949 when Rama idols were sneaked into Babri Masjid in Ayodhya, claiming that the Masjid site was the precise birthplace of Rama, the Ram Janmabhoomi. The Indian state managed to keep the whole issue suspended for nearly forty years by locking up the premises. The BJP and the Hindutva brigade once again began to rake up the issue in 1989, riding on the reactionary wave among Brahmin, upper-caste groups dismayed by the implementation of the Mandal Commission recommendations by the V. P. Singh government in 1989, paving way for reservation in educational institutions and Union government services for the backward classes (communities).[3] Scholars have observed and argued that the national telecast of a serial based on the Ramayana, produced by Ramanand Sagar, helped the Hindutva brigade to mainstream the sentimental claim to the Ram Janmabhoomi in the north (Mankekar 2003; Rajagopal 2005). All this led to the illegal demolition of Babri Masjid in 1992 by the *kar sevaks* lead by L. K. Advani, the BJP leader. The triumphalism associated with the act, and the communal riots that followed in many parts of the country, helped political Hinduism, or Hindutva, to consolidate its base and pose a challenge to the benign ideological amalgam of the Indian National Congress and a still-effervescent coalition of the so-called "third front" consisting of non-Congress, non-BJP political parties with strong regional holds. Ultimately, the BJP could become a mainstream party ruling at the Center from 2014 with a disturbing rise of acts of oppression against minority religions, most particularly the Muslims. The Supreme Court has recently, in 2019, adjudicated on the long-drawn suit on the title deed of the land where Babri Masjid stood, in favor of Hindu claims, asking the Indian state to form a special purpose vehicle to construct a Rama temple on the land. The possible political fallout of such a construction will have to be awaited. It could either take the steam off the politics in the name of Ram, or it may institutionalize Hindutva as a permanent part of Indian politics.

While this is predominantly a story of north India, a section of the Tamil-speaking south, Dravidianists, had an entirely different take on the Ramayana narrative. They read the Ramayana as the narrative that inscribed the north Indian conquest of the south, or, more precisely, the Aryan conquest of the Dravidian land, a point of view shared by none other than Jawaharlal Nehru (Nehru 1985). Many thought the ethnic difference of the Dravidian population was caricatured as monkeys of Kiṣkintā and demonized as the *asura*s and *rakshasa*s of Sri Lanka. As we shall see in the following chapter, the qualities of an *asura* are never a settled issue. It is also unclear what the difference is between an *asura* and a *rakshasa* (*arakkar* in Tamil). The terms "asura" and "rakshasa," or "asurar" and "arakkar" in Tamil, are used almost synonymously. Both are often translated as "demon" in English. In what sense are they demonic? In fact, in many versions of the Ramayana, Ravana, the *asura* king of Lanka, is described as a person of great valor, a just ruler, a pious devotee of Shiva, an exponent of the musical instrument *veena*, a learned man, and so on. We can complement his virtues with a patriarchal value as well: his wife Maṇṭōtari is remarked to be as chaste as Sita. In many narrative traditions in many languages, including Sanskrit, Ravana has nearly been made out to be a tragic hero, a great man who fell due to a tragic flaw, his all-consuming desire for Sita, Rama's wife whom he abducted, thus greatly blurring the difference between *asura*s and other beings like *deva*s or humans. Nevertheless, there are two issues that underscore the difference between the two sides of the Ramayana battle: one is that the travel of Rama to the south defeating a southern king in battle to recover his wife has a geographical template in which the north conquers the south. The other is the ethnic difference that is inscribed as in the physiognomic figures of *asura*s and *vanara*s, the peoples who are different from allegedly the normative Aryans.

There have been objections that the Lanka of Valmiki's Ramayana, considered the urtext of the many narratives, folk and classical, or at least the most widely accepted standard version of the story, is not the island of Sri Lanka across the peninsular coast of India but a lake island located in western Orissa (Farzand 1981). The evidence shown in this respect is rather persuasive. In all likelihood, the geography of Valmiki's imagination did not stretch beyond present-day Madhya Pradesh or Chhattisgarh. However, later versions stretched it unmistakably to peninsular India. One pertinent marker is the sacred site of Rameswaram, one of the closest points on the peninsular coast to the coast of Sri Lanka, where Rama, supposedly on his way back from Sri Lanka, worshipped Shiva in a ritual absolution for the crimes of war, particularly the murder of Ravana. Narrative has it that it is from here that he built the mythical bridge, Sethu, to Sri Lanka over the ocean, a subject of hotly fought case in the Supreme Court currently over the Sethu Samudram Canal Project, the second time Rama has compelled the court to reckon with his alleged historicity. Many in Sri Lanka take the island to be the abode of Ravana as well. There is a flourishing Ramayana tourism in Sri Lanka, where different places are ascribed to be the sites where Ramayana events and the war took place. All these go to show that the north–south, Aryan–Dravidian distinction cannot easily be dismissed in the critical approach to the Ramayana today, which is a supreme nationalist cartographic allegory, an idea that Presenjit Duara also discusses (Duara 1997, 75).

Before we attend to the Dravidianist contestations with Ramayana, we should first take a brief note of the *long durée* absorption of the Ramayana in Tamil. The central icons of Tamil Vaishnavism during the Bhakti period were Lord Ranganatha, the reclining Vishnu on the serpent bed, and Lord Venkatachalapathy, a Vishnu incarnate with a local lore at Tirupati. The *dasavatara* of Vishnu, that is, the ten incarnations of Vishnu, were also widely known and sung about. Rama is of course one of the celebrated avatars of Vishnu and hence is mentioned with reverence and devotion in Bhakti-period hymns. What brings Rama as an avatar of Vishnu very strongly into Tamil reckoning is the twelfth-century Tamil rendition of the Ramayana as *Irāmavatāram* by Kamban, which, as said earlier, is popularly known as *Kamparāmāyaṇam*. The Tamil public sphere, at least as it emerged in the late nineteenth and early twentieth century, regarded Kamban to be a pinnacle of literary achievement as did many wealthy connoisseurs of literature from agricultural and trading communities. A particular example would be a hegemonic group made up of people like Rajagopalachari, Kalki Krishnamurthy, and their close acolyte T. K. Chidambaranatha Mudaliar, all adulators of the poetic prowess of Kamban, who is commonly known as the emperor of poetry, *Kavicakravartti*. Another example would be the Sahitya Akademi-winning Tamil critic, a highly regarded figure in modernist literary circles of the late twentieth century, K. N. Subramanian, who proposed that Kamban was one of the handful of great epic poets of the world, particularly on par with Dante, whom he probably preceded by a century or two (Cupramanyam 1998, 26–31). K. N. Subramaniam notes that the architectonic of Kamban's epic and its closeness to the brilliance of the narrative structure of Dante's work, *Divine Comedy*, awaits to be fully explored by critics. If literary works are expressions of certain flowering of collective consciousness in a language, we do agree that Kamban is eminently comparable to Dante, for all the reasons Dante is considered to prefigure the renaissance in Italy. What is pertinent to our purposes here is to note that such poetic genius of Kamban did not result in a widespread popular Rama Bhakti, akin to what appears to have happened with the Hindi rendition of the Ramayana by Tulsi Das in the sixteenth century. Kamban was a court poet with a literary finesse that was perhaps not intended for popular audience. At any rate, there was no institutionalized or popular Rama Bhakti in the wake of *Kamparāmāyaṇam*, even if the work strongly and insistently articulated that he was the avatar of Vishnu, a divine being, as against a more humane Rama presented by Valmiki and later works in the history of Sanskrit literature. Lord Ranganatha and Lord Venkatachalapathy continued to be the reigning deities of the Vaishnavite world.

The fact that of all the ten incarnations of Vishnu, Rama is the incarnation in human form with human consciousness sans divine consciousness, powers, and prowess appears to have made the name a great preference among the people. The Rama Nama is in inverse proportion to the prevalence of Rama as a deity. The eleventh- or twelfth-century Vaishnavite philosopher, the founder of Vishishtadvaita (qualified monism) school of philosophy, was named Ramanuja, brother or kin of Rama. We should note that on the one hand, Rama is not a god who is widely worshipped in Tamil Nadu with relatively fewer and less popular temples dedicated to him, often taking a shrine in other major temples; in fact, Hanuman is a far more popular deity than Rama, with some famous temples dedicated to him. On the other hand, Ramas(w)amy and other conjugates of the Rama Nama are extremely popular choices as names among Shaivites as well as Vaishnavites and people belonging to all castes. If there is a census of names given to people in Tamil Nadu in the twentieth century, Ramasamy may win hands down. After all, the most iconoclastic critique of the Rama story, Periyar himself bears the name E. V. Ramasamy (he never bothered to change the name).

Periyar's Engagement with the Ramayana

Periyar is known for his atheism and iconoclasm. It is necessary at this moment to qualify this statement before we proceed to see his specific, lifelong engagement with the Ramayana story, even if we cannot afford a full-length explication of his political philosophy that should be carried out only in a book-length exposition. Suffice it to say that atheism and iconoclasm are only supplementary to the mainstay of his politics of self-respect, as he had clarified many a time. In the early days of propagation, he did not emphasize atheism much, saying that the eternal agonism between believers or theists and non-believers or atheists is but a necessary condition of human intellection. While he made his subscription to a naturalist–materialist immanence clear early on in a tract called *Pirakirutivātam* (Periyār 2010, 5:2359–2365), such an orientation did not result in campaigns against worshipping of any deity in the initial phase of his activist life. He only reiterated that the caste system is perpetuated by Brahmins and other dominant castes in the name of God, which makes it necessary to challenge the authority of God. It is only in the post-independence period, after the birth of the DMK as a party of the people who "deserted" him, as part of his agonistic challenge to consensual politics pursued by the DMK, that he started laying far greater emphasis on atheism. Likewise, his best-known instances of iconoclasm were reserved for two specific godheads: Rama and Ganesha. In the 1950s, he announced two demonstrations: one, breaking the images of Ganesha (usually made of clay) and second, the burning of Rama's pictures. It is not merely incidental that these are the two godheads used by political Hinduism, the RSS and its subsidiaries, for mobilization. Though Periyar might have made agonistic remarks against devotion to many other gods and practices of worship, he never announced an iconoclastic demonstration against any of them, even if they were far more popular among the masses. Lord Murugan, the Tamil god superimposed with the image of Skanda of Puranic imagination, the second son of Shiva, did not attract any of Periyar's iconoclastic protest in spite of the god's popularity among Tamil masses. Of course, the cadres of his movement questioned very many practices associated with gods and temples on the basis of rationalist thought, which he often endorsed. This brief note is necessary to understand his specific engagement with Rama and the Ramayana.

Periyar appears to have had a lifelong engagement with the Ramayana story and the figure of Rama. As early as 1928, Periyar published an essay in *Āṉanta Vikaṭaṉ*, nearly a century-old premier journal of Tamil Nadu now. The magazine was launched by one Budalur Vaidyanatha Iyer but was purchased a few years later in 1924 by S. S. Vasan, a young Brahmin entrepreneur who was to become one of the early media magnates of free India with his highly successful filmmaking career under the banner of Gemini Studios. The Periyar essay was titled "Taṉi Ārāycci" (Independent Research). He wrote in detail of the idea of many Ramayanas, with wild variations in plot structure and the relationships among characters, like Sita being the daughter of Ravana, to draw the conclusion that any speculation about the actual historical events forming the basis of the Ramayana is untenable since actual events could not have led to such wildly differing narratives. He subscribed to the view, and propagated the same, that the Ramayana story is an allegory about the Aryan–Dravidian conflict, or rather the corruption of the Dravidian mind by Aryan deceit.

In 1930, he published a long pamphlet titled *Irāmayaṇa Pāttiraṅkaḷ* (Characters in Ramayana), which saw several reprints (Periyar 2012). The book is a compendium of all the flaws, foibles, and inconsistencies the characters of the Ramayana in Valmiki's version had. In 1956, Periyar announced a program to burn pictures of Rama. He was promptly arrested by the Congress government but still many of the cadres did manage to burn the pictures on the sands of Chennai beach, the designated venue. We should conclude with noting that as late as 1971, in a conference on eradication of superstition, a certain denigration of Rama's image took place, which is held against him even today (Kumar and Ramani 2020), with so much of nationalist sentiment built around Rama after the demolition of Babri Masjid. The conference, held in the town of Salem, concluded with a procession in which many floats depicting the irrational and compromising acts of Hindu gods were depicted. Apparently, there was also a float with Ramayana characters. Those opposed to such a conference, allegedly the cadres of the Hindutva brigade, hurled slippers on the procession as a mark of insult to Periyar. Enraged by the act, a Self-Respecter climbed on the float and hit the image of Rama with a slipper, which was perhaps photographed by a journalist, creating a sensation at the time. Periyar was far behind in the procession from where this incident happened. This act of denigration was not premeditated, though the purpose of the float was, of course, to question the divinity and respectability of Rama. This stray incident, sought to be blown up by Hindutva forces since then to enrage the minds of a new generation of Rama Bhaktas, completes Periyar's engagement with Rama and the Ramayana for our purposes in this chapter. It is as part of this long engagement that the Self-Respect Movement decided to burn copies of two Tamil literary texts of the twelfth or thirteenth century, *Periya Purāṇam* and *Kamparāmāyaṇam*, in 1943. *Periya Purāṇam* is the compendium of the life stories of Shaivite saints and their devotion to Shiva with many a miraculous act of God in recognition of the devotion of the Bhaktas. These two texts represent the hegemonic place Shaivism and Vaishnavism attained by the twelfth and thirteenth centuries in Tamil Nadu under the rule of Imperial Cholas and later extinguishing the Jain and Buddhist lineages of Tamil Nadu under the rule of the Nayaks, Marathas, and Nizams in the period from the fifteenth to the eighteenth century.

Let the Fire Spread

"Let the Fire Spread" (*Tī Paravaṭṭum*) is the title of a popular tract sold in DMK fora in the early phase of mobilization. It comprises the select transcripts of the two debates Annadurai was involved in to defend the decision to burn *Periya Purāṇam* and *Kamparāmāyaṇam*. Before we delve into the details of the debate, we should note an added dimension to the purpose of the agitation to the engagement with Rama and the Ramayana that we have discussed till now. The additional dimension is challenging the canon formation in Tamil literature. This may not have been a great concern for Periyar, but for Annadurai and the DMK this was extremely important. They wanted the earlier epochs of Tamil literature, particularly the Caṅkam age, *Tirukkuṟaḷ* by Thiruvalluvar and the epic *Cilappatikāram* of Ilango Adigal, to be celebrated as the true works of Tamil culture. Many of these texts were immanent to human life, though gods might have been mentioned or had a minor role to play in *Cilappatikāram*. They also have a Jain and Buddhist imprint, though not heavily into their versions of supernatural or cosmology. The earlier corpus of literature listed above is more about human action, their limits and an aesthetic of life that is immanent to the natural environs. The Dravidian intelligentsia felt the sobriety of the early first millennia literary corpus so welcome in comparison to the Bhakti literature that followed them and the two twelfth- or thirteenth-century classics, which were all about pious veneration of the "Hindu" gods, Shiva and Vishnu. While this political preference is appreciable, the contemporary literary sensibility as noted earlier was somewhat at odds with this preference, particularly in the case of *Kamparāmāyaṇam*.

The nineteenth- and early twentieth-century connoisseurs of Tamil literature appear to have held Kamban in an unquestionable esteem as the greatest of Tamil poets. As a somewhat tendentious evidence to the problem, we would like to cite a well-known line from Subramanya Bharathi (1882–1921), Tamil poet and Indian nationalist, a foundational figure of Tamil modernity. There is hardly a second opinion that Subramanya Bharathi is a person of incomparable poetic genius that signaled the birth of modern consciousness in Tamil, something perhaps akin to the place Rabindranath Tagore would hold in Bengal, to whom he is often compared by zealous admirers. Bharathi was a polyglot trained in Tamil, Sanskrit, and Hindi; he was also educated in English and apparently had some learning of Bengali and French as well. The line is from a poem in which the poet celebrates the singular and unique virtue of the Tamil language. We will attempt a translation of the poem to contextualize the line that refers to Kamban, situating him alongside Thiruvalluvar and Ilango Adigal. In the agonized mind of the poet torn between the past glory of Tamil and its present deplorable condition, his confirmation of the pride in Tamil identity, and the desperation of the agenda setting for the restoration of the same, the names of these three great poets get listed.

Of the languages known to us
There is none as sweet as Tamil
What good it is to live on Earth as we do,
Calling ourselves Tamil, beasts of ignorance,
Having lost the noble quality of life,
Despised by the whole world? May you dare.
Ways need be found to spread the
Sweet sound of Tamil all over the world.

Of the poets known to us
None ever lived on earth that was
Like Kamban, like Valluvan, like Ilango.
Being true, this is no empty praise.
We live dumb, deaf, and blind; Oh Listen!
If we are to redeem ourselves may
Tamil reverberate on the streets everywhere!

Scholarly yields of great minds of all nations
Needs to be rendered in Tamil
There should flourish new works in Tamil
That will attain immortal praise
There is no glory in whispering of
Past greatness amongst us in the shades
If our works today are born of talent
They should fetch the awe and respect
Of the people of other lands

If there be true light in the minds
There shall be light shining forth in the words

If like the flooding of water, if art floods,
If poetry floods into every corner The blind fallen into pits
Will gain vision and status.
Having tasted pristine nectar of Tamil
Shall the undying spirit be exalted.
(Pāratiyār 2008)

This is the sort of poem that the DMK thought would have hardly had a problem in identifying with even if Subramanya Bharathi was a Brahmin and a nationalist. They are also, after all, caught between "pledge made long, long years ago in the tryst with destiny" and the need to "redeem the pledge."[4] There is one single line that stands out as a problem. In picking up and ordering the three greatest poets of the language, Valluvan, Ilango and Kamban, Bharathi for some strange reason names Kamban first. In historical chronology, Valluvan and Ilango lived sometime between second century BC and second century AD, though determining the exact period has remained controversial for want of definitive and conclusive evidence. However, we can reasonably affirm that they preceded Kamban by a millennium. In terms of what the works comprise, *Tirukkuṟaḷ* written by Thiruvalluvar is a non-narrative composition, 133 chapters of 10 couplets each, divided into 3 large sections of dimensions of life: *Aṟam* (Dharma or Ethical Life), *Poruḷ* (Artha or Material Life), and *Iṉpam* (Kama or Erotic Life), with a stunning depth of vision and astounding precision of expression deploying a range of literary tropes to make the point; *Cilappatikāram* of Ilango is an epic with a certain austerity of expression and philosophical vision, perhaps rare for the period in which it was composed; *Kamparāmāyaṇam* is a work of indulgence, of creative abandon and abundance, dazzling in the affective potential of the language. In listing the three poets of singular accomplishments, it would have been prudent to have adopted the widely followed chronology of Valluvan, Ilango and Kamban; or though it is rare in Tamil, go alphabetically as Ilango, Kamban and Valluvan (the order is the same as per the Tamil alphabet as well). Bharathi's mention of Kamban first in the list of the three greats betrays, unmistakably, an early twentieth-century common sense of according pre-eminence to Kamban as *kavi chakravarthy*, the emperor of poets. This is precisely what Annadurai was keen on contesting since, after all, Kamban wasted all his genius in the service of a Brahminical, north Indian idea of *Ramavathar*. Notwithstanding every other merit the work may have, it is fundamentally flawed by the capitulation to a dangerous superstition, the divine incarnation from which the other two poets are resplendently free of contamination. Hence, the need to burn *Kamparāmāyaṇam* along with the Shaivite adulatory compendium of blind devotion, *Periya Purāṇam*.

The First Debate

It was on Tuesday, February 19, 1943, that the first debate took place in the law college auditorium in Chennai. Though there were four speakers in all, the debate was primarily between Annadurai and R. P. Sethupillai, senior lecturer of Tamil at the University of Madras, who was to become the first recipient of the Sahitya Akademi Award in Tamil and a reputed Tamil scholar. It is reported that in spite of the absence of publicity for the event, a considerable crowd had gathered to hear the debate. Self-Respecters, law college students, Tamil scholars, and womenfolk were part of the audience. The law college Tamil association secretary welcomed the gathering, saying that the proposal to burn the two texts considered to be the wealth of Tamil language needs to be discussed by people who are proponents of the idea and those who are opposed to it. He likened Annadurai to Indrajit of Ramayana and R. P. Sethupillai to Lord Rama. He mentioned that the event would be chaired by Ramachandran Chettiar, commissioner of the Hindu Charitable Endowments Board, whom he likened to Janaka Maharaja, father of Sita, known for his wisdom.

Annadurai began by clarifying that they were not opposed to literature but seek to revolutionize it. All through the speech, Annadurai referred to the two literary works as *kalai*, a term that today refers to art, instead of *ilakkiyam* that refers to literature, as the latter term perhaps had not gained much currency at that time. He averred that Aryan literature is absolutely distinct from Dravidian literature. Aryan literature is full of the supernatural and the fantastic, riddled with obscenity. Since it corrupts the minds of Tamils, Aryan literature needs to be opposed. There are many cultures in the world that are self-contained, nourishing the people who belonged to it. However, Aryan and Dravidian cultures are conflictual and contradict each other. Aryan culture sought to dominate Tamil culture. He clarified that when he said Tamil culture, it did not just refer only to Tamil speakers but Dravidians. They, the Self-Respecters, were not opposed to Tamil works like *Naṟṟiṇai*, *Akanāṉūṟu*, *Puṟanāṉūṟu*, and *Kuṟuntokai* (all works of the Sangam corpus) but only those works that seductively presented Aryan culture. The division with the Aryans was not imagined by just Dravidianists but by several scholars before them; if Max Müller celebrated Aryan culture, John Marshall argued for Dravidian culture. There was a time when everyone was made to believe that Indian culture was all Aryan. People like Manonmaniam Sundaram Pillai and Shaivite scholar V. P. Subramanya Mudaliar demonstrated the superiority of Dravidian culture. Maramalai Adigal was scathing in his criticism of Aryan stratagem, making Aryan king Rama a supreme God, reducing the gods of Tamils into minor deities. Even Pandit Jawaharlal Nehru, who was politically opposed to Dravidianists, stated that the Ramayana is the story of Aryan–Dravidian conflict.

The major problem with Kamban's work, Annadurai continued, is that he used all his skills to extol the virtues of Aryan characters, vastly improving on Valmiki's depiction of them by removing the blemishes Valmiki showed them to have, as ordinary mortals. Further, to say Ravana abducted Sita because he fell for her charms is to belittle the stature of the Dravidian king, who Kamban concedes as a valorous, scholarly, musically gifted king living in splendor and dispensing a just rule. If one makes a character so easily fallible on a sheer caprice, it will not have a good influence on anyone reading the text. It is more as a strategy to provoke the enemy in retaliation to the violence meted out to his sister, Surpanaka, that Ravana abducted Sita, which was a norm of warfare. There was no personal emotion involved in it. It is claimed that there were great examples of valor, sacrifice, friendship, and chastity in the Ramayana; Tamils do not need to seek them in the Ramayana story since their own literature had provided far more glorious examples of such human traits. Thus, Tamils have nothing to lose except Aryan seduction in burning the texts *Kamparāmāyaṇam* and *Periya Purāṇam*, concluded Annadurai.

In his rebuttal, R. P. Sethupillai disputed this reading of Ravana as a Dravidian king. Sethupillai preferred the term Tamil to Dravidian. He pointed out that Kamban had made clear the basic flaw of Ravana's character, which is a total lack of capacity for sympathy. Would a Tamil king ever be incapable of sympathy? Further, Sethupillai argued that Ravana was in fact an Aryan Brahmin. Hanuman, when he met Sita secretively in her state of imprisonment, hesitated to speak in Sanskrit since he thought Sita would mistake him for Ravana taking the form of a monkey. This implied that Ravana spoke Sanskrit. Further, Rama is said to have earned Brahmahathi Dhosham for killing Ravana; it accrues only in the case of killing a Brahmin. Hence, the whole theory of Aryan–Dravidian conflict in the Ramayana falls flat. Kamban wanted to narrate a powerful story to house his poetic vision and hence he chose the Ramayana. In fact, he made Sita a Tamil woman; for, in Valmiki's version, there was no meeting of Rama and Sita before marriage; but Kamban made them exchange glances when Rama walked past her palace, leading to their falling in love with each other in the tradition of Tamil literary narratives. Kamban patterned Sita on Kannagi, the protagonist of the Tamil epic, *Cilappatikāram*. Kamban made most characters without blemish due to his larger vision; Ravana met with his fate only for want of capacity for sympathy. Thus, there was no need to burn *Kamparāmāyaṇam,* Sethupillai concluded his argument, denying that Ravana was a Dravidian.

Annadurai responded to him saying that merely speaking a language does not make one part of a group of people who spoke the language as their mother tongue. Tamils who speak English are not Englishmen. Tamils who speak Sanskrit are not Aryans. Annadurai alleged that it was not the broad vision of Kamban but a deceit to make Aryan characters look good. He regretted that Sethupillai evaded the debate on the baseless assumption that Ravana was an Aryan. Ramachandran Chettiar, the chair, concluded by appreciating the quality of the debate and reserved his comments for a future occasion.

The Second Debate

The second debate relating to the burning of *Kamparāmāyaṇam* and *Periya Purāṇam* took place a month later, on March 14, 1943, at Salem in the Devanga Padasala Auditorium. Annadurai was joined by a formidable Tamil scholar Somasundara Bharathiar on that occasion. Somasundara Bharathiar (1879–1957) was a childhood associate of Subramanya Bharathiar, the nationalist poet we discussed above, in the court of the Raja of Ettayapuram. Both these child prodigies, Somasundaram and Subramaniam, were given the title "Bharathi" by a visiting Tamil scholar from Jaffna for their capacity to write poems according to a given meter. Somasundara Bharathiar studied law; when he practiced as a lawyer in Tuticorin, he was associated with the native or Indian shipping corporation launched by the nationalist V. O. Chidambaram Pillai. He was variously associated with the Indian National Congress and the freedom movement, eradication of untouchability, and so on. He wrote extensively on Tamil literature, both in English and Tamil, and was a staunch Shaivite opposed to Brahmin superiority and domination. He joined the Tamil department at Annamalai University in 1933 as the head of the department where he served till 1938. He is most remembered for his leading role in opposition to the imposition of Hindi learning in schools by the Rajaji government in 1937, which brought him into the fold of the Dravidianists. Since then, he was a supporter of Periyar and Annadurai, with whom he joined in the advocacy of a separate Dravidian–Tamil country. Somasundara Bharathiar was a reluctant participant in the debate; he had performed a critical reading of the *Kamparāmāyaṇam*, arguing that Kaikeyi was right in claiming the kingdom for her son Bharatha, and King Dasaratha was remiss for having reneged on the promise made to Kaikeyi to crown her son as the king. It was only that he was against harsh measures such as burning of the literary texts, since he regarded them primarily as "Tamil" literature. He was persuaded by many friends to join the debate. The debate was chaired by A. Ramasamy, a professor at Salem College. Reports indicate that there was a huge gathering to listen to the debate.

Annadurai elaborated on how Tamil culture was distinct from that of the Aryans, but, however, due to chicanery of the Aryans, the distinction was blurred. The two texts in question, *Kamparāmāyaṇam* and *Periya Purāṇam*, were absolutely pivotal for Vaishnavites and Shaivites. Annadurai argued that Vaishanavism and Shaivism were not Tamil religions but Aryan imports. Though Tamils had a distinct idea of ethical life (Anna uses the Tamil word *neṟi*, which has a semantic range that includes personal conduct and religious life), they embraced Shaivism and Vaishnavism and as a result came to be thought of as Hindus and Aryans. For instance, in the distinct *neṟi* of Tamils, there were no gods that incarnate in different forms. Similarly, there was no god that would put devotees to such cruel tests like it happens in *Periya Purāṇam*. If Tamils are made to believe in such incarnations and divine interventions, it is because they were made to read texts with Aryan ideas. If Ramayana characters were to be appreciated for their qualities, Bharata comes out as a far nobler soul than Rama. Why then is Bharata not worshipped anywhere? It is only because Rama is believed to be an incarnation that he is extolled as the ideal.

If one takes a historical point of view, in many countries the literary field did undergo many changes, generally moving towards emancipatory ideas. For example, in the English language, there is much difference between John Bunyan's *Pilgrims Progress* and the poems of Robert Burns. Only in Tamil Nadu are the great works of ancient Tamil period neglected in favor of twelfth-century Aryan inflections like *Kamparāmāyaṇam* and *Periya Purāṇam*. Annadurai pointed out that if Muslims could quickly build a strong case for a separate nation, it was because they maintained their cultural distinction, their art and literature as distinct; since Tamils lost that distinction, conflating their own culture with that of the Aryans through Vaishnavism and Shaivism, it had become hard for them to claim a separate nation. If Tamils are to regain their distinct identity, it is necessary to exorcise Vaishnavism and Shaivism represented by the texts *Kamparāmāyaṇam* and *Periya Purāṇam*, hence burning them would be the right way of raising the consciousness of Tamils against them.

Somasundara Bharathiar, in his speech, made it clear that he was uncompromisingly opposed to Brahmin claims of superiority in his life. He was of such a Shaivite upbringing that he refused to let Brahmin *purohit*s officiate at his wedding, who, he claimed, Shaiva Agamas proscribed as polluting temples by their entry. He also clarified that he was not such a Shaivite who would approve the abjection of the devotees in *Periya Purāṇam*. He belonged to a distinct creed of Shaiva tenet that differed from Brahmin-influenced Shaivism and Shiva devotion. Hence, he had always stood in the forefront of many a struggle to defend the distinction of Tamils. In the case of *Kamparāmāyaṇam*, he was all for a rigorous critical engagement with the text that exposed its many weaknesses. He, however, was opposed to the burning of a literary text instead of critically engaging with it. There are two kinds of people opposed to burning the text: there are those who opposed the burning, saying that it is a religious work, and there are those who oppose, saying that it is a literary work. He belonged to the second category. If the text is antithetical to Tamil *neṟi* on occasion, we should burn the wrong ideas expressed in the text through our critique but not burn the text. How could ideas be destroyed by burning a text? Kamban only made use of what was accepted by common sense of his times to write poetry. We should not lose out on the poetry because we were opposed to certain ideas expressed. Even if *Periya Purāṇam* is opposed to the Shaivite creed he followed, he would only want the text to be critically exposed for its weaknesses, like in the works of Ilathu Adigal. If we started burning all texts bearing Vaishnavite and Shaivite devotion, there would be no end to it. Instead, we should only ignite the minds of the people, which should make these texts ineffective. With these sets of arguments, Somasundara Bharathiar went on to say that Rama of Kamban does have many virtues that are worthy of being studied too. *Kamparāmāyaṇam* flowered only on the soil of earlier Tamil literature and was not antithetical to Tamil ethos. If he were to opt between Kamban and Tamil Nadu, he would only opt for Kamban; such was the greatness of his poetry. His significance does not diminish since he wrote on Rama as an avatar of Vishnu. In fact, gods like Vishnu were appropriated by the Aryans from Tamil folk imagination. There is even a view that Rama was a Dravidian, which he would not want to insist upon. Finally, Somasundara Bharathiar said Tamils had no need to call themselves Dravidian. The Sangam corpus does not use the term Dravidian. Hence, to enlighten the Tamil masses it is enough to propagate against the pitfalls of Aryanism instead of burning Tamil literary works.

In his response, Annadurai noted that there was no fundamental disagreement between him and Somasundara Bharathiar in standing for Tamil distinction and against Aryan supremacy. The difference was more about the ways in which opposition to Aryan influence should be articulated. Somasundara Bharathiar contradicted himself when he claimed that he had been consistently critiquing Aryan influence and continuing with it was also the best way to counter Aryanism since the critique, obviously, had not worked sufficiently in countering Aryan influence. If Somasundara Bharathiar likened critique to orally administered medicine to cure the disease without hurting the patient, acts like burning the texts are like necessary surgical procedures to remove an abscess from the body. The strong preference of Somasundara Bharathiar for Kamban should be a new phenomenon since he had earlier strongly condemned Aryan influence. In fact, he had compared how Roman civilization absorbed Greek civilization selectively with due discrimination, without allowing their own civilization to be contaminated, to how Tamil civilization had uncritically allowed Aryan influence to pervade all of their cultural life with no barriers. If such was the case, how could the situation be rectified without serious exorcism through such acts as burning of the *Kamparāmāyaṇam* and *Periya Purāṇam*? Annadurai concluded by assuring Somasundara Bharathiar that while the latter safely rested, Self-Respecters would ensure no harm came to anyone by their protest action. In his concluding remarks, A. Ramasamy, who chaired the session, remarked that there was no fundamental difference between the two speakers with regard to their ends, but they differed only in their means. He pointed out that burning of foreign clothes by the Congress did make an impact on the minds of people. He also asked, if Ravana was indeed an Aryan, as some claimed, why should a text narrating the war among two Aryan kings be read by Tamils with such reverence as their own culture? He emphasized that it was important for Tamils to learn to be wary of the obscenities of Aryan culture.

Many Affects of Kamban

Egged on by the two debates with Tamil scholars, Annadurai published two more texts as a sequel to the debates and the tract comprising the debates titled "Let the Fire Spread." One of the sequels is a play called *Nītitēvaṉ Mayakkam* (The Lord of Justice Fainted). We will discuss this in the next chapter. The other text is the one that was mentioned at the beginning of this chapter, *Kamparacam* (The Taste of Kamban). The term "rasam" refers to the *rasa* theory of Indian aesthetics, widely shared in Tamil discourse on arts and literature. There are basically nine *rasas* possible in any work of creative expression. There has been many a debate about how to translate or interpret the term "rasa". The favorite candidates are Taste, Mood, Sentiment, and so on. We would like to propose that Affect is a good candidate too.

In the popularly shared discourse on aesthetic experience, *rasa* is about *anubhāva*, that is the determination of the same *bhava*, or expressive feelings, in others. It is the experience that flows from the text to the reader and hence is affective in its function. The tile *Kamparacam* is ironic in the sense that certain indulgence of the poet in explicit sexual references is said to be the desired affect sought to be produced in the reader. It is more like tastelessness than taste. If we are to understand the problem in terms of Sanskrit aesthetic theory, while *śṛṅgāra*, the erotic, is one of the *rasas*, the problem Annadurai raises is one of *rasābhāsa* (*rasa* + *abasa*), the inappropriate mixture of *rasas*. Annadurai wrote this with the sole purpose of challenging the consensus around the preeminent place accorded to Kamban among Tamil poets. More than the challenge to Rama and the Ramayana as such, the purpose here is to challenge the canonical status accorded to Kamban in comparison to others like Valluvan and Ilango, who we discussed with the example of the Subramanya Bharathiar's poem. Annadurai, in spite of the highly polemical tone of his tract, an overindulgent and scathing attack on the long-deceased poet Kamban, has a genuine literary argument. Even if one does not agree with his objections, it is necessary to acknowledge and engage with the objections he raises to certain indiscriminate use of affect in Kamban. However, we are not aware of any of the critics or scholars of repute having responded to Annadurai's exercise in critical hermeneutics. The tract is dismissed as lowbrow engagement with classical literature or as lurid polemics unbecoming of scholarly attention. As with most things connected with the DMK, this is nothing but elite prejudice. Of course, Annadurai's exercise is not the kind of criticism that we noticed K. N. Subramaniam as suggesting, something that unravels the architectonic of the Kamban's text. However, it is still a serious exercise in critical hermeneutics, particularly for those interested in *rasa* theory. Annadurai is rather persuasive that Kamban was culpable of *rasābhāsa*, of inappropriate expression. We need to see how Annadurai was able to demonstrate the same.

In taking the other meaning of *rasam* to mean "delectable fluid," Annadurai structured his *Kamparacam* in a certain number of "doses." He numbered the sections with the English term as Dose 1, Dose 2 in Tamil. He has a list of twenty-eight doses or instances in *Kamparāmāyaṇam* that are inappropriate or distasteful. For the sake of brevity, we will only look at a few examples and not the entire list. It is enough to check on a few doses to judge the merit of the case.

The first instance occurs when, after the death of Dasaratha and after Rama's departure to the forest, Bharata returns to Ayodhya. Bharata does not accept the crown, chides his mother for all the misery she has caused, and leaves with everyone to go and request Rama to come back and assume the throne. It is during this journey of grief and guilt-stricken people to meet Rama that the said instance occurs. When they needed to cross a river, the womenfolk and soldiers board a boat rowed by hunters. Water splashes on people from the oars and the boat's movement. Kamban remarks that the soldiers who were fatigued were relieved when the water drenched the women's clothes and revealed their large *alkul* to the gaze of the soldiers.[5] The Tamil lexicon gives the meaning of *alkul* as vagina. However, the defenders of Kamban interpret it as "waist." Vagina or waist, the male gaze involved in the description does no justice to the honor of the soldiers or that of the poet. Annadurai paraphrases the verse in detail. More significantly, Annadurai points that the predominant mood or *rasa* of the moment was *soka*, or grief. The royal queens have been widowed; everyone has become sorrowful at the unfortunate turn of events. Is that the moment to speak of how the soldiers' gaze feasted upon the body of the women whose clothes got drenched by water? They were not on a happy excursion or a joyful ride. How could Kamban belittle the sorrow of the women or the dignity of the soldiers by remarking on the lustful gaze of soldiers feasting on women's body?

The other telling instance is when Sita hears the news that Rama had broken the bow kept by her father, King Janaka, which qualified him to marry her. When Rama entered the city of Mithila and walked through the streets, he walked past Sita's palace. As she was on the balcony, they exchanged glances that resulted in the proverbial love at first sight. When Sita was later told that someone had broken the bow that qualified the person to marry her, she wanted to confirm whether it was the same person whom she saw walking on the streets. When she comes to know that it was indeed him, she burst with joy. Kamban gave the burst of joy a physical dimension; he said that her waist girdle broke since her *alkul* expanded fast with joy.[6] This sure is an extreme description, whether the expanding organ was vagina or waist. The problem for Annadurai again is the crude description accorded to a woman and a princess, a divine incarnate for Kamban, who exchanged glances with a man and was bewitched by him. A vulgar direct reference to the genitals in this context is certainly unwarranted.

Annadurai does think of the age in which Kamban wrote the poem. He suggests that Kamban must have included such explicit references to sexual organs and feelings to titillate his rich or royal patrons who could have the pornographic affect while listening to a sacred literary text. He alleges that it was a compromise to cater to such a need to titillate the readers or listeners. While this charge is speculative, Kamban rather appears to be defenseless in such wanton descriptions involving the female body in contexts where they were not called for. As a counterpoint, Annadurai makes a rather predictable reference to Tennyson, the English poet of the Victorian age, and his poem "Godiva." When Godiva, to free the residents of Coventry from an unfair toll, takes up her husband's challenge to ride around the town seated naked on a horse, the poet describes the scene in a cryptic line: "Then she rode forth, clothed on with chastity." Annadurai's point is, even when there is room to mention the woman's naked body, the poet discreetly says that she was clothed on with chastity. In comparison, Kamban appeared to have "x-ray eyes" that saw through clothed women to describe their private sexual organs.

There can be no question that a dismissal of Kamban's enormous poetic gift on the basis such unsavory, explicit, and contextually inappropriate references to the female body would be unfair. However, Annadurai's criticism needs to be placed in context as well. If we read the two debates on *Kamparāmāyaṇam* he had with Tamil scholars, we could see Tamil scholars swearing by Kamban's poetic genius even when they were in agreement with Self-Respecters about the hegemony of the Brahmins and the Hindi-speaking north. Annadurai wanted to challenge them on the turf of textual exegesis. While his dismissal of Kamban *tout court* based on such lurid references is untenable, the need to bring down Kamban from the pedestal where uncritical adulation placed him was substantial as well. This was part of the larger gamut of culture wars that were being fought as we will have occasion to note in Chapter 9 on mobilization.

In effect, the Dravidian movement succeeded in according a preeminent place to Valluvan among Tamil poets. It should be noted that Valluvan also wrote 280 couplets on love life under the heading *Inbam* or *Kamathuppal*, which should go to show that the Dravidian movement did not exhibit any puritanical tendency in treating literature. Annadurai was deliberate in resorting to this mode of critical reading of Kamban since he had to challenge the preeminence accorded to him; they did otherwise retain Kamban as a major Tamil poet. As it stands, there is a statue of Kamban on the Marina beach arcade not far from the entrance to Anna Memorial. What appears unfair is the silence surrounding Annadurai's critical text *Kamparacam* in the traditions of literary criticism. It is a significant moment in which cultural politics entered the realm of literary criticism, particularly in reading the classics of yore on a popular political platform. The excessive polemical energy of Annadurai's text can be no reason not to accord it the attention it deserves in the annals of serious literary criticism. The question of propriety of expression, *aucitya*, or being out of tune with the predominant sentiment or affective mood, *rasābhāsa*, is of course a serious issue in literary exegesis as much as the contemporary concerns about the male gaze, which gets discursively inscribed in such contexts. Annadurai's questions need to be rearticulated in contemporary critical idiom as much as there is a need for the re-exploration of Kamban's poetic genius, as suggested by K. N. Subramaniam.

Notes

1. Milind Wakankar's personal correspondence.
2. For a discussion of this mutation of the Rama idea, see Kapoor (1993). Also see Patwardhan et al. (1992).
3. Many commentators have pointed out that the pivotal moment was Rajiv Gandhi's gamble in allowing for worship of the Shilanyas at the Babri Masjid site in 1985. In a forecast of a certain post-secular politics, Rajiv Gandhi enacted a law to strengthen the laws of the Sharia as Muslim personal law to counter a Supreme Court judgment in the Shah Bano case, granting alimony to an estranged wife, which was purely in the purview of the Sharia or community adjudication. Allegedly to compensate for that, he also opened the locks to the Babri Masjid site. How far the opening of the lock is instrumental to the Rath Yatra and subsequent mobilizations is a matter of conjecture since the Hindutva brigade could anyway have raked up the issue, lock or no lock. If they could demolish a mosque, they could as well have broken a lock. However, the removal of the lock in the hope of winning over the "Hindu" support or a new balance among communities was counterproductive. The Congress had always tried to adhere to the sentiments of all religious communities as much as possible to keep the state at an equidistance from all religions in a precarious balance of secularism, which sort of failed in this instance.
4. These are taken from the famous inaugural address of Jawaharlal Nehru at the hour of Indian independence.
5. Iyalvuṟu celaviṉāvā yirukaiyu meyiṉar tūṇṭat
   tuyalvaṉa tuṭuppu vīcit tuvalai kaṇ makaḷiṉ meṉṟū
   kayalvuṟu paravai yalku loḷi puṟattaḷippa vuḷḷat
   tayarvuṟu matukai maintark kaya uyiyarp paḷitta tammā!
   (Kamparāmāyaṇam, Ayōttiyā Kāṇṭam, kukappaṭalam, Ceyyuḷ 56)

   See Vai.Mu. Kōpālakiruṣṇamāccāriyār (2006, 1:745).

6. Kōmuṉiyuṭaṉ varukoṇ ṭaleṉṟapiṉ ṟāmaraik kaṇṇiṉāṉeṉṟa
   taṉmaiyā lāmavaṉē koleṉṟaiya nīṅkiṉāḷ
   vāme mēkalaiyiṟ vaḷar talkulē!
   (Kampa Rāmāyaṇam, Pāla Kāṇṭam, Kārmukap Paṭalam, Ceyyuḷ 62)

   See Vai.Mu. Kōpālakiruṣṇamāccāriyār (2006, 2:576).

7 Counter-Narratives

The extent of diffusion of the Hindu Puranic corpus over a couple of millennia among the people of Tamil Nadu is inestimable. Innumerable would be the extent of local variations and interpretations as circulated through folk performances, oral narratives, and many a mode of textualizations from palm leaves to early access to print during the eighteenth and nineteenth century. Hence, it is hard to hazard a guess whether a commoner would, in the middle of twentieth century, be aware of, say for example, the story of churning of the "ocean of milk" to extract *amṛta,* or nectar, a signal Puranic incident, is difficult since a lot would depend on what kinds of access he or she had to folk cultural forms and oral narrative traditions, let alone print literature. We could think of the example of Menocchio, the sixteenth-century miller of Italy, whose cultural world was so painstakingly laid out to us by Carlo Ginsberg, for thinking of what constitutes a common person's view and knowledge of things, say as he or she is immersed in "popular culture" (Ginzburg 1992). Unlike the Italian case, much of what informed a commoner in Tamil Nadu should be oral and folk narratives, occasionally, if ever, supplemented by reading due to the high rate of illiteracy reported in mid-twentieth century. What notion of the *asura* of the puranic lore the commoner might have carried is a matter of speculation. We can however be certain that he or she had a rich and varied sedimentation of cultures to choose from. It is in such an open field of imaginations that the Dravidianists sought to make a case for the assertion of the *asuras* over the allegedly unjust characterizations the Puranic imagination had cast them in.

If we, the authors, were to speak of our own assimilation of the cosmic scheme of the Puranas, not from studying the Sanskrit texts or the works of Indologists but as people who had been immersed in popular culture as we grew up, we should first note that there were three worlds to contend with. The Devaloka is the heavenly abode where the *devas* resided. The Bhuloka is the world of the humans. The Patalaloka, the netherworld, is where the *asuras* and *rakshasas* lived. All worlds were of course ordained by the trinity of Gods: the creator Brahma, the protector Vishnu, and the destroyer Shiva. The three have the constitutive role of all things: the positive, the negative, and the creative or mutative. The trinity also had their abodes adjacent to Devaloka, or the upper worlds, since at least early cinema put them up in the sky. Some of the famous *devas* are embodiments of the very elements that constitute nature, like Agni being fire, Vayu being wind, Varuna being water, and so on. However, the total number of *devas* aggregate to thirty-three crore, a fact often rhetorically stated, and a whole lot of them are anonymous and non-descript. The *asuras* are generally powerful, a sort of brute force with no particular head count. The humans of the Puranas, whenever they make a presence, owe their allegiance to the *devas* and the trinity of gods; they also fear the *asuras* and *rakshasas*. The Puranas often do not make it clear what is fundamentally wrong with the *asuras* and *rakshasas*. They come into the picture whenever there arises a stellar figure from among them who challenge the *devas* over the control of the worlds. Often times these characters appear to possess virtuous qualities; they are also pious towards the trinity of gods, empowered by boons received from them through penance, and are learned, valorous, and just. For example, an *asura* king like Mahabali does not appear to have any blemish except taking over the rule of the three worlds, thus spiting Indra, the Lord of the *devas*. Hence, Vishnu tricks him into self-annihilation. Generally, the problem with the *asuras* appear to be a political one, with their aspiration to control the three worlds. Such pursuit of power constantly places them at war with the *devas*, which they usually lose. In the general template of Puranic narratives, there certainly is a Manichean dualism of light and darkness, good and bad, distributed to the *devas* and *asuras* respectively, though we don't see such a stark difference in the specific deeds of both groups in terms of indulgences, avarice, and meanness, except for the charges of despotism laid against *asura* exemplars. The trinity of Gods is partial to the *devas*, though they often get compelled to grant boons bestowing extraordinary powers to *asura* exemplars as a reward for the hard penance undertaken. Many *asura* exemplars, including the famous examples of Hiranya and Ravana, go through the cycle of hard penance, boon, excesses of the reign, and divine retribution. The *devas* do not boast of such heroic stories. They just hang in with their ontologically granted dominance. The humans are present and active more in the epics, the Ramayana and Mahabharata, than the Puranas or the Vedas. In the Puranas, humans are just spectators, if they have any presence at all, in the *deva–asura* conflict.

The Vedas, Puranas, and the epics are primarily the imaginations of the Aryans, the group that is held to have migrated from central Asia or the region of Persia to the north west initially and later to the Gangetic plains. The consensus among ancient historians is that they encountered native populations in India like those of the Harappan civilization. Whether all of the pre-Aryan peoples of ancient India were Dravidian or not, as speculated by some, the Dravidians of south India certainly were of a different stock than the Aryans. More than ethnology or the still-emerging field of genetic studies, the stark distinctions between Aryans and Dravidians are suggested by linguistics and philology. Romila Thapar glosses the term "mleccha" as referring to "indistinct speech," that is, a speech that is different from Sanskrit, which the Aryans spoke. This latter became a name for those belonging to the foreign lands, *mleccha desa*, where people not only did not speak Sanskrit but also did not observe the rituals of the Aryans. Interestingly, she also uses the term "asura" in the context of such alien non-Aryan people being described by the Aryans:

> That speech was the chief component in distinguishing the Aryan from the others is clearly indicated in a text from the later Vedic literature. An example of barbarian speech, that of the Asuras, is quoted in the Satapatha Brahmana, and is later quoted and discussed by a grammarian of the fourth century B.C., Patanjali. (Thapar 1971)

We notice here the slide from non-Aryan *mleccha* to *asura*. In her latest magnum opus *Past Before Us* (Thapar 2013), Thapar uses the composite phrase "asurarakshasa" to refer to people other than the Aryans, though in the context of arguing for a mix in the case of Puru, a key figure in the lineages of kings, who had an impure speech and descended from an *asurarakshasa* (Thapar 2013, 118). There is much discussion in the text as to what exactly the term "Aryan" referred to. It is certainly not a race; not an unmixed endogamous group; many a time the term "Arya" perhaps referred to "respectability." Nevertheless, Aryans, as a group of people, certainly meant those speaking Sanskrit and those with a certain adherence to rituals and largely a *varna*-based society which *mleccha*s and *rakshasa*s do not adhere to. Overall, there appears to be a certain overlap between the Puranic imagination and the cultural world of Aryans who composed the Vedas, Puranas, and the epics. Many Indologists have said *asura*s and *rakshasa*s referred to non-Aryan peoples. For example, Alain Daniélou, French Indologist writing in the 1960s, has this to say:

> Tales referring to the peoples and the aboriginal tribes with whom the Āryas were first in conflict when they settled in northern India came to be incorporated in the myths of the asuras and the rākṣasas. The allusions to the disastrous wars between the asuras and the suras, found everywhere in the Purāṇas and the epics, seem to include many episodes of the struggle of the Āryan tribes against earlier inhabitants of India. (Daniélou 2017, 176)

Hence, there is a general concurrence that all that is fabulous and fantastic in the Puranic and epic imagination had its social base in the conflicts the Aryans had with other peoples, the earlier inhabitants of India who they chose to describe as *asura*s and *rakshasa*s. Aryans themselves could be identified as the people who composed the Vedas, Puranas, and epics in Sanskrit. Whatever has been the nature of interactions and assimilation between the Aryans and Dravidians all through the millennia, at the dawn of modern public sphere in Tamil Nadu the Brahmins who were identified with Sanskrit knowledge and adherence to rituals, identified as priests in agamic temples and as *purohits* officiating life cycle rituals for others, were seen as descendants of Aryans, a view actively abetted by Brahmins themselves. The non-Brahmins consequently thought of themselves as descendants of Dravidians, primarily through linguistic difference and secondarily through physical features such as a dark skin and so on. Hence, in spite of sharing the Hindu pantheon of gods and Puranic imagination, there were many a conflict with Brahminic or Vedic Hinduism from which others had a historical distance. They, like in the cases of sterling examples of Maraimalai Adigal and Pandit Iyothee Thass, further sought to distance themselves from Brahminical Hinduism at the inception of the modern public sphere through print culture in the late nineteenth century and early twentieth century.

As a consequence of a definite antagonism with Brahmin orthodoxy and Brahminical social order, the practice of writing critical readings of the Puranas and epics, the superstitious practices of Brahmin ritualism and reimaging the tales of Puranas from the vantage of point of the *asuras*, began in the late nineteenth century.[1] In as much a sense of "embedded history" could be discerned in the Vedic, Puranic, and epic narrations in the words of Romila Thapar, Dravidianists sought to reimagine and rewrite such embedded histories from the vantage point of non-Aryans or Dravidians. This was the origin of what we propose to discuss as counter narrations in this chapter.

Iraṇiyaṉ or the Inimitable Hero

Bharathidasan (1891–1964) has a special place as the bard of the Dravidianists in general and the DMK in particular. As we had noted earlier, he was there at the venue of the executive committee meeting of those who were estranged from Periyar when they formally decided to launch the party. Though he did not become an office-bearer of the party, his works and songs were certainly a major source of inspiration for the party. Annadurai had fervently and elaborately argued for a preeminent status to the poet, which he alleged was denied to him due to the Dravidianist, Tamil sentiments that informed his works. Annadurai, in a significant moment, during the days of intense estrangement from Periyar, raised a purse for Bharathidasan and bestowed the title "Puraṭci Kavi" (Revolutionary Poet) on him. Bharathidasan is also widely referred to by his other title as "Pāvēntar," king of poetry. Bharathidasan's given name was Kanaga Subburathinam and belonged to Pondicherry; he met the nationalist poet Subramanya Bharathi, whom we encountered in the previous chapter, in his youth.

The young Subburathinam was inspired to write poems by Subramanya Bharathi and was a member of his group of acolytes. It is in admiration of the poetic genius of Bharathi that Subburathinam changed his name to Bharathidasan, meaning a devotee of Bharathi. However, he was soon to come under the influence of Periyar E. V. Ramasamy, which lead him to the cause of rationalism and Tamil, superimposing on the various investments he had on the rich tapestry of cultural moorings of the Tamil language. It is during the days of intense involvement in the Self-Respect Movement of Periyar, apparently prompted by the activist Kuthoosi Gurusamy, that he wrote the play *Iraṇiyaṉ*, or "the Inimitable Hero" (Bharathitdasan 2005). Gurusamy produced the play in 1934, a sort of forerunner to the later-day advent of the stage play as political propaganda under Annadurai. As was usual, it was first performed in the presence of Periyar. It was performed many times before the Madras state government, in the post-independence years, who thought fit to ban the play as part of their streak of repressive measures, which we will discuss in Chapter 10. *Iraṇiyaṉ* in the title of the play refers to Hiranyakasipu, the *asura* king who was annihilated by the man-lion hybrid avatar of Vishnu, known as Narasimha. It is one of the most popular of the Puranic tales found in many Puranas and the epic Mahabharata. It is widely recounted in oral narrative cultures as well as a wide range of folk performances. We should first take a look at the brief outline of the Puranic story before discussing the counter-narrative offered in the Bharathidasan play. For the sake of parity with Puranic versions of the story, we will refer to the *asura* king as Hiranya rather than the Tamil *Iraṇiyaṉ* that the play uses.

While there are considerable variations of the Hiranya story in the Puranas, we will go for the most popularly known or widely retold plot structure. Hiranya performed severe penance, at the end of which Brahma was constrained to give him the boons he asked for. Hiranya sought immortality but in an elaborately conceived paradoxical exclusions from causes of death. He was not to die indoors or outdoors, during the daytime or at night, nor on the ground or in the sky. He was not to meet death brought by any being created by Brahma, nor by any weapon, nor by any human being or animal. Thus empowered, he ruled over all the worlds. He wanted everyone to offer salutations to him rather than Narayana or Hari, that is, Vishnu, the supreme God.

The problem arose in the person of his son, Prahalada, who, according to some versions, was interpellated with devotion to Narayana or Hari, right when he was in the womb of his mother. As Prahalada grew up with devotion, offering salutations only to Narayana and not Hiranya, the enraged father tried to threaten him with severe penalties for disobedience. As no threats worked, he ordered Prahalada to be executed by several means, only to be saved each time miraculously by divine intervention. Finally, the enraged Hiranya asked Prahalada to show him where Hari was. Prahalada famously stated that he was omnipresent, as in a speck of dust as in a mighty pillar. Hiranya, who was in his palace when the exchange took place, showed one of the pillars there, asking whether Hari would be present in it. Prahalada answered in the affirmative. Hiranya with his weapon hit the pillar, splitting it into two. From inside the pillar emerged the form of man-lion, Narasimha, part man and part lion. The supreme God Vishnu took a hybrid form to beat the paradoxical stipulations of the boon; he chose the liminal space of the doorstep, which is neither inside nor outside, manifesting at dusk, which was neither day nor night, pulled Hiranya on to his thighs, which was neither earth nor sky, disemboweled him with the sharp claws of the man-lion, which was no weapon. Beating all the binary oppositions with emergent manifestation of difference, the Vishnu avatar Narasimha annihilated Hiranya. The steadfastly pious Prahalada was anointed the king. The tale has been explored for its rich symbolism and its potentially vast philosophical import by religious and literary scholars.

The Tamil *Iraṇiyaṉ* is an exact counter-narrative to the Puranic story. Iraṇiyaṉ is a pragmatic, brave, and just Tamil king. The group of Aryan settlers are desperately trying to spread their ritualism, Gods, and caste hierarchy among Tamils, to which Iraṇiyaṉ is stoutly opposed. He never hesitates to punish the Aryans when they are found aggressive in their propagation of deceit. The Aryans naturally see him as a great impediment to advancing of their hegemonic sway over the people. They were persuaded that there was no other option than to plot to kill Iraṇiyaṉ. At the beginning of the play, we find Pirakalātaṉ (Prahalada), son of Iraṇiyaṉ, sent on a journey through many countries to learn the affairs of the world as preparation for his being anointed as the crown prince. Kajakētu, the chief of Aryan clan, had managed to get his son Kāṅkēyaṉ to accompany Pirakalātaṉ in the guise of an aide. Kāṅkēyaṉ contrives to bring Pirakalātaṉ to a garden where Citrapāṉu, the daughter of Kajakētu and sister of Kāṅkēyaṉ, is made to run into Pirakalātaṉ. In an elaborate ruse, she feigns to have already fallen in love with Pirakalātaṉ, who anyway is defenseless in front of the considerable charms of the woman. Kāṅkēyaṉ pretends not to know her; he takes leave of them, enabling Pirakalātaṉ to freely court her. Things proceed fast; Pirakalātaṉ is quickly married to Citrapāṉu in her father's palace. Kajakētu then explains to Pirakalātaṉ the superiority of their God Vishnu, the sanctity of their Vedas and rituals, the sanctity of the social order of caste hierarchy they propose, and so on. Pirakalātaṉ, bewitched by the love of Citrapāṉu, fully accedes to whatever is professed by Kajakētu in return for access to his beloved. In the meantime, Iraṇiyaṉ and his wife ruminate on the first-time separation from their son. Iraṇiyaṉ is particularly worried that his son should not fall for Aryan deceit if he encounters them. At that moment, messengers bring the news that a horde of Aryans had blocked a highway saying that their god, Narayana, would destroy Iraṇiyaṉ and all those Tamils who do not accept the Vedas and the rituals taught by them. They demand that everyone should adhere to Aryan norms. They claim that they were here to redeem Tamils to the right path. Hearing of such an impetuous act, Iraṇiyaṉ orders all of them to be brought to the court in chains. When Kajakētu hears of the king's orders, he feels that Pirakalātaṉ should rush to save the Aryans to be imprisoned by his father, saying that there are many close relatives of theirs among the crowd to be arrested, including Citrapāṉu's mother. Pirakalātaṉ promises to save them at any cost. The Aryan priest advises him to exercise caution as he is to be crowned as prince. He suggests that Pirakalātaṉ should sneak into the prison and release the prisoners surreptitiously. Citrapāṉu insists that she too would accompany Pirakalātaṉ. She decides to kill Iraṇiyaṉ while he is asleep.

When they approach the palace, she learns from Pirakalātaṉ the location of Iraṇiyaṉ's bed chamber. Entering it through the balcony, she throws a spear at Iraṇiyaṉ, which fortunately misses him and only ends up waking him up and his wife. The soldiers apprehend Citrapāṉu. On seeing that she is an Aryan woman, he chides her for the cowardice in attempting to kill him while he is asleep. Since he does not want to execute a woman, he lets her take back the spear and leave. Thus, shamed at being forgiven, Citrapāṉu tells Pirakalātaṉ, who is waiting elsewhere, that she was apprehended because the spear fell from her hands; that Iraṇiyaṉ abused her rudely but she managed to escape from the clutches of the soldiers. They leave the palace forthwith.

The attempt to release the prisoners thus spoiled, they are brought to the king's court. Iraṇiyaṉ gives a rousing speech about the cunning and deceitful nature of the Aryans who do not meet him in the battlefield but try to spread canards like "God Narayanan would punish him" and so on. He declares that no self-respecting Tamil would fall for such Aryan deceit. However, he also has a prescience that the Aryans may manage to kill him, like the attempt on his life the previous night and also spread fantastic tales about the dastardly deed. He only hopes that in the future Tamils would discern what actually happened. Hence, Iraṇiyaṉ is shown to anticipate Bharathidasan's play from within the text. Following the speech, several batches of Aryans are tried for various crimes. One batch is tried for denouncing the Tamil ways of life, celebrating the devious ways of the Aryans, and also for proclaiming that God Narayanan would manifest and kill Iraṇiyaṉ. A group of Aryans is tried for claiming that they had magical incantations that would make Iraṇiyaṉ burn to death instantaneously. Another batch is tried for burning Tamil texts of poetics and exegesis. Yet another is tried for propagating that Tamils are the *asuras* and *rakshasas*.

Finally, a group of Aryan priests are tried for plotting to overthrow the government. Iraṇiyaṉ condemns all these crimes and imposes severe penalties like amputation of limbs, blinding, beheading, and torture to various groups. In the meantime, Citrapāṉu had already seduced the commander of Iraṇiyaṉ's army, promising him that she would marry him once her ritual vows are fulfilled. When the commander takes the prisoners to the execution dock to carry out the punishments, Citrapāṉu appears there to plead with him to let them go. Under her influence, he kills his own soldiers and lets all the prisoners escape. Citrapāṉu asks him to report back that when they approached the execution arena a mysterious light appeared in the sky, which rendered the commander unconscious, killed all the soldiers, and released the prisoners. When the king's emissaries reach the spot, they find the commander pretending to be unconscious and when woken up repeats the tale verbatim. When a furious Iraṇiyaṉ accosts the commander, he holds on to the story, pleading that his mind could be hallucinating. In the meantime, Pirakalātaṉ returns to the palace. When Iraṇiyaṉ asks him about Aryan manipulations, Pirakalātaṉ replies that people are happy taking to the Aryan faith. They could solve their problems by placing faith in the Aryan God. Iraṇiyaṉ remarks of his being upset with both the commander's and Pirakalātaṉ's disposition. The audience knows both were seduced by Citrapāṉu, who is a metaphor of Aryan deceit.

In a crucial scene in the play, the king Iraṇiyaṉ and his minister, both in disguise, mingle among the common people when the royal proclamation is made that Prince Pirakalātaṉ was to be anointed crown prince the next day and that the people were to prepare the city for festivities and also attend the ceremony. They hear people openly talk in defiance of the king, saying that he had fallen out with the Aryans who had God on their side. They ruminate that the Aryan claim about an almighty God must be true since the world could not have sprung up on its own. Since the Aryans were sent to redeem Tamils through inculcating a faith in God, the Aryans should have the support of the almighty God. After all, God did send a light that killed all the soldiers and released the Aryan prisoners. It is due to the goodwill the commander had earned with the Aryans that he was spared death. They hear people talk about an incident that had happened the previous day to Kuppan in Thimman's house who died but was resuscitated to life by an Aryan priest. The king had better fall in line with the Aryan faith like his own son Pirakalātaṉ. On hearing all this, Iraṇiyaṉ realizes that the people had fallen prey to Aryan fabulations. He wondered what could not be achieved by the sword has been achieved by the power of the deceitful words of the Aryans. Even at that moment, Iraṇiyaṉ was not worried about his suzerainty. He was only concerned that Tamils would lose their precious honor and self-respect if they got enslaved to the ideas of the Aryans. He wondered how the commander and his own son fell prey to Aryan beguile. The minister suggests not to rush to an opinion about the prince.

The next day at the coronation platform, the minister asks Pirakalātaṉ to honor the name of Iraṇiyaṉ as a mark of respect and to take oath to follow the path of his father. Pirakalātaṉ stuns everyone by saluting Narayana, the god of the Aryans. He was aware of being watched by Citrapāṉu, who was disguised as a man. An enraged Iraṇiyaṉ demands to know what happened to Pirakalātaṉ's Tamilness; he warns Pirakalātaṉ to change his mind at once, saying that he was given an opportunity not because he was Iraṇiyaṉ's son but because he was the prince of Tamils. The minister and other kings assembled ask Pirakalātaṉ to salute Iraṇiyaṉ. Pirakalātaṉ adamantly repeats his salutation to Narayanan. His mother Leelavati rushes forth to plead with him not to incur his father's wrath. Pirakalātaṉ responds by saying it is only God Narayana, the Almighty, who is the most powerful in all the worlds and hence only he could be saluted. When Iraṇiyaṉ decides to kill Pirakalātaṉ, Leelavati pleads that he be given some time to mull things over. Iraṇiyaṉ agrees to give him a day to reconsider his attitude.

Back in his chamber, Pirakalātan̲ is confronted by Citrapān̲u, who assures him that Iraṇiyan̲ could not have hurt him for two reasons. The commander had placed archers around to stop anyone from approaching Pirakalātan̲. More than that, the Aryan priests had cast a spell that would have bent Iraṇiyan̲'s sword if it ever came anywhere near Pirakalātan̲. She retires to the inner chambers when the commander comes in. Pirakalātan̲ learns from the commander the level of his connivance with the Aryans in faking the story of the mysterious light that liberated the prisoners. As they speak, soldiers come on Iraṇiyan̲'s command to chain Pirakalātan̲ and take him to the assembly hall. The commander tells the soldiers to go back and tell the king that the chain miraculously broke and there are flames that prevent anyone from approaching Pirakalātan̲. The soldiers obey his command and leave. Realizing that Iraṇiyan̲ would come now personally to accost Pirakalātan̲, the commander leaves to prepare an ambush. Likewise, the Aryan clan also gets into the act. Kāṅkēyan̲ puts on a lion's hood and hides behind a pillar. Soldiers hide behind other pillars.

Iraṇiyan̲ and Leelavati come to the hall and ask Pirakalātan̲ as to who had corrupted him. Pirakalātan̲ replies it is the grace of Lord Narayanan. Iraṇiyan̲ demands to know where he could find this Narayanan. Pirakalātan̲ replies that he resides everywhere in every particle or in every pillar. When Iraṇiyan̲ kicks a pillar, asking whether he would be there, Kāṅkēyan̲, hiding behind the pillar with a lion's hood, jumps up and claims to be Narayanan. Soldiers approach Iraṇiyan̲ from behind. Iraṇiyan̲ laughs at the trick, saying, "When I kicked the pillar you appeared; let me see if I kick you a pillar would appear"; he kicks Kāṅkēyan̲, who falls and dies. Soldiers stab Iraṇiyan̲ in the back and he also dies. Leelavati takes the sword from Iraṇiyan̲'s hand to kill herself. Citrapān̲u runs in to fall on Kāṅkēyan̲, her brother, and cry for him. Pirakalātan̲ tries to kill the commander, as instructed by Citrapān̲u. But the commander gives him a slip, managing to kill Pirakalātan̲ in retaliation. He finds a note on Pirakalātan̲'s person written by Citrapān̲u instructing that the commander be killed. Realizing the depth of her cunning, the commander kills her as he finds her weeping by the side of the dead Kāṅkēyan̲. Amidst all this mayhem and fury, the commander realizes how Aryan treachery has brought down the great king Iraṇiyan̲. He is full of remorse at his own act of betrayal, having fallen for the charms of Citrapān̲u and her deception. The play ends with a long monologue where he attests to the fact that the fall of Iraṇiyan̲ was caused neither by Vedic chants nor by a Vishnu avatar but by the treachery of Aryans. He wonders whether poets in the future would dare tell the true story. He only hopes that one day the blood shed by the brave king Iraṇiyan̲ would make Tamils realize the truth and be rid of Aryan deceptions and falsehood. Finally, handing over the land to future Tamils who would redeem their honor and self-respect, the remorseful commander kills himself.

The fabrications of the Aryans within the play where they re-narrate ordinary events with the invention of supernatural elements in a way constitutes the whole of the Puranic narration of the Hiranya–Prahalada story. The whole Purana is but a fabrication to besmirch Iraṇiyaṉ's greatness and his principled opposition to Aryan hegemony and deceit. The truth of the story now stands revealed in the counter narration of the play. The banning of the play as a work that would cause communal disharmony by the Madras provincial government lent further validity to the power of counter narration.[2]

As with Annadurai's play on Shivaji, in *Iraṇiyaṉ* too we could see that the power of Aryans or Brahmins to seduce the minds of the people is taken to be the primary problem. The valorous kings and sovereigns are vulnerable against such propagation of ideas that undercut their power. The Aryan or Brahmin problem is primarily an ideational one. They are a self-perpetuating, self-validating group who claim ritual status and priesthood, creating a social hierarchy in the wake, placing themselves on top of it. It does not matter to them who actually rules the land as long as they frame the laws of society and the realm.

The Lord of Justice Fainted!

At the end of the debates on whether *Kamparāmāyaṇam* should be burnt or not, which we discussed in the previous chapter, Annadurai was perhaps piqued on two counts. One was Somasundara Bharathiar's assertion that while events of the plot of Kamban's work could be critiqued, his poetic genius itself however was unimpeachable; he went to the extent of claiming that given to choose between Tamil Nadu and Kamban, he would choose Kamban. Such an unmitigated adulation of Kamban's poetic prowess perhaps made Annadurai write *Kamparacam* (The Taste of Kamban), which we discussed in the previous chapter. The other provocation was made by R. P. Sethupillai who argued that Ravana was not Dravidian but Tamil who brought about his downfall only because he lacked any capacity for mercy, an inherent quality of Tamils. He cited Kamban's famous phrase, "Iṟakkam eṉṟa poruḷillā arakkaṉ," or in short "Irakkamillā arakkaṉ" (The *rakshasa* sans mercy) as the primary reason for the destruction of Lanka and the defeat of Ravana. Hence, the story could not be read as Aryan–Dravidian conflict was the argument of R. P. Sethupillai. Annadurai responded to this provocation "Irakkamillaa Arakkaṉ" and the result was a play, *The Lord of Justice Fainted!* (Annadurai 1980), which is a sort of counter narration to exclusively focus on the charge of Ravana being a *rakshasa* without mercy. Though playfully written, the polemical vigor of the text against the proposition that Ravana lacked capacity for mercy is remarkable.

When the play opens, we hear a voice calling out to the Lord of Justice amidst thunder and storm. It is the voice of God, referred through the common noun *āṇṭavaṉ*. God says that there are new ideas spreading on the earth that call into question the old verdicts issued. Hence, if people are to have some respect for fairness and justice, it is necessary to go for retrials of some of the cases. God suggests that the charge of Kamban that Ravana lacked capacity for mercy and hence met with his downfall and destruction be taken up first. The Lord of Justice sends an emissary to Ravana, asking him to appear for the retrial. Ravana, however, firmly demands that Kamban, who laid the charge, needs to come for the trial without which he would not appear as well. The Lord of Justice persuades a highly reluctant Kamban.

Ravana chooses to argue his own case. He begins by accepting that he did not show mercy to Sita when he abducted her and kept her in captivity. He also admits that he killed Jatayu, who tried intervening during Sita's abduction. As Kamban becomes jubilant at Ravana's elaborate and meticulous confession, Ravana adds a couple of caveats. He says the abduction was nothing personal but an accepted norm in warfare; as Rama and Lakshmana had attacked his sister Surpanaka, mutilating her face, and killed his brother Karan, he decided to announce hostilities with Rama by abducting Sita. Secondly, he never caused her any harm during abduction or captivity. It was purely as part of a sovereign charge in challenging an enemy who caused an affront that Ravana had to abduct Sita without mercy and hold her in captivity. It was his call to do so like a hunter having no mercy for what he hunted. Having said that, Ravana brings Surpanaka as a witness. He points out that Rama and Lakshmana displayed no capacity for mercy when they mutilated her face by chopping off her nose. Kamban protests that it was because of her audacious sexual advance towards Rama. Ravana says that it would have been enough to refuse her and, if necessary, report her behavior to him instead of inflicting such cruelty on her.

He then summons Kaikeyi. He shows Kaikeyi had no mercy whatsoever when she demanded that Rama should go to the forests for fourteen years over and above the demand that Bharata should ascend the throne. Her husband, King Dasaratha, fell at her feet, asking her to spare Rama the ordeal; the whole of Ayodhya cried its heart out on hearing that Rama was to be exiled to the forest. Kaikeyi showed no mercy. Kamban himself remarked that her conduct would put a harlot to shame. Ravana asks, why is she, queen mother of Ayodhya, a noble human being, and not an *asura*, so incapable of mercy? Why did Ayodhya face no destruction for the queen so lacking the quality of mercy? How could Kamban praise Rama, who killed Vaali mercilessly while hiding behind a tree? Would any of the *deva*s show as much restraint as Ravana in not dishonoring Sita while in captivity? Why is it then that only he be accused of having no capacity for mercy? Hearing the relentless argument, the Lord of Justice faints for the first time.

In an interlude, we see Rama mercilessly killing Sampuka, a lower-caste person, for performing penances that Rama says only upper-caste people are eligible to perform. Sampuka's mother elaborately laments on the brutality of the injustice committed without knowing that it was King Rama who had killed her son. She dies appealing to Rama for justice. Ravana takes the Lord of Justice around when they overhear Sita speaking to Akalya, complaining how merciless was Rama in banishing her to the forest when she was pregnant just on the basis of some vague aspersions cast on her by a random subject of Ayodhya.

When the court resumes, Ravana takes on the members of the jury. The first was the sage Vishwamitra, who refused to accept his own daughter born of Maneka, showing no mercy to the infant. Apart from that, he inflicted so much misery on Harischandra just to win a whimsical wager he made with a fellow sage that he could make Harischandra lie. Though the ostensible purpose was to demonstrate the speckless integrity of Harischandra, the ruthlessness of the hardships imposed on him betrays a lack of capacity for mercy in the sage's heart. The next was Parasurama, who beheaded his own mother at the behest of his father on the mere suspicion of some unchaste thoughts crossing the mind of the poor woman; he showed no mercy to his own mother. Dronacharya, a revered exponent of archery, when accosted by Ekalaiva, a low-caste archer of extraordinary skills matching that of Arjuna, demanded the right thumb of the man as *guru dakshina*, his honorarium. He made such a cruel demand on the unsuspecting self-anointed student only to prevent Ekalaiva from practicing archery even for his survival as a hunter. He showed no mercy to the man since as a hunter his livelihood depended on his ability to wield the bow, a capacity he was deprived of by losing his thumb.

Finally, Ravana addresses Kotpuli Nayanar, a Shiva *bhakta*, whose extraordinarily passionate devotion is narrated in *Periya Purāṇam*. We need to recall that *Periya Purāṇam* was also to be burned along with *Kamparāmāyaṇam* in 1943 by the Dravidar Kazhagam (DK). The gruesome episode related to Kotpuli Nayanar is narrated by Ravana. Kotpuli had accumulated a huge quantity of rice in his cellars, which was meant for Shiva temples. When he was away, there was a famine in his village. People, unable to bear starvation, broke into the cellar and took the rice stored. When Kotpuli came to know of the theft, of people consuming the rice meant for Shiva, he was enraged. He killed all those who had consumed the rice he had kept for the god since his devotion found the act of consuming the rice sacrilegious. When he killed men and women, he found a baby among them. Since he thought the baby would also have been fed with its mother's milk after eating the stolen rice, he threw the child up and cut it in two with his sword. Ravana did not need to ask where mercy in this gory act of revenge by the devotee was. After all these declamations, Ravana shakes up the pedestal on which the jury was seated, asking them what right they have to adjudicate on the question of mercy. The Lord of Justice faints again. Kamban, scared out of his wits, stumbles as he tries to scurry out of the courtroom. Ravana kindly escorts him.

Annadurai not only manages to show that the phrase "Irakkamillaa Arakkan" (*Rakshasa* without mercy) lacks substance but also unravels in the process many contradictions of the Manichean dualism the Puranic imagination tries to set up conceptually between *asura*s and others. The deeds of *asura*s are no worse than others: the sages, the *deva*s, and humans. All others appear to lack mercy, grace, and generosity to a far greater extent than the *asura* who is charged with such a lack. If we encounter a mid-twentieth-century Menocchio, Carlo Ginzberg's protagonist we mentioned at the beginning of the chapter, in Tamil Nadu who had come into possession of Annadurai's text lent to him by a friend, well, we will sure have a convert to atheism and "blasphemy."

Mookaji Counters Rajaji

After stepping down from the office of the chief minister of Tamil Nadu in 1954, Chakravarthy Rajagopalachari (shortly Rajaji) decided to write a prose version of the Ramayana in contemporary Tamil. He decided to serialize it in the weekly magazine *Kalki*, run by the eponymous author Kalki Krishnamurthy, who was a close acolyte of Rajagopalachari. We have already noted in detail the Dravidianist contempt for and opposition to the Ramayana. Hence, Rajaji's decision to rewrite the epic in contemporary prose in Tamil cannot be seen as a politically neutral act. We also need to take note that he had to depose office due to the stringent opposition of the Dravidianists to the vocational stream of education he proposed, known as "Kulakalvi tiṭṭam" that uncritically accommodated caste-based distribution of occupation.[3] Consequently, there was an acute polarization of views on Rajaji at that moment in his life. His recourse to writing the Ramayana in contemporary Tamil prose at such a juncture is thus significant on many counts. *Murasoli* was the twelve-page weekly tabloid launched by Muthavelar Karunanidhi that year. It was later to become the chief organ of the Dravida Munnetra Kazhagam (DMK), which it continues to be till this day. Karunanidhi decided to write a serialized critique of the chapters of Rajaji's prose Ramayana in Tamil. His initials in Tamil sound as "Mu. Ka," standing for Muthavelar Karunanidhi. If one added the honorific suffix "ji" to it, it read as Mookaji. Rajaji called his version of Ramayana *Cakaravartti Tirumakaṉ*, meaning "the noble son of the emperor." Mookaji called his serialized critique that ran parallel to the serialized Ramayana, *Cakravarttiy-iṉ Tirumakaṉ*, meaning the offshoot of Chakravarthy, since Chakravarthy is the family name of Rajaji. Hence, the intention to polemically satirize Rajaji's writing is apparent from the very beginning.

Rajaji had undertaken a challenging task. He had to couch the unbridled primitive imagination of the epic in contemporary prose that stood for different sensibilities and common sense. Usually, the Ramayana storytellers had the benefit of pious listeners to whom they glossed the epic events in a suitable mode of interpretation with varied intonations. However, writing in prose and in print, Rajaji had to abstract many incidents to make them read well for the educated public in Tamil. For example, the instance of childless Dasaratha performing a *yagna*, and Lord Agni coming out of the sacred fire, giving a jar of *payasam*, which was to be drunk by his three wives, after which they would get impregnated, is difficult to narrate in contemporary prose. The Dravidianists, including Mookaji, had access to the original Valmiki version and could quickly point to the evasions in Rajaji's descriptions. However, these are minor issues. Rajaji's greater difficulty was in deciding whether to treat Rama as a noble character of an epic imagination or a human being, a valorous and just king who could have lived in history or as an avatar of Vishnu, a god incarnate. This is aligned to the difficulty of how far he should write in the mode of piety. Apparently, the conundrum led to many inconsistencies in Rajaji's writing that Mookaji pounced on. Further, Rajaji's own infelicity in expression was also very uncharitably picked up in the spirit of relentless polemics. After all, the Ramayana story itself had many inconsistencies that had attracted a tradition of critical reading by many exponents. All these consisted of Mookaji's serialized critique of Rajaji's prose version of the Ramayana. While we will not be able to detail many interesting moments in the critique but we need to make one quick note of the objection to the invocation of the character traits of the *asura*s.

Rajaji wrote:

> On the whole, devas are of good nature. Some of them do make mistakes and suffer the consequences. The Rakshasas, on the other hand, have no regard for morality and ethical behavior bent on making trouble for others. There are of course some wise and just ones among them too. (Rajaji 1956, 70)

Mookaji is quick to challenge the Manichean dualism, though stated with caveats, to point out the many misdeeds of the *deva*s. Particularly, Rajaji himself had conceded that Indra, the leader of the *deva*s, took the form of sage Gautama to have sexual intercourse with his wife Akalya; the woman, Rajaji wrote, even when she realized the trick, was flattered that Indra himself fell for her charms and acquiesced. This was the woman who, on being resurrected from having been cursed to turn into a stone, was worshipped by Rama. Mookaji asks if these are the moral standards with which the *asura*s are measured. Rajaji further said that it is sheer ignorance that some Tamils hold the *asura*s as their ancestors for which there is no basis. Mookaji retorted that he should read Pandit Nehru, who wrote in his letter to his daughter that the Ramayana is the tale of the Aryan conquest of Dravidians of the south, to know who is ignorant. As a result of such discursive assertions, the stark difference between the *deva*s and *asura*s in the Puranic imagination came to be displaced to Aryans and Dravidians in ethnological terms and, more significantly, to the internal frontier created between Brahmins and non-Brahmins in political terms. It is instructive to note that the tradition of such counter narration of the Puranic tales extended to a modern short story due to such displacement of *deva–asura* and Aryan–Dravidian antagonism to Brahmin and non-Brahmin identity in contemporary society.

Poṉṉakaram and Akrakāram

Pudumaipithan (1906–1948) is widely held as a literary genius as a short story writer. He is of a modernist persuasion, as his pen name "lover of the modern or new" suggests. He wrote a short story titled *Poṉṉakaram* – City of Gold (Putumaippittaṉ 2016) in the famed literary journal *Maṇikkoṭi* in 1934.[4] It is a story of hardly seventy–eighty short sentences. Half of it is a description of a slum called Poṉṉakaram. The other half narrates an incident, an evening in the life of Ammalu and her husband Murugesan. Poṉṉakaram is a narrow lane that nestles still narrower alleys with matchbox houses. The people who live in Poṉṉakaram are poor. Some of them are coolies in spinning mills close by while others do sundry jobs to eke out a living. They live in squalor and in hunger. Children fish in the open ditch and sneak into the railway line adjacent to the street to hail the passengers in the trains passing by. The street bustles with activity in the evening as women struggle to fetch water from the municipal pump. Generally, everyone drinks to shore up their sinking morale and forget hunger.

Ammalu works in a mill. Her husband Murugesan drives a horse cart. On the evening in question, Murugesan has one too many to drink and ends up capsizing the cart. He sustains an injury in the leg and is carried home by onlookers. Ammalu nurses him. He wants "milk gruel." Ammalu has no money since wages were still two days away in the mill. She goes out to fetch water. It is a cloudy and dark evening. On the way home she is accosted by someone who had an eye on her from one of the alleys. She goes with him for a while and earns some small money to buy milk gruel for her husband. Those who wax eloquent on chastity should know Poṉṉakaram. The cryptic last line of the story has earned it much attention. The exact translation would be: "You keep ranting on chastity. This is Poṉṉakaram for you." The story evokes sympathy for the inhabitants of the slum; it has the power to pierce middle-class conscience and its smugness in universalizing its values. However, there is also an unmistakable tone of condescension in the story, which employs biting sarcasm in describing the squalor of the living conditions of and life in Poṉṉakaram.[5]

It could be surprising that this story produced a counter narration. The counter story was published in the DK journal *Kuṭi Aracu* in 1948 (Cīlaṉ 1948). It was titled "Akrakāram," which is the common noun referring to the Brahmin residential street. The story is written by someone with the name "Seelan," who is otherwise unidentifiable. It is acknowledged in the end that the story is a *taḻuval*, an "adaptation" of the Pudumaipithan story *Poṉṉakaram*. It follows the exact structure of Poṉṉakaram. It describes the splendor and décor of Akrakāram in the same tone of biting sarcasm. Instead of squalor, the affluence of Akrakāram life is etched in clear terms. If Poṉṉakaram street was so narrow that only four people could walk side by side holding hands, the Akrakāram street is wide enough for four military trucks to ride side by side with space to spare for smaller vehicles. The activities of men, women, and children are described in a line-to-line matching of Poṉṉakaram.

In the later half, in the place of Ammalu and Murugesan, we encounter Sambasivam Iyer, a clerk in the *taluk* office, and his second wife, a particularly beautiful Saroja. Sambasivam Iyer is habitually corrupt; as long as his superiors were also Brahmins, they turned a blind eye or perhaps were conniving with him. Unfortunately, a Shudra *tahsildar* gets posted as his superior. The *tahsildar* apprehends Sambasivam Iyer red-handed and decides to legally proceed against him. Sambasivam Iyer has no other option than to have Saroja plead with the *tahsildar*. The *tahsildar* is of course impressed with her considerable charms. This leads to a dinner invitation; the dinner is followed by entertainment that eventually leads to a predictable "indulgence in bodily pleasures." Sambasivam Iyer is confirmed in his position with additional responsibilities. Those who wax eloquent on talent and merit should know Akrakāram. The punch line, which exactly intones the one in *Poṉṉakaram*, can be exactly translated as: "You keep ranting on talent and merit. This is Akrakāram for you." The story, for all its unmistakable polemical vigor and sarcasm, has the same potential to shock middle-class common sense and its smug universalization of values.

The counter story has so far not received the attention of connoisseurs of literature since the world of Pudumaipithan readers, in the last seventy years, and the world of *Kuṭi Aracu* readers do not normally overlap. It is hard to hazard a guess how far readers of *Kuṭi Aracu* would have been aware of Pudumaipithan's short story in 1948 or how far readers of Pudumaipithan would have had occasion to take note of Seelan's story. If it did not happen in 1948, the chances of anything of the kind happening after that is thin, unless the gaze of researchers happens to note the *Kuṭi Aracu* story. Our purpose in discussing this poignant counter narration is threefold. First is to understand the cultural location of the Pudumaipithan story and the counter narration. The second is to speculate on the conditions of possibility of the counter narration. The third is to think of the displacement of values in the final punch lines of the stories.

Whatever be its sterling literary merits, the habitual location of modernist literature in the cultural matrix of mid-twentieth-century Tamil Nadu was upper castes and the middle class. Pudumaipithan, though not prosperous, was a graduate who belonged to the dominant Shaivite Vellala caste. The whole of *Maṇikkoṭi*'s group of writers and readers belonged to such a class, the caste location of either being Brahmins or non-Brahmin upper castes. This is the social segment that would also be heirs to Puranic tales and Brahminic Hinduism. *Kuṭi Aracu* and its readers belonged to the educated sections of what would now be considered Backward Castes, Other Backward Castes, and Dalits. We need to bear in mind the work of Pierre Bourdieu and his rich account of sociology of taste in France in this context (Bourdieu, Nice, and Bennet 2015). The distinction between the social groups was stark in the mid-twentieth century. In the last seventy years, however, there has been considerable democratization of culture when the best critical appreciation of Pudumaipithan comes from Dalit intellectuals, which of course has not completely displaced the politics of distinction related to taste for all.

Second, it is indeed remarkable that the writer of the *Kuṭi Aracu* story would think of juxtaposing Akrakāram with Poṉṉakaram. In fact, *Poṉṉakaram* as a short story primarily speaks of economic conditions, poverty, and deprivation, of urban slums and their unhealthy condition. A reader of the story would mostly read it as sympathetic to the plight of the urban poor. A few might note the tone of condescension in the story, which might make them slightly uncomfortable. However, to think of the world of *Poṉṉakaram* as something that could be juxtaposed with Akrakāram could happen only as the result of a long chain of displacements. We have repeatedly noted the internal frontier erected by Dravidian populism as between Brahmin and non-Brahmin. This distinction is mapped on to the historical distinction between the migrant Aryans and pre-Aryan Dravidian inhabitants of the subcontinent, particularly in the south. It is further extended to the distinction in the imagination of the Aryans as the opposition between the *deva*s and *asura*s. The short story *Akrakāram* as well as much of polemical writing of Dravidianists refer to Brahmins as *boodeva*s, that is, the *deva*s on Earth. We argue that it is only in the backdrop of such elaborately forged Dravidian common sense, a counter-narrative to the short story *Poṉṉakaram* with Akrakāram as the oppositional trope is conceivable.

The final and most pertinent issue is the displacement of values in the final punch line. While the Pudumaipithan short story speaks about the irony of waxing eloquent about chastity, the counter story displaces it to waxing eloquent on merit and talent, the privilege of cultural capital. We will not be able to devote space to excavate fully the significance of such a displacement except to remark that in the cultural politics in which the shorty story *Akrakāram* is rooted, the Brahmin claim to the naturalness of talent and merit has a far more serious consequence than mere adherence to the value of chastity. Hence, even if Saroja is compromised as offering sexual favors, what stands revealed as hubris is Brahmin dominance in governance based on claims of talent and merit. That the non-Brahmin officer yields to the seduction is but a continuation of Pirakalātaṉ and the commander of *Iraṇiyaṉ* yielding to the guiles of Citrapāṉu, the Aryan woman. We may further note women themselves operate only as metaphors for the far greater ideological seduction and *Aryan Allure*, which the Dravidianist critical vocabulary was keen on articulating. Such are the workings of an "intimate enemy," to borrow the famous phrase from Ashis Nandy (Nandy 2015).

Notes

1. Sundar Kali, writing on the Dravidian rereading of "mythic texts," argues that this was an essential part of the reshaping of a nascent Tamil public sphere. Contesting the view that such work merely anachronizes and literalizes the mythic texts, Kali explores the varied manners in which the above-mentioned rereading is accomplished. See Kali (2018).

2. In a hilarious incident, the entire cast of the play in full costume were arrested, prompting a headline in the party organ *Dravida Nadu*: "Iraniyan Gets Arrested along with Narasimha," *Dravida Nadu*, December 9, 1949.
3. Officially titled "The Modified Scheme of Elementary Education," this scheme proposed the introduction of two shifts or sessions in elementary schools. In one session, regular teaching would be done at school and during the second session, the students would be sent home to learn the occupations of their parents, that is, their caste occupation. The scheme was initially deferred and later dropped by Kamaraj, Rajaji's successor as chief minister of Madras State. For more on this, see Anandhi (2018).
4. *Maṇikkoṭi*, a Tamil literary journal that flourished from 1933–1939, was launched by Stalin Srinivasan Chokkalingam and Va. Ramasamy. It launched the careers of literally the who's who of Tamil modernist literature—people like short story writers Pudumaipithan and Mouni, poet Na. Pichamurthi, and novelists R. Shanmugasundaram and M. V. Venkatram. It is considered as a watershed period in modern Tamil literature.
5. Recently, the story was removed from Madras University's syllabus since there were apprehensions that it would affect Dalit sensibilities. However, Dalit intellectuals like Dr D. Ravikumar were not in favor of the removal. See Kolappan (2014).

8 Power of Fiction

Namakkal Ramalingam Pillai (1888–1972), a poet and a nationalist, was arrested during the Civil Disobedience Movement in 1932 and was incarcerated in a B-class cell in Vellore where many frontline Congress leaders were also jailed. Bulusu Sambamurti of Andhra Pradesh was one of them. Sambamurti was a well-groomed person, genteel and energetic, who took a liking to Ramalingam while the latter was already an admirer of the former. One day, at the prayer gathering in the evening, one person sang Ramalingam's poems. Sambamurti was impressed with the lyrics, which as a Telugu speaker he couldn't understand and took help to comprehend fully, asking whether the poems sung at the prayer were written by Subramanya Bharathi, the famous nationalist poet. People replied that they were written by Ramalingam who was present there. Sambamurti was delightfully surprised. After this incident, he started discussing Ramalingam's poems and songs in their private conversations, which were conducted mostly in English as Sambamurti could somewhat understand Tamil but could not speak the language, same as Ramalingam who could not speak Telugu, though he could understand it to some extent. Sambamurti's cell was located next to that of Ramalingam, which perhaps allowed them to meet often. Ramalingam describes one significant conversation that led to his writing a novel, *Malaikkaḷḷaṉ* (Thief of the Mountains):

> On one of the days when we had such conversations Sambamurti wanted to know what kinds of works I have written in Tamil. I mentioned a few. The conversation turned to the need to write fiction in prose, short stories and novels. Sambamurti spoke of many English, French, Bengali and Marathi writers; he then insisted that I too should write fiction in prose like a teacher would prevail upon a disciple. As I had earlier toyed with the idea, after listening to Sambamurti, I felt a definite impulse that I try some writing in prose. I started writing *Malaikkaḷḷaṉ* the next day.[1]

The context and tenor of the conversation in the prison almost makes it appear like writing a novel in prose is in public cause akin to the service of the nation. Much has been theorized about the intricate link between nation and narration. Before we add to those speculations, we will stay with *Malaikkaḷḷaṉ* to track its fate beyond the prison walls where it was born. Though written in 1932, the novel could, owing to many reasons, find a publisher only in 1944. It was still a decade later that it struck a fortune to become famous through its film adaptation in 1954. Sriramulu Naidu of the legendary Pakshiraja Studios, Coimbatore, decided to make it into a film. He hired a script and dialogue writer, who was a sensation in the early 1950s with a slew of box-office hits, M. Karunanidhi of the Dravida Munnetra Kazhagam (DMK). Once he wrote the dialogue in Tamil, they were translated into Telugu and Kannada, and the film was made in three languages simultaneously. Two future chief ministers, M. G. Ramachandran and N. T. Rama Rao, acted in the Tamil and Telugu versions respectively. Rajkumar, who perhaps could have become a chief minister too in Karnataka, acted in the Kannada version. As the film was a great success in all the three languages, it later saw a Hindi version with Dilip Kumar in the lead and also a Malayalam and a Sinhala version, all shot in the same location of Pakshiraja Studios, Coimbatore, not to speak of other possible adaptations. An idea or a sign that germinated in the prison cell in Vellore in 1932, *Malaikkaḷḷaṉ*, did travel far and wide in the whole of the subcontinent.

Arrival of Fiction

The term fiction is not synonymous with literature. People did not always write fiction. For example, Kambaṉ, when he wrote *Irāmavatāram*, would not claim to have written fiction. Not only was the work epic poetry but the idea was that it was a free mixture of imagination and possible history. Though what was imagined could always be distinguished from what actually happened, the creative vocation had no specific need to call itself fiction since the line of demarcation was not a central concern as poets freely added to what actually happened.

Ranajit Guha's discussion of "use of adbhuta" as juxtaposed to the "prose of the world" is a relevant case in point (Guha 2003, 62–74). However, this turn to realism eschewing the fantastic or supernatural is not merely gesturing to historical facticity. Fiction seeks to achieve something more than a mere reference value to the real. Nicholas D. Paige has recently argued persuasively that there were three regimes of novel: romance or fable, the pseudo-factual, and the fiction; he also names them as poetry, pseudo-factual, and fiction—Homer, Rousseau, Balzac (Paige 2011). His argument is that in both England and France, the seventeenth century produced a mode of representation in which the author pretended to present material as he found them: diaries, letters, documents, and so on. This interregnum is significant in that it was followed by fiction, in which a model of the real was sought to be created without the ruse of presenting the actual document. The author freely imagined or invented particular characters and situations through which he hoped to model a world that was analogues to the actual world.

In a different grid, the initial separation, according to Aristotle, was that history referred to what happened in a particular instance, whereas poetry referred to a general condition of what might happen. The pseudo-factual tried to sink the difference by posturing to present only the particular. Fiction invents the particular to arrive at a model of the general. More than the use of prose and the realist effect, what characterizes fiction is the invention of the particular characters and events that purport to point to the truth of the general condition of human affairs like, for example, the operations of power, money, and the like. What matters to Paige is not a simple denunciation of realism but the question of how people hope to arrive at the truth of human affairs through free invention of characters and events as an act of creating analogues models. This particular mode of creative effort called fiction is distinct from all previous modes of literary imagination. This is a mode that has to declare that the characters and events do not refer to any actual person when in fact they may aspire to do so. It is not pseudo-factual but free invention providing a modelling of the real or actual.

Like in most things that are brought under the canopy of modernity, Tamil prose writing compressed a 300-year process in Europe into a few decades, not necessarily going through the conceptual transformations that could be mapped like Paige does in the case of European fiction. It is possible to say that the pseudo-factual arrived simultaneously with fiction in Tamil. Tamil fiction was obviously borrowing several models of European writing at the same time from Richardson to Joyce, from Scott to Maupassant. This is also the key to understanding the constitutive heterogeneity of the Tamil public. The multiple conceptual mappings of genealogical and historical transformations in Europe roughly in the 500 years since the discovery of America will find a baffling co-presence of the many phases and elements in the Tamil twentieth century. As Tamil professor, scholar, and writer Indira Parthasarathy hyperbolically coined it, it was like "thirty centuries in one century."[2] We need to stay with this idea awhile to consider the constitutive heterogeneity of the Tamil public.

Many Publics of Heterogeneous Time

The construction of a people is not a singular event. It is a composite of multiple processes involving the many constitutions of the public. We may not talk of a particular "public sphere" since the substantive "sphere" indicates a stability that is characteristic of the bourgeoise public sphere that Habermas sought to delineate. As he rightly remarked, there are other publics as well with one significant dividing line separating their characteristics: literacy (Habermas 1991, 91). The publics constituted by folk theater, musical theater, and later cinema that almost developed as an extension of these cut across the literacy divide to include the illiterate. Fiction however could only constitute a literate public. The publicness of a putative public was being constituted through many vectors of governmental action and address, the public articulations of political actors through public meetings, the publications of print material, newspapers, journals, and books that circulated through many networks, causing in its wake distant solidarities alongside many a performative and ritual tradition. It is in this broad overlap of the publics constituted jointly and severally that the so-called hybrid formations of subjectivities thrived.

The public constituted by fiction writing is naturally a literate public. It could experience two key processes through its access to fiction. One is the modeling of social life, its everydayness, materiality, and the like through mimesis offered by realist fiction; we just noted with Paige that this modeling is specific to the power of fiction as a distinct mode of literary creation. The second aspect is an even more significant process, which involves the transformation of "private" into "public". The "private" has a two-fold meaning: the privacy of domestic and personal life and the lack of publicness of office or station in terms of power. The second meaning can be understood by the habit of calling a soldier in the army with no designated office as a private. Fiction rendered both kinds of privacy, the domestic and the subaltern, as public in terms of social modeling. This gave fiction a power to model subjectivities like no other discourse.[3] The privacy of thoughts and feelings of iconic characters reached the privacy of the reader through the publication of the fictional work. In other words, the publicness of the private thoughts and feelings of the model subject of fiction that fed into the private subjects contracting to constitute the public is where the power of fiction is housed.

In the case of mid-twentieth-century Tamil Nadu, the fiction-reading public bore a clear distinction from the publics of other performative traditions and the emergent film-viewing public, the wall of separation being, as we noted, literacy. There are two vectors that needs to be understood here. The percentage of literate population stood at 7 percent in the 1940s. However, this 7 percent will naturally not be even across caste hierarchy. The Brahmin and non-Brahmin upper castes with miniscule share in demography like Chettiars, Mudaliars, and Naickers would have a far greater percentage of literate people among them; this implied that among the literate population, the percentage of Brahmins and other upper castes would be high. This made the fiction-reading public a privileged section of the society. The mimetic charge of fiction and the power of its social and subject modeling were keenly celebrated by the reading public. Particularly, the English educated who encountered Scott, Dickens, and Hardy were so enamored of the novel that they could hardly wait for similar fiction to be written in Tamil. The strides made in Bengali and Marathi literature in India provided further impetus. We should recall the conversation Bulusu Sambamurti and Namakkal Ramalingam had in prison that we recounted in the beginning of the chapter. Tamil fiction had to happen so that Tamil modernity could happen. There was a sense of urgency in catching up with the lack of fiction.

It is best to understand this "incentive to write novel or prose fiction" as a desire to constitute a public, perhaps a self-transforming public, which might play a role in the construction of a people and the formation of the political. We have consistently preferred the description "construction of a people and the formation of the political" to the idea of "nationalism." The belabored debate on the links of the novel as a literary form to the so-called imagined community of the nation, in the wake of Anderson's famous thesis, does not connect to our present engagement with Tamil mid-twentieth-century urgency to write fiction (Anderson 1998). It does not mean that representations of the Indian nation or invocation of Indian nationalism is not present in some of the novels. It, as Jonathan Culler has noted, plays a small part in the process of narrativizing a nation in historical terms and builds a nationalistic discourse, which is primarily sustained by externalizing an enemy figure; in the case of India, the colonizing British provided that external figure, the Firangi (Cheah and Culler 2013).

There is no doubt that there are some fictional works that do seek to represent such antagonism in the Tamil novel, but they would pale in significance to the role songs, ballads, and folk imagination played. It hardly provides any critical yield to say that the conditions of possibility that enable writing of the novel also enable the narrations and discourses of the nation since there is nothing particular to be gained from such a broad canvass, all encompassing postulations. Hence, it is best to stay with the formulation that the novel-reading public is one of the publics constituted heterogeneously in the construction of a people. The DMK investment in fiction can only be read as the urgency to have a foothold in the construction of a people as Dravidian Tamil by constituting its own fiction-reading public. This has to be understood in the context of Brahminical dominance in fiction writing, which would monopolize the fiction-reading public in the absence of contestation from non-Brahmin politics. It will be fascinating to map the culture war that was being shaped in mid-twentieth century between the Brahmin and non-Brahmin blocks of literary production, but the task will have to await a full-length treatise later. We will restrain ourselves to capturing the DMK investment in fiction writing as part of it.

The DMK Leader–Activist as Fiction Writer

We will be, in the next chapter, discussing a case study of grassroots activism. The case study will be based on the memoirs of a small-town activist, Pannan ("Kāviyap Pāvalar" Paṇṇaṉ 2020). He was a party activist in the small town of Udumalpet; his mentor was Udumalai Pa. Naraynan (Pa. Na). Pannan had a bachelor's degree in Tamil and was called by friends as *pulavar*, a scholar–poet in Tamil. One of the events that Pannan recollects relates to his writing a play as entry for a literary competition announced by the magazine *Ananda Vikatan*. As it happened, it was Pa. Na who showed him the advert for the competition asking for entries in different literary forms like play, short story, and so on, asking Pannan to send an entry. Pannan was hesitant since his mind was preoccupied with party work then. However, Pa. Na insisted that he could do it. He arranged with a local sympathizer to accommodate Pannan for ten days in his farmhouse for him to write without any hindrance. Pa. Na arranged for everything including papers, pen, and ink for him to go and settle in the farmhouse and write. In the event, Pannan did manage to finish a play based on a heroic lore from the Tamil Sangam corpus. Though Pannan came to know later that *Vikatan* did not send the work to the jury; it was later published as a book and was received well in certain academic circles. The keenness Pa. Na showed in asking the party worker who was capable of writing a literary work to send an entry to the competition is demonstrative of the cultural ethos that the party sought to cultivate at the grassroots level. It is remarkable that writing fiction gets treated as part of party work. The work was being sent to *Ananda Vikatan*, a magazine run by S. S. Vasan, who was a nationalist and had produced the film *Auvaiyar* the year before, a film that reveled in *bhakti* (devotion) to counter the influence of Dravidian films with atheist intonations. Nevertheless, it was important to send an entry to the competition as part of the culture war.

The leaders set an example. Many frontline leaders of the party edited and published magazines and newsletters. Many of them also wrote fiction in the magazines. It is difficult to explain fully such an investment in writing fiction. Many leaders did not ask, like Pa. Na did, someone else to write fiction in their journals. They wrote fiction themselves. Annadurai set the example. He was writing several short stories and novels. M. Karunanidhi, with his phenomenal success as a script and dialogue writer in cinema, followed suit. Following the example of Annadurai, many other frontline leaders wrote fiction. Many of the novels were serialized first in party journals and then were published as books. Some fiction writers like Thillai Villalan, who wrote in the journal *Dravida Nadu*, were active in the party but did not become frontline leaders later. It is hard to speculate on the circulation of the fictional works, but we have found through our field work that they were actively read by party workers. At least one party member, who headed the municipal corporation in a small town during the 1980s, told us that he was drawn to the party as a young man after reading the novel titled "Rangoon Radha" written by Annadurai. We also see that these books were widely in circulation from a rare document shared by poet T. K. Kalapriya, which lists the books gifted in a family wedding in the year 1951.[4] It is a wedding in a Shaivite Vellala family in the Tirunelveli district; the family had no direct connection to politics. The list consists of many kinds of books including fictional works of Annadurai and Thillai Villalan, among others, probably gifted by DMK sympathizers or by members of the reading public.

The DMK leaders–writers possibly constituted a different kind of fiction-reading public. This could have consisted of those who were literate in Tamil but were not bilingually educated enough to read fiction in English. The English-educated bilingual readers engaged with Tamil fiction writing in a comparative mode; they measured Tamil writers against similar models from English and European authors. They were certainly aware of how fiction was produced. The DMK writers were likely writing for a public who had no similar acquaintance with fiction even if they had heard of writers from abroad. Let us consider an instance where a certain anxiety is expressed by a writer about the nature of the fictional work. S. S. Thennarasu, a party leader, wrote a short story in *Murasoli* in January 1955. It is a historical fiction about a Chola princess in Thanjavur falling in love with a brave young lad, a visitor from elsewhere who is apprehended by the soldiers. She decides to elope with him; she accomplishes the task in the middle of the night with the help of an aged guard. It turns out that the young man was after all the prince of the rival kingdom, Vengi; more surprisingly, the aged guard was none other than the emperor Raja Raja Chola, who outwitted his daughter's maneuvers while still being sympathetic to her choice of partner.

While the story is a routine fare in historical fiction, what is remarkable is the disclaimer the author provided at the end of the story. It says: "The story does not recount things as they were. It is based on several essays on Pulikesi, Nedumaran, the princess and South India" (Es. Es. Teṉṉaracu 1955). Such a disclaimer is after all redundant for those who are familiar with the genre of historical fiction. However, Thennarasu was perhaps anxious that his readers might not be familiar with such a mode of creative writing. The DMK writers were conscious of constituting a different public accessing fiction through them. It is important to understand this, since 1954 was when Kalki Krishnamurthy was completing his magnum opus *Ponniyin Selvan*, a historical fiction on palace intrigues during the younger days of Raja Raja Chola, a work of fiction widely read by the educated classes at that time and since then. The disclaimer of Thennarasu at the end of the short story, hence, can only be understood as addressing another group of readers who are not anticipated to be familiar with the work of Kalki; a subaltern reading public not yet acquainted with historical fiction.

Given such a social historical context, it is necessary to know what the fictional narratives of the DMK leaders consisted of. Within the scope of this chapter, we can only afford to pay attention to a couple of seminal works. We select two novels, one each by Annadurai and Karunanidhi, *Raṅkōṉ Rātā* (Rangoon Radha) and *Puthaiyal* (Treasure) as specimens of DMK fiction writing. As both these novels were also made into films, this would also help us to remark on the distinction that apparently prevailed between the putative fiction-reading public and film-going public, at least as it was perceived by the DMK leaders and associates. These novels were also significant in the sense that they were written by these frontline leaders amidst intense political engagement.

Rangoon Radha

The novel was serialized by Annadurai in his journal *Dravida Nadu* in the years 1946–1947.[5] These were tumultuous years, which considerably preoccupied the important leader of the Dravidar Kazhagam, the first lieutenant of Periyar, as could be gleaned from his other writings and activities. It is indeed puzzling that he found the time to write a novel, which he initially published under the pseudonym Soumiyan, though subsequent editions mention the author as Anna. The novel continues to be in circulation, though it is not a work that is discussed much when compared to the plays, short stories, and essays of Anna. In fact, the biography of Annadurai in English written by R. Kannan does not even mention the novel. The film version of the novel was made subsequently after ten years in 1956, which we will return to later.

The novel is written as a first-person narrative, though there is a relay of three people doing the narration. The main narrator is Parandaman, a young man, affluent and educated, who belongs to a trading family of Naidu caste, engaged in his family business. He comes to know about Radha, whose family had migrated from Rangoon after the Japanese bombing, through his friend Nagasundaram, a person belonging to a similarly affluent trading family from the Mudaliar caste. After initially piquing the curiosity of Parandaman, Nagasundaram becomes extremely reticent about "Rangoon Radha." When one day the restive Parandaman corners him with a demand to know what happened with Radha, a highly hesitant and circumspect Nagasundaram opens up after extracting oaths of secrecy and loyalty from Parandaman. It turns out Radha was a younger sister of Nagasundaram, born to his still secretly surviving mother, out of wedlock. Nagasundaram then starts narrating how he came to learn the terrible truth.

Nagasundaram comes to know from servants that Radha is the daughter of a quiet and dignified woman and a decadent alcoholic called Burma Naidu, who was working as a postal superintendent in Rangoon before migrating to Tamil Nadu. Burma Naidu drinks heavily every evening, returning home to harass his wife; the diligent Radha, who has finished her school finals, keeps to her books in spite of the ruckus. On the day Nagasundaram first mentioned Radha to Parandaman, Burma Naidu turned particularly violent, hitting his wife with sticks and whatever else he could lay his hands on. When Nagasundaram heard the woman wailing in agony, he decided to rush into the neighbor's house, interceding between the drunkard and his wife. Once the drunkard was contained and taken to bed, Radha's mother, bleeding from injuries, thanked Nagasundaram, enquiring after him. When Nagasundaram revealed that he was the son of Kottaiyur Dharmalinga Mudaliar, the woman froze. She then turned rapturous, checked on a mole under the right ear of Nagasundaram and declared that she was his mother. Nagasundaram knew that his mother Rangam died when he was a year old, after which his father married his mother's younger sister, Thangam. He was incredulous when the woman in the next house claimed that she was his mother. After the initial astonishment and the emotionally charged exchanges, Rangam started narrating how she went astray due to his father's avarice.

Rangam and Thangam were daughters of rich landowner, *mittadar*, Veeraraghava Mudaliar. Dharmalingam, a self-made wholesale commission agent who was proud to have gained the hands of the elder daughter of a reputed landowner, had cultivated an image of respectability and moderation as a façade hiding his greed for money and wealth. Rangam initially led a happy family life with him till she realized that the greedy Dharmalingam wanted to marry her younger sister Thangam as well as his second wife so that the whole of the estate falls into his hands. When an infuriated Rangam protested his evil design, he spread a canard that Rangam was possessed by evil spirits. The conniving Dharmalingam, aided by the superstitions, misogyny, and stupidity of the people around, managed to convince the village society of the terrible fate that had befallen Rangam who was possessed by evil spirits. The situation led to the logical conclusion of people proposing that Dharmalingam be wedded to the second daughter Thangam, who then would take care of the household. Rangam, in the meantime, became pregnant, which did not deter Dharmalingam from getting married to Thangam. He started spending most of his time with Thangam, being completely indifferent to Rangam and her newborn son.

It was at this juncture that Dharmalingam befriended a scamster, who promised to make a talisman that would bring forth untold riches. The avaricious Dharmalingam yielded to his proposal to perform black magic to obtain the talisman. As part of the ritual, they killed Tulasi, a destitute woman whom Thangam had kept as a household help, as a human sacrifice. The scamster, then impersonating the police, started demanding a hefty ransom from Dharmalingam to cover up the murder. Rangam, who had overheard the scamster's schemes, intervened to save Dharmalingam by knocking down the scamster. Realizing that Dharmalingam was still culpable of the murder of the old woman, Rangam made a supreme sacrifice. She told Dharmalingam to cremate the old woman as Rangam, who was supposed to have died from smallpox, while she left town in the disguise of a religious mendicant. Her one request was that Dharmalingam raised her son Nagasundaram well.

Unfortunately, life as a mendicant did not go well for Rangam. When she fell ill one day, a fellow mendicant with a criminal past forced himself on her, and left her in a brothel. Rangam, no longer in control of her fate, met Burma Naidu in the brothel and went with him to Rangoon where she gave birth to Radha. After the Japanese bombing, they migrated to Tamil Nadu where, unexpectedly, she landed next door to her estranged son and husband. Nagasundaram, realizing the terrible past that his father had concealed from him, decides to help his mother and Radha. They move houses to another location so that they are not seen by Dharmalingam.

Nagasundaram steals from his father and arranges to admit Radha in a college in Madras, where she stays in the hostel.

After hearing this sad story from Nagasundaram, Parandaman feels a deep sympathy for Radha. Both of them go to meet her during a college festival, where Radha stages a play. Extremely impressed with her impeccable demeanor and high intelligence, Parandaman falls in love with her. Nagasundaram is elated that unmindful of his mother's unsavory past and Radha's birth out of wedlock, Parandaman had come forward to marry her. Parandaman's father was of a progressive outlook; when Parandaman proposes that he was marrying a girl born to a person called Burma Naidu who migrated from Rangoon, he does not object to the humble economic status of the girl's family since Parandaman vouchsafes for the character of the girl. Dharmalingam, meanwhile, is angry with his son for taking so much money for personal use. When he learns that his father threatened to disinherit him through Parandaman, Nagasundaram sends a draft notice of a play titled "Kottaiyur Murderer," indicating that he was aware of his father's murky past. When Parandaman tells the shell-shocked Dharmalingam the fact of Rangam's survival and of Radha, the old culprit suffers a stroke, paralyzing him completely. When Parandaman marries Radha, he sends a diamond necklace as an anonymous gift. After the wedding, it is further revealed that Parandaman was not the natural born son of his father; he was adopted from an orphanage as a newborn baby. He is rather a casteless person since no one knew his parents. Radha and Parandaman are then happily united in a casteless bond.

The pivotal point of the novel is a reflection on the ignominy suffered by the women who lose their "chastity." It is the patriarchal society and its gender normativity that work against women, which results in such a sad plight for many of them. In showing Rangam as an honorable woman in spite of having lived in a brothel and become an unwed companion to a man to escape from the brothel, for whom she bore another child, the novel demonstrates that the character and the sense of dignity of a person does not change due to such mishaps. Further, in making Radha the ideal girl full of charm and intelligence in spite of her birth not sanctioned by a proper marriage of her parents, the novel also argued for dignity of the children who were born to a mother who is supposed to have lost her "chastity." The novel speaks highly of both these women in such a way that the taboo society attaches to such people is nullified in the narrative thrust.

However, this was to change when the novel was filmed in 1956, ten years after its initial publication. As we noted earlier, the public constituted by the novel differed strongly from the public constituted by the film. As M. S. S. Pandian had noted in the case of the iconic DMK film *Parasakthi* (Pandian 1991), consensual politics had to be pursued in films since it catered to a far wider audience, who were still not ready to accept a narrative that questions the norms of society. Karunanidhi wrote dialogues for the film and hence both he and Annadurai should have been aware of the crucial change made in the story. In the film, Radha is not the natural born daughter of Rangam. Rangam, who left Kottaiyur in the disguise of a mendicant, reaches Rangoon where she falls ill. One of the shamans who ill-treated her in Kottaiyur had migrated to Rangoon, setting up a clinic there as a quack with the name Burma Naidu. He identifies Rangam and saves her from disgrace and illness. At that very moment, his wife dies in labor. He leaves his newborn daughter with Rangam who, with the help of his assistant, brings her up. In the film, it is Nagasundaram who falls in love with her, since she was only brought up by his mother and not born to her. The film drastically reduces the role of Radha and jettisons her bitter critique of patriarchal norms and values that were the highlights of the novel. The film instead highlights the criticism against superstitions, the hypocrisy of the rich and untamed avarice, but leaves the critique of patriarchy out. Obviously, while the film could reach out to a far wider public, it was not ready to take up the task fiction could take up with the narrow public it constituted.

Puthaiyal (Treasure)

Karunanidhi serialized *Puthaiyal* in *Murasoli* in the years 1954–1955 (Kalaiñar Mu. Karuṇāniti 2000). It was made into a film soon after in 1956 with his own screenplay and dialogue. Still, there were variations between the novel and the film, but nothing as significant as in the case of "Rangoon Radha." Probably the possibility of filming the novel was already being considered when it was written. It is a plot-driven novel full of twists and turns and an element of suspense about the actual treasure. The novel is set in the actual geographical location of Manora in the east coast of Tamil Nadu. Manora is a fort-like tower on the seashore built by the Maratha ruler Sarfoji of Thanjavur in 1814, apparently to commemorate the British advances against Napoleon Bonaparte. The name "Manora" is derived from the Persian term "minaret." Marungappallam is a village in the vicinity of Manora. The novel makes detailed reference to the geography of the coastal region. It is widely rumored that a treasure was buried near the Shiva temple on the outskirts of Marungappallam.

Velliambalam, the village strongman and landowner with considerable riches, is greedy and seeks to unearth the treasure for himself. The novel is centered around the idea of the treasure: gold and further untold riches buried somewhere in the sands around the Marungappallam temple. There is a cryptic code carved in stone in the temple, giving rise to wild speculations. The avaricious Velliambalam is desperate to secure the treasure. Mayandi alias Kumara Vadivu, a renunciate, is the antithesis. Though he is in possession of the secret of the location of the treasure etched in a tiny copper plate, he does not want to access the treasure for himself. He is still in a dilemma as to how to unearth the treasure and use it for common good. There is a village thug Murugappan who is also independently after the treasure.

The hero of the novel is one Durai. He is an orphan, an idealistic young man who runs a theater group. When he was performing in the high school where Parimalam, a woman from Marungappallam, studied, they fell in love. Parimalam is nevertheless worried that her father, Thandavan, a peasant of the village Marungappallam, would not let her marry Durai, who is an orphan. The lovers get ensnared in the treasure hunt due to several accidents. Thukaram, a dim-witted suitor of Parimalam, gets involved in this too. Murugappan, the thug, and a woman consort of Velliambalam get killed in the many intrigues of the plot. The murder charges are laid against Durai by a scheming Velliambalam.

The mendicant Mayandi alias Kumara Vadivu masterminds the situation in such a way that he gets the couple Durai and Parimalam married through the dictate of Velliambalam and finally hoodwinks the villainous landlord in the matter of the location of the treasure. In the climactic duel, Durai and his friends manage to overpower Velliambalam's henchmen. Velliambalam chases Mayandi to the seashore and shoots him as he tries to escape in a boat; however, finding himself pursued by police who witness the murder, Velliambalam ends it all by drowning himself in the sea.

There is a lengthy flashback separately recounted by Durai and Mayandi at the beginning and end of the novel, which finally reveal that they are father and son. Mayandi, who was Kumara Vadivu in his youth, married Thandavan's sister. He left with his wife to work in a tea plantation in Sri Lanka. Durai and his younger sister Thangam were born in Sri Lanka. Unfortunately, a white man, the owner of the tea estate, cast his lecherous eyes on Durai's mother. When he attempted to molest her, she gave him a fight and died in the scuffle. The white man, through his enormous influence, managed to convict Durai's father, Kumara Vadivu, for murdering his wife in a domestic quarrel. The orphaned children were brought to Marungappallam by another mendicant who used the girl child, Thangam, by lowering her into a well to fetch the copper plate with the secret of the treasure etched on it. The mendicant got the copper plate, but the child died in the process and got buried on the seashore. Durai, the male child, was a mute witness to the sordid event, hiding away from the evil man. He survived and, not knowing that his father was from the same place, grew up as an orphan. Kumara Vadivu in the meantime escaped from the prison and on not finding his children, came to Marungappallam in the guise of Mayandi, a mendicant. He managed to meet with the other evil mendicant in possession of the copper plate. The latter died, handing over the copper plate to Mayandi that contained the secret location of the treasure. When Durai recounts his background in the beginning of the novel, Mayandi realizes that Durai is his son but does not reveal his own true identity since he is a convict who escaped prison. Only before his final departure attenuated by the bullet from Velliambalam's gun does he leave a letter revealing the secret to Durai. Durai and Parimalam, as it turns out, are after all cross-cousins, ideally suited to wed each other. Thandavan is happy at the family reunion.

At the closure of the novel, Durai and Parimalam are once again alone on the seashore when the dead body of Velliambalam washes ashore. As they recognize who he is, they also find the precious copper plate coding the location of the treasure clutched in his hand. Durai plucks it and throws it away into the ocean. Durai finally proves to be a worthy son of Mayandi when he gets rid of the secret of the treasure forever. The real treasure is after all love in human relationships.

Modeling of Sociality in Fiction

If we take these two novels by Annadurai and Karunanidhi, written in the years they were immersed in intense political activity, as examples of DMK fiction, though not as representative samples, we can note a few significant elements. The foremost is, contrary to the general thrust of the Dravidian movement, the novels do not foreground the social contradiction between non-Brahmins and Brahmins. There are simply no Brahmin characters and there is not even a mention of Brahmins. The social space is fully modeled as a non-Brahmin space. The conflict in the novels is caused by the greed and avarice of the rich non-Brahmin merchants or landlords. Though the novels have a strong didactic tonality, the criticism against avarice of the rich is not merely moralistic; it is also about critiquing the preservation of the status quo. The status Dharmalingam as a rich merchant and Velliambalam as a landlord enjoy connotes a certain power and means to control the lives of others. In that sense, it is also restrictive of the free agency of the people around. What young, progressive-minded people like Parandaman, Nagasundaram, and Durai and his friends seek is to destabilize the status quo. One particular trope in which this destabilization is done is through love and the other is through friendship. In other words, the modeling in these fictional efforts were premised on solidarities outside the caste and kinship structures.

Another articulation is the subjection of women. The novels present articulate women who take destiny in their own hands. While the young girl Radha is portrayed as a contemporary woman, intelligent, assertive, and self-conscious, both Parimalam of *Puthaiyal* and Rangam of *Raṅkōṉ Rātā* are also self-reflective and assertive. They take crucial decisions in the scheme of plotting of action. There is a significant remark in *Raṅkōṉ Rātā* on the nature of conversations between men and women that is perceptive of the patriarchal power structure in which there is no social interaction between men and women. The narrator, Parandaman, remarks:

> Radha displayed whatever ideal characteristics I expected in a woman. Her skill for amiable conversation was far more than what I expected. In most houses there is no such thing as conversation. Either pointless chatter or angry

> outbursts fill the everyday routine of a family. Where does one find a family that has a relaxed conversation on various issues? Most particularly, there is never such conversation between men and women, between a son and his mother, between a brother and sister or between a husband and wife. They have a unidimensional relationship. If they start conversing it would only end up in a quarrel or unpleasantness. Since they do not know how to converse with each other, they are unable to do it. How could people with differing perspectives and inclinations discuss anything in common? Women and men are not able to strike a conversation beyond their roles and duties. They would not know what to talk and how to talk. Radha not only possessed this skill, she had cultivated conversation as an art … it was not merely a sweet chatter of a young girl; it had clarity and intelligence that made one feel it was worth the time … she had both sophistication and firmness in her articulations. (Pērariñar Aṇṇā 2005)

Interestingly, both the novels mention the staging of plays as the moment when the lovers came together. In *Raṅkōṉ Rātā*, Radha stages a play, narrating the mythological story of how Tara, the wife of Brihaspati, falls in love with Brihaspati's student Chandran. Radha makes it a self-conscious decision on the part of Tara since she could not find the kind of love with her pedantic and much older husband. Hence, she strongly felt that the love Chandran held for her should not go unrequited, deciding to reciprocate his love out of her own volition. Tara is shown to have no remorse or guilt in deciding to relate outside the wedlock even if it is considered inappropriate since, as a woman, she found her marriage unfulfilling. The play proved controversial among the audience but still it was productive in stimulating a discussion. Radha took the responses of the audience with equanimity and poise. In *Puthaiyal*, Parimalam meets Durai during the school annual fest when Durai's troupe was asked to perform a play based on the life of Nur Jahan and Jehangir. The novel does not say anything about what transpires in the play. The principal has a modern outlook and considers it proper to invite a play to be performed in the school. Regressive elements who don't like such innovations like having a play staged in the school festival contrive to sabotage the event by creating a ruckus. In the commotion that follows, Durai who had dressed up as Nur Jahan was stranded; Parimalam who was asked to be a volunteer takes him to be a woman. She escorts the actor to the safety of a classroom. They stay the night there to avoid troublemakers. Parimalam complements the actor on "her" looks. When she discovers that it is a male who performed as Nur Jahan, she is highly embarrassed but falls in love with the charming Durai.

The model of the society imagined in the novel is transformative. Performing plays is symptomatic of the transformation. Though there are elders who are open to change, it is the youth who are harbingers of self-reflection of society and its eventual transformation. It appears that the DMK leaders believed in the efficacy of fiction in offering such a transformative model of society. Since the intention was to reach to a subaltern audience, the novels are written as transparent narratives without much suggestion and ambiguity of characters that are considered marks of good literature. The novels are melodramatically plotted and didactically articulated. As already noted, there was competition in the constitution of the reading public and it is possible that the DMK, which was keen on working on the cultural front to counteract the overarching influence of Brahminic modeling of society, was keen to create other models of sociality through fiction. Though it is hard to imagine the spread of reading public of seventy years ago, there is no doubt that the frontline leaders of the DMK thought it was important for them to write fiction as well. Perhaps the power to imagine a model of society in fiction is taken as the will to imagine a society politically.

Notes

1. See the foreword written by Namakkal Ramalingam to the first edition of the novel reprinted in a recent edition (Ramalingam 2001, 9–10).
2. Parthasarathy delivered this talk in Tamil to be aired by All India Radio. A transcript was published in 1975 in the little magazine bearing the title *Kacaṭatapaṟa* (the letters of Tamil hard vowel-consonants strung together). We have a personal transcription copied from the magazine.
3. For a good discussion of this aspect of literary production and public sphere, see Pask (2004).
4. T. K. Kalapriya, one of the best modernist Tamil poets, shared on Facebook the image of the original list of gifts received and recorded at his sister's wedding in 1951. The list included several books (with cost and author details). He also sent images of the notebook recording the gifts through personal correspondence.
5. The novel has seen many editions since then. See Pēraṟiñar Aṇṇā (2005b).

MOBILIZATION

9 The Grassroots

The most remarkable part of the DMK history is the incredible energy that went into grassroots mobilization, which has remained so elusive to being captured gainfully by the theoretical or analytical lens. We have already noted in Chapter 2 the sacrificial figure of Kilapaluvur Chinnasamy as an exemplar of the spirit of self-immolation that Charles Taylor invokes in discussing the newer forms of the transcendental aspirations or moral dispositions in the age of modern political imaginary. However, such extreme acts of sacrifice should not distract us from the predominantly pragmatic and programmatic aspects of associational life, social mobility, and political empowerment that characterized the lives of hundreds of thousands of Dravida Munnetra Kazhagam (DMK) party workers at grassroots level all across the state in the eighteen-year period of our study. However, it is obviously impossible to condense qualitatively, let alone measure quantitatively, the myriad forms the grassroots mobilization assumed in the period, though this precisely is the most significant aspect of history. It should be possible to write an ethnographic account of the history of the organizational formation in a given place but that would demand a book-length narration.[1]

When that is the case, to pick from the extensive material of ethnographic accounts we mobilized from various locations in a short chapter like this is likely to render it purely anecdotal. For the sake of brevity, we opt to provide a synoptic overview as an extraction of salient features from all that material, ethnographic and archival, in which we will study the phenomenon under five distinct rubrics: *the historical backdrop*, *the new sociality*, *the organizational structure*, *fostering of political culture*, *the political insurmountable*, and finally a case study which would illustrate all of these.

The Historical Backdrop

It will be useful to conceptually segregate three distinct dimensions of the formations of the political to begin with: civil society organizational formations; discursive formations that include both ideational synthesis and diffuse articulations; and finally, popular uprisings, protest events of mass participation, organized agitations, electoral victories, and so on. It should be borne in mind that these three dimensions are not always welded together; it will often be difficult to ascribe causal relationships and strict correspondences between them, as Shahid Amin has convincingly shown in his abundantly illustrative account of the Chauri Chaura "event" in 1922 (Amin 1996). More importantly, it would be misleading to identify one for the other. We would like unambiguously to state at the outset that what we mean by grassroots mobilization is the extension of civil society organizational forms of the party among the "common people," infusing ideational synthesis as well as promoting diffuse articulations around the organizational forms, thereby creating scope for protest or electoral events of mass participation. *The party organization is like a metaphoric stirrer that would seek to infuse the ideational sedimentations into the actions of the masses but there are far too many factors that determine the levels of saturation.* In other words, when the primary act of extending organizational form among the people as the structure of a political party is accomplished, it becomes possible to harness the other two dimensions with far greater coherence than otherwise. Nevertheless, this perception has to be accompanied by the fact that the popular support gained for the party has always been in an arbitrary relationship to both organizational growth and ideational dissemination with a host of factors playing a role in the conjectural possibilities that allow for the staging of historical events, as we shall see in the following chapters. Hence, it is necessary to study each of these dimensions, of organizational growth, ideational dissemination, and popular manifestations, in their own respect without attempting an overarching explanatory framework. This is the necessary precaution we adopted as we found both Marguerite Ross Barnett's and Narendra Subramanian's detailed documentation of the DMK mobilization falling into many an interpretive pitfall, diminishing the critical yield of their otherwise useful inputs on the period we seek to study (Barnett 1976; Subramanian 2004). Our approach, as it should be obvious, starkly differs from theirs in the framework in which we seek to analyze mobilization; we will return to their works later.

The historical backdrop of the grassroots mobilization undertaken by the DMK should consist of two key aspects for the purposes of our account: one is the brief summation of the state of political economy during the period and the other a snapshot of the history of the political that preceded DMK mobilization. When we refer to Tamil Nadu in the context of historical backdrop in 1949, we only speak of the post-bifurcated linguistic state of Tamil Nadu (then called Madras) formed in 1956 and named so in 1967 after the DMK came to power, though in 1949 it still was the Madras Presidency of the colonial times. The putative state consisted of 30 million people in 1949; as is well known, it was predominantly an agrarian society with over 70 percent living in rural areas (Rukmani 1994). The literacy rate was a meagre 7 percent; the electricity generation in the state was a negligible 156 MW.[2] If we are to grasp the dimensions of transformation in the last seventy years, we need to note that the population today is 73 million with nearly 50 percent living in urban areas. The present literacy rate is 80 percent and the power generation is 32843 MW.[3] In short, a largely illiterate agrarian society of approximately 30 million people with the still-evolving standardized Tamil as language of mass mediation was ushered into democracy and universal adult franchise in post-independent India, which set the ground for DMK mobilization. The evolution of de-Sanskritized and non-colloquial Tamil of official and media usage today is a crucial part of the evolution of the DMK and its rule after 1967, a phenomenon that holds vast significance.

In terms of political mobilization, we should note that both the Congress and the Justice Party were largely civil society organizations with the rich and the learned not only constituting the party but also the electorate before independence. The Justice Party was in power under diarchy from 1920 to 1937 since the Congress did not participate in the elections directly. When the Congress decided to enter the electoral fray, the Justice Party, marked by considerable political lethargy of the rich and powerful top brass, was trounced under the anti-colonial sentiment that swept the limited electorate, adding to the considerable political clout the Congress had earned as a civil society organization negotiating for a free country with the British. The Justice Party never recovered from the blow; many middle-class aspirants in the party brought a large section under the leadership of Periyar E. V. Ramasamy, eventually forming the Dravidar Kazhagam (DK) in 1944.

When we consider discursive formations, the anti-colonial sentiment had a widespread popular appeal from the early decades of the twentieth century; for example, the memories of the Poligar wars were circulated as ballads in chapbooks and folk performances which formed the latent common sense about foreign domination, though the Congress was not particularly geared to mobilize it for building the organization. The reform programs like promotion of homespun khadi, anti-arrack, and Harijan upliftment gave some political thrust to the party amongst the people. The popular face of the Congress distinct from its Brahminic civil society formation, it was claimed, was primarily constituted by four non-Brahmin leaders: Pillai, Mudaliar, Naicker, and Naidu, the caste surnames standing for V. O. Chidambaram, V. Kalyanasundaram, E. V. Ramasamy and N. Varadharajulu respectively. Of these, E. V. Ramasamy was to become a major adversary of the Congress due to the failure of the Congress high command to accommodate the demand for communal reservation (the early form of compensatory discrimination introduced by the Justice Party). Varadharajulu was the one we encountered in Chapter 1 in the discussion of the seminal text by Annadurai, the *Aryan Allure,* wherein he was critiqued for his brief dalliance with the Hindu Mahasabha, Savarkar, and Moonje before fading into oblivion. V. O. Chidambaram died early in the 1930s with some noted sympathy for the non-Brahmin cause. V. Kalyanasundaram stayed away from electoral politics but endorsed the idea of Dravida Nadu in the early 1950s.

It was the estranged Congress leader Periyar E. V. Ramasamy who galvanized the anti-caste, non-Brahmin sentiments among the people through incessant propagation between 1925 and 1937. A network of non-Brahmin elite, scholars, traders, and landlords did lend their support to the work of Periyar and his Self-Respect Movement irrespective of the so-called "heretical" views of the movement and its iconoclastic leader. However, Periyar did not attempt to build a party organization, given his disinterest in both state power and civil society orientation of politics. He was keen on reaching out to the people at large à la Gandhi, whose populist orientation and reformist vision he admired when he was in the Congress. The diffusion of sentiments about abolition of caste and gender inequity, that is, the ideas of liberty and equality promoted by Periyar, superimposed itself on the diffuse anti-colonial sentiments. Several local patrons moved between the two formations, the Congress nationalist formation and the "Self-Respect Anti-Caste Non-Brahmin formation," with ease that included, for example, prominent civil society actors like R. K. Shanmugam Chettiar.[4] When the elected Congress government under the premiership of Rajagopalachari presented the historical opportunity of an anti-Hindi block to emerge in 1938, Periyar was the natural leader of the opposition, which led to the crystallization of separatist sentiments of the Dravidian plank.

C. N. Annadurai, a young, educated, lower-middle-class political aspirant in the Justice Party, had a firsthand experience of the political lethargy of the Justice Party elite. He naturally found Periyar's populist orientation and intensity for propagation extremely welcome. He wholeheartedly became the lieutenant of Periyar after the anti-Hindi struggle. When he became the co-architect of the DK with Periyar in 1944, he hoped to inaugurate and extend an organizational network gradually among the supporters of the DK. However, he was soon becoming dismayed with Periyar's lack of interest in nurturing a party organization with structural units and elected representatives. Annadurai also began to employ an ornamental rhetoric, promoting literature and art, particularly the drama stage, for purposes of propagation in marked contrast to Periyar. Much of the party structure of the DK was oriented to Annadurai as a result of his efforts to build an organization involving scores of youngsters. Periyar responded with his own ideas like the black shirt brigade, which seems to have struck a chord in creating a sense of belonging and identity among the followers, though Annadurai was not happy with such unilateral decisions of Periyar as the party president.

When their differences came to a head with Periyar's remarriage to find a reliable successor to lead the party, Annadurai tried to mobilize the nascent party organization to apply pressure on Periyar to desist from the course of action. However, Periyar, who only trusted his own judgement and banked only on his ability to propagate his thoughts and positions, hardly bothered about Annadurai's hold on the party structure that Annadurai had built. The crucial issue, as we already noted, was Periyar's apprehensions about and disdain for the "office seeking" culture in politics. This extended to a disregard and suspicion of organizational structure of the party, deliberative bodies, evolving consensus, appealing rhetoric, all of which appeared geared towards electoral participation, governance, and state-centered politics. More importantly, Periyar did not want to appeal to the common sense of the people; he wanted to challenge, provoke, and agonize people into forging *a critical sense*. As a result, he was not comfortable with employing affective and emotional tools of art and imagination, or ornamental rhetoric in speech. Periyar was conversational, blunt, and provocative in his speeches, though he invariably qualified most of his articulations with an appeal to critical scrutiny by the listeners. Likewise, he was not keen on evolving consensus within the party machinery or taking decisions through deliberations since this could be the first step in the direction of politics of consensus to which he was opposed. In other words, adapting the model of the civil society form in the organizational structure implied its readiness to assume state power and govern. Periyar was resolutely against moving in that direction even though he did not mind having a large number of followers who would share his spirit of agonism and dissemination of critical sense among the masses, using it to apply pressure on the state.

Annadurai, however, was dismayed how a demand for a separate republic can be made without organizational strength. The spirit of agonistic and radical articulation is fine, but without the embodiment in the form of an organizational structure based on the model of civil society associational life, how could people be rallied for the cause of demanding a nation-state for themselves? A mere demonstration of the conceptual validity of Dravida Nadu as a nation to be carved in the southern peninsular region of India would hardly be adequate to realize it in real terms. Frustrated initially with the political isolation of the Justice Party elite and subsequently with the "agonism as an end in itself" model of Periyar's avowedly power-distancing politics, Annadurai was pushed to leave with the nascent organizational structure he was building in the DK to found the DMK. At last, he was free to build a proper party organization to counter the Indian National Congress to achieve self-governance of Tamil non-Brahmins, the plebs, if not a sovereign nation-state. Hence, as could be seen from the extant archival material, an incredible channeling of subaltern energy to create a party organization followed the founding of the party. The rallying cry was to form the branches, form the district committees, and to hold district conferences to realize the dream of a grassroots party organization, like giving shape to a body that would have flesh, bones, sinews, and of course, muscle.

The New Sociality

A quick perusal of the advent of print culture in the late nineteenth and early twentieth centuries would go to show the slow and steady emergence of a new public marked by a different form of sociality that appeared to possess an eagerness to exceed the boundaries of caste. In other words, the need to create a sphere of social interaction beyond the confines of caste while personally people still organized their life as members of a given caste was the call for new sociality. There is a long list of social and cultural phenomena that contributed to and were strengthened by such forms of sociality beyond caste. While the new mode of governance and the introduction of a legal system called forth a public, the expansion of production processes and markets, augmentation of transportation and print, and introduction of gramophone and radio, all contributed to the shaping of the public sphere, which in turn brought about the sites of new sociality beyond the confines of caste.[5]

The participation in political activity by the commoner, first invited by the Congress and to some extent by the Justice Party, was further extended by the Self-Respect Movement. While the Congress had to resort to a clientelist model of mobilization, since it was mobilizing the rich civil society segment against the British rule, the Self-Respect Movement could emphatically appeal to the reasoning capacity of the commoner to question the mores and boundaries of the discriminatory and patriarchal caste society. While the Congress had to uphold the cultural forms of the nation, which it sought to reform in an incremental fashion in dialogue with the conservatives, the Self-Respect Movement could be unbounded in its criticism of the traditional values promoted by the Brahminical caste order. Hence, many who organized caste conferences of the non-Brahmin castes began to be attracted by the promise of collective action unmarked by caste against Brahminical caste order. Many caste associations invited Periyar to their conferences and listened patiently to his critical assessment of their attempts to gain greater status through refashioning their caste identity (Vī.em.es.Cupakuṇarājaṉ 2018). It is well known that Annadurai first met Periyar in the conference organized by his caste group of Senguntha Mudaliars. If we recall Annadurai's discussion of *paṟṟu*, in the context of associational life that we elaborately noted in Chapter 3, it would be easy to see how these caste associations perhaps slowly merged into the DK and the DMK as a federation of non-Brahmin castes seeking to rid society of the Brahminical caste order. In other words, the caste-based non-Brahmin interests and the desire for new non-caste-based social formations and emergent sociality coalesced to create the grassroots environment for the DMK.

While the core aspiration of the DMK was to transcend caste in its mobilization of the plebs as Dravidian–Tamil, it naturally had to operate within the social field of caste-based allegiances as well, in a society organized through rock-like striation and stratification of caste. We can conceptually list three categories of people who were available to and also saw the need for new forms of associational life transcending caste barriers, while these forms of associational life do not demand the liquidation of caste *tout court* immediately, a task that would have been unrealizable then as now. The first group would be those who worked and studied in educational institutions, primarily schools and colleges, with a definitive layer of citizenly disposition formed over the caste subjectivity. The second group consisted of merchants, professionals, workers, and service providers of new forms of commodities and lifestyle requirements, the last of which needs some parsing. For example, while in a village the people belonging to the washermen caste collected and delivered clothes to each household, the small towns and cities began to have laundries where people went to give their clothes for washing and ironing. The same was the case with barbers; the barber shop was the very epitome of new sociality where the service was paid in cash by individuals unlike the obligatory service rendered by the caste of barbers to the village community by visiting individual households. The reference to the barber shop as a site of dissemination of party news and ideas, of everyday gathering and of reading party newsletters and magazines is ubiquitous. Likewise, the tea shops, tailor shops, and cycle shops had no prior existence in the caste system, but just came about as sites of modernity. Alongside, the newfound mobility of goods through road and rail transport created several kinds of merchants, small-scale producers of commodities, and sellers in markets, many of whom provided their space as nodes for party activity. The third important category of people would be the artists of the drama stage and later cinema: writers, publishers, and the like whose nature of work was inalienably linked to the emergence of the new public unmarked by caste at least in so far as the activities related to their profession is concerned. They were united by their gift for art, writing, and creativity.

The idea of political empowerment through associational life in the party forum had an immense appeal to these segments of the common people, the educated class, the emergent networks and forms of material life, and the new modes of entertainment, media, and creative expressions. The DMK emerged out of these segments and naturally aspired to mobilize them as these segments expanded over the years. What sustained and galvanized the party at grassroots level was the very idea of empowerment, capacity to bargain for better stakes, and eventually a better standard of life in the immanence of social life as an assemblage of power. It was brought under the discursive canopy of the transcendental goals of social equity, formal equality, and political liberation of the putative collective identity through a democratic transformation, which provided the imagination and energy. If grassroots is to be understood in its own terms, it is necessary to see what political association made possible as personal gains in a comprehensive sense of betterment of life for the individuals who joined the party organization.

In our interviews with party workers and in the perusal of biographic narrations, there is always the allusion to the element of personal gain through association with the party. This needs to be understood as a composite part of social transformation rather than being dismissed as lack of altruism common sense ascribes, rather arbitrarily, to political work with the lofty idea of sacrificing personal good for common good. The forms of empowerment in casteist society are many which are not purely impersonal. Social and economic advancement of each individual mattered as forms of empowerment. Hence, the pragmatic and programmatic aspect of associational life in the extended spaces of civil society should be seen complementing the moral imaginary of the common good and sacrifices made for it. One particular small-town party supporter told us that after his arrest under the infamous Maintenance of Internal Security Act (MISA) during the state of national emergency declared by Indira Gandhi in the years 1975–1977, the party leadership insisted that he contest at least the local civic poll to become municipal chairman for a term. He also made it clear to us while he accepted and did become the municipal chairman, he did not want to profit from the position since he anyway had a thriving business. However, he obviously appeared gratified by the recognition for his selfless interest in party activity.

Extracting from various written accounts and oral narratives gathered, it can be gleaned that in the initial years, the richer non-Brahmin landowners obviously chose the Congress, which appeared to ensure status quo vis-à-vis the DMK articulating empowerment of the common man and the poor. The middle level and small landholders tended to sympathize with the DMK and lent support initially from outside the party organization, slowly joining in once electoral participation and success became a possibility. We have encountered in many small towns early party activists and functionaries who gradually got sidelined as further mobilization occurred, bringing more resourceful people into the fold of the party. Some of these now inactive early functionaries are of course unhappy about not having been recognized or not having gained much socially and economically through their involvement in the party even as compensation for the time and effort they put in. However, there are also many erstwhile activists who have gained some social ascendancy from their humble origins and economic advancement through the connections made possible by party work.

Irrespective of the variations in individual accounts, it is unmistakably clear that the party infused a social energy that paved the way for many a people of humble origin to rise up in the social structure through individual and collective effort. Having emerged from the widespread nascent sphere of new sociality, the DMK mobilization created a political vehicle that would advance the prospects of the common people individually and collectively. A dhobi here, a tailor there, a load man here, a bullock-cart driver there, all inspired by the idea of political participation and self-rule, collectively etching a mammoth story of social transformation in which they found their own life changing drastically, leading them to or giving access to corridors of power. In the drawing rooms or verandas where we would be seated when we visited the house of the erstwhile party activist, irrespective of the account of his engagement with the party, his levels of satisfaction or disappointment and present degree of estrangement or involvement, the walls were always adorned by the photographs of the party leaders, particularly the ones in which the activist is seen to stand beside the leaders like Annadurai and/or Karunanidhi, among others, and many other party paraphernalia.

The Organizational Structure

The DMK organization was conceived as an elaborate four-tier structure with a vision to build the party from the grassroots. The base consisted of branches; branches of a *taluk* constituted a circle; each revenue district had a district committee; the apex body was the general council, which elected the executive committee and the office-bearers at the state level. In spite of the fact that C. N. Annadurai and a group of other leaders were considered the ideologues or the brain of the organization, they deliberately and resolutely avoided a top-down model of organization building through nominations. The organizational structure was carved, and elections were conducted to fill various positions in all the tiers with utmost care and meticulousness, allowing for local-level leadership to emerge from among the basic members. In fact, all that was different about the politics of the DMK had everything to do with this empowerment of the grassroot structures, which metonymically represented the political empowerment of the commoner that the party aspired to bring into reality. Right from the outset, the party functionary at the local level was not necessarily the richest person in the area. In fact, most often, the functionaries of moderate means drew on the support of the marginally richer sympathizers and party members, since political work demanded the time that those involved in agriculture, commerce, and industry could not afford due to their occupational constraints. All that the party did was to make the local branch the primary node of the party, which led to the emergence of the party functionary or political aspirant from a moderate or humble background. Such a functionary could be the conduit for the effective distribution of political power within and gradually outside the organization.

When the party was launched, it initially formed a 133-member general council, sixteen-member executive council, a set of office-bearers and a few committees entrusted with specific tasks like propaganda, organization building, finance, and most importantly the drafting of the party constitution. C. N. Annadurai assumed the charges of the general secretary; the secretary of the propaganda committee was Era.Nedunchezhian; organizational secretary was N. V. Natarajan; drafting committee secretary was K. A. Mathiazhagan; and the finance committee secretary was Kanchi Manimozhiar. The constitution drafting committee consisted of E. V. K. Sampath, Era.Chezhian, P. Vanan, N. V. Natarajan, Era.Nedunchizhian, and K. A. Mathiazhagan (secretary). The drafts prepared were discussed in the general council meetings held at Chennai and Kancheepuram, were adopted at the general council meeting held at Madurai, and finally passed at the State Conference held in December 1951. A revising committee was formed on June 6, 1958, in the meeting of the central executive committee with N. V. Natarajan as secretary, and E. V. K. Sampath, M. Karunanidhi, Era.Chezhian, and V. P. Raman as members. The revised bylaws were presented to the executive committee, which met at Chidambaram on July 10, 1959, and was adopted in the general council meeting held at Mayavaram in the subsequent days. It is obvious that considerable thought went into the laws governing the organizational structure, which the party believed as its core strength.

Anyone aged eighteen and above who agrees to abide by the aims, principles, and rules of the party was eligible to become a member. They should not be members of other political parties or caste or religious associations. Only those with official identity cards issued by the party headquarters will be deemed as members. The initial subscription was 50 paise for three years. Of this, 25 paise would be retained by the branch and another 25 would be sent to the headquarters. The headquarters will retain 10 paise and give the district committee 10 paise and circle committee 5 paise. The percentage of fund distribution is illustrative of the party's grassroots vision. Fifty percent of the subscription is to be retained at the branch; the headquarters takes only 10 percent, the district committee 10 percent, and the circle 5 percent. The branch directly sends money to the headquarters; the headquarters distributes funds to the district and the circle. These factors go to show how central the local branch was as the basic unit in the imagination of the party.

A branch should have a minimum of twenty-five members. A branch is a territorial entity. A village, a small town hosting a *panchayat* union office, a larger town designated as *taluk* headquarters, or district headquarters, can only have one branch. Only a city with more than 50,000 people can have a branch in each ward of the municipality or corporation. A member can transfer the membership from one branch to another on application. A branch general body meeting should take place at least once in six months and executive meeting should take place at least once in two months. Branch members should elect ten to twenty members, depending on the size of the town, as the executive committee. From among the executive committee, it should elect a forum president, secretary, assistant secretary, treasurer, and a representative to the circle.

In every *taluk* with at least ten branches, a circle unit will be formed. The branch secretaries and the branch representatives will be the members of the circle general body. They should elect a fifteen-member executive council, including a forum president, secretary, assistant secretary, and a treasurer. The circle secretary will be the ex-officio member of the district council. The circle general body will also need to elect, apart from the circle secretary, five members to the district council. The circle will coordinate the activities of its branches.

A district council will be formed in each revenue district. The circle secretaries and the circle representatives will be the members of the district council. The district council will elect a forum president, district secretary, assistant secretary, and treasurer. The district secretary will be the ex-officio member of the party general council. The district council members will also elect ten representatives to the party general council (Chennai district will elect fifteen). The district office-bearers and the party general council members of the district can be any registered member in the branches of the district, which implies that they need not be members of the district council formed by those elected from the circles or even the branch executive committee. While the second and third tier derive from the base of the first tier of the local branches, there is also mobility and flexibility in terms of representation at the top level. A party general council member will be free to do the work for party headquarters while he is a member of a certain local branch. He will be free of responsibilities of the branch, of the circle, and even the district since he could straightaway become a general council member if the elected bodies in all these tiers chose him as the party general council member.

The party general council thus elected by all district councils will then elect the office-bearers, executive committee, governing council, and other requisite party functionaries. The elections were to be held every three years to elect office-bearers at all levels. The rules relating to the elections were also meticulously framed. The drafting and approval of the party constitution was in itself an exercise in self-governance. The party became a site of learning for party workers, the rudiments of representative and deliberative democracy. As we shall see, this paid rich dividends to the party in the years of its inception. The organizational skeleton was well-formed with fully lubricated and flexible joints.

Infusing Political Culture

When the party held its first district-level conference in the town of Trichy in January 1950 just a few months after the founding of the party, forty branches were formed in the district. It is likely that some of these branches were just renamed as the DMK branch from being the DK branch. However, new branches were also being formed with newfound vigor. By the time the party held its fourth district-level conference of Madurai district in Sholavandan by June 1950, eight months after the launch, 500 branches had been formed throughout the state. C. P. Sitrarasu, an ideologue, mentioned on that occasion that he travelled 2,000 miles on an average in a month to address various meetings, indicating the vibrancy of the fast-spreading party network. The special edition of *Dravida Nadu* on the first anniversary of the party had the following list as accomplishments in the first year of its existence.[6]

- Total number of members enrolled: 3,500 (the party launched a massive membership drive only after the state-level conference and the completion of inner party elections under the party constitution in 1952)

- Number of branches: 505
- Number of district units: 12
- Number of district conferences held: 7 (apart from a women's conference demanding amendments to the Hindu code of law and a conference on the growth of the Tamil language)
- Number of public meetings organized: 2,035

All the leaders expressed their excitement that the party had started taking roots, belying their anxiety at the moment of its founding and parting from Periyar Ramasamy.

It is possible to detect a great deal of autonomy in the initial years in the functioning of the branches, district committees, and the frontline leaders. A branch or a local-level functionary decided on what kind of public meeting is to be organized, choosing the theme and the speaker. Karaikudi Rama. Subbiah, belonging to an influential Chettiar family, provides a good instance in his memoirs of the movement years. He was an activist from the days of the Self-Respect Movement who decided to follow Annadurai, becoming a functionary in the DMK. Rajaji, who held the position of the last governor general of India, had come to Karaikudi to attend a festival organized by the Kamban Kazhagam in honor of the poet. He had said in his address on that occasion that the Ramayana, Mahabharata, and Bhagavata Purana are as essential and indispensable to the life and well-being of the people as plants needing sunlight for their survival.

The party members in Karaikudi were incensed by his exclusion of Tamil sources like Tirukkural, a great fount of wisdom and ethics. They suggested to Rama. Subbiah that they should conduct a meeting to protest this biased outlook of the governor general. When Subbiah thought of who he shall invite to speak on this issue, he felt Karunanidhi would be the appropriate person. He likens Karunanidhi to late Alagiri of the Self-Respect Movement who combined wit, passion, and simplicity in his speeches. Subbiah came to know that Karunanidhi and M. G. R. were coming to Madurai to appear in a promotional event for a film. Subbiah went to Madurai to ask Karunanidhi whether he would agree to speak on the issue. When he got the assent of the speaker, he sent information to party cadres in Karaikudi to go about organizing the meeting a couple of days later, saying that he would personally escort the speaker, Karunanidhi. The meeting was a success, which paved the way for the annual celebration of Tirukkural in the town in juxtaposition to Kamban festival. Many notable orators evolved from these exercises like Thirukkural Thenappan and Mudiyarasan.

In fact, in many towns not only were party branches formed but forums like Thirukkural Kazhagam were also formed. These forums conducted cultural activities in tandem with party activities. It was common to conduct workshops and seminars specifically to inculcate the art of public speaking called *coṟpayiṟci*, literally "training with words." It was left to the imagination and initiative of the local organizers to decide what kinds of forums they would form. There were places where Ambedkar Mandrams were formed. The incessant touring of the leaders was made possible with modest means of hospitality afforded by the cadres. Leaders often stayed in the houses of local activists and traveled in public transport or whatever was available locally, bullock carts, bicycles, and the like. The use of cars for touring places was resorted to sparingly in some cases, particularly after the electioneering phase by busy leaders like Karunanidhi. Alongside this operational flexibility, there was also organizational flexibility. The party innovatively responded to emergent situations. For example, when the handloom workers faced distress, the party took to selling handloom clothes in an organized campaign as against and similar to the Congress campaign for khadi in the 1920s and 1930s.

The party journals also published brief news on branch meetings and the resolutions passed there. For example, when police resorted to firing in Salem jail to suppress an allegedly communist-led agitation inside the jail, the *Dravida Nadu* reported the resolutions passed by several branches condemning the police excess.[7] However, each branch had a different set of resolutions apart from the one on the Salem firing. The news items give the names of persons who presided over the meeting and so on. The branches thus functioned as citizenship training forums as well. The party members not only learned the art of speaking but also began to style themselves differently in the way they dressed and presented themselves. An elderly member of the Communist Party in a small town told us, admiringly, that what attracted people to the DMK was a certain charm exuded by the distinct air and style adopted by the DMK party workers. Like the black-shirt-wearing members of the DK, the DMK also made a mark with their style of dressing. Such cultivations of social distinction and style, we learned in one particular case, even lead to a marriage arranged by parents between a Dalit young man and a backward caste woman. Of course, other factors like education and social status matched but it is still remarkable that the families that became connected through organizational work went to the extent of arranging an inter-caste alliance without the cause being love interest of the people who got married. This is just indicative of the infusion of political ideals in spaces of new sociality that we discussed earlier.

In fact, the party organized social reform conferences too apart from regular party conferences. In one such conference held at Tindivanam on May 20, 1951, for example, the following are the "noble reformers of the world" about whom the DMK leaders mentioned against each spoke: Socrates: Anbalagan; Mustafa Kamal Pasha: E. V. K. Sampath; Sun Yat Sen: N. V. Natarajan; Martin Luther: C. P. Sitrarasu; Abraham Lincoln: Era.Nedunchezhian; Voltaire: Kanchi Kalyanasundaram; Rajaram Mohan (surname Roy omitted): K. A. Mathiazhagan; Vemanna: N. S. Ilango; Rousseau: Ma. Ilanchezhian; and Narayana Guru: Manoharan. Apart from these special lectures, a long list of party leaders was also given who were also said to participate in the event. The conference, as is routine in other district conferences, would end with the play *Chandramohan*, which we discussed in Chapter 5, in which Annadurai would act along with the professional actor and party affiliate K. R. Ramasamy. The conference was ticketed at 10 rupees (donor), 5 rupees (delegate), 1 rupee (audience), and 50 paise for women. Most of the district conferences were also ticketed with the proceeds used to strengthen the district committee organizing the conference as the corpus fund.[8]

Apart from such efforts at dissemination through public meetings, conferences, and so on, the reading of a plethora of party journals run by various leaders also played a key role in infusing the political culture. A branch or cultural organization like the Thiruvalluvar forum will have a reading room where party journals and later newspapers would be available. It is usual for one person to read aloud with several others listening in. The more efficient ones would mimic the voice of Annadurai while reading an essay in epistolary form by him, giving the listeners the feel of listening to Annadurai himself. The journals also contained essays on many international personalities like Tolstoy, global affairs like the Korean War or the rebellion in Morocco, and political leaders of different counties like Ho Chi Minh. The DMK sought to make the political awakening a part of global history and universal humanism. They thought globally while they acted locally.

The Political Insurmountable

There are at least three major issues that appear to have daunted the party in this period: one is the lack of funds for mobilizational activities and propagation, second is the difficulty of overcoming caste prejudices, and the third is the inevitable issue of differences among frontline leaders. We will take a brief note of all the three as impediments created by the uneven social terrain in which mobilization was undertaken by the party.

The expenses of the meeting in which the party was launched at Robinson Park was met by contributions from the following: Annadurai: 1,000 rupees; Pethampalayam Palanisamy: 100 rupees; K. K. Neelamegam: 100 rupees; P. U. Shanmugam: 100 rupees; S. Needhi Manickam: 100 rupees; and Avudayappan: 51 rupees (Tirunāvukkaracu 2017, 1:350). Two-thirds of the expense was borne by Annadurai personally. The desire of the party to launch a daily newspaper with a stable run could not be easily realized for several years, though *Malai Mani* appeared intermittently as the party newspaper. The Annadurai-edited weekly organ, *Dravida Nadu*, was being run with such a skeletal staff that there was an announcement that due to the district-level conference at Trichy the journal for the week would not be released. There were constant efforts to raise funds for party headquarters, state-level conferences, to face cases filed against party activists, to pay penalties imposed by the courts, and so on. Raising funds for elections appeared a daunting task. The party resorted to staging plays with the announcement that the proceedings would go for such and such fund.

Gradually, once the network of branches was established in all districts, it was possible to request the district committees to organize fundraising drives. It was decided that for the first state-level conference to be held in December 1951, each district committee should collect 2,000 rupees, remitting 1,000 rupees in May and another 1,000 rupees in June. It is with a certain euphoria that Annadurai announces that about 1 lakh rupees[9] could be collected for the conference and for the purchase of a building to serve as the party headquarters called Anbagam. The conference ticket collection was 48,434 rupees. The donation from the district committees was 21,933 rupees. The fee collected for renting stalls at the conference was 3,700 rupees and in total it came to 74,067 rupees. The donation collected for the headquarters building was 25,300 rupees. It is by adding both that Annadurai speaks of 1 lakh rupees as the money donated by people for the party (Tirunāvukkaracu 2017, 1:455). In all these proud announcements of the success of fundraising campaigns, it could be seen how acutely the need for the party to fend for itself was felt, since it did not have the support base in the class of rich landlords, entrepreneurs, and professionals. It also did not have the support base in organized working classes like the Communist Party. The party had to rely on its skills of propagation and persuasion and hence every success in fundraising was celebrated with great joy and euphoria. The party repeatedly relied on writing and staging plays to raise funds through the ticket proceedings on various occasions. There were also regular advertisements for books and pamphlets authored by party leaders, both fiction and nonfiction. It is possible some personal income could be generated from the proceeds.

However, the resource crunch perhaps always provided the incentive to solicit at least people of moderate affluence to get involved in the party. Particularly when the party entered the electoral fray, it had to find candidates who could have some partial means to spend on the campaign. This necessarily resulted in certain tensions at the grassroots level between various stakeholders like the activist, ideologue, and persons with means to spend. As a party intending to mobilize a vast number of people initially into a mass movement and later seeking to win a popular mandate, the balance to be struck between various stakeholders remained a challenge as one could discern from various personal accounts. It is not possible to forget or ignore the necessary ingredient of need for funds when thinking of mobilization. As a corollary, gaining certain prominence in the party could either mean a capacity to spend or raise funds for expenditure. As a party trying to wrench power and also give thrust to a counter-hegemonic formation, working against the Indian National Congress that had captured state power, funds for party activity were indeed a major concern, which certainly had to be balanced with its pro-poor vision and orientation.

This aspect is also tied to the caste question. While the desire was to bring together all the non-Brahmin castes, the hierarchy separating the Dalits and other land-holding castes was not easy to surmount, particularly in the rural areas. The initial radical spirit earned the party the reputation of being a *Paraiyar Party* (Paraiyar being a Dalit caste) as testified by S. V. Rajadurai, a prominent left Periyarist intellectual (Es. Vi. Rājaturai 2018). This created some apprehension in the minds of the landholding, rich peasants who depended on farm labor by Dalit castes. While some accepted the need to come to terms with notions of equity and equality, there were many who could not associate with such a party mobilizing the untouchable castes. In an extreme instance, we find a report that two of the party activists belonging to landowning castes were beaten up by the members of the caste *panchayat* for going to the *cheri* (Dalit habitat) for party work.[10] One of them was tied to a pole and was beaten up for the transgression of defiling himself and thereby the caste by entering a *cheri*. A passerby rescued him and a complaint was filed with the police on the violence meted out to party activists. The news item ends by stating that the police promised to act.

In another oral account, a party activist recalled how an upper-caste landlord was shocked when he was addressed with the prefix *thozhar* (an equivalent of comrade or friend) by a speaker when he was on the dais for a public meeting. The speaker was from a Dalit caste. His entreaty was that while he wanted to support the party and work with others, it goes too far for him in everyday life to completely lose caste distinction by being publicly addressed as *thozhar* by a Dalit. While the situation varied from place to place, the difficulty on the ground was hard to surmount, particularly in the rural areas, to simultaneously mobilize both Dalits and the landed castes, due to the servile conditions imposed on the Dalits for ages. There is no detailed account of how far the party was able to handle this challenge, but it is not difficult to see that there was a concerted effort to bring Dalits into the fold. The reports of Ambedkar Kazhagams or Manram's as ancillary units of the party and reports of their holding meetings point to the participation of Dalits in party-building activities in the period we study. Among the frontline leaders, Sathiyavani Muthu and Ilamvazhuthi represented Dalit castes and were regular speakers in conferences. There have been district and circle secretaries from Dalit castes. As we already noted, the party had to bank on sections that became part of the new sociality to work against the bulwark of a caste stratified society.

The DMK successfully instituted inner-party elections to ensure internal democracy. Annadurai was keen to break from the tradition of a singular leader acting as a sovereign figure or party supremo. If Gandhi held sway over the Indian National Congress, Periyar acted as the unquestionable leader of the DK, which Annadurai felt was inimical to the spirit of organization-building. While party elections at the branch, circle, and district level appeared to have been successful, there was some difficulty in rotating the apex position of the general secretary. At the time of inception, Annadurai was the natural choice for the position since he was about to be the successor to Periyar in the DK. After the election of the first general council in 1952, Annadurai was elected unopposed to the position since the party was still in its infancy. However, since the idea was to rotate the post, certain tensions started building in the party as to who was to succeed Annadurai to the post or, in other words, who could be the second person in command of the party. It should have been obvious to anyone that Annadurai would still hold the steering wheel, but it was nevertheless important to see who commanded the number two position.

The rise of Karunanidhi as the most prominent leader next to Annadurai was not to the liking of many other leaders, most particularly E. V. K. Sampath. Sampath was Periyar's nephew and was anticipated to take over the reins of the DK itself as he was also the personal heir to Periyar's property since Periyar had no children of his own. Hence, his parting company with his uncle, following Annadurai by joining the DMK, was seen as a vindication of the position of those who departed from the DK. It was deemed as an act of sacrifice by Sampath. The affluent background and formal education set Sampath as a contrast to Karunanidhi who hailed from a humble background with no formal education. This was contravened by the incredible array of talent and the extraordinary vigor and passion Karunanidhi displayed in propagation and party activities. Karunanidhi surpassed Annadurai's success as a screenplay and dialogue writer in films. He also wrote plays for fundraising purposes and acted in them. He was successful as a fiction writer. His journal *Murasoli* was fast becoming the most widely read magazine among the cadres. His rapport with the cadres from all over the state was remarkable even at the early stage as could be gleaned from oral testimonies. He was a passionate, firebrand speaker, leading the party agitations from the forefront and changing the script of protest action at Kallakkudi by spontaneously deciding to lie down in front of the train, which dramatized the struggle in 1953. We will discuss this in the next chapter.

In spite of his formidable stature as party ideologue and thinker in his own right, Karunanidhi was perceived as representing the film fraternity within the party. The educated sections of the party were not happy with the attraction held by film people among the masses. This began early on as even the great thespian N. S. Krishnan, a popular comedian in the 1930s and 1940s who was a party aficionado, felt sidelined when the district conference was held in Nagercoil, his hometown. Karunanidhi records bringing about a rapprochement between him and Annadurai prior to the state-level conference, as a result of which N. S. Krishnan performed his folk musical event during the inaugural ceremony of the conference.

Though Sampath acted in Annadurai's plays, it does not appear that he ever took to writing fiction or plays. He came to represent a section of ideologues who wanted to maintain ideological purity against the corrupting influence of the affective forms of attraction through fiction, stage, and cinema. As these differences were getting sharpened, Nedunchezhian was chosen as the consensus candidate for the rotation of the general secretary position instead of the competing figures of Sampath and Karunanidhi. However, it was a matter of time before Sampath would engineer a split in the party, citing untenability of the demand for Dravida Nadu as the reason in 1961. He formed Tamil̲ Tēciya Kaṭci (literally, "Tamil Nationalist Party"), claiming the demand for a Tamil nation was more practical but soon merged with the Congress, betraying his actual orientation. Periyar was at that time a fervent supporter of the Kamaraj-led Congress government at the state level. Sampath's term as a member of parliament between 1957 and 1962 is also perhaps something that influenced his thinking during the period.[11]

It appears that the party gave up its illusions about rotating the apex position after the term served by Nedunchezhian. Annadurai occupied the position again, which he retained till his death; Karunanidhi became general secretary succeeding Annadurai and then moved on to become the first president, the position that was kept vacant for Periyar notionally. The party continued to hold elections for various tiers of party organization. But the position of the general secretary first and the president later in the 1970s became the preserve of a singular leader. It is possible even to speculate that such stability at the apex position enabled the leader to be the arbiter in all the power struggles in the lower tiers.

Observing that the phenomenal success story of grassroots mobilization by the party was still circumscribed by such insurmountable factors, we should now move on to an instructive case study written by Pannan, a Dalit activist of the party from Udumalpet in Coimbatore district, belonging to the caste of Pallar, now known as Devendra Kula Vellalar. Pannan's intention is to record memories of his relationship with his mentor, Udumalai Narayanan, a notable Dravidian activist who eventually became a member of parliament in 1967 and in 1971, terminated by his untimely death. While Pannan's admiration for Narayanan bordering on adulation is remarkable, our interest in the book comes from several insights it provides about the grassroots situation in the 1950s.

Politics and the Everyday: A Case Study of Grassroots Politics

Pannan's memoirs of the years of his association with Udumalai Narayanan, *Sixteen Years with Pa. Na* (*Pā. Nā. Vuṭan̲ Patin̲ār̲u Āṇṭukaḷ*) (2000), amply demonstrates grassroots political activity as something that sows the seeds of history in the everyday, mundane, and material life of the people. As Pannan clearly states in the preface, Narayanan was neither Tamil nor Dravidian by birth. He was initially known as Narayan Singh and belonged to Bundelkhandi Rajput stock that had migrated to Tamil Nadu. Annadurai, Pannan states, used to call him Udumalai Desingu, the Tamil elision of Tej Singh, who was a popular hero as Desingu Rajan in Tamil folk renditions, the ruler of Senji fort who sought independent dominion but was conquered by Sadatullah Khan of Arcot in the eighteenth century. Tej Singh of Senji, as said earlier, was also of Rajput lineage, whose forefathers must have migrated as a retainer in the Moghul or Maratha army. Narayanan was of a humble origin; he ran a cycle shop in Udumalpet town. A cycle shop usually rented cycles by the hour, mended cycles and cycle tires, including pumping air.

From Pannan's description, it does not appear that much income was generated by the shop as Pannan further celebrates Narayanan for displaying nobility in poverty. However, Narayanan was already a familiar name in the Dravidian movement even before the DMK was launched. A few months before the launch of the DMK, Narayanan was implicated in a case along with Periyar, K. A. Mathiazhagan, and others for defying ban orders. Pannan was studying in his final school year when Periyar and others were brought to the court adjacent to the school compound. Pannan, along with other students, jumped over the compound wall to get a close view of the revered leader. Later, while in college, Pannan became actively involved in organizing meetings for the DMK in the years 1950–1953. This continued after he took up the job of a Tamil teacher at Kangeyam in the years 1954 and 1955. Though he once met Narayanan as he came to address a meeting in Kangeyam, Pannan maintained a respectful distance from the speaker.

Pannan's contract with the school was not renewed in 1955 not only because he was actively involved in the DMK, opposing the Congress, but also because of his altercations with an arrogant principal of the school. The school was run by the district board and presided over by a Congress leader who had initially allowed Pannan's appointment as he was deemed a good teacher "in spite of" his DMK affiliation. Since the principal fell out with him, the DMK affiliation caused more consternation with the president of the board, resulting in Pannan losing the job. Pannan recollects that he had two personal resolves at that moment: not to work in a district board school again and to wipe out the Congress. As he was writing the exams at Coimbatore city to clear arrears of the English language papers that he had not passed in his Bachelor's degree, one of his relatives brought a letter to the examination center. It was an invite from Narayanan (hereafter Pa. Na) to come to Udumalpet to campaign for him in the municipal election. For Pannan, it was a call of destiny. Pa. Na was contesting in a ward where many of Pannan's relatives and those belonging to his caste lived. Pannan could no longer focus on writing the exam and left for Udumalpet the same evening. When he accosted Pa. Na the next morning in the cycle shop, the latter called him *pulavar*, the title denoting a Tamil scholar, which threw Pannan into raptures. Thus, began the relationship that shaped Pannan's life for the next sixteen years.

In spite of Pannan's campaigning with his kinsmen for Pa. Na, the result was negative since the Congress moneybags treated the voters to a meal and paid cash, extracting a promise to vote for the Congress. Pannan then decided to stay on with Pa. Na. After spending a few days sitting around in the cycle shop, one day he noticed a building across the street with a name board saying "The DMK Branch,

Udumalpet." But the wooden planks covering the entrance to the room were shut and the flag at the top of the flagpole in front of the building was torn. Pannan asked Pa. Na why the flag was in such a bad shape, to which Pa. Na suggestively replied that someone should take the onus to change it. At that time, an affluent supporter came by. Pa. Na asked for 5 rupees from him, sending his friend's driver to buy black and red cloth. He then beckoned an assistant from a tailor shop close by and asked him stich the flag forthwith. Once it was ready, he looked at the wonderstruck Pannan. Pannan realized that it was up to him to hoist the flag. So began his initiation into party work. Immediately, Pannan opened the room, lit a lamp, spread out a couple of mats, and threw in party newspapers and journals. When workers from nearby mills and factories paid a visit, Pa. Na directed them to go to the now-open branch office.

The branch had become dormant since a few people opposed to the rise of Pa. Na in the party became office-bearers, while many Executive Committee members were ardent supporters of Pa. Na. Instead of using the opportunity to build their own base, the elected office-bearers fell out with Pa. Na supporters and went inactive. Pannan's arrival and his involvement revitalized the branch. Pannan organized a public meeting by inviting Sathiyavani Muthu, a frontline Dalit leader. The elected branch office-bearers took offence with Pannan's independent initiatives; they decided to initiate disciplinary proceedings against him. However, the party headquarters had already decided to dissolve the branch executive committee citing dormancy and conflict. This gave Pannan a free hand to work under the guidance of Pa. Na to promote the party in Udumalpet. He also became a familiar figure after the public meeting addressed by Sathiyavani Muthu, which Pa. Na made him preside over.

What constituted Pannan's basic revitalization of the party was his everyday routine. Each day he would go around the town as if he were going somewhere on purpose, but the very purpose was to go around and meet people. If party members and sympathizers passed by, he would just greet them. If they stopped for a chat or invited him to have tea, he would oblige, discussing things with them. He would also pass by the narrow lanes and by-lanes; if he spotted the house of a party worker or sympathizer, he would stop by; if they extended hospitality, he would accept it. Pannan describes the party base in the following words: "Many party affiliates ran petty shops, cycle shops, tea shops, retail grocery shops, laundries, barber shops, milk shops and similar. Many others were working in handloom, textile mills, private commercial and industrial enterprises. Only a few were affluent" ("Kāviyap Pāvalar" Paṇṇaṉ 2020, 57). His daily sojourns in the town were such that there was hardly a household of a party worker where he had not had tea. He thus gained much proximity with the members and supporters of the party.

Next to this everyday routine, he also wanted to broad base the activities of the party. Common people in different parts of the town would not come to the branch office situated in one particular area. Hence, he initiated the formation of affiliate forums in different parts. He encouraged the forums to conduct public meetings in their areas. He would coordinate with them, facilitate, and guide them. This way residents in many parts of the town became familiar with the party's presence and its activities. The affiliate forums had reading rooms, where party journals were available. Teachers and government officials residing in those areas supported these efforts. At one point, Pannan asked all the party members to hoist the party flag in their houses; those who were in rented facilities where the owner would not allow it were asked to erect a flagpole in their street corner. About 400 flags were hoisted in Udumalpet town that year, 1956, on Pongal day.

Pannan was then inducted into the Kalasi workers (load men in the market) union. He streamlined the wages for loading and unloading different kinds of goods. Once the wages were negotiated and fixed, he distributed the table of agreed wages to all traders in the market. The load men then became a source of strength for party activities. His success with Kalasi workers led to his getting inducted into the mill workers' union, where again he streamlined the functioning of the unions against the Congress-backed and left unions. The growing profile of the party led to the induction of more upcoming businessmen and professionals, like the photo studio owner Manickam and a young Muslim lawyer, Sadiq Basha. Pannan and Pa. Na decided to hand over the positions of branch office-bearers to the newly inducted prominent people of the town. While Pa. Na had planned to become the district secretary, Pannan became fully immersed in the trade union activities, but also guided and coordinated party activities in Udumalpet.

E. V. K. Sampath who was the district secretary of Coimbatore district became a member of parliament in 1957. There was a contest for the position between Pa. Na and Kovai Chezhian, who was a classmate of Pannan in college and hailed from an affluent family of the dominant Gounder community. As Pa. Na easily won the election, having done the groundwork for years, a visibly upset Chezhian left the venue in a huff. Pa. Na asked Pannan to bring back Chezhian by reasoning with him about the election process. While Pannan went with much trepidation, he was able to convince Chezhian not to take the results personally. He could persuade Chezhian about Pa. Na's commitment and intentions and the need to work with him in the interest of the party. When he returned with Chezhian to the party office, Pa. Na was waiting to ask Pannan whether he would take the position of a general council member. Pannan inexplicably declined, suggesting the young lawyer Sadiq Basha for the position. This was the first of the three occasions on which Pannan declined important offers from the party in recognition of his party work. Sadiq Basha who was thus inducted into the general council was to later become a member of the Legislative Assembly, finance minister of the state, and the party treasurer of the DMK.

Pannan narrates a few instances in which his growing influence with the public, police, and government officials in the town is clearly demonstrated. Pa. Na fully backed him in all his decisions and actions, offering gentle course corrections.

However, the conflict between Kalasi workers and the merchants came to a head. Pannan concedes that some of the actions of the people of the Kalasi union were also excessive. The merchants, with the support of some prominent DMK members, demanded that the Kalasi union be disbanded. Pannan and Pa. Na suggested a more moderate response but the interlocuters were adamant. After the negotiation, Pa. Na asked Pannan to come with him to Chennai that evening after handing over the responsibilities of mill workers' trade union and the rest to the right kind of people. Thinking that Pa. Na was taking him on a break, Pannan did as he was told. It was only in the train later that evening that Pa. Na revealed he wanted Pannan to relocate to Madras to work with poet Kannadasan in his journal *Thenral*. Pannan was completely taken aback by this proposition; only then did Pa. Na share the stark situation in the town. Because of Pannan's work in the textile trade union, there were already forces seeking to eliminate him. Given his caste background, which Pannan only hints at, the considerable influence he had come to wield in the small town had irked many powerful people who were also inimical to the party. However, as the party was trying to induct more affluent people of the trading class, it was a risky situation that could cause grievous harm to someone like Pannan with uncompromising attitudes. Sensing the levels of enmity on the ground, Pa. Na had already asked a couple of Kalasi workers to offer shadow protection to Pannan without his knowledge. Pannan had in fact noticed those shadow guards but did not understand or bother much as to why they were around. In a certain sense, Pannan appeared to have outgrown his brief in the small town.

It took several years and many different assignments for Pannan in Chennai, like journalism, dialogue writing in films, full-time writing, and so on, before he could finally settle as a teacher in a reputed school in Chennai. Six months after his taking the job, Pa. Na paid him a visit to say that he himself and a few other friends were contesting in the 1967 elections. He asked Pannan whether he was willing to contest from the Dharapuram (reserved) constituency. Pannan, explaining that he had just begun a regular job with a good pay, entreated Pa. Na to make the decision for him. A deeply reflective Pa. Na just left with his entourage. The DMK made a landslide victory, with Pa. Na getting elected from the Pollachi parliamentary constituency. A few days after the results were declared, Pa. Na made an unannounced early morning visit to Pannan along with other freshly minted members of parliament and legislature. He cried out to Pannan as to why he declined the offer. Pannan politely pointed out that he did leave the decision to Pa. Na. Of course, Pa. Na acknowledged that he did not want to push Pannan into taking the risk since no one was sure of the outcome of the elections. He did not want to make life uncertain for Pannan once again.

Pannan regularly met Pa. Na on his visits to Madras. The DMK friends including Pa. Na helped out Pannan when he wanted to buy a house in Chennai with a generous contribution of funds. However, Pa. Na was no longer a happy person since there was mounting pressure from those who wanted to taste the spoils of power, including the persistent demands of his family. Pannan vaguely hints at certain weaknesses of Pa. Na as well that lead to a fast deterioration of his health.

Some of the influential leaders of the DMK in Coimbatore district once again suggested that Pannan contest for the Dharapuram assembly constituency in the 1971 elections. For the third time, Pannan firmly declined the offer. He does ruminate that he might have agreed had Pa. Na insisted on his contesting the election. It appears that Pa. Na had a certain regard for Pannan's Tamil scholarship as well as certain apprehensions about his inflexible attitude in politics, which perhaps did not allow Pa. Na to insist on Pannan's return to active politics. Soon after the elections in 1971, Pa. Na succumbed to illness, thereby attenuating any possibility of Pannan's return to politics in the absence of his mentor. There are two incidents that stand out in Pannan's narration that deserves attention.

Pa. Na was not just a mentor in politics but took full care of Pannan's well-being and pursuits. He would push him to send entries for literary competitions, he would train him on how to eat chicken properly, chewing the tender bones, and so on. However, there was an occasion when Pa. Na was disappointed that Pannan did not suffer injuries. Strange as it may sound, the context is very revealing. Due to the intense rivalry among the mill workers' trade unions, the majority unions launched an attack on a "gate meeting" organized by Pannan's union. They were raining stones from a distance on the gathering. Some of them were grievously hurt, while some of attackers were also hurt in the counterattack. Pa. Na who was touring elsewhere heard of this and returned to town to check on what happened. When he visited Pannan, Pa. Na asked whether he sustained injuries. Pannan happily told him that he had miraculously escaped from getting hurt even as people around him sustained injuries from the raining stones. Pa. Na looked upset, taking abrupt leave of Pannan. A much-perplexed Pannan later pondered about the speculation that since most of the leaders of oppositional trade unions belonged to Pannan's community, had Pannan been injured that might have drawn many of them to the Dravidian trade union. Pannan never thought much in terms of his caste identity, but he notes that Pa. Na did perhaps need to have such political calculations.

A more interesting anecdote, particularly considering the present status of party machinery, was a casual everyday occurrence. After he was elected as the district secretary, Pa. Na had to go to Coimbatore on some work at the district office. He asked Pannan to accompany him. They left in a bus in the morning. After finishing the work in the party office, they walked towards the railway station. A poor old man approached them on the pavement asking for alms. Pa. Na asked Pannan whether he had some money with him; Pannan just had a 25-paise coin with him, which he gave to the poor man. After a few steps ahead, Pa. Na asked him whether he would like to have some tea. Noting that he had parted with the only coin he had, Pannan asked Pa.

Na whether the latter carried some money. Pa. Na was shocked as he had assumed Pannan would have brought money. Realizing both were broke, Pa. Na then decided to go to a tea shop of a party member close by. Both were treated to *masal vadai* and tea. Pa. Na asked the owner whether he could part with 5 rupees. The owner of the tea shop was delighted to be of some assistance, extending two 5-rupee notes, asking whether that would suffice. Pa. Na answered in the affirmative, introducing Pannan to the tea shop owner, Pa. Gopal, who later became a member of the Legislative Assembly. What is even more remarkable is the way Pannan prefaces the anecdote with an explanation that in those days party functionaries did not have vehicles of their own so that people who read his account do not find the story unintelligible or incredible. Such is the chronicle of the relationship between Dhandapani alias Pannan and Narayan Singh alias Udumalai Narayanan alias Pa. Na.

Notes

1. For example, the party enthusiasts lead by Senthalai Gauthaman in Sulur have brought out a pamphlet chronicling the party history in the small town. They have also produced a history of the town in the twentieth century in terms of key cultural and political events and structural growth.
2. See for literacy, Office of the Registrar General and Census Commissioner, India (2011).
3. See for energy related statistics, "TEDA | Tamilnadu Energy Development Agency," Teda, http://teda.in/ (accessed June 26, 2020).
4. R. K. Shanmugam (1892–1953) hailed from Coimbatore. He was a founding member of the Justice Party and was also the first finance minister of independent India. He was a lawyer, economist, and politician. He served as *dewan* of Cochin Princely State from 1935–1941 and deputy president of the Central Legislative Assembly from 1934–1935.
5. See literature on this by scholars like Blackburn (2006), Hughes (2002) and Venkatachalapathy (2015).
6. *Dravida Nadu*, September 24, 1950, 2.
7. *Dravida Nadu*, February 19, 1950. Also see Ka Tirunāvukkaracu (2017, 1:366).
8. *Dravida Nadu*, May 13, 1951.
9. "Lakh" is a unit followed in the South Asian numbering system, where 1 lakh=100,000.
10. See news item in *Malai Mani*, July 9, 1951.
11. For finer details and an understanding of Sampath's political career, see his biography recently complied by Vivēkāṉantaṉ, Campat, and Kalpaṉātācaṉ (2013).

10 The Waves

When the Dravidar Kazhagam (DK), formed in 1944 under the leadership of Periyar and the stewardship of Annadurai, made a concerted effort to moot the demand for an independent south Indian republic to be known as Dravida Nadu, one question that had to be confronted was, if a plebiscite was to be held on the question, would people vote for the idea of Dravida Nadu? This naturally formed the corollary, whether there could be mass participation in protest action or agitation to press for Dravida Nadu. Annadurai realized that they were in no position to be assured of either. The origin of the Dravidian idea was a counter-hegemonic assertion against Brahminic and casteist hegemony. If the Justice Party elite who ruled the state under dyarchy were keen on ensuring that Brahmins did not monopolize power in the emerging state machinery and civil society, the Self-Respect Movement of Periyar was waging a battle on the turf of the common sense of the people against Brahminism and casteism, and patriarchy.[1] As we have repeatedly noted, it was only after the attempt to make Hindi learning compulsory in 1937 by the Congress ministry under Rajagopalachari did the threat of Brahmin hegemony transforming into north Indian hegemony become a palpable reality, in and through the political vehicle of the Congress party with leverage from fringe groups like the Hindu Mahasabha with the ideational content of Hindutva, as we noted in our reading of *Arya Mayai* (*Aryan Allure*) in the first chapter. Since the transformation from counter-hegemonic struggles and articulations to a demand for an independent Dravidian country was recent in origin, there was a long way to go to mobilize people towards that end. Annadurai was prescient in realizing that the idea of freedom, the desire to become a self-governing republic, that had spread in the process of the independence struggle that the Congress had led should now form the basis for the demand for an independent Dravidian country as well. He saw them as successive stages of history. This was in contrast with the still counter-hegemonic approach of Periyar, which made him declare August 15, 1947, as a day of mourning. Annadurai had to publicly disagree with Periyar to claim it as a day of celebration since it was the first step in achieving an independent Dravida Nadu. As we already noted, Annadurai was keen on construction of a people to achieve their self-governance, while Periyar placed a premium on counter-hegemonic propagation.

Subsequently, Periyar appeared invested in exposing what he thought was the chink in the armor of the Dravida Munnetra Kazhagam (DMK) in not taking up certain forms of struggles, displaying radical antagonism. One such moment that may serve as an example was Periyar's decision to burn the Indian national flag in 1955. Annadurai was piqued that Periyar was not coming forward to consult him to forge joint action of the Dravidian formations, while extending an indirect and open invitation after the form of struggle was decided. More than that, he did not think burning the national flag would be useful in winning over people's allegiance since many had developed warm sentiments about the new independent nation and its insignia (Tirunāvukkaracu 2017, 2:815). He wrote that the DMK was interested in convincing and winning the minds of Congress men and Congress supporters, who he termed as "Congress Dravidians" for the cause of the independent Dravidian nation. Such acts of desecration of national emblems might alienate them from the genuine political aspiration of the DMK. Periyar did succeed in making the DMK appear tame, but Annadurai was not afraid of facing the charge, relying on his strength to reason with party cadres and followers. He categorically asserted that they, the DMK, were an independent party and they had their own modes of agitation; after all, they had displayed sufficient capacity for facing state repression since the founding of the party. Earlier, Periyar also organized an agitation, breaking idols of Ganesha—of course, the idols were made specifically for the purpose and were not the ones worshiped in any temple. Again, not wanting to alienate the pious, Annadurai distanced the DMK from such iconoclasm. He famously quipped that he would neither break coconuts in front of Ganesha (a routine offering) nor break the idol of Ganesha. However, Periyar's actions seemingly did apply some pressure on the DMK to match up in terms of oppositional politics to the Indian state. Interestingly, Periyar had extended support to Congress Chief Minister Kamaraj who had assumed office in 1954 saying that it was the rule of a pure Tamil.

While Annadurai's consensus-building approach contrasted with Periyar's agonistic approach, both placed the emergent post-colonial state in a quandary as to how to deal with them. As much as Annadurai posited that the DMK has now taken on the role of the Congress in Tamil Nadu to work for an independent Dravida Nadu, the Congress did inherit the colonial state. It was unclear to the rulers and administrators how to deal with these peaceful, symbolic agitations that was reminiscent of their own anti-colonial struggle. More than Periyar, who was anyway not interested in governance, Annadurai appeared to enjoy every moment of serving the Congress rulers with their own recipe. Day after day, the frontline leaders of the DMK relentlessly pointed out the similarity of approach of the colonial state and the now independent Indian state when it came to matters of governance and grievance redressal. In such a context, the work of the DMK became the remainder of the freedom struggle waged with British imperialism now replaced by north Indian imperialism. The government obliged the DMK with knee-jerk reactions, curtailment of civil rights, unwarranted measures of repression, thereby walking with eyes wide open into the role of the dictator or oppressor cast for them by the DMK.

Annadurai still had to cautiously weigh the repercussions for the mobilizational efforts of the nascent party structure in undertaking protest action. Hence, the strategy was to build a grandiose rhetoric about valor, sacrifice, and honor on part of the party cadres, and of the brutal, reprehensible acts of suppression on the part of the government, even when a limited confrontation took place. It is to the credit of the inexperienced state actors that such a strategy paid rich dividends to boost the morale of the fledgling party as an oppositional force. The new nation was so desperate for consensus that even minor acts of dissension appeared like "treason," the much-brandished charge in colonial governance. We will quickly capture some of the salient features of these waves of protest action that helped the party substantiate its rhetoric of liberation struggle in three parts: the protests and confrontations of the initial years, the famed three-front agitation of 1953, and protests of the later years. We will reserve the massive anti-Hindi uprising of 1965 for the following chapter.

The Protest Actions of the Early Years

The first year after the party's inception, September 1949 to August 1950, almost passed off in forming the branches and organizing district conferences. There were several provocations against which the party articulated opposition along with others like renewed attempt to introduce compulsory Hindi in schools, the implementation of judgements against "Communal GO" (government order), the nomenclature used for the early system of reservation or compensatory discrimination. The party did not call for any agitation to reinstate the communal GO but appeared to have organized or supported student protests. Eventually, protests from various quarters led to the requisite constitutional amendment to legalize reservations. Attempts to impose Hindi teaching in schools were also repelled without the party directly launching any protest action. However, there were a slew of cases against publication of propaganda tracts and books by the party activists. One of the first instances of provocation by the state was the arrest of two party activists, A. V. P. Asaithambi and Thuraiyur Thangavel Kaliaperumal, on July 21, 1950, for publishing books titled *Gandhiyar Santhiyadaiya* (Appeasing Gandhi) and *Azhiyattum Dravidam* (May Dravidam Be Destroyed) respectively.[2] Immediately bail was moved, but before the court order could reach the prison, the weekend ensued. In spite of being informed orally of the granting of bail, the jail authorities decided to tonsure the heads of the remanded prisoners as if they had been convicted. This vengeful attitude of the authorities triggered much anger among the cadres. *Dravida Nadu*, the party journal, published the pictures of the tonsured young men. A slew of cases against journals and publications followed, obviously trying to intimidate the DMK in their articulation of dissent. In many instances, the cases were foisted on publications from many years ago. The most significant of such cases was of course the banning of the *Aryan Allure* by Annadurai, which was published in 1943. We will return to this case soon.

As there have been sufficient provocations as listed above, the party felt compelled to launch some form of protest action on a sustained basis. While there were concerns about the ability of the nascent formation to undertake such a task, some testing of waters was necessary if the party was to stall further repressive measures from the government. In many instances, the party had to raise funds to face legal action against writers and publishers; such a situation, if it continued to prevail, was likely to cause much stress on the activists. It is possible that the party felt that it had to mount some form of counterattack. In its seventh district-level conference held at Kovilpatti in August 1950, the party executive brainstormed about forms of protest action.[3] One idea was to erase names written in Hindi at railway stations and other Union government facilities; this was sporadically carried out on many different occasions with varying degrees of local initiative since then. A proper call was reissued in the general council meeting held on July 2, 1952, on the elaborate modus operandi of how to carry out this struggle of erasing Hindi letters at railway stations and post offices on August 1, 1952 (Tirunāvukkaracu 2017, 1:494–497). This was peaceful, methodical, and was widely participated in most cities and towns.

The other novel idea mooted by the Kovilpatti executive was to travel in trains without buying tickets; if arrested on checking, either serve a prison term declaring the act of ticketless travel as protest action, or pay the fine in the court, which then would only go to the state government and not to the centrally administered railways. There is no evidence to the effective launch of this form of action, though Pannan reports that his friend and mentor Udumalai Narayanan practiced this.

However, the most significant form of action that was properly called for with full emphasis was the idea of holding black flag demonstrations whenever any Union minister visited the state with the rallying cry demanding them to "go back" (*tirumpi pō*). The idea was to protest on all those issues of affront caused by the actions and inaction of the Congress governments at the state and the Center (Tirunāvukkaracu 2017, 1:376). These black flag demonstrations were carried out to considerable effect and were in fact the first wave of protest action initiated by the DMK within a year of its founding.

The first such demonstration took place when Information and Broadcasting Minister R. R. Diwakar visited Chennai on September 9, 1950. Being the first such event, many frontline leaders came to the Hindi Prachar Sabha in Chennai where

Diwakar was to participate in the graduation ceremony. It appears that there was some attempt to avert the minister confronting the demonstrators by advancing the function an hour earlier but the DMK volunteers had gathered on the spot several hours before. Diwakar did happen to see the flood of black flags; some of the demonstrators presented him with black flags as well. Those who could not reach the venue by that time went to his next event and waited to wave black flags at him. In the photograph published in the subsequent *Dravida Nadu* issue, there was a prominent display of a placard saying in English "Go Back Diwakar" held by the demonstrators. While this demonstration was both peaceful and successful, subsequent demonstrations were beginning to be met with police repression, preventive arrests, lathi charges, and so on. The confrontation was most severe when Rajaji, who had joined the Union ministry after being demoted from the office of the governor general, visited the state. A scholar activist of the party, Ka. Appadurai sustained serious injuries in Chennai while participating in a black flag demonstration against Rajaji (Tirunāvukkaracu 2017, 1:378–379). A couple of anecdotes would serve to illustrate the panic mode in which the government handled such demonstrations.

The first anecdote is narrated by Pannan, whose memoirs we discussed in the previous chapter. This incident happened in 1954 by which time Rajaji had become the chief minister of the state. Pannan, an active student leader of the DMK, was studying at a college in Coimbatore. Rajaji was coming to Coimbatore to lay the foundation stone for a dam to be constructed on the river Amaravati. The previous night a police official in the intelligence wing who knew Pannan well since he had worked with Pannan's elder brother, who was also in the police, paid a surprise visit to Pannan's hostel room. He was just enquiring after Pannan's well-being for a while. When he prepared to leave, he asked Pannan to step out with him. Then he asked Pannan whether the students had planned to hold a black flag demonstration. When Pannan told him that there was no such plan, the official still insisted that Pannan spend the night with him in the latter's house so that he did not get to organize any such activity. It was only after a solemn promise from Pannan that he would not step out of his hostel room at all that the police official let him go. In fact, the idea was to place Pannan, a student leader, under preventive arrest to avert any black flag demonstration. Since the police official knew Pannan's family, he decided to personally keep an eye on Pannan instead of arresting him. The whole situation apparently arose because of some policemen overhearing a couple of students casually remarking that they should hold a black flag demonstration to protest Rajaji's visit while actually there was no such plan at all at the organizational level (Paṇṇaṉ 2020, 100–102).

We should recall that the black flag demonstrations were reserved only for ministers of the Union government in the years 1950–1951. It was only because Rajaji had joined the Union ministry that he was being given the same treatment, in spite of hailing from Tamil Nadu. The second, far more significant anecdote related to the black flag demonstrations can be read in Karunanidhi's memoirs titled *Nenjukku Needhi* (Fair to the Heart) (Karunanidhi 2019, 1:173–176). In fact, it was Karunanidhi, presiding over the Tirunelveli district conference at Kovilpatti, who had insisted on some programmatic protest action, which resulted in the idea of black flag demonstrations against Union ministers. Hence, when Rajaji planned to visit Thiruvaiyaru in Thanjavur district to which Karunanidhi belonged, he suggested to Annadurai that a black flag demonstration should be held there as well. The senior party leader K. K. Neelamegam was hesitant. Thanjavur district was still a stronghold of Periyar's DK on the one hand, and the Congress on the other. The communists, banned at that time, had a presence too. The DMK was yet to consolidate its base there. Hence, Neelamegam was hesitant. He consented to the demonstration on the condition that Karunanidhi would take charge of a month-long mobilizational activity to make the demonstration a success. Having agreed to the idea, Karunanidhi set on a relentless, nonstop propaganda in the villages of the district about the need for the black flag demonstration, inviting people to participate. Slowly they became confident that the demonstration would be a success. On the day before Rajaji's visit, Karunanidhi, with a few other activists, was going to Thanjavur by train. As the train approached Thanjavur station, Karunanidhi realized that the police were waiting to arrest them on the platform. He removed his shirt, wrapped a towel around his head like a villager, got off the train on the other side of the platform on to the tracks, and walked along the railway track for a kilometer, eventually reaching a friend's place in Karanthai. The police, surprised by his absence among the group that arrived, arrested the rest. They sent a special team to search for him in all the likely places in the town with the aid of a party worker who finally expressed his inability to locate Karunanidhi for them. The next morning Karunanidhi avoided riding any vehicle through the main fares, knowing that the police would be on the lookout, and took to walking through alleys and fields to reach the place where the demonstration had been planned on the route Rajaji was to take. When he appeared among the demonstrators at the last moment, the police were unable to arrest him. The demonstration was peaceful and effective. The demonstrators then marched in a procession to the railway station. Once he boarded the train, Karunanidhi contracted a high fever due to the exhaustion resulting from the intensity of the month-long mobilizational activity. Scarcely would have he imagined that twenty-two years later he would be the chief minister of the state when Rajaji would be laid to rest.

The extraordinary efforts the police took to prevent black flag demonstrations went to enhance the symbolic value of the act that the DMK desired it to have. The lore of the preventive arrests and such strategies as Karunanidhi's to evade them made heroes out of the party activists in the eyes of the public. The government was also refusing permission for public meetings to be held by the party, imposing regulatory orders under Rule 144. It was then decided by the party that they should violate the orders to hold the meetings. In a place called Kundrathur on the outskirts of Madras, the party was planning to hold a meeting to condemn the proscriptions imposed on party publications and the cases foisted on the writers. The government kept refusing permission; when the party finally decided to go ahead with the meeting on October 26, 1950, in spite of the imposition of 144 ban orders, the police opened fire on the crowd. A report in the *Dravida Nadu* claims that seven rounds were fired. Three party workers sustained bullet injuries. The leaders who were to speak in the meeting, about fifteen in all, were arrested and charged with breaking of the law and order. Scores suffered injuries in the lathi charge. Police broke into the houses of party volunteers who hosted outsiders coming to attend the meeting. Such an excess naturally called for the iteration of the constant theme of the metamorphosis of the erstwhile freedom fighters into oppressors. In reporting on the Kundrathur incident, the *Dravida Nadu* recalled Jallianwala Bagh and Kumaran of Tiruppur, who died sustaining injuries from a police lathi charge during the freedom struggle, saying that history is being repeated with the Congress in power this time.

Karunanidhi wrote a play *Vethanaik Kural* (Voice of Anguish) to raise funds towards the legal expenses to fight the cases filed against the organizers of the Kundrathur meeting. He also acted in the play along with several leading party activists like Kannadasan (who was to become a much-celebrated lyricist of film songs later), Arangannal, Thillai Villalan, and so on. The play was performed in Wallahjahbad, close to Kundrathur. Two-thirds of the proceeds of the play went to the corpus fund to meet the legal expenses of the Kundrathur detainees and the rest to the district committee which organized the performance.[4]

There were locally initiated protest actions everywhere. This included organizing meetings defying ban orders, erasing Hindi from nameboards in railway stations, and removing caste names in commercial outlets like hotels (particularly the Brahmin tag to coffee houses that were considered prestigious). The *Dravida Nadu* issue dated October 8, 1950, for instance, gives a list of names of towns where these activities took place, congratulating the resolve with which these activities were carried out peacefully.

In the meantime, the case against the *Aryan Allure* reached its final stage. Annadurai was convicted and the book was banned from circulation on September 9, 1950. He was asked to pay a fine of 700 rupees or face imprisonment for six months. Annadurai, of course, decided to court arrest. The government decided to release him after ten days fearing widespread unrest. However, they confiscated several bundles of newsprint he had purchased to start a daily in lieu of the fine of 700 rupees imposed on him (Tirunāvukkaracu 2017, 1:408). Annadurai wrote a scathing editorial questioning the logic of the punishment meted out to him. The tract in question, *Aryan Allure*, was published in 1943, had sold about 15,000 copies approximately and had been widely discussed and internalized by thousands who constantly referred to it in speeches. What purpose does it serve to sue the author and publisher so late and ban the circulation of the book that had already been well circulated?

However, such inexplicable action on the part of the government gave scope for an innovative form of protest. The North Arcot district committee decided that they would hold public reading sessions of the *Aryan Allure* in street corners. From every town, they informed the district collector a week ahead about their intention to perform the public reading of the book in a chosen place, mostly a specific street corner. The activist-reader went to the place at the announced time, held the book in his hand, shouting "Arya Mayai" a few times and read the whole book aloud to all those who gathered. This public act of defiance created a sensation while the district administration watched helplessly. The event was held in 105 towns; the list of names of the activists and the towns were later published in the *Dravida Nadu*. We note that the activist who performed this act of defiant reading in Wallahjahbad was called Irraniya Dasan, Irraniyan being the name of the *asura* Hiranya in Sanskrit, as we noted in Chapter 7.

There is another interesting minor episode connected with the arrest of Annadurai for writing the *Aryan Allure,* which allows us to imagine the reaction to state repression among the party cadre. This narration is part of the memoirs of Rama Subbiah of Karaikudi we had occasion to refer to in the previous chapter in giving an instance for local initiatives in organizing party events, when he invited Karunanidhi to critique Rajaji's exclusion of Thirukkural as a text foundational to Indian civilization. Subbiah was involved in organizing the first district-level conference of Ramanathapuram district. He had chosen, after consultations, Sivagangai as the venue for the conference. He had printed tickets and donor receipts to mobilize funds. All the frontline leaders were to participate in the conference as was the case with other district conferences held so far. Of course, what was crucial was the presence of the general secretary and founder of the party, Annadurai. Since Annadurai was arrested just before the conference, there was widespread anxiety about the success of the conference. Rama Subbiah wanted to discuss with Annadurai but thought they would not permit him to see the leader in custody. He decided to disguise himself as the lawyer's assistant to go to the prison. As long as the jail superintendent was present, Annadurai discussed the legal aspects of the case with the lawyer. Once the jailor stepped out of the room, he could not contain his laughter at Rama Subbiah's attempt to disguise himself as the lawyer's assistant. The anxious Subbiah asked him how to go about the conference. Annadurai told him to go ahead with the preparations since he was likely to be set free before the conference. He was indeed freed two days before the conference. Rama Subbiah and other organizers distributed pamphlets everywhere that Annadurai would attend the conference and also act in a play. Crowds thronged to the venue on the conference day to listen to Annadurai's emotionally charged speech. Such were the occasions, says Rama Subbiah, that consolidated the movement among the people.

Apart from the insecurities of the newly formed post-colonial government, it appears that the Congress party workers were not tolerant of the dissension as well. Many people, activists, and sympathizers of the DMK have reported the hostile activities of the Congressmen, like causing disruptions in the meetings, attacking speakers and organizers, and so on. One such occasion was the DMK meeting organized in Theni where Nedunchezhian was invited to speak in 1950. One of the local Congress leaders and his men were intent on disrupting the meeting. Apparently, the police asked the DMK organizers to bring forward the meeting to 3 p.m. Congress workers still launched a severe attack with sticks and sickles, which had the crowd gathered run in panic. They demolished the stage, trying to throw a big stone at the guest speaker, Nedunchezhian, which might have killed him or caused grievous harm. Luckily, he was saved by the local organizers and the police. The police personnel who charged at the attackers were later suspended by the government. This further infuriated the DMK and its sympathizers. The DMK again collected funds to file a case against the offenders and the government, which finally reinstated the police personnel and imposed fines on the violent Congressmen. In short, the confrontations with the government and the Congress party were leading to trials, and there was a constant need to raise funds to defend party workers or secure justice. These experiences prepared the party for a major event in July 1953 that was to go down in history as the Three-Front Struggle.

Three-Front Struggle: July 1953

After the first general elections held in 1952 for the united Madras province, in which the DMK did not participate, the Congress cobbled up a majority by inducting Rajaji who did not contest the elections as the chief minister in an awkward extra constitutional maneuver. It was only a year later that Andhra Pradesh was formed as a state to be followed by a country-wide re-organization of states on the basis of language. Even before the partition of Andhra Pradesh, Rajaji felt compelled to initiate a measure in elementary education that provoked a storm. Officially known as Modified Scheme of Elementary Education, or Madras Scheme of Elementary Education, the scheme, introduced in 35,000 schools in different districts of the state, provided for education at the school in the forenoon and vocational training at home, in whatever profession the parents were engaged in, in the afternoon. According to Anandhi, "This new education scheme, Rajaji claimed, was modelled on the ideals of basic education formulated by Gandhi as the Wardha Scheme (1936) and later as *Nai Talim*. The central feature of this scheme was to teach children spinning, handicraft, agriculture, weaving and so on with the idea of productive manual work which could self-sustain the expenditure on school education by meeting the salary of the teachers and so on" (Anandhi 2018). However, the difference in the implementation by the Rajaji government happened to be that the child had no other option than to learn the caste-based occupation of the father since the primary schools could not afford a range of craft practitioners needed to give options to the children. Rajaji was aware of this as he had said: "… the shoes are stitched, the scavenging is done, the cart-wheels and the ploughs are built and repaired, because thank God, the respective castes are still there and the homes are homes as well as trade schools … children are automatically apprenticed" (Anandhi 2018). As can be expected, this infuriated the DK and the DMK as well as many in the Congress as it appeared to perpetuate caste-based occupation, which was hoped to be replaced by individual choice of vocation through universal education. The scheme was dubbed as *Kulakalvi Thittam* (Education in Caste Occupation). The DMK decided to launch a protest by gheraoing the chief minister's residence in Habibullah Road in Chennai. This was the first front of the concerted three-front struggle (Tirunāvukkaracu 2017, 1: 558).

Another major provocation came from Prime Minister Nehru himself. When asked about the DK and DMK efforts to erase Hindi letters from signboards of railways, post offices, and the like, he had quipped, calling the action "Nonsense." The DMK naturally took this as an insult to their most serious concerns about Hindi imperialism. Hence, they proposed to block trains all over the state on a given day as symbolic protest against Nehru's dismissive and arrogant attitude. This was the second front.

A cement factory was started in a place between Lalgudi and Ariyalur in Trichy district by the Dalmia group. They named the factory township Dalmiapuram and the railway station on the Trichy–Madras route was also called Dalmiapuram station as against Kallakudi, the original name of the village. The renaming of a Tamil village with the name of a north Indian industrialist was seen to be a demonstration of north Indian imperialism, which was the mainstay of the critique of the Indian nation forged by DMK politics, as we may recall from our discussion of Annadurai's *The Garden of Money (Panathottam)* in Chapter 4. In the second Trichy district conference held at Lalgudi on April 23–24, 1953, a resolution was passed to carry out protest action to demand changing the name of the railway station. Karunanidhi was nominated as in charge of the protest. This was to be the third front of the struggle.

While the three-front struggle was planned in April itself, with Annadurai announcing it on April 28 in the meeting held to conclude fundraising efforts for cyclone relief, the dates were set for mid-July. The gheraoing of the chief minister's house was to begin on July 13, the blocking of trains all over the state was to take place on July 15, and the overwriting on Dalmiapuram railway station nameboard with its original name Kallakudi was to also take place on July 15. The party elaborately campaigned and prepared the cadres and people before the struggle. In the event the party executive met on July 13 at Chennai, which decided to gherao the CM's residence the next day. E. V. K. Sampath was to lead this action. However, by the time the meeting concluded, the police swooped in to arrest five of the frontline leaders present—Annadurai, E. V. K. Sampath, Mathiazhagan, Nedunchezhian, and N. V. Natarajan. The media began calling them the "Five Big Leaders" (*aimperum thalaivargal*) allegedly after the fashion of Lenin and five other comrades being called the Big Six in the American press during the Russian Revolution. The five leaders were placed under preventive arrest and charged with conspiring to disturb peace by planning agitations. Annadurai personally defended their actions in the court, heroically claiming that it was their democratic right as the elected government refused to listen to their views. They were sentenced with two months of imprisonment.

About 3,000 people were arrested throughout the state on July 15 in trying to stop trains with instances of police lathi charge and firing in Thoothukudi. A case was foisted on party activists in Thoothukudi with far more severe charges that included a plan to attack Brahmin residential quarters known as Agraharam. The party once again had to raise funds to defend those charged in the Thoothukudi conspiracy case (Tirunāvukkaracu 2017, 1:594).

However, the most dramatic action was to take place at Dalmiapuram or Kallakudi railway station as Karunanidhi improvised the struggle on the spot to give it a revolutionary fervor. As per the original plan, he was to lead a group of people to cover the nameboard of the railway station with a sheet in which the desired name Kallakudi was written. If they were prevented from doing it or if the new name was torn down, another team was to repeat the action a couple of hours later and then a third team was also to repeat the action. It had been decided that Karunanidhi would lead the first team, Karaikudi Rama Subbiah the second team, and finally Kannadasan was to lead the third team. When Karunanidhi led the first team of protestors and pasted the name board, they were not stopped. On seeing the protest action turning into a tame affair, Karunanidhi walked to the tracks and laid down in front of train that was about to leave. He was accompanied by his team of five volunteers. The police were taken by surprise by this action. Thinking that they would get off if the train started, the driver was asked to move the train. But the demonstrators lay firmly on the tracks, forcing the driver to stop the train a few feet short of a defiant Karunanidhi (Tirunāvukkaracu 2017, 1:578–580). This bold action impressed the crowds gathered there beyond measure. The police had to arrest him and the others.

The event turned into a huge sensation, drawing more crowds to the station. The second team repeated the protest action of laying before the train and were also promptly arrested. By this time, the crowds began to pose a problem to the police in controlling the situation. Hence, when the third team headed by Kannadasan arrived, a lathi charge was ordered. This led to a confrontation with the police resorting to firing at the crowd to bring the situation under control, killing six people with only one of them being a party member. The five others were civilian commuters, including two in a train moving through the station at that time. The Kallakkudi front thus became the highlight of the three-front struggle, though the nomenclature of the "Five Big Leaders" also stuck in popular memory. However, Karunanidhi became a leader of independent stature, though there was much consternation in party circles about his improvisation of plans on the ground exceeding the mandate of the party. As the gains for the party in the public image was considerable, he could also not be disowned publicly. Kannadasan, who suffered injuries in the lathi charge, being the victim of the aggravated situation following the arrests of the first two teams and their defiant action could not manage to convert the experience to increase his stature in the party, perhaps owing to the peremptory nature of his involvement and his uneven temperament. Karunanidhi, apart from initiating the idea of the protest, was after all mobilizing people from the surroundings for more than a month preceding the event, like in the case of the black flag demonstration we noted earlier. Kannadasan arrived there at the last moment, perhaps hoping to participate in the symbolic protest of inconsequential nature. He was much embittered by the unexpected turn of events, which eventually turned him against Karunanidhi, his mentor, subsequently making him align with Sampath when the latter split the party in 1961. Following Sampath, he was soon to join the Congress and remain opposed to the DMK for the rest of his life even as he turned out to be one of the most famous lyricist-poets of all times. Those arrested in the three-front struggle were punished with prison terms ranging from a few months to one year or more.

The three-front agitation marked the evolution of the party as a serious contender to power, as Annadurai claimed in the court in defense of their protest action. It proved that they could inspire people to struggle and court arrest for the cause of Dravidian self-rule. The three fronts also captured the three dimensions of the party's ideational structure: one was against the perpetuation of the caste system (the education scheme); the other was against the imposition of Hindi and the dominance of the Union government (Nehru's insult); and the third was against the economic exploitation of Tamil Nadu by north Indian capital, the most serious form of north Indian imperialism (the naming of the railway station after the north Indian capitalist). The struggles performatively etched these dimensions of the party's politics in the minds of the people of Tamil Nadu.

The Congress and the elite press of course condemned all the protests as redundant and unruly. The common people perhaps thought otherwise as it signaled the mobilization of subaltern political energy to them.

Later Day Struggles

It will not be useful to go into a complete listing of various local struggles that the party was involved in the long years between 1953 and 1967. However, we shall note a few struggles, local as well as statewide, to understand various transformations in the political thrusts of the party.

A significant local struggle was the Nangavaram farmers struggle, again led by Karunanidhi, this time as a member of the Legislative Assembly from the constituency to which Nangavaram village belonged (Karunanidhi 2019, 1:307). A conflictual situation existed between tenants or farm laborers and the landlords in the village of Nangavaram, a fertile tract of land. Soon after the three-front struggle, there was the second round of inner party elections, culminating in the selection of Nedunchezhian as the general secretary, replacing Annadurai in 1954. In a couple of years, the party took the historic decision in 1956 to contest in the general elections. In the 1957 elections, Karunanidhi was elected from Kulithalai constituency. His maiden speech in the assembly mentioned this conflict situation in Nangavaram eloquently. Subsequently, Karunanidhi led the struggle along with the farmers against the exploitative tendencies of the landlords. It was a peaceful struggle that lasted for twenty days with scores of farmers courting arrest each day. Finally, the landlords relented to grant the demands placed on them. This struggle is notable since the DMK took up the cause of the farmers, usually organized by the communists in such confrontational situations, with a sitting member of the Legislative Assembly personally leading the struggle.

The year 1958 once again saw the DMK deciding to hold a black flag protest against Prime Minister Nehru who was to visit Madras State on January 6, 1959. The reason was the persistence of the prime minister's dismissive attitude towards the demands and concerns of Dravidian formations. Having now elected representatives to both the Legislative Assembly and the parliament in their ranks, the party had a far better public profile to compel the prime minister to take notice. The state government was resolved to crush the opposition. The DMK decided to hold a public meeting at Triplicane beach in the city of Madras on January 3, 1959, to explain to the public their reason for a black flag demonstration against Nehru. Annadurai was to address the meeting. The police refused permission for the meeting, imposing a blanket ban on rallies and public meetings for a fortnight from December 31, 1958, under the Chennai Police Act, rule 48 (Karunanidhi 2019, 1:342–343).

Annadurai gave a call for peaceful assembly against such state repression. The party only desired to demonstrate their unhappiness in a democracy through a black flag demonstration, which was unnecessarily met with hostility by the government. Hence, he decided to defy prohibition and address the meeting. The police arrested him and other frontline leaders when they approached the venue of the meeting. The cadres gathered were agitated, raising slogans against state repression. The police burst tear gas shells and lathi charged the gathering, causing grievous hurt to many. Hundreds of leaders and volunteers were arrested. Still, the cadres managed to outmaneuver the police to raise a sea of black flags when Nehru emerged from the airport. Once the offended Nehru left, the police unleashed merciless violence on the demonstrators. The police atrocities continued in many parts of the city where people gathered to demonstrate, even going to the extent of entering the houses of people to beat up who they thought were involved in the demonstrations. Two of the party workers died after sustaining injuries. Many leaders were punished with imprisonment for ten days or a fine, which they anyway refused to pay. As in the *Arya Mayai* case, the police once again released the leaders and confiscated goods in lieu of the fine imposed.

In the course of the year, that party underwent the tremors of the first internal dissension; the upcoming inner party elections and the need to elect the next party general secretary perhaps were the triggers. As we already noted in the previous chapter, the animus between factions led by Karunanidhi and Sampath were getting further entrenched. In order to avert a showdown, Annadurai had to take over as the general secretary once again. Further, Sampath's experience in parliament also made him wary of the rhetorical insistence on the demand for an independent Dravidian republic, a federation of four southern states. Many other leaders, including Karunanidhi, were also keen on marching towards electoral capture of power in the state under the Constitution of India to which the demand for a separate republic appeared to be contrapuntal. Annadurai however advised restraint as the emphasis on Dravidian difference through the demand of a separate Dravidian federation was necessary as the premise of the oppositional politics. The internal dissensions became more serious, resulting in Sampath and allies leaving the party to form the Tamil Nationalist Party in 1961.

In the meantime, the year 1960 saw the party once again preparing for a massive struggle to forestall the plans for incremental increase in the use of Hindi as the official language of the state jettisoning English. As we shall soon see in detail in the next chapter, the constitutional assembly left the time bomb ticking with its setting fifteen years as the period after which Hindi might be implemented as the sole official language. The DMK wanted to resort to a far more formidable black flag protest when the president of India planned to visit the state. This time Nehru relented. In his correspondence with Sampath, who was a member of parliament, he extended a promise that English too would be retained as an official language till such time all the states consented to the implementation of Hindi as the sole official language. He also publicly articulated the promise, requesting that further agitations be canceled. The DMK then withdrew the plans.

The party geared up to participate in the general elections in 1962, this time harvesting fifty members of the Legislative Assembly, though Annadurai lost the election in his hometown of Kancheepuram.

This created the opportunity for him to go to the parliament as a Rajya Sabha member. In his maiden speech, he explained the historical need for the separatist demand in terms of political theory in true parliamentary spirit. Annadurai's eloquent pleading for the right to self-determination in the upper house of the parliament rankled the Congress government to such an extent that they were quick to bring in a constitutional amendment that mandated elected representatives to abide by the integrity and sovereignty of the Indian Union.

The party was aware of widespread discontent among the people about the rise in prices of essential commodities. A decision was taken to picket the offices of revenue officials as a mark of protest against the price rise and the apathy of the elected Congress governments (Karunanidhi 2019, 1:381, 387–388). As the party had gathered considerable strength by this time, the demonstrations were powerful and widespread.[5] All the leaders and scores of volunteers were arrested all over the state. The picketing was done by successive groups of five or so volunteers who would go and block the entrance of the offices of district collectors or *tahsildars*. In Chennai, the police started manhandling the protestors while heaving them into police vans after arrest. This led to considerable unrest. The picketing and arrests went on through the day. Thousands were arrested in Chennai. The police once again unleashed violence on prisoners who had been remanded in blatant violation of all established procedures. The police also threatened those arrested to sign letters of apology. Annadurai intervened to stop such torture inside the prisons. Most leaders including Annadurai who led protests in various district and *taluk* headquarters were arrested and punished with several months of imprisonment. They were received by cheerful demonstrations when they were released after the prison term. When Annadurai went to receive other leaders getting released in Trichy, Karunanidhi walked out in the prison uniform to add to the impact of the highhandedness of the government (Karunanidhi 2019, 1:392). He was after all serving his second term as a member of the Legislative Assembly after the second successive victory at the hustings.

The year 1963 became eventful for the party. The party, having accepted Nehru's promise that English would also continue as official and link language, was insisting on a formal amendment to the Constitution. However, the Chinese aggression at the border became a major concern; the party threw in its lot to support the Indian government in its war efforts to defend the borders against the Chinese. Annadurai distinguished the parties' demands and the need to support the Indian Union against Chinese aggression. However, in spite of such expression of goodwill, the Center was keen on a constitutional amendment that would require all parties that contest elections to abide by the unity and integrity of India, failing which the parties may have to be banned from contesting elections and holding offices. Annadurai eloquently argued against such use of force against a reasonable debate on the question of right to self-determination of peoples who constitute the republic. Anyway, as the Center pressed ahead with the amendment, the party officially gave up the demand for a separate republic, rearticulating Dravida Nadu as a group of autonomous states within the Indian federation.

The year 1964 brought the country close to the deadline set by the Constitution for implementing Hindi as the sole official language. The DMK and other non-Hindi speaking constituencies managed to bring about a constitutional amendment in which the possibility of English continuing to be the official language beyond the fifteen-year deadline was enacted. However, it was only provisional and not binding on the Union government to continue English also as an official language. Nehru passed away without resolving the ambiguity of whether English shall continue as an official language, or it "may" continue as an official language alongside Hindi if the government so pleased. The shrill voices of Hindi zealots in the north aggravated tensions in the south. The DMK, with all its experience for protest action, geared up for a final showdown on the question of official and link language. The party launched a series of agitations once again; however, as the Republic Day of 1965, the deadline enshrined in the Constitution, approached, the situation erupted in such a scale far beyond the control of the party. We will consider the chain of events from the agitations of 1964 to the cataclysmic events of the fortnight following Republic Day, January 26, 1965, and its far-reaching ramifications in the next chapter.

Notes

1. Dyarchy is the form of double government through which the British shared governance with elected Indian representatives. Through the Government of India Act, 1919, enacted following the Montagu–Chelmsford reforms, a system of double government was introduced by the colonial state for the provinces of British India. It marked the first introduction of the democratic principle into the executive branch of the British administration of India.
2. For a list of banned books, see Tirunāvukkaracu (2019, 1:364–365).
3. For details of the discussions and resolutions, see *Dravida Nadu* 9, no. 10, September 3, 1950.
4. For more on this, see *Dravida Nadu* 9, no. 27, December 17, 1950, 8.
5. *Dravida Nadu*, October 24, 1962.

11 The Eruption

In the months of January and February 1965, Tamil Nadu witnessed the eruption of mass protest and violence that shocked almost all political actors in its intensity and scale. The protests carried several features of subaltern uprisings such as lack of central directives, spontaneity of action, role of rumors, destructive and homicidal violence, state repression, and finally, unverifiability of the precise nature of events in many places where several lives were lost. Though the Dravida Munnetra Kazhagam (DMK) had spearheaded anti-Hindi movements until the moment of eruption, it was the students who took the lead in "direct action," which then propelled mass action in many places, the scale of which is still a matter of oral histories and "folk" narratives. A perusal of the events between January 25 and March 15, 1965, most particularly the three cataclysmic days between February 10 and 12, would scarcely leave anyone in doubt that these days transformed Tamil politics forever. The party, as an organization, was not directly involved in the waves of spontaneous agitations in most places, even though students and activists belonging to the party joined the "public" in action. However, the events were bracketed by the DMK's sustained opposition to the imposition of Hindi as well as a demand for Dravidian political independence from its inception and its subsequent gain of popular support in the electoral arena. It was as though the DMK was airlifted in the most difficult part of its climb to power by the event of anti-Hindi uprising of 1965, as we will have occasion to analyze in detail in the subsequent chapter on electoral participation.

In what follows in this chapter, we need to focus on making sense of the scale and spread of the uprising within a span of a month, though a short-lived one. Before we narrate and analyze the event itself, we need to gather the larger historical context in which it happened. We shall do so under three rubrics: the constitutive roles of the elite and the subaltern in the linguistic public sphere, the constitutional conundrum of designating the national or sole official language, and the Damocles sword of official language implementation that the Constituent Assembly left hanging on the Indian republic.

Language of the Elite, Politics of the Subaltern

India was imagined and articulated in many languages during the freedom struggle. This is so obvious that it requires no special mention or substantiation. However, understanding the implications of this fact is where there has been considerable difficulty or rather an enigmatic failure that needs to be parsed carefully even if briefly before we begin narrating the sort of eruption that occurred in Tamil Nadu in January–February 1965 against Hindi becoming the sole official language of the Union. This is necessary to understand the context of the eruption, which otherwise may become unintelligible in its historic significance.

Let us begin with how the colonizers articulated their difference from the colonized first.

It consisted of the claim that "India" lagged behind in the march of history as indicated by the retardation of the formation of modern state, mature technologies of governance, scientific advancement, and the related epistemological tool kit. The explanations for this lack, the insufficiency in historic maturation in comparison to Europe, had a wide range, touching upon various aspects of civilization and social life. While this claim of the colonizing British might not have gathered the weight of hegemony, it formed the discursive template for colonial governance. The anti-colonial response consisted of two aspects: one is the claim to have the capacity to replicate, adapt, and run the state as formed by the colonial machinery; the second being the sovereignty of the cultural, inner, or the spiritual self of the nation that demanded its independence. This particular mapping of the nationalist thought is of course famously well developed in the oeuvre of Partha Chatterjee.

In his first book on nationalism as derivative discourse, he forged a dialectic, non-sublative, as one may describe it, between departure, maneuver, and arrival, in which the departure staked the claim for the sovereignty of the spiritual inner world, maneuver used it for effecting mass action articulating nationalist difference, and arrival signified the materialization of the nation-state, as a sort of incomplete closure (Chatterjee 1993). The next book mapped again the dialectic between the arrival of the nation-state and the still recalcitrant components of nationalist imagination not being fully assimilated into the state of the nation but remaining fragments still trying to redefine the nation (Chatterjee 1995). Though he does not treat linguistic regions or "vernacular" public spheres as fragments in the book, language is recognized as the primary site in the constitution of the spiritual inner domain, the necessary source for imagining the nation. Recently, Chatterjee has spoken of the distinction between the nation-state and people's nation where he has accorded a fuller treatment of the differences between the historic trajectories among linguistic regions of the country and how they constitute a people's nation.[1] There are other analogues distinctions made by Chatterjee elsewhere that we would like to recollect as well. Narratives of capital–narratives of community, right to property–other fundamental rights, and civil society–political society are some of the key distinctions. In all these mapping of binarization of historical forces, we may perhaps elucidate two key sites of action in history: the elite aspiration for sovereignty based on cultural distinction or state-making capacity and the subaltern aspiration for democratic self-governance that promises equity and participation.

Once we derive these two distinct forces in history, one being the elite claim to distinction and sovereignty and the other subaltern aspiration for equity and participation, it should be possible to speculate on how they figure in the constitution of linguistic public sphere under colonialism. It is possible to see the same forces in operation in the formations of the linguistic public sphere as well. There are elite constructions of polity based on language with aspiration for legal recognition of the power held by the group invested in ensuring perpetuation of dominance; there are then subaltern assertions that need to use the same language polity to ensure democratic participation and share in power. In the case of each Indian language, the way in which the dialectic played out marks the political history of the people speaking the language. The elite, subaltern dialectic may play out in many ways depending on historical circumstances in which such groups arrive to participate in the linguistic public sphere.

We will make bold to list some of the paradigmatic components of the constitution of linguistic public spheres in India that may be deduced as roughly common or similar with a certain degree of variance in emphasis in each case. It begins with the missionary activity introducing print, with the determination and consolidation of script as a consequence.[2] This is followed by a revival of texts of yore through print, wide dissemination, and cannon formation (Venkatachalapathy 2005). The next step is a sort of philological inquest in which the language exorcises the influence of other languages that had dominance over it for various political reasons, eventually redefining itself through a certain purity of idiom. It also produces a prose that can express contemporary concerns, where it maintains a distinct semantic from the language from which it claims to have been derived. Popular narratives, oral traditions like ballads, and folk narratives also find their way to print, paving the way to a public sphere as well as its subaltern counter public. Journals and broadsheets appear in which political concerns are expressed as well as themes of social change and reform. A wide variety of fiction and poetry appear in dialogue with European and particularly English language cannon, deriving, refracting, and modifying in many ways the forms of expression and forms of content. One can say the strength of the distinction of the language primarily depends on both the revival of ancient or medieval texts and the vibrancy with which the contemporary use is stabilized. A comparison between the emergence of Maithili and Bhojpuri public sphere may become instructive in understanding the relative role of these various components. Maithili had a head start due to the literary corpus that it could lay claim to, gaining recognition as an independent language in the schedule of national languages.

Bhojpuri is still fighting for similar recognition, though interestingly its historic lack in terms of literary corpus appears to have been compensated by a blooming film industry in the final decades of the twentieth century where Maithili has made no mark whatsoever. It appears, prima facie, that insofar as this pair of Maithili and Bhojpuri is concerned, Maithili had a predominantly elite orientation and Bhojpuri a subaltern one.[3]

The constitution of the Hindi public sphere was an act of schism, by now well researched, where Hindustani was rendered schizophrenic with the ghosts of Sanskrit and Arabic or Persian pasts tearing the language to make two distinct languages, Hindi and Urdu (Orsini 2012). It was certainly the most violent exercise of linguistic exorcism where the exorcised assumed a form of a new language called Urdu to be identified with the religion of Islam and finally a newly carved nation in the form of Pakistan. It only took a little more than two decades for the Bangla-speaking East Pakistan to free itself from the Urdu nation of Pakistan located in the west. The Tamil case of exorcism was strident as well. In the case of Tamil, the exorcism related to the *longue durée* influence of Sanskrit, which came to stand for Aryan–Brahmin hegemony and north Indian dominance. In spite of the differential role played by Sanskrit in the emergence of Hindi and Tamil public spheres, these sister public spheres had no need to develop any antagonism, as both were in fact emerging out of the shadow of a colonially inflicted notion of subordination. It is only because of the strange circumstances in which Hindi gained subaltern endorsement as against elite preference for English in the north of India, thereby resulting in a call for its recognition as the national language or at least the language of governance, that is, official language, that elite machination of promoting Hindi appeared antithetical to the interests of Tamils in Tamil Nadu.[4] This is because, unfortunately, the emerging nation endorsing a Sanskritized Hindi included Tamil Nadu, where the making of the Tamil public sphere was intrinsically connected to exorcising Sanskrit. This was initially the concern of the elite Tamil scholars, both Shaivites and Vaishnavites. However, the Tamil cause was soon endorsed by the subaltern as the ground had been prepared for non-Brahmin assertion, to which opposing Hindi became a natural corollary since the Congress tried to impose it at the behest of the north. In other words, both Hindi and Tamil, though initially constituted by the elite as languages of the public sphere, soon had reasons to become the sign of subaltern assertion. The subaltern of the Hindi heartland wanted Hindi to become the official language of governance for the same reason the subaltern in Tamil Nadu opposed it. The leadership of the Indian National Congress could not address the problem at all, given its elite common sense.

Tamil Nadu was not the only non-Hindi-speaking state to oppose Hindi becoming the sole official language of the Indian Union. The specificity was that it was a state in which the long traditions of exorcising Sanskrit and a revival of markedly Tamil traditions of religious life like in the case of Tamil Shaivism joined hands with non-Brahmin as well as the rationalist Self-Respect Movement to create a resistance to Hindi in 1938. This inspired, in the subsequent decades, the subaltern to endorse the cause of Tamil as a mark of self-respect and self-rule. In other words, the conditions in which the elite investment in forging and sustaining a linguistic public sphere could be effectively and fully transferred to subaltern political mobilization, that is, to generate the conditions that enabled the DMK to mobilize so successfully in the first two decades after independence. These conditions primarily consisted of the newly constituted democratic polity and the most exciting political experiment with the introduction of universal adult franchise, in short, the possibility of the rule of the commoner that the DMK championed. *It is because the commoner in Tamil Nadu realized that he had a stake in governance that he was most agitated about the alien language Hindi becoming the official language of governance in the country.* The exasperated Hindi zealot, in pointing out that English too is an alien language, does not realize that the Tamil common sense would prefer English as it was equally alien to all. It would obviate the enormous power differential with the north that would follow suit if they were to accept Sanskritic Hindi as the official language; further, one can afford to learn one alien language and not two, since English would anyway be required for global connectivity.

The Constitutional Conundrum

It was English that made the Indian National Congress possible. In the absence of a contingent of English-speaking Brahmin lawyers from Madras, it might have been hard for the Congress to include Tamil Nadu in the nationalist imagination. The ties between Bal Gangadhara Tilak and V. O. Chidambaram Pillai in the early decades of twentieth century, the intimacy shared by Gandhi and C. Rajagopalachari in the 1920s and 1930s, or even the possibility of collaboration between Dr B. R. Ambedkar and Alladi Krishnaswamy Iyer in drafting the constitution would not have been possible without English. For that matter, the veneration Vivekananda and Rabindranath Tagore generated in Tamil Nadu was due to English education. Of course, it is understandable that the Congress leadership was embarrassed about their dependence on English, the language of the colonizer. They certainly wished the participation of the masses in the political awakening, which meant business was conducted in the languages of India.

It is in the process of this English-born imagination of the nation that the question of a national language reared its head. When Gandhi, a Gujarati, wrote to Rabindranath Tagore, a Bengali, in English, in January 1918, asking whether Hindi, "as bhasha or Urdu," was not the right language to be made the national language or the language for intercourse among the provinces, the die was cast. Tagore answered in the affirmative. However, to the question of whether Congress should transact business in Hindi, Tagore was not in favor of hasty transition. He pointed out that for the "people from Madras," it was entirely a foreign tongue. Further, people would find it hard to express themselves in Hindi, since political thought itself was formed in English. Hence, Tagore suggested English for making politics possible and Hindi to unite and make people a nation. It was obvious that English, the language of the colonizers, cannot continue to unite India. A "national language" had to take its place; the sheer numerical figure of those who could speak Hindustani (*bhasha* or Urdu, said Gandhi, a little ambiguously in the letter) naturally appeared to make it the best candidate to become the national language. Gandhi also asked whether Hindi should not be made a compulsory language in all post-primary schools in the country. Tagore did not respond to this question (Bhattacharya 1997, 50–51).

The conundrum of bilingual nationalism was acute. For the intelligentsia to come together, gather their political thought, and negotiate with the British, English was necessary. As for mobilizing people for the nationalist cause, the Indian languages, the so-called vernacular, were absolutely essential. The irony of having to use the colonizer's language to fight with them while mobilizing people through Indian languages made even great minds like Gandhi and Tagore yield to the desire for a national language that all the people in India would speak, at least as we evidence in this exchange in 1918, though Tagore notes the difficulty people from Madras would face as Hindi was "foreign" to them. It is interesting to note that he did not think of Bengalis having similar difficulties with Hindi as much as Gandhi did not have to worry about Guajarati acceptance of Hindi. Whatever be our speculation about it, we need to know that even for them Madras had already marked itself out as foreign to the sphere of Hindi accommodation. In spite of it, the Congress leadership hoped that asking aspiring Tamils to learn Hindi for official purposes would not be hard. Perhaps the Congress Brahmins, who imagined Sanskrit as their language even when they did not learn it, assured them that it would be so.

When the first Congress ministry under diarchy was sworn in with Rajaji as premier in the Madras Presidency, he decided to impose mandatory Hindi learning in schools. As we had occasion to note earlier, this provided the historical opportunity for various strands of Tamil adherents and non-Brahmin political formations to rally under the leadership of Periyar to launch a struggle that could pave way to the demand for a separate nation. The death of two subaltern figures, Natarajan, a Dalit, and Thalamuthu, a Most Backward Class person, in prison during the struggle, started the long list of martyrs for the cause of Hindi opposition and Tamil protection. There was a moment of amusement in the state assembly when Chief Minister Rajagopalachari responded to a member's question as to why illiterate people are worried about what language is taught in school (Pandian 2007, 231). They were soon to realize that such people could make imagination of another republic, a Dravidian republic, possible. Though the separatist demand for a south Indian Dravidian republic could not make the British reckon with it for want of consolidation of elite support and the lack of popular mobilization in favor of it, it was sufficient to make many of the Congress leaders, particularly those from the Madras Presidency, feel cautious and ponder upon the inadvisability of pushing for Hindi as the national language or even as the sole official language of the Indian Union. This sense of caution could not perhaps match the passion generated by the apotheosis of the Hindi–Urdu schism in the partition of the country. The debates in the Constituent Assembly are framed by the interplay of the caution and passion thus derived, peppering the long-felt unease about the persisting role of the colonizer's language in post-colonial governance.

Gandhi had his own idea of what this Hindustani was; four months before his death in January 1948, Gandhi wrote in the *Harijan Sevak*,

> This Hindustani should neither be Sanskritized Hindi nor Persianized Urdu but a happy combination of both. It should freely admit words wherever necessary from different regional languages and also assimilate from foreign languages, provided they can mix well and easily with our national language. Thus, our national language must develop into a powerful instrument capable of expressing the whole gamut of human thoughts and feelings. To confine oneself to Hindi or Urdu would be a crime against intelligence and the spirit of patriotism. (Austin 2011, 51)

The Nehru report too made it clear that they were "strongly of the opinion that every effort should be made to make Hindustani the common language of the whole of India as it is today of half of it." However, the report went on to say that it is "axiomatic that the masses can only grow educationally and culturally through the medium of their own languages" and therefore the "provincial languages will have to be encouraged" (Austin 2011, 48).

The language question cropped up in the Constituent Assembly early on or, in other words, even before the assembly could commence its business. The Rules Committee under the chairmanship of Rajendra Prasad decided on December 14, 1946, that in the assembly business should be transacted in Hindustani or English and that, with the president's permission, a member could address the house in his mother tongue. When the draft rules were taken up for debate in the assembly, held in camera on December 22, 1946, Seth Govind Das, a prominent Central Provinces representative, said that that he found it painful that the Constituent Assembly of free India

> should try to make English its national language… I want to tell my brethren from Madras that if they, after twenty-five years of efforts on part of Mahatma Gandhi, have not been able to understand Hindustani, the blame lies at their door. It is beyond our patience that because some of our brethren from Madras do not understand Hindustani, English should reign supreme in the Constituent Assembly… (Austin 2011, 53)

and went on to argue that the language of the Constituent Assembly was equal to the national language of future India.

K. Santhanam, a distinguished academic and lawyer from Madras who represented the south Indians, proposed an amendment that all motions and amendments in the assembly be tabled in English, and that English must be spoken on the floor whether or not the member knew Hindustani. This was received favorably by the south Indians and Bengalis in the assembly, to the extent that Alladi Krishnasamy Ayyar requested a translation of Govind Das's speech demanding Hindustani be the national language, in English. However, the assembly passed the rule as proposed originally by the Rules Committee relating to the language of transaction, unamended, by a large majority. The matter did not die there—it cropped up again with the Fundamental Rights Sub-Committee and it was proposed that Hindustani written in Devanagari or with Persian script shall be the national language. This was submitted, with a minority dissent, to the Advisory Committee. The Advisory Committee at the meeting on April 22 postponed consideration of the language provision, and subsequently the clause was dropped from the rights. Hindustani as the national language died very soon as a consequence of Partition. "Partition killed Hindustani and endangered the position of English and the provincial languages in the Constitution" (Austin 2011, 57). The Hindi extremists kept pushing for Hindi. However when the Draft Constitution came out in 1948, it had no separate language provision but it established that the language of parliament was English or Hindi and that these languages could be used in the provincial legislatures as alternatives to the provincial language. In response to the Draft Constitution between February and November 1948, the Hindi extremists proposed twenty-nine amendments, basically demanding that Hindi be the sole national and official language of India and Devanagari the national script, and that English should not be used after a five- to seven-year period. The south Indians believed that the official language should be English for fifteen years, after which Hindi should be recognized as the official language, and Hindi and English would be the language of the parliament.

When the question of the language of the Constitution came up again and again, people like Rajendra Prasad and other Hindi extremists insisted on adopting a Hindi version of the Constitution, much to the annoyance of south Indians and other non-Hindi speakers. By the middle of 1948, the translation of the Constitution into Hindi and Hindustani was completed. Nehru wrote to Prasad on seeing the Hindi version, "I don't understand a word of it." The Sanskritized Hindi adopted by people like Prasad, Purushottam Das Tandon, and Ravi Shankar Shukla had made it incomprehensible. Notwithstanding the lukewarm reception of the Hindi version, Constituent Assembly members like G. S. Gupta and S. L. Saksena insisted that the Hindi version passed by the assembly should be considered as the original version of the constitution. A sub-committee of the Central Province and Berar Legislative

Assembly made three recommendations: that Hindi should be the official language of the Union, with English optional during a transitional period; that a knowledge of Hindi was mandatory for entrants into the civil service; and that the Constitution should be framed in Hindi. The transitional period was to be five years and that the source of learned terms should only be from Sanskrit. T. T. Krishnamachari's reply to these recommendations sums up the reaction from Madras in the assembly:

> I would, Sir, convey a warning on behalf of the people of the south for the reason that there are already elements in South India who want separation and it is up to us to tax the maximum strength we have to keeping those elements down, and my honorable friends in UP do not help us in any way by flogging their idea "Hindi-Imperialism" to the maximum extent possible. (Austin 2011, 63)

The language question, especially at the state level, became even more important because of bilingual areas like Ganjam in Orissa, Manbhum in Bihar, and Belgaum in Maharashtra. If education is to be in one's mother tongue, how is this to be done in bilingual areas? What about other rights of linguistic minorities? To address these questions, the Congress Working Committee drafted a resolution, largely drawn by Prasad. The main provision of this resolution was that

> there should be a State language that the Union business should be conducted in … and this will be the language of correspondence with the Provincial and State Governments. All records of the Centre will be kept and maintained in that language. It will also serve as the language for inter-Provincial and inter-State commerce and correspondence. During a period of transition, which shall not exceed fifteen years, English may be used at the Centre and for inter-Provincial affairs that the State language will be progressively utilized until it replaces English. (Austin 2011, 71)

On August 8, 1949, when the assembly met, the order paper bristled with language amendments to the Draft Constitution. These amendments included, apart from the usual litany of Hindi as national language and Devanagari as script, a ten-year transition period and that parliament could provide for the use of *either or both* Hindi and English for Union purposes. The south Indian block led by Santhanam (and supported by T. T. Krishnamachari, Mrs Durgabhai Deshmukh, Alladi Krishnasami Iyer, M. Ananthasayanam Ayyangar) passed a counter resolution the next day, August 9, 1949, in which they said that English will be the official language for at least fifteen years; they flatly refused to the progressive substitution of Hindi during this time. They conceded that a two-thirds majority of the parliament could authorize the use of Hindi *in addition* to English in the transitional period. The Hindi extremists objected that only progressive substitution could replace English with Hindi. Amidst such acrimonious exchanges, one thing that was agreed upon unanimously was that Hindi was to be the official language and Devanagari its script.

With no resolution in sight, Ambedkar presented a compromise on August 22, 1949, according to which English would be used for fifteen years for official Union purposes and that parliament could extend the period if it deems fit at the end of the period. The final compromise after much bitterness and to the chagrin of the Hindi extremists that was adopted was that the official language of the Union was to be Hindi with Devanagari script and that international numerals would be used, with the proviso that English was to be used as official language for a period of fifteen years and parliament could extend that period. Further, the language of the Supreme Court and high courts, the language of authoritative bills, acts, ordinances, and so on should be English. It was the duty of the Union government to promote the use of Hindi, and for its vocabulary Hindi should draw primarily from Sanskrit and secondarily from other languages. An attached schedule listed thirteen living Indian languages, but not English and Sanskrit. The compromise would be called the Munshi–Ayyangar formula, proposed by K. M. Munshi and Gopalasamy Ayyangar. This amendment suggested that no language will be called the national language and only mention official languages of the Union. The Hindi extremists were once again up in arms and refused to accept this formula, with the south Indians refusing to give in. After three years, and nearly 400 language amendments (which were all withdrawn), the Munshi–Ayyangar formula was passed on September 14, 1949, amidst deafening cheers (Austin 2011, 90).

Damocles Sword of Official Language Implementation

The Hindi enthusiasts had to be content with the victory of Hindi with Devanagari script over Hindustani and the promise of implementation of Hindi as the official language fifteen years later. If the period was meant to prepare non-Hindi speakers to accept Hindi as the official language, it also gave them time to mobilize people further against such implementation. In any case, that is what transpired in Tamil Nadu. The DMK developed an impeccable logic. It argued that for international relationship, higher education in most disciplines including the sciences, for business and commercial transactions with those outside India, English had become necessary. In the context of the Commonwealth and beyond, English made it easier to access various nationalities as translation from and into English was essential for most countries since English was spoken by a large number of people in the world, particularly with the rise of the United States as a superpower alongside the erstwhile global hegemon England.

Taking the apocryphal story of a scientist or wise man making a large hole in the door for the big cat to pass through and a smaller hole for the kitten, the DMK asked why make people learn English for global connectivity and Hindi for connectivity within India. English should be allowed to serve both purposes. This logic appealed to most people as naturally it was hard for the common people to learn either of the two because most were just becoming literate and were first-generation learners. The fear of becoming unequal to those who have Hindi as their mother tongue, if and when Tamils were forced to learn Hindi, and more particularly to Brahmins who swore affinity with Sanskrit, appeared almost as a more lasting form of colonization. Surprisingly, the Brahmins and the elite do not appear to appreciate even today what it meant for the common folk who already had much to cope with in the school curriculum. Moreover, that some of the people of India would be more comfortable with the official language than others appeared to create a two-tier citizenship replicating caste hierarchy. The DMK was in fact propelled by such sentiments against Hindi among the people rather than having to propagate anti-Hindi sentiments, as could be gleaned from accounts such as Paṇṇaṉ's that we read in Chapter 9.

After the symbolic anti-Hindi protests in the early years like tarring the sign boards in Union government facilities and offices, the DMK protest action shifted to opposing the Union government on various issues. Resistance to Hindi took a back seat in the mobilization as against the concern for overall welfare of the people of Tamil Nadu. Further, the Congress showed enough involvement stalling the "Hindi only" approach to official language. Many other non-Hindi-speaking states also showed definite concern and resistance.[5] However, as the fifteen-year deadline drew close, Hindi advocates in the north grew restive, prompting the DMK to relaunch struggles against Hindi as the sole official language of the state. It was then that Prime Minister Nehru extended a promise on the floor of the Parliament on August 7, 1959, that English would be retained as an additional official language till such time all the states of India were ready to accept Hindi as the sole official language. He had also conveyed this to Sampath, the DMK member of parliament, when the party proposed to hold a black flag demonstration against the visiting president, requesting the party to drop the agitation (Vivēkāṉantaṉ, Campat, and Kalpaṉātācaṉ 2013). While this provided some reprieve, the DMK asked for a constitutional amendment to convert the promise into a law. The DMK did not launch any agitation to press the demand due to Chinese aggression in the border in 1962; the Union government publicized Nehru's assurance in dailies to ensure people's support for the war effort.

The problem reared its head again in 1963. When President Radhakrishnan addressed the joint house of the parliament on February 18, 1963, the Jan Sangh and Socialist members heckled him, demanding that he should address the houses only in Hindi. After the commotion they walked out. Such acts of aggressive push for Hindi implementation provoked others into action as well. After much pressure, finally an amendment was tabled in parliament on April 23, 1963. It failed to satisfy the members from the south since they found the assurance was not categorical but equivocal. Nehru insisted that there was no intention to sneak in Hindi as the sole official language and such quibbles about whether the conjunction "may" should be replaced with "shall" should not be of any importance since the government intended to stand by its commitment to evolving consensus on the issue before use of English was discontinued. His demise in the subsequent year on May 17, 1964, certainly fanned wild anxieties about the fifteen-year deadline the Constitution mandated in spite of the equivocal amendment that left continued use of English to the discretion of the government.

Annadurai heard the news of Nehru's demise in prison. He had been sentenced to six months' imprisonment following the struggle launched to protest the equivocation of the constitutional amendment. We need to go to the events leading to his imprisonment. The party general council that met in the second week of June 1963 at Chennai decided to form a committee to plan and launch a struggle under the stewardship of Karunanidhi. The committee decided on four-fold action: conducting zonal conferences against Hindi imposition; to draw lists of those who were prepared to court arrest for a long term and those who could court arrest for a short term; to hold various programs like speeches, musical programs, and stage plays highlighting the danger of Hindi imposition at the grassroots level to spread awareness; and to observe Hindi opposition week from September 15 to 21, 1963. At the end of these programs, the party drew up a plan to hold a chain of periodic demonstrations at different districts in which Article 17 of the Constitution providing for Hindi as the official language would be burnt (Pērāciriyar A. Irāmacāmi 2015, 1:240). Such events were to be held till the fateful Republic Day of 1965 when the hour would strike for Hindi to replace English as the sole official language of the state. The leaders who burnt the Constitution were sentenced up to six months of rigorous imprisonment. Annadurai was undergoing the sentence when he came to know that Nehru had passed away on May 27, 1964, as they lowered the national flag in front of his prison cell.

An event of far-reaching significance happened in January 1964. On the twenty-fifth of that month, a day before Republic Day, a young member of the DMK, Kilapaluvur Chinnasamy, who grew desperate with the obstinacy of the Union government to impose Hindi as the sole official language of the state, and endless struggles of the party and its leaders going vain, decided to take his life in an act of self-immolation. We discussed this singular act in Chapter 2 when we engaged with Sumathi Ramaswamy's text on the passion for Tamil language. Reading the act as part of this larger narrative may perhaps reveal the necessary political meaning of the act rather than some atavistic fixation with the mother tongue. After all, Chinnasamy was apparently influenced by the example of self-immolation of Buddhist monks in Vietnam (Pērāciriyar A. Irāmacāmi 2015, 1:153). Chinnasamy's act however proved to be the real trigger for the conflagration that was to begin a year later on the same day (Pērāciriyar A. Irāmacāmi 2015, 1:270). All the way through the year 1964, the DMK continued to burn the Constitution at periodic intervals. The signals from the Congress leadership after Nehru's death were confusing at best. While Kamaraj and other southern leaders seemed confident that Hindi would not be thrust on them, many utterances of Union ministers and circulars from the ministries indicated a concerted effort to make Hindi be used as widely and regularly as possible, pushing the envelope with the southern states. The new prime minister Lal Bahadur Shastri mentioned the impending transition in his speeches. There was still simultaneous talk of Nehru's assurance on the meaning of "English may continue" as unambiguously permitting the use of English along with Hindi as long as southern states wanted. It all now depended on how the Indian government would act with the leverage offered by the open-ended conjunction of "may." While the Congressmen in non-Hindi states tended to believe that English would continue to be used alongside Hindi, there were others who felt that Hindi may become the sole language of official communication of the Union. The periodic assurances were not categorical enough; the Hindi proponents were constantly demanding removal of English from government use. The Congress leaders were chiming in with them as well.

It appears that the DMK decided to adopt a wait-and-watch strategy as the fateful fifteenth Republic Day neared. The party decided on a strategy of symbolic protest on Republic Day of hoisting black flags. They made it clear that they were not mourning the day but the imposition of Hindi on that day. However, the Congress government in the state, in the post-Nehru scenario, embarked on a more aggressive response to thwart the peaceful demonstration of protest by the DMK. Both the police machinery and the Congress party workers were to take on anyone hoisting black flags. The Congress planned an elaborate street battle where all black flags hoisted would be burnt and destroyed. Annadurai was intent on avoiding confrontation and violence. He advised the party people not to hoist black flags in public spaces but to do so in the party office and other private venues (Pērāciriyar A. Irāmacāmi 2015, 1:274). He reduced the number of public meetings to be held on that day from 1,000 to 100. The Congress party, on the other hand, was becoming belligerent. Periyar, who had been backing Kamaraj and thus the Congress rule in the state, was blaming the DMK for causing unnecessary panic around the speculation about Hindi imposition through official language implementation.

It was in this explosive situation of great anxiety that had built up around the vagueness of the constitutional amendment, the vulnerability of the Congress moderates after Nehru's death to the pressures of Hindi zealots, that students in Tamil Nadu took the initiative to launch a concerted protest against the possibility of Hindi imposition. The student bodies of course had the presence of the DMK affiliates or sons and relatives of the DMK cadres; however, there were also student leaders who were definitely outside the fold of the DMK influence. At any rate, the students were not acting on the basis of any directive from the party. They were persuaded that making Hindi the sole official language of the country would ruin their future and equitable participation in government machinery. Furthermore, this was also the moment when safeguarding the interests of Tamils was actively undertaken by Telugu- and Kannada-speaking groups in Tamil Nadu, as we could repeatedly encounter in our fieldwork. When we asked a Kannada speaker, a later-day party functionary, how he identified with the cause of Tamil during the agitation, he was perplexed by the question. For him it was a political question of not getting subordinated to north Indian Hindi dominance. Likewise, students from Congress families actively participated or even led the agitation in many places. The "public," unnamed multitude of people were also to join students soon in direct action. Their passions were high on that count.

The Eruption of Anti-Hindi Agitation

The students chose to hold rallies on January 25, a day before Republic Day. One reason was that it was the death anniversary of Kilapaluvur Chinnasamy, the first martyr in the anti-Hindi struggle who self-immolated. Another reason appears to be that at least a section of them was keen on not synchronizing with the raising of the black flags by the DMK. From reading several accounts closely, most particularly the chronicling of the January 25–March 15 agitation by A. Ramasamy, it almost appears that if only the Congress governments at the Center and in Madras State had acted with due diligence, consideration, and sympathy, the situation in Tamil Nadu might not have deteriorated so much.[6] Chief Minister M. Bhakthavatsalam refused to meet with the student delegation on January 25. The government wanted to prevent students from taking out rallies in most places. The government unleashed heavy repressive measures like lathi charge, tear gas, and so on to disperse student rallies. In Madurai, two students, Kalimuthu and Kamarajan, decided to burn Article 17 of the Constitution and were arrested. The student rally was attacked by the Congress cadres at Madurai, resulting in injuries to many students, which was another act of provocation. The Union home minister Gulzarilal Nanda told the press that change of official language was a constitutional obligation. The Congress party and the government were geared to launch a frontal attack on the DMK wherever they erected the black flag.

It was in such a tense atmosphere that Sivalingam, a DMK branch-level functionary at Chennai, burnt himself in the wee hours of Republic Day. He wanted to and gave true substance to the day of mourning. His cryptic suicide note read, "Uyir tamiḻukku! Uṭal tīyukku!" (Life for Tamil! Body to flames!). During the day, the DMK leaders were arrested en masse; 1,569 people were arrested throughout the state. The DMK party office buildings and houses of the party functionaries where black flags were hoisted came under attack. In many places, enraged DMK members launched a counterattack, cutting down the Congress party flags. In many colleges, students also joined in hoisting black flags. In Chennai, police went into the student hostels and beat up students, creating horrible scenes of violence. The next day, another DMK functionary, Ranganathan, immolated himself in Chennai after writing appeals to many. These extreme acts of sacrifice grabbed headlines and worked as triggers.

More such sacrifices were to follow in the days to come. The students decided to continue with their agitation. On January 27, students of Annamalai University in Chidambaram went in a procession from campus to the city. The police denied permission for the rally to enter the city. The students squatted on the road. The crowd swelled. A minor altercation with the police led to a full-scale conflagration, with the police resorting to lathi charge and tear gas shells. Finally, when the police resorted to firing, a first-year undergraduate student, M. Rajendran, succumbed to bullet injuries on the spot in full view of the police and the students. The police refused to allow the students to take him for treatment. Ironically, he was the son of a police constable. The enraged students ransacked and set fire to the house of the university registrar, thinking that he had colluded with the police. The police in turn entered the campus, launching a full-scale attack on the inmates of the hostel. As a result, the university was shut down.

As the news of Chidambaram firing and Madurai excesses spread, of course with added force as rumors took wings, school students also got into the act. The agitation spread from cities to villages. In many places, school students came out and held processions. In Tirunelveli, when a procession went past the house of the Congress member of the Legislative Assembly (MLA), those in the procession got into an altercation with the husband of the MLA, demanding the Congress flag in the house be brought down. As this escalated into a scuffle, the husband of the MLA allegedly fired at the rally, hurting a 10th standard student who luckily survived the bullet injury. As the agitation spread, school students boycotted classes and took out processions. In most places they would target the post office, erasing Hindi letters in the boards there and damaging the office as well. In some places, students halted trains by squatting on the tracks. The police often lathi-charged the students; some policemen were also hurt in the melee in some places. There was continuous sporadic action by the college and school students in the days following Republic Day, as news of incidents at Madras, Chidambaram, and Madurai spread. The government responded by closing all colleges till February 8.

In Chennai, student leaders from several institutions gathered to form an umbrella association. It was called Tamil Nadu Students Anti-Hindi Agitation Council (Pērāciriyar A. Irāmacāmi 2015, 1:280). It was of course preceded by hectic parleys and a statewide tour of a group of students to network nodal points. Such a tour was obviously helped by some of the DMK functionaries in their individual capacity. The state-level student body was headed by one M. N. Ravichandran of Madras Law College, who was not affiliated to any political party and was the son of a police officer. Of the three secretaries, one was from the DMK student wing, P. Seenivasan of Law College, who would go on to defeat Kamaraj in the Virudhunagar constituency in 1967 elections. L. Ganesan, who also was to become a DMK MLA later, was active in forming the association. In fact, many later-day DMK leaders were part of the student organization, including Durai Murugan, who is the general secretary of the party at the time of writing this book. One could say the party harvested a generation of young leaders from the agitation even if it was not organizationally involved in rallying the students. At the time of the agitation, the student body was keen on being autonomous, as exemplified by choosing Ravichandran as the president. It could further be understood by the subsequent differences the students had with the party in concluding the struggle. Anna appealed to the students many a time to withdraw the struggle.

On February 6, the students' council had a prolonged deliberation in Madras on the future course of action. They met with the chief minister that night. Their main demand was that Article 17 of the Constitution should be removed. The talks failed as Chief Minister Bhakthavatsalam was unable to convince the students that the state government would protect the interests of Tamils. The students then resolved that they would observe a fast on February 8 when colleges reopened. A. Ramasamy documents that during the deliberations one student categorically declared that they should resort to violence (Pērāciriyar A. Irāmacāmi 2015, 1:282). The degree of frustration among the students about the repressive measures of the government was high. Their impulse was to retaliate with a violent insurrection. One of the student leaders interviewed by us shared a similar episode. When students gathered in the town where he was organizing protests, one student from a rural background had brought country-made bombs to the meeting. In such a volatile situation, a largely peaceful action of fasting on February 8 did not satisfy the students. Hence, they announced picketing of post offices on the ninth and tenth, stopping of trains on the eleventh and a complete statewide *bandh* on February 12. The die was cast.

On February 9, student leaders picketed the head post office in Chennai in batches and were all arrested. As the news spread, at different parts of the city incidents like stone throwing and clashes with police started occurring. In most places in Tamil Nadu, a pattern was emerging in the agitation. There would be the symbolic action by the students; the police would arrest them. The action would attract a gathering of public. Police would try to disperse them in many places with lathi charge and so on. This would trigger the people into regrouping, indulging in arson, and attacking public buildings and offices. These confrontations began on a small scale on February 9 but flared up into full scale the next day.

There are two incidents that will show the intensity of confrontations on February 10. At Coimbatore, a crowd gathered in front of Naaz cinema hall, ironically showing a film titled "Aya Toofan," meaning "The Storm Has Arrived." The crowd asked the theater to stop the screening of the Hindi film. The owner hesitated. The irate mob entered the theater, tore the screen and set it on fire. They ransacked the theater. A part of the theater burnt down. The crowd prevented fire services from approaching the theater. The police rushed to the spot and opened fire. Four people died on the spot; Mohan, a seventeen-year-old student studying in the tenth standard at a municipal high school, was hit in the chest and died. The three others who died were fifteen-year-old schoolgirl Hamsa; Abdul Kadar, aged thirty; and Sarojini, also aged thirty. A far more gruesome confrontation happened in Tiruppur, the industrial town close to Coimbatore. About 500 students at a local high school marched, defying the ban order. The police asked them to disperse. They refused. As was the pattern, a huge crowd gathered as well. The police lathi-charged. The crowd pelted stones. Then the police opened fire. A schoolboy, the son of an influential Congress leader in the town, died on the spot. This infuriated the mobs that regrouped in many places and attacked government offices, the magistrate's court, and so on, ransacking and burning whatever they could lay their hands on. A particularly frenzied mob noticed two police sub-inspectors standing at a corner and charged towards them. The constables ran from the scene while the two sub-inspectors stood hoping to pacify the crowd. When they sensed the danger, it was too late. Both of them were dragged, beaten, tied up, and finally burnt alive.

The program for the next day was blocking trains from running. All over Tamil Nadu, students, frequently joined by the public, got onto the tracks and stopped the trains. In some places the train compartments were burnt, and the railway stations were ransacked and set on fire. The day sufficiently raised the tempo for the total strike the next day, February 12. The events in Tamil Nadu caused great concern in Delhi. The cabinet met on the evening of February 11 and decided that Prime Minister Lal Bahadur Shastri should address the nation on radio that evening, reassuring non-Hindi speaking states. In the cabinet meeting, C. Subramaniam, the food minister, insisted on introducing a categorical assurance in the Constitution on the continuation of English alongside Hindi as the language of governance as long as the southern states wanted it. But the ministry was reluctant, fearing reprisal in the north. As a result, even as Shastri was proceeding for the broadcast, C. Subramaniam resigned. It was soon followed by the resignation of another minister, O. V. Alagesan, a relative of the then Tamil Nadu Chief Minister Bhakthavatsalam.

Meanwhile, the Tamil Nadu government had requisitioned State Armed Police Forces from many other states to control the crowds in Tamil Nadu. These special forces were active from February 10. Further, the government also requested the deployment of the army in several districts, though the army was called into action only at Pollachi. In analyzing the events from newspaper reports and oral testimonies, it appears that it is only by imposing a curfew and curtailing peaceful and symbolic demonstrations that the government was actively inciting violent action. In most places, if the students and public had been permitted to organize rallies, demonstrations, and symbolic acts like hoisting black flags and so on, mob violence might not have been instigated, leading to lathi charge, tear gas bursting, and firing on the part of the police or army, and stone pelting, arson and burning of public properties, and hurting and killing police personnel on the part of the crowd. Police repression in the early days of the agitation intensified it, taking it beyond the control of police, requiring the army to step in in many places. The government continued the same confrontational strategy even on the fateful day of February 12. The government announced over the radio that inspectors were empowered to give shoot-at-sight orders to control the crowds. In many places throughout the state, the police opened fire. Post offices, public buildings, trains, and other vehicles were burnt by angry mobs in many places. The government claimed that fifty people had died in police firing in this phase of the struggle. However, independent observers felt the number would be about 500.

There are two incidents that stand out from all the violent confrontations that happened all over the state. Both these occurred in otherwise quiet and scenic small towns situated close to the Western Ghats that functioned as a border with the neighboring state of Kerala. One was Gudalur in Theni district in the south and the other Pollachi in the west. We will narrate the events in these two places to give a sense of the intensity of the agitation. Anyone visiting these two towns today will find it incredulous that such violent conflagration could have happened in these places. While the incident in Gudalur is the touchstone for mob frenzy, the event of the army firing on the public in Pollachi, Jallianwala Bagh style, is perhaps forever shrouded in the enigma of oral history typical of subaltern uprisings.[7]

Gudalur

The protest action in Gudalur appeared to have started very peacefully. A group of school students were pasting anti-Hindi bills on vehicles passing by. As Gudalur was on the road from Kerala to Madurai, a foreign tourist, accompanied by a couple of Kerala state police constables, was traveling in a car. Students stopped it to stick bills. The Kerala police beat up the students and dispersed them. The tourist decided to return to the resort in Thekkadi instead of proceeding with the journey. Then a few policemen came by in a lorry. The students stopped it to stick bills. The policemen lathi-charged the students. As the lorry started, it ran over a student who was crossing the road in front of it, crushing his legs. The angry students and the public pelted stones on the lorry. The police inspector in the lorry started firing at the crowd. Three were injured of whom one succumbed to the injury.

A huge crowd gathered to check on the dead person and the injured. The crowd became furious and went to the post office to attack it. The policemen guarding the post office fired again. Some people fell to the bullets but the crowd overpowered the police, who ran away to the police station. In its fury, the crowd ransacked and burnt the post office. It then went to the police station. Again, the handful of policemen fired at the crowd. As the crowd was uncontainable, the policemen took to their heels, this time running into the woods behind the police station. The crowd then vented its fury on the police station, burning furniture, records, and setting fire to the station building. They found the lorry in which the policemen had traveled and set fire to it. It is then that they noticed constable Devarajan in the vicinity. He tried to hide in a motel nearby. The crowd pulled him out, beat him up, and threw him into the burning lorry. They also apprehended a head constable, Ramachandra Singh, lynched him, and threw his body in front of the police station. After all this carnage, an uneasy quiet descended on the town. However, the district police superintendent and the district collector came with a posse of police force; they took it out on all the inhabitants of the small town. Women were sent into the fields from every household and the men were beaten up all through the night. They arrested more than 200 persons. The DMK MLA of the constituency, Rajangam, who was not present in Gudalur at all during the day, was also arrested and tortured. In our interviews with the local people who were young men at that time of the incident, it was hard to figure out or even guess why such extreme acts of violence took place in the quiet and scenic small town in the mountains. A similar event in a city like Madurai or Chennai or even an industrial town like Tiruppur should not be so surprising since there would be a mass of people involved in protest action there. It is difficult to imagine a town like Gudalur becoming the site of such extreme violence, which perhaps serves to indicate the spread of emotions relating to Hindi imposition.

Pollachi

Pollachi was certainly a larger town than Gudalur; it was primarily a trading center surrounded by fertile rural hinterland and the Western Ghats. At the time of the incident in 1965, the town had a college and a polytechnic institution. It also had many schools. In our interview with a student leader of those times, we could gather that the students were highly charged up with pent-up fury about the imposition of Hindi as the official language of the Indian Union. It was no different from the rest of Tamil Nadu. There is nothing we could gather as to why a military posse was asked to be sent to the town or why the army opened fire on the agitating crowd. It is the only place where the army opened fire on civilians, allegedly using machine guns. The itinerary of the agitation is unremarkable and is similar to what happened in most other places: students and public marching to the post office and erasing Hindi letters from the board; police lathi-charging the crowd in front of the post office; an irate mob then going about with acts of vandalization and arson. A school building was set on fire. What is inexplicable is why the army was asked to take on the crowd. Was the crowd so huge? Was it so violent?

From the accounts gathered by A. Ramasamy and our own interviews, it appears that the people resisted the military in many parts of the town. They erected barricades and went about committing acts of arson. The military repeatedly opened fire. There are many accounts of how many people died sustaining bullet injuries. The army occupied the town for about twelve days, holding it under strict curfew. What is reported to have transpired is that since the army occupied the town, no one came out to claim the corpses that were strewn on the streets. The army arranged for mass cremation of the bodies at two different places. Owing to fear of reprisal, no one came forward to complain about missing persons or to claim the bodies. While this is possible, what eludes comprehension is how many could have died on that day. Most people believe about 300 people died in the army firing. While it appears to be too huge a number to be simply erased in history, the official figure put out by the government as a mere ten persons also appears improbable. Further, it is not clearly stated who those ten persons were. We are not able to ascertain the name of anyone who died. One young man who sustained an injury to his leg has been interviewed by a group of local historians according to some of the people we spoke to. But this man too was unable to mention who lost his or her life in the firing. Ramasamy, who conducted interviews in 1969, is of the view that about 80–100 people must have been killed (Pērāciriyar A. Irāmacāmi 2015, 2:580). There are no official records to confirm this figure. Almost all the people we talked to have heard of the mass cremation of bodies by the army. Is it possible that a terror-stricken people decided to go silent on missing members of their families? Was it that all those killed were people who came from the villages around, whose families did not want to speak of their involvement in the agitation? There are no easy answers to these questions, but oral history firmly believes that hundreds died.

Since it is hard to understand why the military was brought to the town and why they started firing at people, it is also difficult to understand who exactly stood up to the army, raising barricades and street fighting before falling to the bullets of the army guns. An anonymous multitude seem to have sprung into action. More than one person has said even Brahmins were on the streets resisting the army; Ramasamy recorded an eyewitness account of a Brahmin setting fire to a cart in the middle of the street to stop the army. We have heard of a narration in which another Brahmin rushed to save a dying man on the street, sustaining a bullet injury himself. These stories, while possibly exaggerated, point to a widespread involvement of the people in resisting the repressive onslaught of the army. Ramasamy has titled the chapter of his book as "Pollachi Massacre." Contemporary newspaper accounts have spoken of army firing and controlling the town without giving specific details about number of causalities or the details of the agitation (Pērāciriyar A. Irāmacāmi 2015, 2:578). There are details of the damage to the public buildings, shops, and schools but no details of the people who were responsible. The crowd. Anonymous martyrs. An enigmatic account of massacre in an innocuous-looking small town.

Aftermath

All the leaders were pleading with students to withdraw their agitation. Annadurai called up L. Ganesan, a student leader and a DMK affiliate on the night of February 11 and prevailed on him to stop the agitation the next day. As most of the student leaders had been arrested, Ganesan and the rest deliberated on it and announced that after the *hartal* (general strike) on the twelfth, there would be no further program of agitation. Every leader, including the prime minister of the country, welcomed the decision. There were demands and negotiations about releasing all the arrested students. However, since there was no central command for the agitation, sporadic action continued in many parts of the state. When schools and colleges opened on March 8, many boycotted classes. Again, processions were being taken out. There was police firing in the hill station Ooty, killing three. It was only by March 15 that all further agitation ceased and students returned to classes. In spite of its intentions, the Union government could not bring about a legislation categorically assuring the continuation of English as the official language in addition to Hindi. The anti-English, pro-Hindi zealots kept applying pressure on discontinuing English. Every piece of legislation drafted was a compromise between the two positions. They satisfied neither side. In the meantime, when Independence Day approached in August, the student leaders were taken into preventive custody. But as nothing happened, they were released. They resolved to support the DMK in the forthcoming assembly elections in February 1967.

The victory of the DMK did not end the student unrest. They were still demanding a total abrogation of Article 17 relating to official language. They were demanding that Tamil also should be announced as an official language of the Indian Union. When the agitation simmered again, Chief Minister Annadurai announced a special session of the assembly to discuss the language issue. The assembly resolved that Tamil Nadu would follow only the two-language formulae in schools, which meant only English and Tamil would be taught. The command words in Hindi used in the National Cadet Corps (NCC) were removed to be replaced by English words. It was resolved to appeal to the Union government to find a solution to the official language question. With these moves, most particularly the one that discontinued the teaching of Hindi as an additional language in schools, the student action subsided. A lingering discontent had a group of students in Coimbatore led by an Agricultural College student, Ramasamy, declare a free Tamil Nadu, rising the flag of the state.[8] He was later called for a discussion with Annadurai. He was persuaded to subsist from further adventures and leave it to the state government to work on protecting the interests of Tamils. Even if the question of official language of the Indian Union was not fully resolved, it had become clear that Hindi could not become the sole official language of the Union. Nearly half a century later, it looks more impossible than ever to have Tamil Nadu accede to Hindi being the sole official language of the Union. No national party is likely to attempt imposition of Hindi on Tamils.

Notes

1. In precise terms, Chatterjee writes, "A relativist view provides a more adequate ontological account of the object called Indian nation as the political identity of the nation state with the people–nation grounded in the material field of linguistic practice" (Chatterjee 2020).
2. For more on missionary contribution to script standardization and print, see Blackburn (2006).
3. In an interview to *Himal* magazine, M. K. Jha, speaking about the nationalist period, says,

   > In that historical–political context the print played a very significant role and through print then, Maithili writers and intellectuals began to establish the rich tradition of Maithili and its continuous production since fourteenth and fifteenth century Jyotirishwar Thakur, Vidyapati and so on. So Chanda Jha and Harshanath Jha and many others in the 18th, 19th, and 20th century, their literary works began to establish the richness of Maithili literary tradition.

   Whereas speaking about Bhojpuri, he says,

   > In comparison to that [to Mythili], many other linguistic groups such as Bhojpuri or Awadhi did have a rich literary tradition—but that was not written. Print was not available as easily as it was available to Hindi writers and intellectuals. So these linguistic groups did face many obstacles in terms of print or expressing their identity through print. But with this audio-video culture, that disadvantage has gone.

   See Jha (2020). See also Jha (2018).
4. For an appreciation of the complexity of the issue of Hindi language politics, see Rai (2007).
5. "Hindi Thrust Dubbed North Indian Imperialism," *The Hindu*, February 2, 1965.
6. All events mentioned in the section are drawn either from Ramasamy's two volumes chronicling the agitation in Tamil or the monograph in English, which were independently corroborated with newspaper reports and fieldwork wherever possible.
7. We did considerable fieldwork in both Pollachi and Gudalur and spoke to several participants in the agitation on these fateful days, apart from cross-checking the information with archival sources both governmental and news media.
8. This was confirmed by Ramasamy himself in his interview with us, who gave us a copy of the photo taken on that occasion.

12 The Climb

On the day the Dravida Munnetra Kazhagam (DMK) was founded, September 17, 1949, the debates on the Draft Constitution of India were being held in the Constituent Assembly. They were concluded in a month's time; the draft was approved by November 14, 1949, and was formally adopted on January 24, 1950, four months from the day the DMK was founded. It could be said that the Republic of India and the DMK were born simultaneously. The information is significant because the party mirrored and shared an antinomy of the new republic. The DMK vowed to work for another republic, the south Indian federation of states known as Dravida Nadu. It decided to work for the goal under the conditions of possibility made available by the Indian republic, a Union of States. We can thus say that the political mobilization of the DMK is constituted by an antinomy. This antinomy immediately mirrored the antinomy of centrifugal and centripetal tendencies of power consolidation in Indian polity. As per the Constitution, the term "state" is applied to the regional governments that constitute the Union. The "union of states" is centrally governed. There is a lasting antinomy in the formation. On the one hand, in effect, the powers are largely concentrated at the Union, making the Union government a unitary state with the provincial governments, grandiosely called States, increasingly becoming dependent on the central power. On the other hand, popular politics, particularly electoral outcomes, have been strengthening party formations at the regional level, thus constituting the antinomy of the republic in the practice of popular electoral democracy.

The DMK was an exemplar of the autonomous political formations at the regional level. It was also distinguished by the fact that the very building of the party structure involved elections to various tiers of party positions. The way the party wrote its constitution and conducted organizational elections pointed to the liberal streak of politics it endorsed, which aligned it with a possible electoral participation. Its inherent possibility, as a party formed by the people of plebeian stock, was to achieve the rule of the commoner that was promised by universal adult franchise; the party's hopes for and belief in electoral democracy as a historical game changer was hence genuine and palpable from the beginning as enshrined in the oft-repeated dictum "Ellorum Innattu Mannar" (translating to "Everyone is Sovereign in the Country," or more directly "All are Kings in the Country"). In a personal sense, Annadurai had in fact contested in local body elections in the mid-1930s before joining Periyar, which indicates that he bore no disdain for electoral politics like Periyar. Hence, it could be said that the party was destined to participate in the elections from the very moment of its inception. It was only the larger goal of demanding an independent republic that ran counter to its inherent interest in electoral democracy. However, even to work towards the goal of an independent republic the party needed to demonstrate the support of the people. In popular parlance, the choice in front of the party was between "ballot" and "bullet." As a party trained in counter-hegemonic and agonistic propagation in the style of Periyar, the DMK naturally believed in peaceful and civil organization of the people, which made it necessary for the party to be armed with the ballot rather than bullet to wrench power. Seventy years later, it is now commonsensically held that the reason for the DMK to branch out from the DK was to move towards electoral participation. While this wisdom in hindsight is appreciable, things were certainly not that simple in the years between 1949, when the party was founded, and 1956, when the party officially decided to enter the electoral fray. It is necessary to understand the concerns and dilemmas of the party in the seven years before it yielded to the inevitability of electoral participation. If the country spent the two years between 1950 and 1952 to prepare for the general elections, the DMK spent that period in forming branches, having district-level conferences, and drafting a party constitution. When the party general council met in Madurai on November 17, 1951, to finalize the party constitution and the agenda for the first state-level conference to be held in Madras, the first general elections had already been announced.

The foremost concern naturally was whether participation in the first general elections in 1952 would result in the dilution of the demand for a separate country, Dravida Nadu, a south Indian federation of states. Hence, in his address in the first state-level conference of the party, Annadurai described the election as a lure and possible distraction from the goal (Tirunāvukkaracu 2017, 1:426). The party had to register its protest to the way the republic was formed through a Constituent Assembly, which was not elected through universal adult franchise and, consequently, not being inclusive in its nature. Further, immediate participation in the election could be read that the DMK was interested only in coming to power in the state and not in its demand for a separate country. The party would compromise its capacity to rally people around the demand for a separate country if they immediately participated in the elections. Sufficient propagation of the ideal of Dravida Nadu needed to be made before risking electoral participation so that the goal remained etched in the hearts and minds of the people. Moreover, the party hoped to mobilize popular support to such an extent that they could appeal to the United Nations for a directive to the Indian government to conduct a plebiscite in south India on the question of a separate country like in the case of Jammu and Kashmir, or they would initiate a referendum in 1954 to demonstrate that most people were behind the demand for the Dravidian republic.

Immediate electoral participation could jeopardize such a possibility if it were to happen. The DMK in the years 1949–1952 was just a group of spirited youngsters with some support base among the unorganized laborers and small entrepreneurs in the cities and small towns, tendentious support from middle-level peasants, and a small section of the landed gentry. It was pitted against the Indian National Congress that was ruling at the Center and had the near total support of all the rich people in trade, industry, and agriculture in Tamil Nadu apart from the mass appeal of leaders like Gandhi and Nehru. The DMK had also separated from the veteran leader Periyar, one who had brushed shoulders with such national leaders, to chalk a path in the uncharted terrain of popular politics. Hence, it could be imagined that there was a genuine difficulty in terms of knowing how much mobilization would actually become possible even if the effort was tireless and spirited. The year 1952 was too soon for the nascent party to gauge its own mobilizational capacity and strength to decide on a possible course of action. It could not decide to join the elections without fully realizing its potential for mass mobilization to demand a plebiscite on a separate south Indian republic.

The Communist Party of India too had decided on a parliamentary path, a peaceful and civil mobilization through trade unions instead of a revolutionary class struggle against the government. Being a vehicle of working-class people against the consolidation of the rich and the powerful around the Congress, the Communist Party was seen as an ally by the DMK, which it was keen to align with. However, the difficulty was the communist disinterest in the call for Dravida Nadu or a south Indian republic. The Communist Party decided to abide by the idea of India. In the first state-level conference of the DMK in 1951, shortly before the first general elections, Annadurai made a fervent appeal to Jeevanantham, the communist leader who was present as a guest of honor, to consider accommodating the idea of Dravidian republic in return for the DMK endorsement of communist ideal so that they could merge their formations. As we had discussed in Chapter 4, the communists had no sympathy for populist reason in which the internal frontier of Aryan–Dravidian or rather Brahmin–non-Brahmin and the empty signifier of Tamil combined to produce the catachrestic–synecdochic demand for Dravida Nadu, a south Indian federation of states as a separate country. In the event, left populism of the DMK had far greater electoral success than the class essentialist mobilization of the Communist Party. Since this historical outcome could not be predicted in 1951, the DMK was anguished about the communist refusal to join them in their demand for a separate Dravidian country of south Indian states.

There was yet another reason for the DMK to skip the first general elections. Periyar had a strong and well-articulated disdain for "office seeking culture" in politics. He believed in relentless propagation to win over the minds of the people to effect far-reaching changes in society. Electoral politics implied a self-interest that is antithetical to the cause of selfless and agonistic propagation. Having parted company with Periyar on the question of furthering the ideal of a separate Dravidian republic, the DMK placed itself in public scrutiny of its true intents and purposes. It necessarily had to exhaust its possibilities of mass mobilization for a separate republic before considering electoral participation as an intermediary stage. Any rush to gain political power might lead to the charge of office seeking and self-interest as against the larger goal of working for a separate nation. This also necessitated that the DMK stayed away from participating in the first general elections. But it did not stay away from the elections altogether; it supported and campaigned for candidates who vowed to work for the cause of Dravida Nadu—more on this later. First of all, we need to understand what a general election meant for a party like the DMK in the period we are studying.

Election as Event and History

Electoral outcomes immensely contribute to the emplotment of the political history of the nation-state. They give a vast scope for causal narratives and teleological interpretation. Nevertheless, an election is also an autonomous event that retains certain inexplicability in spite of the overall outcome in terms of winners and losers. For example, some constituencies will buck the general trend; some will return an obscure independent candidate; there will always be some surprise defeats and so on. Most particularly, reckoning with the number of votes polled will point to a different narrative than the number of seats won. For example, Indira Gandhi lost in Raebareli in 1977, which can surely be attributed to her unpopular regime under the Emergency for eighteen months that preceded the elections. However, she polled 122,000 votes and lost the election only by a margin of 55,000 votes. If the narrative is that the people disapproved of the imposition of Emergency, certainly not all of them disapproved. It is usually common for the losing candidate to speak of the number of votes polled by him or her. The votes polled by the loser point to a counter-narrative, or at least cannot be mobilized by the narrative of the victor. This essentially boils down to the event of a single voter casting her vote in a secret ballot system, a unit of recalcitrant micro history not always yielding to the larger causal narratives.

It is possible to speculate that in order to unpack the complex nature of the electoral event, we need to reflect on at least four key dimensions that constitute the event: the voter, the candidate, the campaign, and the historical context. There is an inherent arbitrariness to the voter's decision underlined by the redundancy of the act from the viewpoint of the voter. The dynamics of the assemblage of power at the level of the state does not immediately connect to the immanence of power relationships in everyday life. As a result, she may or may not be swayed by or seized with any of the factors that may recommend or not recommend a candidate. She can momentarily and arbitrarily decide to vote for a symbol or a candidate. From a sheer lack of cause, there can be several kinds and layers of considerations that may influence the decision. At the kernel of the mystery of the electoral event lies the possible arbitrariness of the voter's choice or the tenuously linked multi-causal chain that led to the choice. It remains unclear what investment the voter would have in studying the implications of her choices since much of that may not appeal to a person immersed in the cares and chores of everyday life. The everyday is a bottomless pit into which all the tumult of history is absorbed effortlessly, often with critical indifference.

As we already noted, the indifference is due to the fissure between the immanence of power relationships one is placed in everyday life and the larger assemblages of power that seek to govern the state. An employee, a salesperson in a textile showroom, drawing 10 rupees as her monthly salary in 1957 would naturally wonder how it mattered to her life which candidate or party won the election. In popular parlance, this is remarked as "How does it matter whether Rama or Ravana rules?" (Tamil: *Raman aanda enna, Ravanan aanda enna*). Hence, the first major task of the political parties was to provide some ground for the voter to develop a capacity for reasoning that would help her make the choice by becoming interested in the causes the parties espouse. The ideal trajectory is a sort of popular political pedagogy that the DMK tried to inculcate as acknowledged by the Congress-leaning journal *Ananda Vikatan* in 1957.[1] Such pedagogic and propagative efforts always came with a range of affective material that sought to interest the indifferent voter as in the case of the DMK, causing the intellectual disdain for popular electoral politics. What is often missed is that in spite of the seemingly catachrestic exercises of political campaigns that seek to overcome voter indifference, there still comes about a condition in which governance cannot fully ignore the concerns of the people and remain answerable to their aspirations in some measure and degree. There rests the meaning of electoral democracy.

Apart from political pedagogy or propagation, whatever be the affective dimensions that accompany them, there were many other modes in which the voter made up her mind. In most situations, as is well known, the landlord of the village to whom the laborers are attached, the headman of a caste group, the elder in a neighborhood, or the grand patriarch of a clan told the voters whom to vote for. The candidates often only met with such patron figures who would ensure all those who were attached to the patron cast their vote for the candidate. It was a challenge in the early elections to reach out to the individual voter and make the person conscious of her ability to decide for herself and also provide sufficient motivation to do so, particularly in the rural areas. In the absence of a political motivation, it was assumed that the voter may make the choice based on the level of affinity she may have for a candidate, as a person from her neighborhood or village, or more extensively, a person belonging to her caste. It is largely believed that caste considerations have a bearing on the electoral choices since caste functioned as the *longue durée* federation of individual families. It is common these days for analysts to speak of the numerical strength of a caste in a given region and the likely party affiliation of the caste group, for example, the Lingayat affiliation in North Karnataka to Yeddyurappa, a Lingayat leader of the Bharatiya Janata Party (BJP). However, in most situations the caste group affiliation to a party is never complete. The opposing party too fields a candidate from the numerically strong caste in a constituency, thus necessarily splitting the caste vote. Increasingly, the voters are also said to vote on the basis of monetary inducements in what is known as "Vote for Money." This is not entirely new, as the Congress candidates were accused of giving money to voters in the 1952 elections by the DMK. Political parties and charismatic leaders have struggled hard to build a committed voter base known as "vote bank" that will not be swayed by inducements or contingent reasons. The "growth" of a political party consisted in increasing its basic membership as a political federation, which would help in garnering votes beyond competitive inducements offered by political formations.

The choice of the candidate can also be an important factor. The personal attributes of the candidate, his or her personality, dynamism in action, and capacity for communication and inspiring confidence would all certainly matter in increasing the tally of votes. It also mattered what recommended the candidate to the voter. Social status and privilege may help insofar as the voter would trust such people to be able to hold power and negotiate for them; having financial resources to spend during the election campaign is certainly a great advantage. It is essential to have the party machinery well provided for during the campaign. If the candidate is not rich enough by himself, he should inspire confidence in some people who would spend for him in return for services. Leadership traits, charisma, communication skills can compensate for lack of resources and may invite sponsors of many kinds. The candidates' standing in his social group, that is, caste and religion, will also help if it is a numerically strong group within the constituency. Merely belonging to the caste group does not mean the candidate will have a standing within the group, which will have to be earned over a period of time.

One of the things the candidate has to ensure is a good campaign. It depends much on the party activists. It is in energizing the party machinery, identifying the right kinds of workers, building strategies to reach out to the voters in many parts of the constituency that the art of the election campaign lies. The right kind of party worker nurtures his pocket of influence all the time by forming social and clientele networks which he would enlist for support during the election. The conversion of such pockets of influence into actual ballots polled depended on the nature of the campaign. There have been instances where a good campaign has overturned an adverse scenario in terms of support for a particular party. A spirited campaign makes a positive impression on the voter. An active campaign is an equalizer to the difference in clout and status of the candidates. A rich landowner may lose to a person of far lesser means and status due to an effective campaign strategy by the underdog. Many a narrative of David triumphing over Goliath are spun out of effective campaign trails.

Finally, the event slowly shapes itself out of the issues that are spoken about in the campaign, style of the campaign, the candidate, the party, and the overall context of the election. Each given election develops a general theme; levels of approval or discontent with the party in power on the basis of governance is one default factor. There can be other particular issues that frame a given general election. The voter preference slowly forms and spreads—the reason why it is often called a wave of support. In the period under our present study, elections were more entrenched in the local moorings than now when extensive media networks often apparently supersede the so-called face-to-face interaction in a given constituency. One can perhaps see a gradual increase in the role of the media in the first four elections in Tamil Nadu we are discussing in this chapter, owing to the spread of transportation and communication networks. If the election in 1952 was more a local event in a constituency, it was more of a trans-local event in 1967. The transformation allowed for statewide trends to emerge in due course, though it never would totally obliterate the local variations owing to the other factors discussed.

The Insurmountable

As we discussed elaborately in the section on grassroots mobilization, the DMK managed an elaborate network of branches, circle committees, district committees, and so on all through the state. They could keep the network active by organizing meetings and conferences and through various protest actions. The journals and newsletters run by the party leaders provided a necessary discursive template for articulating ideational underpinnings. The plays, short stories, and novels of the party leaders added to the political discourse and deepened the sensibility about social transformation and also the Dravidian–Tamil identity. However, all these were not immediately adequate to convince ordinary voters, held fast by the forces of the status quo, to vote for the party. The gap between the grassroots party organization, its supporters and sympathizers, and the vast social space of the voting public was substantial. In 1957, the number of voters in Tamil Nadu was to the tune of 17.5 million. Managing a gathering of 1,000 or 2,000 people for a meeting or conference in a small town was quite different from convincing 100,000 people to vote for the party. This gap was marked by the inherent antagonism between the idea of social transformation and the idea of conserving the status quo. The Congress, already identified with the developmental state, had no problem in gaining the support of the conservative rich and the forces of status quo. For example, to cite a party worker's recollection, the richest landlord in a constituency who was also the trustee of the most important local temple and the correspondent of the local school—a man of high social status—would naturally be a member of the Congress, often the party candidate, or at least a well-known sympathizer. In contrast, the DMK branch secretary would be a *dhobi* who had started a laundry in the small town. In other words, the Congress almost inherited the state from the British, signaling to the power elite that it was in their interest to align with the Congress. The DMK in marked contrast started to mobilize the commoner with sporadic and indirect support from a few rich people here and there. It was only after showing some electoral success in 1957, establishing its reputation as an opposition party in the assembly and marking its presence in the parliament, could the DMK inspire confidence in richer people to align more fully with the party and also come forward to contest in the elections as party candidates.

Given such an overall backdrop, the foremost challenge faced by the DMK since its inception was a lack of funds. As a party of young leaders from the plebeian stock, each and every activity, be it a party journal or newspaper, hiring buildings for party offices, facing trials in cases foisted on activists, paying penalties imposed on protestors and writers, organizing meetings and conferences, depended on funds collected from the public. Raising funds for the elections was a daunting task. The DMK invariably relied on staging plays to do so. It increasingly motivated the party branches to raise funds through their own means and local resources. The crucial role played by election funds was increasing with every election. For example, in all the fifteen constituencies where the DMK had won in 1957, the Congress fielded wealthy candidates in 1962 with the sole intention of trouncing them with money power. Fourteen out of the fifteen candidates lost except for Karunanidhi who had switched constituencies from Kulithalai to Thanjavur, only to face a formidable liquor baron of the Congress. The most shocking defeat was that of Annadurai at Kanchipuram, which was widely attributed to the money power of the Congress party and the candidate, which included charges of monetary inducement to voters.

At any rate, money for campaign expenditure was always a challenge that was spoken about in every party forum. When it came to the 1967 elections, it was Karunanidhi, the treasurer of the party, who proposed that the party should aim to raise 5,000 rupees each for 200 constituencies, a total of 1 million rupees, as early as 1965. He undertook and was assigned the task of raising the funds as suggested. He scripted and acted in a play called *Kakithap Poo* (Paper Flower) that made an incessant tour of fundraising performances throughout the state. The DMK workers' unions and branches in faraway places like Bombay and Ahmedabad pitched in. By the time of the pre-election conclave in 1966, Karunanidhi had raised 11 lakh rupees, exceeding the target by a lakh. The second syllable of his name "nidhi" meant funds, which the jubilant Annadurai pointed out. When he announced the list of candidates, he mentioned Saidapet constituency, paused, and said "Mr 11 lakhs," referring to Karunanidhi.[2]

The DMK suffered from several negative perceptions, the key one being the charge of atheism that connoted it to be a party of upstarts who had no regard for traditional values. In a society where morality was and is taken to be identical to piety and faith in God (in matrimonial advertisements people still demand a "God-fearing" spouse), where patriarchy and the joint family system was widely practiced, the language of transformation articulated by the DMK appeared to disturb most of the common people that the party sought to rally. For example, we were told by a local activist in a village in Uthamapalayam constituency where Christians lived in majority that the local church initially used to ring the bell for a special congregation and the priest would warn the parishioners not to vote for the atheist DMK. In 1962, when Rajangam was fielded as the candidate of the DMK from the constituency, he happened to see the priest standing outside the church as he was passing by. He walked straight up to the priest, knelt in front of him, and sought his blessings. It is an instance that shows the role that could be played by a candidate in mitigating the negative perception carried by the party. Paṇṇaṉ, whose memoirs we discussed in Chapter 9, mentions Muslim elders being unhappy about the young lawyer Sadiq Basha joining the party. If this could be the case with Christians and Muslims, there is hardly any need to speak of the so-called Hindu orthodoxy.

If there is one way in which we could extract the difficulty faced by the DMK in the electoral turf and complexity of the processes, it is by paying attention to the regional variation in the narrative of the climb to electoral success. This should also be able to contest the naïve and superficial attribution of causes like the consolidation of "intermediary castes" or "attraction of cinema and film stars" or "rhetorical flourish in speeches" to the electoral success of the party. If such were the factors at all, we cannot see the sharp difference that took place among different regions in Tamil Nadu.

In order to make it simple, we will divide the state into four regions (Figure 12.1): north, west, central, and south.[3] The DMK had a head start in the north, could only slowly gain success in the central region and in the west, and still later in the south. In 1957, even in the case of number of candidates fielded, we can see the difference. The party fielded candidates in 37 out of 47 constituencies in the north; 31 out of 47 in the west; 26 out of 32 in the central region; however, in the south it fielded candidates only in 26 out of 47 constituencies with no one winning the election. The analysis of Table 12.1 will show a stark variation between the north and the south. In 1957, the north accounted for 80 percent of the seats won and the south drew a blank. In 1962, the north accounted for 48 percent and the south a mere 8 percent. In 1967, the north accounted for 38 percent and the south 23 percent. Likewise, the west and central regions also do not match up with the north. One immediate

Table 12.1 The region-wise electoral success of the DMK in the four assembly elections from 1952 to 1967

Election Year	North					West					Center					South				
	T	C	CA	W	W-A	T	C	CA	W	W-A	T	C	CA	W	W-A	T	C	CA	W	W-A
1952	56	-	34	-	24	43	-	9	-	5	40	-	11	-	11	51	-	8	-	3
1957	47	37	-	12	1	47	31	-	2	2	32	26	-	1	1	47	26	-	0	0
1962	63	50	-	24	2	47	39	-	9	1	39	31	-	13	0	57	23	-	4	3
1967	70	64	6	52	4	55	40	15	31	12	43	33	10	22	4	66	36	30	32	17

Notes: T = Total number of seats in the region; C = Seats contested by the DMK; C-A = Seats contested by alliance partners or candidates endorsed; W = Seats won; W-A = Seats won by alliance partners or candidates endorsed.
North: Chennai, Cuddalore, Tiruvannamalai, Vellore, Villupuram, Tiruvallur, Kancheepuram, Kallakkurichi, Chengalpattu, Ranipet, Tirupattur
West: Coimbatore, Erode, Dharmapuri, Namakkal, Salem, Nilgiris, Tiruppur, Karur, Krishnagiri
South: Madurai, Dindigul, Ramanathapuram, Sivagangai, Tirunelveli, Thoothukudi, Virudhunagar, Kanyakumari, Tenkasi, Theni
Central: Tiruchirappalli, Nagapattinam, Perambalur, Pudukkottai, Thanjavur, Thiruvarur, Ariyalur

Source: Authors.

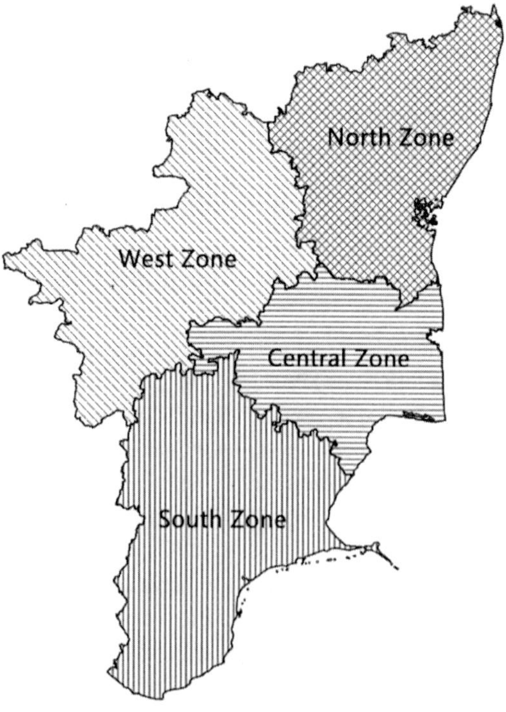

Figure 12.1 Map of Tamil Nadu divided into four zones
Source: Authors.

speculation that offers itself is to think of the numerically strong caste groups in each of these regions. The difficulty in such analysis is to first of all explain why some castes should prefer the DMK when others do not. For example, if the DMK is an ethno-nationalist party, why should ethno-nationalism appeal to one region more than another? If the party drew its dividend by a socially divisive strategy of non-Brahmins against Brahmins, why should that be more effective in the northern region than in other regions? Could it be that the party basically aligned with an urban imagination that the largest city, the capital Madras, provided it with all the mobilizational energy with proximity to Madras influencing the northern region?

There is more to regional variations than the disproportionate success in the north. Between 1957 and 1962, when the party's overall tally increased from 15 to 50, the south recorded an increase from 0 to 4, the west from 2 to 9, and the central region from 1 to 13. We see the central region marking a greater increase than the west and the south. Except for the fact that Karunanidhi contested in the region in both the elections, moving from Kulithalai to Thanjavur, it is hard to speculate why this increase was greater in central Tamil Nadu when compared to the west and the south.

If we take the share of its success across the four regions in the three elections, we are able to see one important factor. The variation among regions comes down drastically in 1967 but it happens incrementally between the three elections. If we make a ratio of the percentage of seats won in the four regions of north, west, central, and south out of the total number of seats won in each of the general election, it is possible to see how the gradual spread incrementally happened, finally aided by the statewide election thematic that became possible in 1967.

Election Year	Ratio
1957	80:13:7:0
1962	48:18:26:8
1967	38:23:16:23

If we also take into account that the 1967 election was fought in alliance with several other parties, which won 37 seats among them, the success in that election would look more evenly spread.

Without prejudice to many explanations that can be proffered for these electoral outcomes, it can be said that in 1967 there was a far greater historical and thematic reason for the electoral outcome than in the two previous elections. In spite of still-persisting local variations, an overall statewide thematic emerged in 1967 that helped the DMK to mainstream its ideational package in the state. Its painstaking grassroots mobilization and electioneering for eighteen years paid rich dividends when the historical moment of change arrived. What is perhaps important is that the DMK had forged a consistent political discourse that constructed a people as

Dravidian–Tamil that could finally consolidate the electoral success as a decisive historical moment rather than as a mere caprice of electoral politics. Hence, we will describe the climb of the DMK to power as a result of two distinct processes: a steady and consistent effort to nurture grassroots politics and a political discourse, a political common sense towards the construction of a people added to the contingent electoral events that helped it to move towards capturing power in the state. As we have discussed the efforts to build a political discourse in other chapters, we will now briefly study the electoral participation that helped the party to consolidate its gains.

History of Electoral Participation

It is necessary to contextualize the role of the DMK in each of the four legislative assembly elections held in 1952, 1957, 1962, and 1967. We need to read them as vastly distinct junctures with a substantial set of historical variables that the DMK encountered. We also need to take note of the local body elections in which the DMK local leaders and cadres participated as their personal initiative. There can hardly be any doubt that it was only by demonstrating that they could secure the votes of the common people, the party could become a force to reckon with, compelling the rich and the elite to negotiate with it. In other words, there is so much that is fascinating in the innumerable life stories of grassroots activists like the memoirs of Paṇṇaṉ or Rama Subbiah, all of which point to the gradual and substantial social change; however, all those changes in the everyday social crystalized better only through electoral participation and taking up governance. It is necessary to reiterate at this juncture that while the form of content of the political aspiration was the rule of the commoner, which was achieved, the form of expression of the political aspiration was initially Dravida Nadu, the republic consisting of the federation of south Indian states, which in 1963 was rescinded as an autonomous state of Tamil Nadu in the Indian federation.

It is beyond the scope of this book to speak of the yield of the electoral success in 1967 and the story of the DMK in power, which it started alternating with its offshoot, the All India Anna DMK (AIADMK) since 1977. The history of Dravidian rule certainly deserves a couple of volumes or more. Our present purpose stops at the moment the party came to power in 1967, closely followed by Annadurai's premature demise in 1969 marking the end of the era of construction of a people as Dravidian–Tamil. Perhaps the act that symbolizes it best is the renaming of the state as Tamil Nadu, a long-cherished goal of the party, for which Sankaralinganar gave up his life, fasting unto death in 1956.[4] While the history of electoral participation does not subsume the larger history of construction of a people and its attendant role in social transformation, it certainly addresses the crucial role of capturing state power, which alone can crystalize and consolidate the historical process.

1952

The party general council that met in 1951 to finalize the party constitution ahead of the first state-level conference in Chennai took a unique decision with the regard to the first general elections. In order to strengthen the opposition to the Congress, which had unleashed repressive measures against the movement, they decided to support any of the individual candidates or the parties willing to sign a pledge prepared by the party. The pledge read:

> I support the call for the independent Dravidian republic. If I am elected as a member to the assembly or the parliament, I will work to support the above cause and other principles of the DMK. I will also function in the assembly or parliament in such a way to mobilize support for the efforts of the DMK to end exploitation and despotism.[5]

We see that about seventy-three candidates for the assembly, state legislature, and thirteen candidates for the parliament, central legislature, signed the pledge. Two political parties, Toilers' Party and Commonweal Party, that emerged from the Vanniar Sangam, an association of the Vanniar caste, signed the pledge as parties. The Congress had many rich people like Poondi Vandayar and Ramnath Goenka in its list of candidates. Basically, the first election was conducted for the composite Madras State, earlier known as the Madras Presidency. It had parts of what is now Orissa, Andhra Pradesh, Karnataka, and Kerala included, as the linguistic state formation was yet to happen. It had 375 seats in all, out of which only 190 were in what was to become Madras State and later Tamil Nadu. Out of those who signed the pledge to earn the support of the DMK, forty-three candidates to the assembly and eight candidates to the parliament won the elections. This gave a considerable moral boast to the newly formed party. Even without contesting the elections directly, it could have its impact felt. The DMK conducted a tea party in honor of the winning candidates.

The Congress failed to get a majority, with the Communists securing 62 seats and independents winning 62 seats, apart from two parties from Andhra, Kisan Mazdoor Praja Party lead by Prakasam and Krishikar Lok Party lead by N. G. Ranga, winning 35 and 15 constituencies each. The Toilers Party supported by the DMK won 19 seats, and the Commonweal Party 6 seats. Rajaji was invited by Governor Tanguturi Prakasam to form the government as a firefighting measure even when he had not contested elections. He was nominated to the upper council by the governor even before the ministry was formed, which should recommend such a nomination. Rajaji offered a cabinet birth to Manickavel Naicker to secure the support of the members of the Commonweal Party. The Toilers Party also voted in support of the government. It was through such adroit moves that Rajaji managed to win the vote of confidence to stabilize the first Congress government. Even as the leaders of the two Vanniar parties defected to support the Congress, the DMK gained the loyalty of the general secretary of the Toilers Party, A. Govindasamy. He functioned as the head of a group that called itself as Dravidian parliamentarians.

Many DMK leaders like Karunanidhi, Sampath, and Nedunchezhian campaigned for the candidates who signed the pledge and were supported by the DMK. The party cadres also worked in the campaign. The fact was highlighted since the DMK lost a party functionary, A. Majeed of Cuddalore, to poll-related violence. He was stabbed by a Congress functionary, Kannan, who admitted to the crime in the court (Tirunāvukkaracu 2017, 1:446). The DMK raised funds for the distraught family of Majeed and bought them three acres of cultivable land. There are reasons to speculate that campaigning for the two Vanniar parties in northern Tamil Nadu helped the DMK to strengthen its support base in that region, particularly in North Arcot and South Arcot districts. The fact that the Congress could win only 96 constituencies out of the 190 in the Tamil-speaking region demonstrated that the mobilization of the Congress was not really at the grassroots level, exposing its inherent weakness. However, after the bifurcation of Andhra Pradesh from Tamil Nadu in 1953 as a prelude to the formation of linguistic states, Kamaraj, a grassroots Congress leader, ousted Rajaji to become the chief minister, which helped the Congress strengthen its organizational base in addition to the support of the rich and the elite.

1957

We noted that the first general elections in 1952 took place a month after the first state-level conference of the DMK when the party constitution, as adopted by the general council, was released. The party initiated a widespread membership drive under the aegis of the new party constitution; more branches were formed and organizational elections were conducted as per the party constitution. In the year 1954, elections were held for local bodies of governance like *panchayat* unions, municipalities, and corporations. We can recall from Chapter 9 that Pa. Narayanan sent a missive to Pannan to come to Udumalpet to help him campaign for the ward councilor position. As the example shows, many DMK activists and aspiring local leaders contested the local body elections in their individual capacity. Some of the victorious candidates like Anbil Dharmalingam were congratulated in the pages of the *Dravida Nadu*, which shows the party leadership was not against the effort. The DMK also launched waves of protest action and the three-pronged struggle, energizing the party cadres and gaining much visibility, as we discussed in Chapter 10. All this prepared the party for entering the electoral fray in 1957.

Nevertheless, the antinomy between the form of content of political aspiration as the rule of the commoner and the form of expression of political aspiration as the independent republic of Dravida Nadu persisted. The party adopted a unique procedure to reconcile the contradiction. In its second state-level conference held in Trichy in May 1956, it instituted a referendum in which all those who bought the entry ticket to the conference could cast a ballot in favor of or against electoral participation. One of the party enthusiasts we interviewed recounted an anecdote as narrated by his uncle, who was a party activist close to leaders like Karunanidhi and Annadurai. He caught Annadurai wistfully looking at the ballot boxes in the middle of the night at the conference venue. He made bold to tell Anna that people would vote in favor of electoral participation and that he need not worry; Anna quipped that indeed was his worry. It was only because the leadership or the general council could not decide on the crucial issue that the party members or in fact all those who attended the conference were asked to vote on the question. In the event, 56,942 votes were cast in favor of electoral participation with merely 4,203 votes cast against. The overwhelming decision in favor of electoral participation indicated that the party cadres were keen to realize the immediate goal of coming to power in the state than the long-term goal of achieving an independent republic of Dravida Nadu.

Annadurai reeled out several metaphors to interpret the decision as the necessary interplay of intermediary goal and the long-term goal. His metaphors indicated that the Congress rule in the state prevented the party from rallying people for the cause of the Dravidian republic. If one went to pluck jasmine flowers in the garden and it started raining at the moment, it is necessary to cover oneself from the rain in order pluck the flowers. The Congress rule is an adverse condition like the rain. Hence, it is important to remove the Congress from power to further the cause of the Dravidian republic. It can be surmised that in fact the articulation of the long-term goal served to energize the immediate goal. The DMK was not merely a political party that wanted to come to power ousting the Congress. It is a party that aspired for the democratic self-rule of the people vis-à-vis the Congress, which only acted on behalf of the Union government at Delhi. It is through this continued insistence on the aspiration for self-rule in the form of Dravida Nadu that the party could continue the task of constructing the people as Dravidian–Tamil.

The decision also coincided with the formation of linguistic states in 1956 that was to be ratified by November. As we noted, the bifurcation of Andhra, the Telugu-speaking regions, had taken place in 1953, leading to the ouster of Rajaji as chief minister and Kamaraj replacing him. Rajaji and his supporters left the Congress to form the Congress Reform Committee. Periyar welcomed Kamaraj as a true Tamil, in the sense that he belonged to the caste of Nadars, a Tamil-speaking non-Brahmin caste. This change of guard did take some wind out of the sails for the DMK since Kamaraj also hailed from a plebeian stock, a person without formal education or wealth, someone who ascended in the Congress party through sheer dedication. He was a total contrast to Rajaji, a rich Brahmin lawyer from a traditional landowning family. However, Kamaraj's proximity to Nehru and a strong nationalist stamp as well as the predominance of rich landowners, traders, and industrialists in the Congress compromised his personal image as a commoner and a Tamil. Kamaraj could be shown as the handmaiden of vested interests by the DMK. Speaking in an election rally in Chennai, Prime Minister Jawaharlal Nehru lashed out at separatist and anti-Brahmin sentiments, describing them as ridiculously barbaric. Apparently, he could not pronounce the name of the party, Dravida Munnetra Kazhagam even as Kamaraj prompted him.

The DMK's decision to contest the elections immediately gave rise to concerns about funds required for the same. Several fundraising campaigns were initiated in the form of special meetings. The party formed a committee to explore the conditions for contesting elections in various constituencies. Out of the total number of 205 seats, the DMK could contest only from 123 seats. Though it made a vibrant campaign effort with innovative posters and street corner oratory, it could win only in 15 seats; it forfeited the deposit in 40 seats. As we noted already, 14 out of 15 seats won were in the north and north-west. Karunanidhi was the only person to win from central Tamil Nadu. However, it had polled nearly 17 lakh votes, making it a serious contender for power. Further, it could send two members to the parliament, marking its presence in the national scene. E. V. K. Sampath, a frontline leader, was one of them. With fifteen of them in the assembly and two in parliament, the DMK had gained a foothold in democratic governance, which it utilized to the hilt in building its image in the subsequent years. The street corner meetings now echoed their interventions in the assembly and also the parliament.

1962

The five years between 1957 and 1962 were relatively a good period for the Congress governments at the Center and at the state with impressionable progress in economic development. The DMK went through a process of transformation as a parliamentary party. There was no major protest action or struggle launched by the DMK between the two general elections in 1957 and 1962. As expected, or feared, the party's long-term goal of the Dravidian republic was increasingly getting weakened with the advent of its new image as a parliamentary party. E. V. K. Sampath, who went to parliament, was pushing for changes in the party. He secured an assurance from Nehru on the question of official language implementation, that is making Hindi the sole official language. As the party's influence grew at the grassroots level, the stakes in party positions were becoming more important, resulting in inner-party conflicts. Sampath finally engineered a split and quit the party in 1961. He initially launched the Tamil Nationalist Party, which he claimed to have a more practical goal than the elusive ideal of a Dravidian republic. However, his Tamil nationalism was to soon merge with Indian nationalism, as he merged his party with the Congress after a poor show in the 1962 elections. The DMK also admitted a high-profile Brahmin lawyer, V. P. Raman, into the party in 1957. Sampath's biography notes that the lawyer's house was the venue where many congregations of party leaders took place in the four years between 1957 and 1961. Rajaji, who had launched the Swatantra

Party in the meantime, absorbing the members of the Congress Reform Committee, was also building bridges with the DMK to fight the Congress led by Kamaraj.

The DMK made a powerful impact in the local body elections in 1959. It captured the Madras Corporation, winning 45 wards out of 100; with the support of the Communists, a DMK member became the mayor of the Madras Corporation. In turn, the DMK supported a communist chairman in the Coimbatore municipality. Winning Madras Corporation further enhanced the stature of the party.

As the election approached, the party was far better prepared this time. It had made it a practice to release election manifestos. In the 1962 manifesto, it listed the interventions it made on the floor of the assembly in addition to several goals and aspirations for the future. The demand for the independent Dravidian republic, a federation of the four southern linguistic states, still occupied a preeminent place. It should be noted that its section on the expansion of the public sector included nationalization of banks that was to be undertaken by Indira Gandhi towards the end of the decade. The manifesto was an elaborate document touching upon core economic sectors and a full-fledged socialist vision. *Murasoli*, the magazine edited by Karunanidhi, also brought out a pictorial version of the manifesto (Po. Taṅkapāṇṭiyaṉ 2008, 45–71). In spite of several parleys, electoral alliances did not firm up. There were localized seat-sharing arrangements within districts, extending mutual support among candidates, but no formal alliance was struck with any party. Both the Swatantra Party and the Communist Party expressed a synergy with the DMK. The Congress roped in all the rich and powerful candidates into the fray. The DMK made a huge stride, contesting in 143 seats, winning 50 seats, and doubling its vote share to 34 lakh. It also won in seven parliamentary constituencies.

1967

Everything changed between 1962 and 1967. Soon after the elections in 1962, the DMK launched an agitation to protest the rise in the prices of commodities, the first struggle launched by the party for a general cause that signified the mainstreaming of the party. Most of its frontline leaders courted arrest, as we discussed in Chapter 10. The Official Language Act was passed after much pressure exerted by the DMK, which allowed for continuance of English as the language of governance in addition to Hindi beyond the fifteen-year period as mandated by the Constitution. However, the term "may" allowed for uncertainty over the implementation of the promise made by Nehru that English would continue as long as all the non-Hindi speaking states insisted on it. This uncertainty was to flare up in 1965 into a major conflagration in Tamil Nadu that we elaborately recounted in Chapter 11. The DMK underplayed its disquiet over the uncertain nature of the act due to Chinese aggression in the border which rattled the nation. The DMK articulated its unstinted support to the Indian Union in the face of Chinese aggression.

Due to several rumblings within the Congress, the Kamaraj plan, or "K" plan, was implemented, in which most senior leaders quit office to take care of the party work.[6] Kamaraj resigned as the chief minister of Tamil Nadu, asking a far less popular Bhakthavatsalam to take over. In a far-reaching legal measure, in spite of Annadurai's eloquent protest, the parliament enacted in October 1963 the sixteenth amendment to the Constitution that required all elected representatives to the parliament and state legislature to abide by the sovereignty and integrity of India, thereby making the demand for secession of any part of India on the floor of the house ultra vires. As a consequence, the DMK officially rescinded its demand for an independent Dravidian republic, substituting it with the demand for state autonomy within a federal India. When the DMK once again upped the ante about the Official Language Act and its implementation, Nehru had passed away, making things more uncertain. The Communist Party suffered a vertical split in the country, giving birth to Communist Party of India (Marxist), or CPI(M). The death of Nehru, absence of Kamaraj at the helm in Tamil Nadu, approaching of the fifteenth Republic Day when the official language switch was about to happen, and apprehensions caused by many articulations of the cabinet ministers, including Prime Minister Lal Bahadur Shastri, combined to produce a massive uprising in Tamil Nadu triggered by student protests in January–March 1965. The Madras State also suffered a food grain shortage, particularly rice, that made the Congress government extremely unpopular. Following a brief military conflict with Pakistan over Kashmir, Lal Bahadur Shastri died in Tashkent, Russia, during peace negotiations in January 1966. Kamaraj played a pivotal role in getting Indira Gandhi, the daughter of Nehru, elected as the prime minister. This left Morarji Desai and many other Congress leaders unhappy. It is at the end of these eventful five years that the 1967 elections were held.

Except for the Communist Party of India, all other parties in Tamil Nadu including the Swatantra Party and the newly formed Communist Party of India (Marxist) were so eager for the unpopular regime of Bhakthavatsalam to end that they were willing to form an alliance. The DMK, having inducted a large number of students after the anti-Hindi uprising, was fully prepared to take on the Congress, which was responsible for the unwarranted, extreme repression that turned what might have been peaceful protests into bloody confrontations. A broad coalition was formed under the leadership of the DMK, which contested in as many as 174 seats. Swatantra Party contested in 27 seats, CPI(M) in 22 seats, Praja Socialist Party in 4 seats, Indian Union Muslim League in 3 seats, and the Sanghata Socialist Party in 3 seats. The DMK was swept to power with as many as 137 seats. The Congress, which contested 232 seats, could win only in 51 seats. Kamaraj was defeated in his native constituency Virudhunagar by the student leader P. Srinivasan. The coalition secured 80 lakh votes as against 62 lakh votes by the Congress. The victory of the DMK was emphatic.

Jawaharlal Nehru repeatedly rubbished Dravidianist politics, both its claims about regional distinction and non-Brahminism, as nonsense. As we have noted in different parts of the book, he was not alone in expressing certain elite disdain for the political language and imagination of the plebeian stock. The DMK was no match to the combined power of the wealth, status, and privileges of those who produced the consensus around the Indian nation. Many a time when the English language media mentioned them or wrote about them, even if adversely, the DMK journals reproduced the articles to share with the cadres that they were being noticed by the powers that be. The frontline leaders of the party slept on the floors of laundries and tailor shops, under the trees in the open, to rally the commoners in the hope of creating a politics of the plebs. If anywhere in the annals of electoral democracy universal adult franchise produced a lasting political formation, cultural awakening, and social transformation, it was Annadurai and his *thambis*—younger brothers—who made such a history possible. If Nehru was alive in 1967, he would have heard a faint murmur of his own words echoing from Chennai: "Long years ago we made a tryst with destiny, and now the time comes when we shall redeem our pledge, not wholly or in full measure, but very substantially."

Notes

1. *Ananda Vikatan* welcomed the entry of Annadurai into the assembly. It also started advertising in DMK magazines. See Tirunāvukkaracu (2017, 3:1255).
2. This is an oft repeated anecdote and widely known. See, for example, T. Muruganantham and S. Kumaresan (2017).
3. Other scholars have approached this problem differently from us. Narendra Subramaniam, for example, has a five-fold classification of the state. See Subramanian (2004).
4. In 1956, after the bifurcation of the erstwhile Madras State, political parties in Tamil Nadu demanded that Madras be renamed as Tamil Nadu. Sankaralinganar, a Gandhian, started a fast on July 27, 1956, and after 76 days of fasting he died in a hospital.
5. *Dravida Nadu* 10, no. 22, November 25, 1951, 6.
6. For details of the plan and its context, see Narain (1963).

Conclusion

Formations of the Political

> Whereas politics represents just one instance of a social totality, the political refers to the way diverse instances are disaggregated and mutually articulated.
>
> —Elias Jose Palti, *An Archeology of the Political*

The central argument of the book has been that the Dravida Munnetra Kazhagam (DMK) accomplished the task of construction of a people as Dravidian–Tamil through or alongside the formations of the political. In borrowing Laclau's formulation of populist reason, we have argued that Tamil functioned as the empty signifier that unified the people while the divide between Aryan–Dravidian or Brahmin–non-Brahmin functioned as the internal frontier. We sketched this proposition through Chapters 1 and 2, providing a sum-up at the beginning of Chapter 3. We will return to this later to fully expand on its significance and also relate to two previous works on the DMK mobilization by Marguerite Ross Barnett and Narendra Subramanian. We will now focus on, in conclusion, our proposition related to the formations of the political. In a certain sense, formations of the political have a lasting validity and importance that provides stability to the construction of a people. Our understanding of the term "political" and its formation in Tamil Nadu needs some parsing now.

Political: Play of Immanence and Transcendence

In his recent work *An Archaeology of the Political*, Elias Jose Palti has suggested that it was with the separation of the spheres of immanence and transcendence and through the play of the two that a historical phase began in which regimes of power were organized in what came to be referred to by the term "political." He has sketched at least three distinct ages: "the age of representation" (the seventeenth and eighteenth centuries), "the age of history" (the nineteenth century), and "the age of forms" (the late twentieth century). Without going into the details of these epochs and logic corresponding to each, what we borrow for our own analysis is his formulation succinctly expressed in these terms: "The political, as we have seen, is a play of immanence/transcendence, and the different regimes of exercise of power we have been analyzing are diverse modes of production of the transcendence effect out of immanence, a justice effect" (Palti 2017, 143).

Our understanding of immanence is to locate the political as generated from the networks of power, structures of power, and the relationships of power that obtain in the social. This constitutes what Carl Schmitt refers to as the "pluriverse" of the political (Schmitt 2008, 53). There are many antagonisms as well as antagonisms muted as agonisms in the everyday social. Until the arrival of the modern age or the age of the political, these were tethered to divinity and sovereignty in an undifferentiated mode. It is only when such articulations of transcendence were critically separated and the social appeared to be self-governing or self-regulating that the age of the political was born. Still, the plurality of the conflictual interests of the social needed to produce a unity, a governing structure, underlining a residual need for a political theology, even as Claude Lefort argued for an ambivalent break with such a need (Lefort 1989). A crucial conceptual operation that is perhaps needed here is not to identify transcendence only with the manifestation of a sovereign entity like the nation-state. Transcendences abound in the immanent field of the political. Let us think illustratively in the context of Tamil Nadu.

The caste system produced a social hierarchy that effectively combined consent generation and coercion through the transcendental idiom of Brahminic Hinduism and its codes or *shastras* variously disseminated, administered, and had become part of the common sense, a caste ontology so to speak. However, the immanent pluriverse of social relationships could never be fully contained or ordained in the way the transcendental scheme articulated it. Nevertheless, the separation of the immanence and transcendental still remained in an undifferentiated mode in which the social was seen to be so ordained to drown the murmur of immanent articulations. It is only with the critical separation introduced by the discourses of law, individual rights and entitlements, and so on that a separation could be articulated between the immanence of the social and the transcendental order. This can be readily understood by the popular re-narration of the story of Nandan at the beginning of Tamil literary modernity by Gopalakrishna Bharathy.

Nandan, an untouchable devotee, who was barred by the priestly class from having a *darshan* of Lord Shiva, was granted *darshan* and redemption by the Lord himself. Though couched in the idiom of devotional literature, the separation of the immanent and transcendental in the story as soulless order of the social and the redemptive potential of the transcendental is both subtle and significant. The reversal of transcendental imaginary is important: the priestly class mobilized God to justify the transcendental castiest order; the devotee mobilized God to defy the normative proscription. In the nineteenth-century rearticulation, though a devotee, Nandan's volition provided him the singularity required to mark the birth of individual consciousness.[1]

The discursive reiteration of the individual with a human essence unmarked by caste began to proliferate and gain strength as the cornerstone of nascent modernity. The advent of such humanist articulations began to yield conscious re-articulations of caste networks as civil society organizations that negotiated various demands for redressal of grievances and injuries with the new secularly informed legal structures of the government. If these became nascent structures of reform axis in the immanence of the social, the discourse of anti-colonial nationalism with its patriotic fervor introduced an axis of sovereignty as a transcendental aspiration. The combination of the two soon began producing a pluriverse of antagonisms and agonism that inaugurated the formation of the political. Instead of imagining the birth of the neutral citizen sterilized of all social identity who rallied for political cause, we need to see that in the social crosscurrent of various mobilizational activities, contingent articulations of the political were born. Further, in spite of hierarchy, a given caste was neither a unified whole and nor was social antagonism only inter-caste. The friend–enemy dyads proliferated on all axes as the countless accounts of folklore reveal. Let us return to Schmitt to clarify this further.

If we keep to the Schmittian dictum in treating the friend–enemy formation as the core of the political, an immanent vision of the political will recognize that friend–enemy formations are extracted from nuclear structures of friendship and enmity in the social, cemented with a transcendent discourse to form the political. This is not hard to grasp in popular electoral politics, where enmity among the members of a kinship or caste group, or even members of the same family get roped into opposing political party formations. This does not fully negate or supersede the earlier forms of solidarities or power constellations but drives a wedge into the social through the production of newer forms of affiliation and transcendence. We can recall here Annadurai's seminal discussion of *paṟṟu*, or affiliation that produces an equivalence to the idea of "good" that we considered in Chapter 3. There are many affiliations and many ways in which associational life is formed; if the social has been stratified and hierarchized in a certain way, the newer modes of association and affiliations to newer organizing principles produce newer transcendences. While we agree with Lefort that there is no question of simple transference from theology to political and that democracy introduces a break with the inception of civil society, we nevertheless should emphasize that discourses of transcendence need to be produced to realize the formations of the political from the pluriverse of antagonisms embedded in the social. Hence, the play of immanence and transcendence in which transcendence produces the justice effect in producing or reproducing the political. The emergence of the modern state, juridical power, and nations to house them as sovereign entities were historical outcomes of the need.

As a result, the historical energy had two axes in the process: one was form oriented—“re-formation” of the society; the other was subject-oriented “sovereignty” of the polity. They often were not mutually exclusive but different political constellations accentuated and prioritized either. Largely, when hegemonic forces try to unify society into a political entity, they work on the subject-driven, sovereignty axis, identifying an external enemy with violent tendencies or war machine formations against the outside of the unity that was sought to be built. Contrastingly, when marginalized, subjugated identities try to unify politically, they work on the structure-driven, reformation axis where the antagonism with “outside” is muted or abstracted by agonism within. The outside becomes a disembodied notion. For example, in a sensational event, the Brahmin patriot Vanchi Iyer (1886–1911) assassinated the British collector Robert Ashe in the year 1911, shooting him at point-blank range in a train compartment at Maniyachi junction in southern Tamil Nadu. He killed himself soon after. In his suicide note, he abusively called the British King George V a beef-eating Panchama—a term denoting the untouchable castes. Around the same time, Iyothee Thass (1845–1914), belonging to one such Panchama caste, was rallying for the cause of marginalized people. He had formed the Panchamar Mahajana Sabha and edited a journal *Tamizhan*. He was in no hurry to seek liberation from the British rule. He was one of the early political activists to use the identities “Dravidian” and “Tamizhan” in a political sense.[2] The political unification of India, a source of transcendence for the Brahmin patriot, meant annihilation of the foreign ruler, the British collector representing the British sovereign king George V, who he ironically described as a Panchama. It is difficult to anticipate Panchama politics to have the same investment against this figure of the Other representing the “outside,” as it had much to contend in the immanence of power relationships in the social.

The extremists and moderates in the Indian National Congress represented the two axes of subject-driven sovereignty and “re-form”-driven self-regulation or rule. Gandhi made a populist innovation in that he marked colonial modernity as the “outside” to transfer the energy of the subject-driven quest for sovereignty or *swaraj* into a notion of self-reformation. But Gandhi still fell far short of the demands of Periyar and Ambedkar in terms of fuller emphasis on social reconstruction. In his speech delivered on the occasion of the birth anniversary of Ranade, titled “Ranade, Gandhi, Jinnah” (Ambedkar 2008), Ambedkar not only clearly points to the difference between “social” and the “political” but also between “social reform” and “political reform.” Explaining how Ranade’s insistence on social reform is the necessary precursor to political reform, he rebukes the intransigence of Gandhi and Jinnah in 1943 when the speech was delivered as leaders of two contending groups, Hindus and Muslims, transcendent entities, which was producing a stalemate. It is possible to read Ambedkar’s criticism as directed towards the gravitational pull of the sovereignty axis of historical energy in the mobilization of the transcendent entities Hindu and Muslim, which ought to have been diverted to the reform axis.

The Congress anchorage in the state-making enterprise at the time of independence left the vast field of social reconstruction open. With the cataclysmic violence engulfing the birth of two nations, marking a religious divide, and with the assassination of Gandhi by another Vanchi like Maharashtrian Brahmin, who wanted national unification under the sign of the Hindu, Congress nationalism fully identified with the state and sovereignty axis with a transcendent Indian nationalism, which they were at pains to distinguish from a Hindu transcendence. They became zealous guardians of their hard-won sovereign possession, rallying all status quo nodes of power in the social. The foundational weakness of their attempt to keep Hindu transcendence at bay was a lack of strident critique of Brahmin hegemony. While Kamaraj in Tamil Nadu did manage to mobilize many sections of society, he was hampered by an allegiance to Indian nationalism, which refused to articulate a repudiation of Brahmin hegemony as expressed by the legalization of dharma *shastras* during the colonial era as vide the judgement in 1943 mentioned in Annadurai's *Aryan Allure*. It is precisely at this moment that the DMK emerged in Tamil Nadu to continue to articulate the discontent of the still vastly unreconstructed social. The history of the DMK is nothing but the history of its grassroots mobilization. The formation of branches, reading rooms, Thirukkural societies, debating forums, and the many allied activities that nurtured a self-reconstructive, reformative discourse, which appealed to the universal humanist claim of emancipation, formed the bones, flesh, and sinews of the party. Its meticulous work of transformation of power relations in the immanence of the social had to be accompanied by a discourse of transcendence, which became the goal of the independent Dravidian republic. In a sense, the demand for Dravida Nadu was the expression of what was left unfinished on the side of the social reformation by the Congress, most particularly the dismantling of Brahmin, casteist hegemony, which manifested in many ways in the production relationships of the vast agrarian hinterland and a new form of Brahmin domination and power consolidation in the cities by combining ritual, spiritual authority with a substantial hold on secular governance, legal and other emergent professions, and cultural production.

In a sense, the DMK inherited the ideational mandate. Since the nineteenth century, several non-Brahmin caste associations were formed with the purpose of furthering their interests in terms of cultural status and secular power-sharing. This paved way for elite political formations like the South Indian Liberal Federation, also known as the Justice Party, which championed communal reservation in government offices and educational institutions to make them more inclusive. Later, Periyar's Self-Respect Movement drew sustenance and cadres from the erstwhile non-Brahmin caste mobilizations. The discourse against caste could only emanate from subordinated castes who found their positions being marginalized in the new dispensations of power ushered in by colonial modernity and governance, most particularly felt through revenue administration and the juridical apparatus. Periyar radicalized the discontent by expanding the scope of opposition to the ritual domain that can also be described as the spiritual and religious domain. Periyar found this necessary since in order to found the political, the spheres of immanence and transcendence needed to be separated so that their interplay could constitute the political. If secularism is the name given to such separation, the same cannot be realized as the common turf of social and political or immanence and transcendence without a rigorous critique of ritual dominance, spiritual discourse, and performativity of the Brahminical social order. It is only because everyone realized the need for the political to be shaped by the separation of immanence and transcendence that many of the non-Brahmin elite as well as common people chose to align with Periyar even when they were not atheists or philosophically grounded in the provenance of materialism or "prakriti vatham" (*pirakiruti vātam*) as Periyar described it in a tract.[3] This is the historical context in which the non-Brahmin critique of Brahminism and Dalit critique of Brahminism merged. Ambedkar and Periyar were in full agreement that the dismantling of Brahmin hegemony was the precondition for building a democracy. It is at this juncture that the party, the DMK, was able to inherit such an ideational mandate, which enabled it to mobilize both Dalits and non-Dalits in the party formation and this possibility was crucial in the formations of the political.

The translation of the inherited ideational mandate as the formation of friend–enemy relations at the local level happened as between the power elite and those in subordinate and subaltern positions. The power elite were not necessarily Brahmins but were adherents to the Brahminical social order. The soil in which the DMK grew was what we described as the ground of new sociality: educational institutions, media industry, including theater groups, sites of new material practice like tea shops, barber shops, tailor shops, laundries, and small scale enterprises in trade and commerce were all sites and nodes where new solidarities were forged beyond caste and kinship networks. The DMK branches and forums became another site where a new solidarity of the subaltern was fashioned alongside these other nodes and sites. As we noted earlier, this gradually manifested in a certain personal style and bearing of DMK functionaries, a specific mode of discourse and conduct that recommended them to people. They marked their difference and they promised a social transformation, a new cultural awakening. The Congress, though it consisted of non-Brahmin castes, was not able to articulate the break with the past, the normativity of Brahminical social order because of the national cultural discourse it forged with Brahmins. However, we should note that in the messy empirical world of the social, there were no strict lines separating the political formations. We can only aspire to trace a conceptual aggregation. If we can produce a table to capture a conceptual map of the political in the period of our study, it might look like Table C.1.

Table C.1 Conceptual map of the political in Tamil Nadu, 1949–1967

Plane of operation	DMK	Congress
Immanence (Friend–enemy structures in the social)	Spheres of new sociality, subaltern aspiration for equality, non-Brahminism social reformation, change or emancipation	Power elite, hegemonic control, status quo, Brahminical Hinduism, nationalism, patriotism
Reform axis (Form of content)	Reform from below	Reform from above
Transcendence Sovereign axis (Form of expression)	Dravidian republic–federation of four southern states, rule of the commoner	Indian nation-state, rule of the nationalist or cultural elite

Source: Authors.

While this particular history provided the conditions of possibility of the political to take shape, on the ground the political returned to an autonomous domain where only the friend–enemy alignments mattered, as Schmitt reasoned. The party formation of the DMK and its success in the 1957 elections, garnering 17 lakh popular votes in the state, posited it primarily as a political vehicle with grassroots strength. As a result, parties opposed to the Congress sought to align with the DMK, particularly during the elections. Rajaji, who was fully opposed to the DMK in 1954, became a benign ally in 1962, though an electoral alliance did not materialize that year. It can be instructive to see how Rajaji's Swatantra Party, an elite formation of Brahmin professionals and landowners, rich non-Brahmin landowners, industrialists performed in the elections compared to the DMK, fully banking on grassroots mobilization and cadre strength. At the other end of the spectrum, the Communist Party, which was a rival formation to the DMK, particularly among the organized working class and trade unions, was tending to align with the DMK on the electoral front against the Congress. Again, there was no alliance yet in the 1962 elections, except perhaps seat adjustments in some parts of the state. To see how the Communist Party of India, CPI before the split, fared in the elections would also be instructive. Let us consult Table C.2 with relevant data from the 1962 election results (see Table C.2).

The fundamental reason for the success of the DMK was the elaborate party organization at the grassroots level, meticulously built over a decade, which was constantly energized by protest action, political propagation, and popular pedagogy of democratic values and practices. At its core, it aspired to form the rule of the commoner. In our gloss, we call this the form of content. The *formation* of the

Table C.2 The comparative electoral performances in 1962

Description	DMK	Swatantra	CPI
Seats Contested	143	97	68
Seats Won	50	6	2
% of Seats Won	35%	6%	3%
Votes Polled	3,435,633	991,773	978,806
% of Votes Polled	27.10%	7.82%	7.72%

Source: Authors.

party organization is the historical content. The cause, goal, or ideals promoted by the party we designate as form of expression. These two attain a degree of autonomy in the electoral process because when it comes to the election what matters is winning enough number of seats to be able to form the government and rule. This is the reason why a certain disdain for popular politics increases manifold when considering the electoral process. If popular politics or populism staked out rhetorical positions about ideology, electoral politics appeared to dilute it even further. If critical theory is invested in learning to theorize elections, it needs to see that the form of content, the party organization, and form of expression, and the ideational scheme, while functioning autonomously, still connect in many ways, since the political itself is nothing but the interplay of immanence and transcendence. In other words, the impure mixture of ideals and realpolitik does not produce a negation of either but produces outcomes that Palti helpfully describes as "justice effect."

If the party machinery is saturated in the power relationships, antagonisms, and allegiances in the immanence of the social, the ideational articulations of the party try to bring about a coherence to the pluriverse of contradictions through a discourse of transcendence, which in the case of the DMK was Dravidianism that sought to construct people as Dravidian–Tamil. It is why it will be unnecessary and futile to explain the successes and failures of the party in terms of allegiances of caste groups since the interests of a caste group itself are not so unified and identifiable as to fully align with a political party. The DMK backed the candidacy of Sivaraj, a prominent leader of the Scheduled Caste Federation in the 1957 election. He became a member of parliament. The party had electoral seat adjustments with Pasumpon Muthuramalinga Thevar of the Forward Bloc, an icon of Mukkulathor castes in 1962, while it also continued to align with Sivaraj, a fact that retroactively appears implausible. Hence, while caste associations and networks play a role in politics, the friend–enemy combinations of electoral politics at best can have only an indefinite and arbitrary connection to such caste interests when it comes to the electoral outcomes, remaining forever a subject of speculation. In common sense parlance, almost everyone in Tamil Nadu who has even a cursory interest in electoral politics knows the adage, "There is no perpetual friend or foe in politics" (*arasiyalil niranthara ethiriyum kidaiyathu; nanbanum kidaiyathu*). The corollary of this common sensical wisdom is the dictum one can derive from Schmitt: "There ought to be some enemy and some friend, a friend–enemy formation at any given moment to constitute the political."

In the event, Rajaji was increasingly aligning with the DMK after 1962. His opposition to making Hindi the sole official language was becoming emphatic. He shared the dais with the DMK and other prominent socialites in anti-Hindi imposition conferences. The Communist Party, in the meantime, suffered a split in 1964, allegedly as a consequence of the souring of Sino-Soviet relationship and Indo-China war. A new party, the Communist Party of India (Marxist), or CPI(M), was formed with apparent allegiance to China, while the CPI retained its affiliation to the Soviet Union. When Indira Gandhi became the prime minister in 1966, she was thought to be leaning towards the Soviet Union and of a socialist persuasion. The CPI decided to support the Congress under her leadership. The CPI(M) however was opposed to the Congress. Hence, in the 1967 election both the Swatantra Party led by Rajaji and the CPI(M) led by P. Ramamurthy struck electoral alliances with the DMK. Annadurai led an alliance with two parties representing the extremes of the ideological spectrum both headed by Brahmins. Periyar supported Kamaraj and the Tamil Nadu Congress headed by him. The 1967 election is a good example of how friend–enemy formations could supersede ideological, ideational considerations when it came to elections and electoral outcomes. The constant use of the metaphor of battle for elections reveals the existential pact of friend–enemy formations of the political. What is significant about the formation in 1967 was the leadership the DMK assumed in the political divide.

What followed the 1967 election was an even more complex unfolding of events that demands a detailed study. We will quickly remark on some of the salient features to drive home our point about how formations of the political guide electoral considerations. As we had noted earlier, Annadurai passed away in 1969. Karunanidhi became the party leader and the chief minister. The Congress party suffered a major split in the same year, allegedly over the left leaning policies of Indira Gandhi. Kamaraj, Morarji Desai, and other leaders, known as the "syndicate," expelled Prime Minister Indira Gandhi. She formed a rebel Congress. The syndicate called their congress Congress (O) with "O" standing for "organization," and Indira Gandhi called her party Congress (R) with "R" standing for "reform." The DMK parliamentary party supported the Indira Gandhi government, finding a common cause in the socialist agenda. When she decided to dissolve the parliament to seek the mandate of the people in 1971, one year ahead of the completion of the term of the elected government, the DMK too dissolved the assembly to have simultaneous elections. The Congress led by Indira Gandhi formed an alliance with the DMK with such terms that could be considered a historical watershed moment. Indira Gandhi's Congress (R) accepted the offer to contest in nine parliamentary constituencies from Tamil Nadu and agreed not to contest anywhere in the assembly elections. Probably, the image Kamaraj carried made Indira feel that she perhaps had no stake in Tamil Nadu politics. Rajaji, alarmed by the more accentuated socialism of Indira Gandhi, aligned with his long-time archrival Kamaraj and also the Jan Sangh led by A. B. Vajpayee. The Congress (O)–Swatantra–Jan Sangh alliance was touted as a Grand Alliance. The Indira Gandhi–Karunanidhi alliance secured a huge victory. Indira won 352 seats in the 534-member parliament and 43 percent of popular votes. Karunanidhi won 184 seats in the 234-member assembly and 48.5 percent of the popular vote. The outcome nearly eclipsed the Congress in Tamil Nadu since the Indira Gandhi faction did not contest the assembly elections, leaving all the seats to the alliance partner, the DMK, and the Kamaraj faction was trounced in the election. The Congress never recovered.

A year later, the DMK suffered a vertical split. M. G. Ramachandran, known as M. G. R., the DMK leader and actor playing the hero in popular film narratives, who had nurtured fan clubs alongside party branches, revolted against the leadership. When expelled, he started a party adding the name of Anna to DMK, naming the party ADMK, claiming to be the true legatee of the deceased founding leader. The singular history of M. G. R.'s transformation from actor to leader through popular film narratives produced against the historical backdrop of the political discourse of emancipation and the rule of the commoner that the DMK propagated needs to be recounted separately.[4] He provided the fictional subject-driven sovereignty axis as a supplement to the structure-driven reform axis of the DMK, particularly since the DMK gave up on the demand for the Dravidian republic of the four southern states. Interestingly, as sovereignty had already coalesced around the Indian state, M. G. R. became more Indianist within the fold of Dravidianism, renaming his party as All India Anna DMK (AIADMK) during the Emergency rule of Indira Gandhi.[5] It is widely held that the Congress and its ally, the CPI, played a role in instigating him to split the DMK. However, neither faction of the Congress could gain from the split as the DMK gained from the Congress split. What happened was, the friend–enemy combinations at all levels of the social found the two Dravidian parties adequate to form electoral battle lines. Slowly and irretrievably, a two-party system emerged in Tamil Nadu with all other political formations having to align with either of the two Dravidian parties that fully entrenched their roots into the immanence of the relationships of power in the social in the half century following the split.

The distinction made by Subramanian between the DMK and the AIADMK as pursuing assertive populism and paternalist populism respectively does not sufficiently capture the difference between the two parties (Subramanian 2004). We propose that the distinction rests more on what we have already discussed as structure-driven reformist populism and sovereignty-driven populism. Partha Chatterjee captures the distinction precisely when he notes, "After his split from the DMK, M. G. R. was no longer the bearer of a political message from the party; he was himself the message" (Chatterjee 2019, 102). While we agree when Chatterjee points out a certain decline of the pedagogic content of populism from Periyar to M. G. R., we propose that there is a need to ponder on the lasting effects of the formations of the political. The well-known Dalit critique of the rule of the Dravidian parties as not having sufficiently offered redressal to the injuries suffered by Dalit constituencies, which Chatterjee also points out, is itself enabled by the formations of the political that has made a relay of contestations possible. The formations of the political, in the scale in which it has penetrated the social in Tamil Nadu, certainly does not seem to reverse what Chatterjee has described as the "passive revolution of the capital" staged on a global scale. However, it needs to be considered whether a latent potency has been nurtured among people for political action, which, combined with the optimism of the intellect he mentions, may open some possibilities in future for the long-deferred arrival of the people. A speculation as this reverberates more with the concluding lines of Chatterjee's *The Politics of the Governed*, where he describes the political present as a learning exercise.[6] Since our present book has covered only the period between 1949 and 1967(69), we need to return to a final summation of the idea of constructing a people.

What Constructs a People?

If Tamil speakers constitute a people, there would be no need to construct them. They are an ontic presence. The construction of a people as "Dravidian–Tamil" was a political process in which a pedagogy of democratic principles for self-governance was undertaken. In short, infusion of the political into the social is what constructs a people. The internal frontier, Aryan–Dravidian or Brahmin–non-Brahmin, provided the requisite energy for the politics of the plebs to realize other internal frontiers like the privileged and underprivileged, rich and the poor, dominant north India and the resistant south India, and many more. In fact, it is the predominance of the internal frontier in the DMK ideation and imagination that took precedence over the empty signifier, the reason formations of the political became central to the task of constructing a people. It implies the play of agonistic social relationships through several matrices was the necessary fulcrum through which the party mobilized. In most places, as we already noted, it meant the agonism of the status quo against transformative imagination. In the larger picture, it manifested in the party's insistence on a Dravidian republic consisting of the four southern states rather than demanding a Tamil nation consisting of Tamil speakers. Further, the semantic range of the Dravidian identity was extended from the racial to the geographical when the party was named with the space-centric adjective "Dravida" rather than the person-centric "Dravidar." Thus, the combination of the twin identities "Dravidian" and "Tamil" produced sufficient porosity for several groups of people to join and endorse the construction of the people which refused to be exclusivist. Though the DMK spoke a lot about the glorious Tamil past, its politics was not premised on any ontological or primordial Tamil identity but on a notion of social transformation towards an egalitarian order.

The work of Barnett provides a good instance of how easily people are misled in reading and understanding DMK literature (Barnett 1976). In spite of knowing that the DMK demanded Dravida Nadu consisting of the four southern states, Barnett keeps repeating that it propagated Tamil nationalism. Further, she describes this nationalism as cultural nationalism once the demand for secession was given up in 1963. She proposes that territorial Indian nationalism based on abstract individualism is in dialectical relationship with the cultural nationalism of the DMK based on collective individualism. The valorous attempt of the DMK to build a party through organizational elections in which every individual member casts a vote in secret ballot is completely ignored when the party is taken to represent "collective individualism." In spite of some interesting ethnographic accounts of party members and functionaries, Barnett's book largely fails in gauging the import of the historical journey of the DMK. Her gloss on DMK's cultural nationalism and its contradictions are vague and unproductive in understanding the lasting importance of the transformative journey.

If Barnett's book bears the burden of "cultural nationalism" as the explanatory framework, Subramanian's work bears the cross of "ethnicity." Saying that the DMK undertook populist mobilization is correct but why call the book *Ethnicity and Populist Mobilization*? What does ethnicity signify here? Subramanian appears to consider all regional political formations that are not pan-Indian as "ethnic." In a footnote he says,

> Jammu & Kashmir was the sole state ruled by an ethnic party until the mid-1960s. Since then, ethnic parties have ruled Tamil Nadu, Andhra Pradesh, Punjab, Assam, Nagaland, Mizoram, Goa, Uttar Pradesh, Madhya Pradesh, Maharashtra, Gujarat, Rajasthan, Himachal Pradesh, Sikkim, and Delhi, in addition to Jammu &Kashmir. Electoral results only understate the increased appeal of ethnic alternatives to pan-Indianism. (Subramanian 2004, 5)

The list of states ruled by "ethnic parties" is astounding to say the least, since he appears to collapse the distinction between Hindu nationalism or Hindutva of the Jan Sangh and Bharatiya Janata Party, and various regional political formations, bringing them under the same rubric of "ethnic politics." Be that as it may, there is another gloss to ethnicity provided in the case of Tamil Nadu, which stems from the threat of ethnic conflict. Subramanian presupposes a ground for violent conflict and argues for the "containment of ethnic conflict as a result of party–society transactions."

What was the basis to presuppose an ethnic conflict? Subramanian states, "The Dravidian movement in Tamil Nadu began during the 1910s by raising militant demands for secession and virulently opposed the upper Brahmin caste with appeals which to some extent resembled those of Nazi anti-Semitism" (Subramanian 2004, 7). It is surprising that Subramanian allows for such an unsubstantiated, uncritical, and odious comparison with anti-Semitism popular among Brahmin diaspora and among the Hindu right to sneak into his work as a working hypothesis.

For a better appreciation of the prehistory of the DMK, it is necessary to refer to M. S. S. Pandian, who produced a genealogical reconstruction of the context of the non-Brahmin manifesto (Pandian 2007). We would like to add that the Justice Party was restricted to the demand for communal reservation, which was just a demand for social inclusivity like what is known in the US as affirmative action and what Marc Galanter called "compensatory discrimination" (Galanter 1984). The counter-hegemonic articulations of Periyar and the Self-Respect Movement were thoroughly liberal in spirit and held nonviolence dear to the heart. Periyar steadfastly regarded any violation of the rights and property of a person as hooliganism. There were many Brahmin writers and intellectuals who held Periyar in high esteem all through his career even if they disagreed with him on different counts. When it came to the DMK, Annadurai and other leaders repeated ad nauseam that they opposed only Brahminism and not Brahmins. The DMK had no objection to Brahmins joining the party.

Subramanian's reading of non-Brahmin or Dravidian politics as a possible source of ethnic conflict, that is, a potential source of violent strife, cannot be historically substantiated. Mere reference to verbal articulations, meant to challenge the superiority claimed by Brahmins as a caste or *varna* as well as the Brahmin obsession with caste endogamy, as potential signs of ethnic conflict completely ignores the relations of power in the immanence of the social. Subramanian himself offers evidence against his own presupposition of the possibility of violent ethnic conflict. In his preface, he mentions his maternal grandfather, P. Venkatarama Das, who was a member of the Congress Party but shared the staunch anti-Brahminism of the early Dravidianists. He writes,

> While conceiving the social world in terms of essentialized ethnic categories, my grandfather engaged very closely across ethnic boundaries. People were to him "Muslims," "Naidus," "Chettiars," yet equally friends. More significantly, he married a woman of a different caste and religion, and warmly accepted a Brahmin as his son-in-law despite his anti-Brahminism. (Subramanian 2004, xviii)

He provides a stellar example of how anti-Brahminism distinguished between individual Brahmins and Brahminism as a normative social principle. Given such a personal acquaintance with the immanence of the social, it is not clear how

Subramanian forges a presupposition about a possible violent ethnic conflict, holding critique of Brahminism as similar to anti-Semitism. As a result, his characterization of the DMK mobilization as "ethnic" robs the history of the party of its core value, a painstaking inculcation of liberal spirit of associational forms.

Our insistence on characterizing the historical exercise undertaken by the DMK as construction of a people is solely based on its potential to steer away from identity-based politics. We elaborately noted, through Pannan's memoir, how Narayan Singh, a person of Rajput lineage, was a respected party activist who rose to become the district secretary and a member of parliament. We met a party functionary, a Vokkaliga Gounder speaking Kannada at home, who saw no conflict in his passion for Tamil.[7] We have heard accounts of innumerous Telugu speakers or even Marwari youth participating in anti-Hindi demonstrations, raising the slogan "Long Live Tamil!" It is our understanding that what inspired these people was a call for democracy in which a people decided their own destiny. If this is what Subramanian describes as pluralism of populist mobilization, it needs to be seen why it should be described as "ethnic" as well.

This pluralism might not have been possible if the DMK had succumbed to the temptation to articulate Tamil nationalism. If they had opted for a populism that unified the people merely on the plane of transcendence, in the axis of sovereignty, it might have ended up as an ethnic and chauvinist party, possibly leading to violence. It was the steadfast orientation to the plane of immanence, the axis of social reformation that helped the DK and the DMK to articulate a Dravidian federation of states in the plane of transcendence, effectively pluralizing the construction of a people as "Dravidian–Tamil." This also allowed for the ideational field of the party to be expansive and emancipatory in echoing universal aspirations of humanism, seeking to participate in the global history of democracy.

Ironically, the DMK is often accused of "compromise" and "dilution" when its vision of politics expanded to be inclusive of several schemes of transcendence to enable the work of the justice effect in the immanence of the social. It is the critics who demand that DMK's opposition to religious sentiments to be strident, when the party stops at the level of contending with Brahmin orthodoxy and superstition. Critics of Tamil nationalist persuasion have accused the party of compromising with Marwari financial and business operations in Tamil Nadu when the DMK stopped at the level of contending with accumulation of power in the hands of the Union government. Most confusions in critical vocabulary stem from the failure to distinguish between what we describe as "form of content," which is the immanence of power relations in the social, and "form of expression," which relates to narratives of transcendence that are needed to provide coherence to political action. The DMK's firm orientation to the form of content as the rule of the commoner and the axis of social transformation in the plane of social immanence is what helped it to make the formations of the political the bedrock of the construction of a people as Dravidian–Tamil. We have elsewhere written and collected accounts of how this played out in the fifty years of rule of the Dravidian parties and our thoughts on Dravidian futures (Krishnan and Sriramachandran 2018). Moreover, economists have helpfully documented the beneficial yields of Dravidian rule as the Dravidian Model (Kalaiyarasan and Vijayabaskar 2021). For now, we will conclude with three brief anecdotal narrations or excerpts as coda pointing to the pluriverse of the immanence of social relations we have talked about.

Coda 1

A party activist took us to meet an octogenarian, a previous member of the Legislative Assembly (MLA) belonging to the DMK, Mr A. P. Shanmugasundaram, in his house in his native village of Devanurpudur, about 30 kilometers from Pollachi. He was gentle, soft-spoken and was without airs. With his humble disposition, there was no distinct mark of a politician in him. He won the elections from the Pollachi assembly constituency in 1967 and 1971. Before him, the constituency was represented by Pollachi N. Mahalingam, a rich landlord, industrialist, and entrepreneur who had contested on a Congress ticket. Mahalingam was a close associate of C. Subramaniam, who held several cabinet positions in successive governments at the Center. Shanmugasundaram in 1967 was a young man with moderate possession of agricultural lands. He had married into a more affluent family. At a time when elections were approaching, Annadurai toured the region. He opted to stay in the house of Shanmugasundaram, a party enthusiast. Shanmugasundaram proudly showed us the spot where Anna had rested. The next day there was a public meeting in Pollachi town. It was in this meeting that Anna surprisingly announced Shanmugasundaram as the party candidate for Pollachi constituency. The young man was taken aback but could not object to Annadurai's unilateral announcement. He knew he had to contest against the might of N. Mahalingam and associates in the constituency. Though Shanmugasundaram also belonged to the same caste of Gounders as Mahalingam and C. Subramaniam, the strength in terms of resources hugely varied. Luckily, Shanmugasundaram's father-in-law offered to support his candidacy one time. It was with the help of the party cadres and a spirited campaign that Shanmugasundaram could defeat the Congress candidate supported by N. Mahalingam.

Encouraged by the success, he decided to contest for the second time in 1971 on his own. He could win again in the massive wave of support for the DMK. After that, when M. G. R. split the party, the DMK was weakened in the region, which ended Shanmugasundaram's tenure as an MLA. His family members, son, and other kin continue to be part of the DMK. When we took leave, Shanmugasundaram had a request. He asked us to visit the Perumal (a Tamil name for Vishnu) temple at the top of a hillock close to his house. He had organized the resources to build the temple, which he mentioned as his lifetime achievement. He had also built a shrine for Vaishnavaite philosopher Ramanuja, believed to have propagated against caste discrimination, in the foothills. He obviously felt no contradiction between his affiliation to the DMK and his pride in having constructed a Perumal temple. We were not sure whether we should be surprised. Though we consented to do as he suggested, owing to the paucity of time we could not visit the temple. Fieldwork can hardly ever be exhausted.

Coda 2

A. Thirunavukkarasu is a reputed Tamil journalist, writer, and a DMK historian. He was a party worker in his youth, closely associated with Annadurai and other leaders. His voluminous and professionally researched chronicle of the DMK history is an indispensable source for efforts like ours. He has an anecdote to narrate that captures the charm of the everyday social. The DMK used to print attractive posters at the time of elections. Meticulous attention was paid in designing the poster and coining the slogans. Hence, the posters would be carefully distributed to the branches, counted, and handed out to individual volunteers to be stuck on walls in the area designated for the person. Thirunavukkarasu worked in the railway security force at the time of the 1962 elections and was volunteering to do party work in his spare time. He lived close to the Mylapore area in Chennai, well known for its concentration of elite and rich Brahmins. Thirunavukkarasu was to stick posters in the area. One morning when he was pasting posters in Abiramapuram, an old man wearing a khadi shirt and dhoti, with sacred ash on his forehead, stopped by. He followed Thirunavukkarasu, watching him sticking the posters in different locations in the street. Once he finished, the elderly person told him that it was a waste of effort to stick posters in the area as no one would vote for the DMK. Thirunavukkarasu told him while that might be the case, it is necessary for him and the party to make people at least be aware of their party candidate. He said there would be a day when the people of the locality would vote for the party. As they walked back, the old man enquired about Thirunavukkarasu. When they reached the gate of a house with an unkempt garden, the old man stopped to say that it was his house. Perhaps charmed by Thirunavukkarasu's sincerity, the old man invited him for a cup of coffee. Thirunavukkarasu politely refused, showing him his hands full of glue from sticking posters. The old man however insisted.

There was a fading nameplate at the gate which read "Shankar Ram." When they went inside, the house almost looked empty. An old woman, very fair-skinned, was sitting on an *oonjal* (swing). She was his wife. The old man said, "The boy's name is Thirunavukkarasu. Please give him a cup of coffee. He works in railways. He is doing election work for the DMK." The woman brought hot coffee in a well-polished Kumbakonam "tapara set." It was the beginning of a friendship; Thirunavukkarasu often visited him to hear him discourse on many things. The person was originally Nadesa Iyer whose pen name was Shankar Ram. He had published fiction in English and Tamil since 1920. His novel in English *Love of Dust* (1938) was translated by himself into Tamil as *Mannasai*. He was also a Congressman involved in the freedom struggle. He had no children. Thirunavukkarasu had many memorable moments from his visits to Shankar Ram. One day Thirunavukkarasu found him talking to a visitor with an impressive look; Shankar Ram introduced him as the communist leader M. R. Venkatraman. On another day, Shankar Ram pointed out that it was scholarship that enabled Anna to inspire the youth to constitute a party. After the demise of Shankar Ram's wife, there was a call in the magazine *Ananda Vikatan* to raise some funds for him. Shankar Ram was not amused. One day Thirunavukkarasu found him walking alone in the hot sun. When asked, Shankar Ram showed him a visiting card he kept in his pocket, saying that he would be identified if he were to die on the streets. As it turned out, Shankar Ram was one day found dead in the local bus stop. He was cremated with all the attendant rituals. Thirunavukkarasu still feels warm about the affection Shankar Ram extended to a non-Brahmin youth, though he was a Brahmin. We should add, likewise that Thirunavukkarasu, the young DMK activist, had no reservations in befriending an elite, lonely Brahmin who was a Congressman.

Coda 3

Imayam is a well-known contemporary Tamil writer with wide critical acclaim who has bagged the Sahitya Akademi award for the year 2020. Though he does not call himself a Dalit writer, he hails from a Dalit caste. In a souvenir published in honor of Karunanidhi by *Hindu Tamil Thisai*, a Tamil daily from The Hindu Group, Imayam recounted his induction into the DMK in his school days in an essay titled "Partyman" (Imayam 2017, 134–136). He was studying in the seventh standard in his native village of Kazhudur, Mangaloor Union, Tittakkudi *taluk*, South Arcot district. One Chinnasamy, a person working as a daily wager in a Chennai market, gathered school students one day to explain to them about the political party, the DMK. He said,

> Only Kalaignar would help our people. Only if he is in power, we can ride bicycles in the streets of the village. We can have tea in the tea shops of the village. We would not be asked to wash the tea glasses after drinking the tea. We will not have a separate glass for our people. We can also sit in bench and eat idly. We need not perform indentured farm labour. You can sport moustache and sideburns like me. You can wear dhoti bordered with party colors and also a shawl on the shoulders. Would you like to join the party? (Imayam 2017, 135)

Imayam stood up as the first person willing to join the party that would ensure all these. The next day he went to ask Chinnasamy how to join the party. Chinnasamy asked him to go to Tittakudi town, meet Circle Secretary Rasu, and ask for a membership form saying Chinnasamy sent him. The boy rode a rented cycle 20 kilometers to reach Tittakudi town. He was directed at the *idli* shop to the brick kiln on the riverside 2 kilometers away where he found Rasu. Rasu laughed when the boy told him of his intention to join the party, quipping about what he plans to do by joining the party (at such a young age). He then took him to the *idli* shop, made him sit on the wooden bench, bought him four *idli*s and *poori* kept in a glass case. It was the first time the boy ate in a hotel while also sitting on a bench. Then Rasu gave him the membership form, one and quarter rupees to pay for the rented cycle, patted him on his back, and sent him off. It was also the first time an upper caste man patted him on his back. When he gave the form to Chinnasamy, he filled all the details and also wrote the names of the other members and signed. He sent the form with subscription money to the party headquarters. After a few months, the boy, Imayam, received a membership card from the party. Imayam then narrates how he used to attend all the meetings in which Kalaignar spoke held anywhere close to where he was. Once he grew up, he started going to party conferences; after his wedding, he also took his wife and children to the conferences. He participated in the protests announced by the party and courted arrest. He campaigned during elections, feeling elated when the party won, despondent when it lost. Though it has been thirty-seven years since he joined, he is still an ordinary member of the party. There are millions like him. They are in the party for Kalaignar, for the DMK. They are the backbone of the party.

Imayam asks himself what has the party done for him. It has not given him anything materially. But it always beckoned him: "Come to the party meeting, come to the marriage of the party man, come to the funeral of the party man." It brought him such invitations, transcending caste barriers; it made him sit as an equal to everyone; it made him place a shawl on others' shoulders as others placed a shawl on his shoulders as a form of paying respect. It made him aware of the social; it made him conscious of the language; consciousness of the social and the language made him a writer. Which is why he is a writer today. He holds no party positions even today; but he has one position that is most dignified in the party—party man (*katchikkaran*).

Notes

1. Nietzsche in *Gay Science* proposed that in polytheism, a person conceiving one's own God is the first inkling of sovereignty of the self (Nietzsche 1974, 191). In terms of south Indian film narratives, the figure of citizen-devotee has been

brought into discussion by Bhrugubanda (2018). For a philosophically rigorous exploration of the links between subalternity and religion, see Wakankar (2011).

2. There is a growing body of work that situates Iyothee Dass as the pioneering figure in the construction of "Dravidian–Tamil" people. This certainly deserves a keen exploration. For the moment, in our scheme of understanding presented in the book, we are informed by the semantic rupture in the use of the combination after the event of the anti-Hindi agitations in 1937–1939.
3. Prakriti Vatam is usually glossed as naturalism. Periyar however provided the subtitle "materialism" to the tract. There are many nuanced articulations in the tract, which are usually overlooked but deserve to be unearthed. See Periyar (1949).
4. For an outline close to the gloss provided here, see Krishnan (2004).
5. It is due to this Indianist slant of the AIADMK, currently at the time of writing this book, the BJP is trying to replace the AIADMK as the main opposition party to the DMK in the state. This naturally demands that the AIADMK should reorient itself to Dravidianism if it is to survive the takeover bid of the BJP.
6. Chatterjee concludes his reflections thus:

> I conclude by reminding my readers of the founding moment of the political theory of democracy in ancient Greece. Centuries before either civil society or liberalism was invented, Aristotle had concluded that not all persons were fit to become part of the governing class because not everyone had the necessary practical wisdom or ethical virtue. But his shrewd empirical mind did not rule out the possibility that in some societies, for some kinds of people, under some conditions, democracy might be a good form of government. Our political theory today does not accept Aristotle's criteria of the ideal constitution. But our actual governmental practices are still based on the premise that not everyone can govern. What I have tried to show is that alongside the abstract promise of popular sovereignty, people in most of the world are devising new ways in which they can choose how they should be governed. Many of the forms of political society I have described would not, I suspect, meet with Aristotle's approval, because they would appear to him to allow popular leaders to take precedence over the law. But we might, I think, be able to persuade him that in this way the people are learning, and forcing their governors to learn, how they would prefer to be governed. That, the wise Greek might agree, is a good ethical justification for democracy. (Chatterjee 2006)

7. For a focused discussion of this phenomenon, see Sriramachandran (2018).

Bibliography

Newspapers

Dinamani
Indian Express
Kudi Arasu
Malai Mani
Murasoli
Nava India
The Hindu
Times of India

Journals

Dravida Nadu
Manram
Thendral

Books and Articles

A. Balasubramaniam. 1961. *Intiyāvā? Tirāviṭamā? Tamiḻakamā?* Pamphlet.

Ā.Irā.Vēṅkaṭācalapati. 2020. *Tirāviṭa Iyakkamum Vēḷāḷarum*. 2nd ed. Chennai: Kālaccuvaṭu Patippakam.

A. Kalaiyarasan, and M. Vijayabaskar. 2021. *The Dravidian Model: Interpreting the Political Economy of Tamil Nadu*. Cambridge: Cambridge University Press.

Ambedkar, B. R. 2008. *Ranade, Gandhi and Jinnah*. Delhi: Siddharth Books.

Amin, Shahid. 1996. *Event, Metaphor, Memory: Chauri Chaura 1922–1992*. Delhi: Oxford University Press.

Anandhi, S. 2018. "Education and Dravidian Commonsense." *Seminar* 708 (August): 28–32.

Anandhi, S., S. Karthick Ram Manoharan, M. Vijayabaskar, and A. Kalaiyarasan. 2020. *Rethinking Social Justice*. New Delhi: Orient Blackswan.

Anderson, Benedict. 1998. *Imagined Communities: Reflections on the Origin and Spread of Nationalism*. London; New York: Verso.

Annadurai, C. N. 1975. *Anna Speaks at the Rajya Sabha, 1962–66*. Bombay: Orient Longman.

———. 1980. *Nītitēvaṉ Mayakkam*. Ceṉṉai: Pūmpukār Piracuram Piras.

———. 1995. *Tī Paravaṭṭum*. Ceṉṉai: Parati Patippakam.

Aṉpaḻakaṉ, Ka. 2000. *The Dravidian Movement, Its Genesis and Growth*. Chennai: Poompuhar Pathippagam.

Aṟiñar Aṇṇā. 2008a. *Āriya Māyai*. Chennai: Va.U.Ci. Nūlakam.

———. 2008b. *Kamparacam*. Chennai: Pāri Nilaiyam.

———. 2010a. *Paṇattōṭṭam*. Chennai: Āḻi Papḷiṣars.

———. 2010b. *Pēraṟiñar Aṇṇāviṉ Kaṭṭuraikaḷ*. 3rd ed. 3 vols. Chennai: Pūmpukār Patippakam.

———. 2018. *Civāji Kaṇṭa Intu Cāmrājyam*. Chennai: Pūmpukār Patippakam.

Arrighi, Giovanni. 2010. *The Long Twentieth Century: Money, Power, and the Origins of Our Times*. London: Verso.

Austin, Granville. 2011. "Language and Constitution." In *Language Politics in India*, edited by Asha Sarangi, 41–92. Delhi: Oxford University Press.

Balakrishnan, R. 2019. *Journey of a Civilisation*. Chennai: Roja Muthiah Research Library.

Barnett, Marguerite Ross. 1976. *The Politics of Cultural Nationalism in South India*. Princeton: Princeton University Press.

Bate, Bernard. 2011. *Tamil Oratory and the Dravidian Aesthetic: Democratic Practice in South India*. New Delhi: Oxford University Press.

Bayly, Christopher Alan. 2005. *Origins of Nationality in South Asia: Patriotism and Ethical Government in the Making of Modern India*. Delhi: Oxford University Press.

Bellah, Robert N. 1968. "Meaning and Modernisation." *Religious Studies* 4 (1): 37–45.

Bharathithasan. 2005. *Iraṇiyaṉ Allatu Iṇaiyaṟṟa Vīraṉ*. Chennai: Kaurā Patippaka Kuḻumam.

Bhaskar, Roy. 2008. *Dialectic: The Pulse of Freedom*. London; New York: Routledge.

Bhattacharya, Sabyasachi. 1997. *The Mahatma and The Poet: Letters and Debates between Gandhi and Tagore 1915–1941*. New Delhi: National Book Trust.

Bhrugubanda, Uma Maheswari. 2018. *Deities and Devotees: Cinema, Religion, and Politics in South India*. New Delhi: Oxford University Press.

Blackburn, Stuart H. 2006. *Print, Folklore, and Nationalism in Colonial South India*. Delhi: Permanent Black.

Bottomore, Tom. 2006. *A Dictionary of Marxist Thought*. Oxford: Blackwell.

Bourdieu, Pierre, Richard Nice, and Tony Bennett. 2015. *Distinction: A Social Critique of the Judgement of Taste*. New York: Routledge.

Buckholz, Jonathan. 2015. "Countering Kampan: C. N. Annadurai's Critique of the Ramayana." *Zeitschrift Für Indologie Und Südasienstudien*, nos. 32/33: 203–232.

Caldwell, Robert. 2012. *A Comparative Grammar of the Dravidian or South-Indian Family of Languages*. Muenchen: LINCOM Europa.

Chakrabarty, Dipesh. 2000. *Rethinking Working-Class History: Bengal 1890–1940*. Princeton, New Jersey: Princeton University Press.

Chatterjee, Partha. 1993. *Nationalist Thought and the Colonial World: A Derivative Discourse*. Minneapolis: University of Minnesota Press.

———. 1995. *The Nation and Its Fragments: Colonial and Postcolonial Histories*. Delhi: Oxford University Press.

———. 2006. *The Politics of the Governed*. New York; Chichester: Columbia University Press.

———. 2019. *I Am the People: Reflections on Popular Sovereignty Today*. 1st ed. Muenchen: Permanent Black.

———. 2020. "A Relativist View of the Indian Nation." In *Rethinking Social Justice*, edited by Karthick Ram Manoharan and S. Anandhi, xv–xxviii. Hyderabad: Orient BlackSwan.

Cheah, Pheng, and Jonathan Culler. 2013. *Grounds of Comparison: Around the Work of Benedict Anderson*. Hoboken: Taylor and Francis.

Cīlaṉ. 1948. "Poṉṉakaram." *Kuṭi Aracu*, August 7, 1948.

Cohn, Bernard S. 1968. *Notes on the History of the Study of Indian Society and Culture*. Chicago, Illinois: University of Chicago, Committee on Southern Asian Studies.

———. 1996. *Colonialism and Its Forms of Knowledge: The British in India*. Princeton, NJ: Princeton University Press; Ann Arbor, Michigan: MPublishing, University of Michigan Library.

Cupramanyam, Ka. Nā, Venkat Cāminātan, and Sahitya Akademi (New Delhi). 1998. *A Movement for Literature*. New Delhi: Sahitya Akademi.

Daniel, E. Valentine. 2001. "The Arrogation of Being by the Blind-Spot of Religion." *Hitotsubashi Journal of Social Studies* 33 (1): 83–102.

Daniélou, Alain. 2017. *The Myths and Gods of India: The Classic Work on Hindu Polytheism*. Delhi: Motilal Banarsidass Publications.

Deleuze, Gilles, and Félix Guattari. 1988. *A Thousand Plateaus*. Minneapolis; London: University of Minnesota Press.

Dirks, Nicholas B. 2002. *Castes of Mind Colonialism and the Making of Modern India*. Princeton, NJ: Princeton University Press.

Duara, Prasenjit. 1997. *Rescuing History from the Nation Questioning Narratives of Modern China*. Chicago: University of Chicago Press.

D.Veeraraghavan. 2019. *Half a Day for Caste? Education and Politics in Tamil Nadu, 1952–55*. Delhi: Leftword.

Es. Es. Teṉṉaracu. 1955. "Tañcai Tārakai." *Muracoli* 1 (47): 1, 2, 10.

Es.Vi.Rājaturai. 1998a. *Periyār: Ākasṭ 15*. Coimbatore: Viṭiyal Patippakam.

———. 1998b. *Periyār, Aṇṇā, and Kēcari: Ākasṭ 15 Tukka Nāḷ-Iṉpanāḷ*. Coimbatore: Viṭiyal Patippakam.

Es.Vi.Rājaturai. 2019. "Kalaiñarum Tirāviṭar Iyakkamamum: Eṉ Aṉupavam." In *Tīvuc Ciṟaiyil Viṭutalai Ilakkiyam*, 140–59. Chennai: New Century Book House.

Farzand, Ahmed. 1981. "Not Sri Lanka, but Sonepur in Orissa Is the Lanka of Ramayana: Archaeologists." *India Today*, April 30, 1981. Accessed July 7, 2020. https://www.indiatoday.in/magazine/heritage/story/19810430-not-sri-lanka-but-sonepur-in-orissa-is-the-lanka-of-ramayana-archaeologists-772872-2013-11-22.

Galanter, Marc. 1984. *Competing Inequalities: Law and the Backward Classes in India*. Delhi: Oxford University Press.

Gandhi, M. K. 1938. *Hind Swaraj, or Indian Home Rule*. Ahmedabad: Navjivan.

Ghosh, Pramita. 1978. *Meerut Conspiracy Case and the Left-Wing in India*. Calcutta: Papyrus.

Ginzburg, Carlo. 1992. *The Cheese and the Worms*. London: Johns Hopkins University Press.

Gramsci, Antonio, Joseph A. Buttigieg, and Antonio Callari. 2011. *Prison Notebooks*. New York: Columbia University Press.

Guha, Ranajit. 2003. *History at the Limit of World-History*. New York; Chichester: Columbia University Press.

Guinness World Records. n.d. "Largest Funeral Gathering." Accessed January 17, 2019. https://www.guinnessworldrecords.com/world-records/65207-largest-funerals.

Guna. 2019. *Tirāviṭattāl Vīḻntōm*. 2nd ed. Bengaluru: Kuṇāviya Aṟakkaṭṭaḷai.

Habermas, Jürgen. 1991. *The Structural Transformation of the Public Sphere: An Inquiry into a Category of Bourgeois Society*. Cambridge, Massachusetts: Massachusetts Institute of Technology.

Hardgrave, Robert L. 1965. *The Dravidian Movement*. Bombay: Popular Prakashan.

Hardt, Michael, and Antonio Negri. 2016. *Empire*. Cambridge, Massachusetts: Harvard University Press.

Hoisington, Henry R. 1854. "Siva-Gnâna-Pōtham, Instruction in the Knowledge of God. A Metaphysical and Theological Treatise." *Journal of the American Oriental Society* 4: 31–102. https://doi.org/10.2307/592273.

Hughes, Stephen P. 2002. "The 'Music Boom' in Tamil South India: Gramophone, Radio and the Making of Mass Culture." *Historical Journal of Film, Radio and Television* 22 (4): 445–473. https://doi.org/10.1080/0143968022000012129.

Imayam. 2012. "Kaṭcikkāraṉ." In *Therkilirunthu Oru Sooriyan*, edited by Camas, 134–136. Chennai: Tamil Thisai.

Irā, Neṭuñceḻiyaṉ. 1953. "Etirppalla Tollai Tavirppē." *Maṉṟam* 1 (4): 3–6.

Jha, Mithilesh Kumar. 2018. *Language Politics and Public Sphere in North India: Making of the Maithili Movement*. New Delhi: Oxford University Press. https://doi.org/10.1093/oso/9780199479344.001.0001.

———. 2020. "What the Maithili Movement Tells Us about Language Politics in India." *Himal Southasian*, October 2, 2020. Accessed November 22, 2019. https://www.himalmag.com/what-the-maithili-movement-tells-us-about-language-politics-in-india/.

Joshi, Shashi, and Bhagwan Josh. 2011. *Struggle for Hegemony in India*. Vol. 1 of *A History of the Indian Communists: The Irrelavance of Leninism*. Thousand Oaks, California: SAGE Publications.

Justice Pandrang Row., and Justice Somayya. 1941. *Swayampakula Subbarammaya and Ors vs Swayampakula Venkatasubbamma*. Indian Law reports, Madras Series. Madras High Court.

Ka. Appadurai. 1954. "Māskōvā? Kāñcipuramā?" *Teṉṟal*, July–August, 1954.

Kailasapathy, K. 1979. "The Tamil Purist Movement: A Re-Evaluation." *Social Scientist* 7 (10): 23–51.

Kalaiñar Mu. Karuṇāniti. 2000. *Putaiyal*. Chennai: Pārati Patippakam.

Kalbag, Chaitanya. 2007. "Buddha Says He Has to Follow Capitalism." *Hindustan Times*, July 19, 2007. Accessed February 21, 2019. https://www.hindustantimes.com/kolkata/buddha-says-he-has-to-follow-capitalism/story-YnzYxn5k8qYEv4V3SMg4MK.html.

Kali, Sundar. 2018. "Making of a New Public Sphere." *Seminar* 708 (August): 45–49.

Kannan, R. 2017. *Anna: The Life and Times of C. N. Annadurai*. Chennai: Penguin Books India.

Kapoor, Anuradha. 1993. "Deity to Crusader: The Changing Iconography of Ram." In *Hindus and Others*, edited by Gyanendra Pandey, 74–109. New Delhi; New York: Viking.

Karunanidhi, Mu. 2019. *Nenjukku Needhi*. 6 vols. Chennai: Tirumagal Nool Nilayam.

Kaviraj, Sudipta. 2012. *The Imaginary Institution of India: Politics and Ideas*. Ranikhet; Bangalore: Permanent Black; Distributed by Orient Blackswan.

Kītā, Va, and Es Vi Rājaturai. 1999. *Towards a Non-Brahmin Millennium: From Iyothee Thass to Periyar*. Samya; in association with Book Review Literary Trust; Mumbai: Distributed by Bhatkal Book International.

Kolappan, B. 2014. "Pudumaipithan's 2 Short Stories Removed from Madras University Curriculum." *The Hindu*, February 24, 2014. Accessed August 24, 2021. https://www.thehindu.com/news/national/tamil-nadu/Pudumaipithan%E2%80%99s-2-short-stories-removed-from-Madras-University-curriculum/article11550812.ece.

Kōpālakiruṣṇa Pāratiyār. 2015. *Tirunāḷaip Pōvār Eṉṉum Nantaṉār Carittiram: Kīrttaṉai - Vacaṉattuṭaṉ*. Ceṉṉai: Srīceṇpakā Patippakam.

Krishnan, Rajan Kurai. 2004. "When Kathavarayan Spoke His Mind: The Intricate Dynamics of the Formations of the Political through Film Making Practices in Tamil Nadu." In *New Cultural Histories of India*, edited by Tapati Guha-Thakurta, Bodhisattva Kar, and Partha Chatterjee, 223–245. New Delhi: Oxford University Press.

———. 2018. "Double Articulation of Sovereignty." *Seminar* 708 (August): 20–24.

Krishnan, Rajan Kurai, and Ravindran Sriramachandran. 2018. "Dravidian Futures." *Seminar* 708 (August): 62–68.

Kumar, D. Suresh, and Srinivasan Ramani. 2020. "Ram, Ramasamy and Rajini: What Happened in Salem in 1971?" *The Hindu*, March 30, 2020. Accessed January 22,

2021. https://www.thehindu.com/opinion/op-ed/lord-ram-ev-ramasamy-periyar-and-rajinikanth-what-happened-in-salem-in-1971/article30618177.ece.

Laclau, Ernesto. 2005. *On Populist Reason*. London; New York: Verso.

Laclau, Ernesto, and Chantal Mouffe. 1985. *Hegemony and Socialist Strategy: Towards a Radical Democratic Politics*. London: Verso.

Lefort, Claude. 1989. *Democracy and Political Theory*. Minneapolis: University of Minnesota Press.

Mahadevan, Iravatam. 2002. "Aryan or Dravidian or Neither? A Study of Recent Attempts to Decipher the Indus Script." *EJVS* 8 (1): 1–19.

Mankekar, Purnima. 2003. *Screening Culture, Viewing Politics: An Ethnography of Television, Womanhood, and Nation in Postcolonial India*. Durham, NC: Duke University Press.

Mitchell, Lisa. 2010. *Language, Emotion, and Politics in South India the Making of a Mother Tongue*. New Delhi: Orient Blackswan.

Mohan Ram. 1968. *Hindi against India: The Meaning of the DMK*. New Delhi: Rachna Prakashan.

Mohanrajan, P. A. 1990. *Glimpses of Early Printing and Publishing in India: Their Contribution Towards Democratisation of Knowledge*. Madras: Mohanavalli Publications.

More, J. B. Prashant. 2004. *Muslim Identity, Print Culture, and the Dravidian Factor in Tamil Nadu*. Delhi: Orient Blackswan.

Mouffe, Chantal. 2019. *For A Left Populism*. New York: Verso.

Mu. Irākavaiyaṅkār. 1929. *Tolkāppiya Poruḷatikāra Ārāycci*. Madurai: Tamiḻccaṅkamuttirācālai.

Nambi Arooran, K. 1980. *Tamil Renaissance and Dravidian Nationalism, 1905–1944*. Madurai: Koodal. Accessed June 4, 2019. http://books.google.com/books?id=WxluAAAAMAAJ.

Nandy, Ashis. 2015. *The Intimate Enemy: Loss and Recovery of Self under Colonialism*. Delhi: Oxford University Press.

Narain, Iqbal. 1963. "The Congress at the Cross-Roads: Hypotheses and Imponderables in the Kamaraj Plan." *Indian Journal of Political Science* 24 (4): 383–393.

Narasimhacharya, Madabhushini, and Sahitya Akademi. 2004. *Sri Ramanuja*. New Delhi: Sahitya Akademi.

Nehru, Jawaharlal. 1985. *Discovery of India (Centenary Edition)*. Delhi: Oxford University Press.

New York Times. 1940. "British Aide on Lost Airliner." March 6, 1940.

Nietzsche, Friedrich. 1974. *The Gay Science: With a Prelude in Rhymes and an Appendix of Songs*. 1st ed. New York: Vintage.

Office of the Registrar General and Census Commissioner, India. 2011. "Census of India 2011." Census. New Delhi: Ministry of Home Affairs, Government of India.

Orsini, Francesca. 2009. *The Hindi Public Sphere, 1920–1940: Language and Literature in the Age of Nationalism*. New Delhi: Oxford University Press.

Pa. Tirumāvēlaṉ. 1950. *Kāntiyār Cāntiyaṭaiya*. 1st ed. Thuraiyur: Erimalaip Patippakam.

Paige, Nicholas D. 2011. *Before Fiction: The Ancient Régime of the Novel*. Philadelphia: University of Pennsylvania Press.

Pa.Jīvāṉantam. 2005. *Matamum Māṉiṭa Vāḻvum*. Chennai: New Century Book House.

Pālā Jeyarāmaṉ. 2013. *Periyar: A Political Biography of E. V. Ramasamy*. Delhi: Rupa Publications.

Palti, Elías. 2017. *An Archaeology of the Political: Regimes of Power from the Seventeenth Century to the Present*. New York; Chichester: Columbia University Press.

Pandian, M. S. S. 1991. "Parasakthi: Life and Times of a DMK Film." *Economic and Political Weekly* 26 (11/12): 759–770.

———. 1992. *The Image Trap: M.G. Ramachandran in Film and Politics*. New Delhi; Newbury Park: Sage.

———. 1993. "'Denationalising' the Past: 'Nation' in E. V. Ramasamy's Political Discourse." *Economic and Political Weekly* 28 (42): 2282–2287.

———. 1994. "Notes on the Transformation of 'Dravidian' Ideology: Tamilnadu, c. 1900–1940." *Social Scientist* 22: 84–104.

———. 1996. "Towards National-Popular: Notes on Self-Respecters' Tamil." *Economic and Political Weekly* 31, no. 51 (December): 3323–3329.

———. 2002. "One Step outside Modernity: Caste, Identity Politics and Public Sphere." *Economic and Political Weekly* 37 (18): 1735–1741.

———. 2007. *Brahmin and Non-Brahmin: Genealogies of the Tamil Political Present*. Ranikhet: Permanent Black.

———. 2019. *The Strangeness of Tamil Nadu: Contemporary History and Political Culture in South India*, edited by David E. Ludden and S. Anandhi. Ranikhet: Permanent Black.

Paṇṇaṉ. 1992. *Toṇṭiṉ Vaṭivam Eṅkaḷ Cāmi*. Punjai Puliampatti: Periyār-Aṇṇā Cintaṉaiyāḷar Pēravai.

———. 2020. *Pā. Nā. Vuṭaṉ Patiṉāṟu Āṇṭukaḷ*. Chennai: Paṇṇaṉ.

Paramasiva Iyer, T. 1940. *Rāmāyaṇa and Lanka, Parts I and II*. Bangalore: Printed at the Bangalore Press.

Pāratiyār. 2008. *Pāratiyār Kavitaikaḷ*. Chennai: Tirumakaḷ Nilaiyam.

Pask, Kevin. 2004. "The Bourgeois Public Sphere and the Concept of Literature." In "When Is a Public Sphere?" Special issue, *Criticism*, 46 (2): 241–256.

Patwardhan, Anand, Apurwa Yagnik, Sushmita Mukherji, First Run/Icarus Films, and Icarus Films. 1992. *Ram Ke Naam, or In the Name of God*. New York City, NY: First Run/Icarus Films.

Pērāṟiñar Aṇṇā. 2005a. *Cantirōtayam*. Chennai: Pāri Nilaiyam.

———. 2005b. *Raṅkōṉ Rātā*. Īrōṭu: Pūmpukār Patippakam.

Pērāṟiñar Aṇṇāturai. 2002. *Tampikku Aṇṇaviṉ Kaṭitaṅkaḷ*. Vol. 6. Chennai: Pūmpukār Patippakam.

Pērāciriyar A. Irāmacāmi. 2015. *Inti Etirppup Pōrāṭṭa Varalāṟu*. 2 vols. Chennai: Nakkheeran Publications.

Periyar. 1949. *Pirakirutivātam Allatu Meṭṭīriyalicam*. 2nd ed. Īrōṭu: Kuṭiyaracu Patippakam.

Periyar. 2008. *Periyāriṉ Eḻuttum Pēccum*. 27 vols. Chennai: Periyār Tirāviṭar Kaḻakam.

———. 2010. *Periyār Ī. Ve. Rā. Cintaṉaikaḷ*, edited by Vē. Āṉaimuttu. 20 vols. Chennai: Periyār-Nākammai Aṟakkaṭṭaḷai.

———. 2012. *Irāmayaṇa Pāttiraṅkaḷ*. Chennai: Periyār Puttaka Nilaiyam.

Pirzada, Syed Sharfuddin. 1981. "Jinnah's Reply to EVR." In *Quaid-e-Azam Jinnah's Correspondence*, 233–234. New Delhi: Metropolitan Book Co. P. Ltd.

Po. Taṅkapāṇṭiyaṉ. 2008. *Tirāviṭa Muṉṉēṟṟak Kaḻaka Tērtal Aṟikkaikaḷ; 1952 Mutal 2005 Varaiyilāṉa Āvaṇaṅkaḷ*. Chennai: Nāḷantā Patippakam.

Putumaippittaṉ. 2016. *Putumaippittaṉ Kataikaḷ*. Chennai: Kālaccuvaṭu.

R. Vijaya Sankar, ed. 2019. *Oru Maṉitaṉ Oru Iyakkam: Kalaiñar Mu.Karuṇāniti (1924–2018)*. Chennai: FRONTLINE.

Rai, Alok. 2007. *Hindi Nationalism*. Hyderabad: Orient Longman.

Rajagopal, Arvind. 2005. *Politics after Television: Religious Nationalism and the Reshaping of the Indian Public*. Cambridge: Cambridge University Press.

Rajaji. 1956. *Cakkaravarttit Tirumakaṉ*. Chennai: Pari Nilaiyam.

Ramakrishnan, Venkatesh. 2018. "A Funeral That Entered Guinness World Records." *DT Next*, September 16, 2018. Accessed January 22, 2021. https://www.dtnext.in/News/City/2018/09/16025820/1088622/A-funeral-that-entered-Guinness-World-Records.vpf.

Ramalingam, Namakkal. 2001. *Malaikkaḷḷaṉ*. Chennai: Maṇivācakar Patippakam.

Ramanujan, A. K. 1994. *The Interior Landscape*. Delhi; Oxford: Oxford University Press. Ramanujan, A. K and Tolkāppiyar. 2011. *Poems of Love and War: From the Eight Anthologies and the Ten Long Poems of Classical Tamil*. New York; Chichester: Columbia University Press.

Ramaswamy, Sumathi. 1997. *Passions of the Tongue: Language Devotion in Tamil India, 1891–1970*. Berkeley: University of California Press. Rāmamūrtti, Pi. 1987. *The Freedom Struggle and the Dravidian Movement*. Madras: Orient Longman.

Redfield, Robert. 1969. *Peasant Society and Culture: An Anthropological Approach to Civilization*. Chicago: University of Chicago Press.

Richman, Paula. 1997. *Many Rāmāyanas: The Diversity of a Narrative Tradition in South Asia*. Delhi: Oxford University Press.

Rukmani, R. 1994. "Urbanisation and Socio-Economic Change in Tamil Nadu, 1901–91 on JSTOR." *Economic and Political Weekly* 29 (51/52): 3263–3272.

Ryerson, Charles A. 1988. *Regionalism and Religion: The Tamil Renaissance and Popular Hinduism*. Madras: Published for Christian Institute for the Study of Religion and Society, Bangalore, by Christian Literature Society.

Sarkar, Jadunath. 1920. *Shivaji and His Times*. 2nd ed. London: Longmans, Green and Co.

Sattanathan, A. N. 1982. *The Dravidian Movement in Tamil Nadu and Its Legacy*. Madras: University of Madras.

Schmitt, Carl. 2008. *The Concept of the Political*. Chicago, Illinois: University of Chicago Press.

Seshadri, Kandadai. 1996. "Ramanuja: Social Influence of His Life and Teaching on JSTOR." *Economic and Political Weekly* 31, no. 5 (February): 292–298.
Shulman, David. 2016. *Tamil: A Biography*. Cambridge, Mass: The Belknap Press of Harvard University Press.
Siegel, James T. 1997. *Fetish, Recognition, Revolution*. Princeton, NJ: Princeton University Press.
Sivaraman, K. 2001. *Śaivism in Philosophical Perspective: A Study of the Formative Concepts, Problems and Methods of Śaiva Siddhānta*. Delhi: Motilal Banarsidass.
Spratt, Philip. 1955. *Blowing Up India: Reminiscences and Reflections of a Former Comintern Emissary*. Calcutta: Prachi Prakashan.
———. 1970. *The DMK in Power*. Bombay: Nachiketa Publications.
Sriramachandran, Ravindran. 2018. "Pluralization of Political Identity." *Seminar*, no. 708 (August): 49–52.
"Statistical Report on General Election, 1952, to the Legislative Assembly of Madras." n.d. Delhi: Election Commission of India.
"Statistical Report on General Election, 1957, to the Legislative Assembly of Madras." n.d. Delhi: Election Commission of India.
"Statistical Report on General Election, 1962, to the Legislative Assembly of Madras." n.d. Delhi: Election Commission of India.
"Statistical Report on General Election, 1967, to the Legislative Assembly of Madras." n.d. Delhi: Election Commission of India.
Subramanian, Narendra. 2004. *Ethnicity and Populist Mobilization: Political Parties, Citizens and Democracy in South India*. Oxford: Oxford University Press.
T. Muruganantham, and S. Kumaresan. 2017. "Karunanidhi, the Man Who Never Gave Up." *New Indian Express*, July 8, 2017. Accessed March 6, 2021. https://www.newindianexpress.com/states/tamil-nadu/2018/aug/07/karunanidhi-the-man-who-never-gave-up-1854600.html.
"Tamiḻnāṭu Aracu - Intu Camaya Aṟanilaiyattuṟai." n.d. Tamil Nadu Government Portal. Accessed July 3, 2020. https://tnhrce.gov.in/hrcehome/index.php.
Taylor, Charles. 1992. *Sources of the Self: The Making of the Modern Identity*. Cambridge, Massachusetts: Harvard University Press.
———. 2007. *Modern Social Imaginaries*. Durham: Duke University Press.
Thapar, Romila. 1971. "The Image of the Barbarian in Early India." *Comparative Studies in Society and History* 13 (4): 408–36.
———. 2013. *The Past before Us: Historical Traditions of Early North India*. Cambridge, Mass: Harvard University Press.
———. 2019. *The Past as Present: Forging Contemporary Identities through History*. New Delhi: Seagull Books.
Thapar, Romila, and Orient Longman. 2016. *Ancient Indian Social History: Some Interpretations*. New Delhi: Orient BlackSwan.
Tirumular. 1991. *Tirumantiram, a Tamil Scriptural Classic: Tamil Text with English Translation and Notes*. Madras: Sri Ramakrishna Math.

Tirunāvukkaracu, Ka. 2017. *Ti.Mu.Ka Varalāṟu Mūṉṟu Pākaṅkaḷ*. 3 vols. Chennai: Nakheeran Pathippagam.

———. 2019. *Tirāviṭa Iyakkamum Tirāviṭa Nāṭum*. Ceṉṉai: Nakheeran Pathipppagam.

Trautmann, Thomas R. 2006. *Languages and Nations: The Dravidian Proof in Colonial Madras*. Berkeley: University of California Press. Accessed June 4, 2020. http://site.ebrary.com/id/10146816.

———. 2007. *The Aryan Debate*. New Delhi; New York: Oxford University Press.

———, ed. 2009. *Madras School of Orientalism: Producing Knowledge in Colonial South India*. New Delhi: Oxford University Press.

Turner, Victor. 1974. *Dramas, Fields, and Metaphors: Symbolic Action in Human Society*. Ithaca: Cornell University Press.

Uddin, Sufia M. 2014. *Constructing Bangladesh: Religion Ethnicity and Language in an Islamic Nation*. N.p.: University of North Carolina Press.

University of Madras. 1985. *Tamil Lexicon*. 6 vols. Madras: University of Madras.

V. Anaimuthu, ed. 1974. *Thoughts of Periyar E. V. R: Speeches and Writings of Periyar E. V. Ramasami*. 3 vols. Tiruchirappalli: Cintaṉaiyāḷar Patippakam.

Va., Kītā, and Rājaturai Es. Vi. 2009. *Periyār: Cuyamariyātai Camatarmam*. Kōyamputtūr: Viṭiyal.

Vai.Mu. Kōpālakiruṣṇamāccāriyār. 2006. *Kamparāmāyaṇam Āṟu Kāṇṭaṅkaḷ: Ēḻu Tokutikaḷ (Urai)*. Chennai: Umā Patippakam.

Vaitheespara, Ravi. 2012. "Re-Inscribing Religion as Nation: Naveenar-Caivar (Modern Saivites) and the Dravidian Movement." *South Asia: Journal of South Asian Studies* 35 (4): 767–786.

———. 2015. *Religion, Caste, and Nation in South India: Maraimalai Adigal, the Neo-Saivite Movement, and Tamil Nationalism, 1876–1950*. New Delhi: Oxford University Press.

Vaitheespara, Ravi, and R. Venkatasubramanian. 2015. "Beyond the Politics of Identity: The Left and the Politics of Caste and Identity in Tamil Nadu, 1920–63." *South Asia: Journal of South Asian Studies*, 38 (4): 543–557.

Vē. Āṉaimuttu, ed. 1974. *Periyār Ī.Ve.Rā. Cintaṉaikaḷ: Periyār Ī.. Ve.Rāmacāmi Avarkaḷiṉ Coṟpoḻivukaḷum Kaṭṭuraikaḷum*. 3 vols. Tiruccirāppaḷḷi: Cintaṉaiyāḷar Kaḻakam.

Vedaratnam, S. 1951. *A Plea for Understanding: A Reply to the Critics of the Dravidian Progressive Federation*. Kancheepuram: Vanguard Publishing House.

Venkatachalapathy, A. R. 1995. "Dravidian Movement and Saivites: 1927–1944." *Economic and Political Weekly* 30 (14): 761–768.

———. 2005. "'Enna Prayocanam?' Constructing the Canon in Colonial Tamilnadu." *Indian Economic and Social History Review* 42 (4): 535–553. https://doi.org/10.1177/001946460504200406.

Venkatachalapathy, A. R. 2015. *The Province of the Book: Scholars, Scribes, and Scribblers in Colonial Tamilnadu*. Ranikhet: Permanent Black.

Vijetha S. N. 2011. "Historians Protest as Delhi University Purges Ramayana Essay from Syllabus." *The Hindu*, October 15, 2011. Accessed September 11, 2019. https://www.

thehindu.com/news/national/Historians-protest-as-Delhi-University-purges-Ramayana-essay-from-syllabus/article13372074.ece.

Vivēkāṉantaṉ, Iṉiyaṉ Campat, and Kalpaṉātācaṉ. 2013. *Ī.Ve.Ki. Campattum Tirāviṭa Iyakkamum (Iṉiyaṉ Campat Patippakam, n.d.). 2013*. Chennai: Iṉiyaṉ Campat Patippakam.

Vī.Em.Es.Cupakuṇarājaṉ. 2018. *Namakku Ēṉ Inta Iḻinilai? Jāti Māṉāṭukaḷilum Jāti Oḻippu Māṉāṭukaḷilum Periyār*. Chennai: Kayal Kaviṉ Patippakam.

Wakankar, Milind. 2011. *Subalternity and Religion: The Prehistory of Dalit Empowerment in South Asia*. London; New York: Routledge.

Index

Adi Dravida/Adi Dravidas, 51, 57, 71
Adigal, Ilango, 129–130, 136
Adigal, Maraimalai, 61*n*6, 71, 82, 144
Adigalar, Ramalinga, 69, 71
Adithanar, 43
Advani, L. K., 124
affect, affective, 10, 56–58, 61, 68, 131, 137–140, 158*n*5, 181, 193, 243, 274
agonism, agonistic, 4, 20, 23, 37, 50, 64, 66, 70, 73, 88, 89, 106, 127, 128, 181, 202, 240, 242, 259–261, 268
    class antagonism, 88
"Akrakaram" (short story), 154–157
Alagesan, O. V., 233
All India Anna Dravida Munnetra Kazhagam (AIADMK or ADMK), 12, 110, 250, 267, 276*n*5
Ambedkar Kazhagams/Mandram, 189, 192
Ambedkar, B. R., 221, 226, 261, 263
America, American, 34, 86–87, 161, 211
Āṉanta Vikaṭaṉ (journal), 128
Anbagam, 191
Anbalagan, 189
Anderson, Benedict, 163
Annadurai, C. N. (Anna or Annadurai), 2, 5, 23–38, 39*n*8, 42–43, 45, 52–53, 55, 58, 64, 66–67, 69–70, 72, 74–80, 82, 83*n*5, 86–88, 90–94, 97–98, 100, 105–112, 114, 121, 122*n*1, *n*2, 123, 129, 132–140, 144–145, 150, 152–153, 164–166, 168–169, 171, 179–182, 185, 188, 190–194, 201–204, 206–208, 210–215, 228–229, 232, 237, 240–241, 246–247, 250, 253, 256–257, 257*n*1, 260, 262, 266–267, 270, 272–274
Annamalai University, 134, 231
Arabic, 220
Arangannal, Rama, 24, 207
Arooran, Nambi, 39*n*6, 49
Arrighi, Giovanni, 94
    The Long Twentieth Century: Money, Power and the Origins of Our Times, 93
Aryan Allure (*Āriya Māyai* or *Arya Mayai*), 23, 25–31, 34, 52, 64, 88, 90–91, 98–99, 105, 107, 116, 157, 179, 201, 204, 207–208, 262
Aryan/Aryanism, 20–23, 25–32, 38, 38*n*5, 39*n*8, 44, 49–50, 52,

55, 62*n*6, 63, 93, 99, 117, 121, 125–126, 128, 132–137, 142–144, 146–150, 154, 157, 220, 241, 258, 268
Ashe, Robert, 261
asuras, *rakshasas*, *asurarakshasa*, 125, 141–144, 147, 150, 152, 154, 157
adukku mozhi, 58
atheism, 66, 69, 74, 79, 81–82, 127–128, 153, 247
aucitya, 140
Auvaiyar (film), 164
Avudayappan, 190
Ayodhya, 124, 138, 151
Ayyangar, Gopalasamy, 225–226

Babri Masjid, 129
  illegal demolition by *kar sevaks* in 1992, 124
  Supreme Court verdict in 2019, 125
  worship of Shilanyas, permission by Rajiv Gandhi, 140*n*3
Balasubramaniam, A., 99
Balasundaram, Pavalar, 121
Balzac, 160
Baniya capital, 92–93, 98
Barnett, Marguerite Ross, 178, 258, 269
Basha, Sadiq, 197, 247
Bate, Bernard, 58, 60–61
Bayly, Chirstopher, 109
becoming a people, 7
Bellah, Robert, 67–70
Bhabha, Homi, 42
Bhagavata Purana, 188
Bhakthavatsalam, M., 230, 232–233, 256
Bhakti movement, 22, 53
Bhakti/Bhakti tradition, 64–65, 82, 119, 126–127, 130, 164
Bharathi, Subhramanya, 69, 130–131
Bharathiar, Somasundara, 134–137, 150
Bharathidasan, 144–145, 147
Bharathy, Gopalakrishna, 259
Bharatiya Janata Party (BJP), 124, 244, 276*n*5, 269
  campaign against Sonia Gandhi's Italian origin, 56
Bhattar, Gaga, 108, 113–119
Bhojpuri, 219–220, 238*n*3
black flag demonstration/protest, 204–206, 212–214, 227, 229–230, 233
Bombay, 46, 91–92, 94, 246
Bourdieu, Pierre, 156
Brahmin/Brahminic/Brahminism, 3, 7, 9, 12–13, 15*n*6, 19–24, 27–32, 35–38, 39*n*6, *n*8, 44, 50–57, 60–61, 64, 65, 86, 95, 106–107, 109, 111–120, 124, 127–128, 131–135, 150, 154–157, 162–163, 171, 173, 179, 182, 207, 211, 221–222, 227, 236, 241, 249, 253–254, 258–259, 261, 266, 270–271, 273–274
  hegemony, 4, 25, 48–49, 66, 72, 83, 88, 96, 98–99, 108, 121, 139, 201, 262–263
  Hinduism, 10, 26, 38*n*5, 82, 123, 144, 264
  shastras, 112
Braudel, Fernand, 93–94
Buddhists, Buddhism, 57, 71, 73, 129, 228

Cakaravartti Tirumakaṉ (prose narration), 153
Caldwell, Robert, 38*n*4, 39*n*11, 44
Cantramōhaṉ or *Civāji Kaṇṭa Intu Cāmrājyam* (play), 53
capitalism/capitalist, 13, 73, 80, 87, 91, 93–94, 98–99, 212
  Baniya, 92
  Bombay, 92
caste/casteist, 12, 26, 30, 39*n*7, 45, 51, 54, 56, 69, 72, 82, 98, 107–108,

112, 114, 120–121, 124, 127, 151–153, 156, 158*n*3, 166, 168, 171, 179–180, 182–184, 186, 189–192, 194–195, 198–199, 207, 210, 212, 243–244, 247, 249, 251, 253, 259–261, 263, 270, 272–275
associations, 22
conflicts, 68
denominations, 115
groups, 58–59, 61, 265
hegemony, 13, 53, 201, 262
hierarchy, 3, 21–22, 29, 31, 36, 45, 50, 57, 67, 83, 83*n*2, 88, 146, 162, 227
identification, 48
inequality, 11, 97
mobilization, 10
modernity of, 64–65
ontology, 56, 259
catachresis, 12, 50, 54
Chatterjee, Partha, 15*n*11, 83*n*4, 218, 238*n*1, 276*n*6
concerns about populism, 13
Nation and Its Fragments, 7
nation-state and people's nation, difference between, 218
on political society, 89
The Politics of the Governed, 11, 268
Chettiar, 98–99, 162, 188, 270
Chettiar, A. V. Meiyyappa, 121
Chettiar, Ramachandran, 132, 134
Chezhian, Kovai, 197
Chidambaram Pillai, V. O., 134, 221
China, 15*n*7, 86–87, 266
Chinese aggression, 215, 227, 255
Chinnasamy, Kilapaluvur, 40–41, 45, 49, 61*n*3, 74, 177, 228, 230, 274–275
Cilappatikāram, 129, 131, 133
civil society, 21–22, 35, 48, 54, 57, 66, 89, 95, 178–182, 184, 201, 219, 260, 276*n*6
class essentialism, 9, 83, 88–91, 94, 101
coercion, 259
Comintern (the Communist International), 85, 87, 95–96
Commonweal party, 251
Communist Party of India (CPI), 241, 256, 264–267
Communist Party of India (Marxist) (CPI[M]), 5–6, 86, 256, 264, 266
compensatory discrimination, 179, 203, 270
consent generation, 259
Constituent Assembly, 43, 217, 223–224, 239–240
constitutionalism, 88–89
Construction of a People, 6, 10, 13–14, 19–20, 38, 51, 57, 72, 85, 161, 163, 202, 250, 258, 268, 271. *See also* becoming a people
corpayirci, 188
Culler, Jonathan, 163

Dalits, 12–13, 51–52, 156, 158*n*5, 189, 191–192, 194, 196, 222, 263, 268, 274
Dange, Shirpad, 96
Daniélou, Alain, 143
Daniel, Valentine, 83*n*7
Dante, 126
Das, P. Venkatarama, 270
Das, Seth Govind, 223
Dass, Iyothee, 57, 71, 276*n*2
Deleuze, Gilles, 115, 122*n*7
Desai, Morarji, 256, 266
Devanagari, 224–226
devas (of Hindu Puranas), 125, 141–142, 151–152, 154, 157
Dharma Shastras or *shastras*, 21, 26–27, 31, 64, 262
Dharmalingam, Anbil, 167–168, 171, 252
dialectical materialism, 80–81, 83, 84*n*12
Dirks, Nicholas, 39*n*7, 64

disenchantment, 73
disengaged reason, 73–74, 79–80
Diwakar, R. R., 204–205
double articulation, 115, 122*n*7
Dravida Nadu (journal), 3, 11, 14*n*4, 24, 28, 32–33, 40, 47, 49, 53–54, 58, 106, 121, 158*n*2, 164, 166, 180–181, 187, 189, 190, 194, 201–202, 204–205, 207–208, 215, 239–242, 250, 252–253, 262, 269
Dravidar Kazhagam (DK), 1–2, 4, 9, 12, 22–24, 34–37, 42–43, 45, 49, 52–53, 60, 66, 92, 96, 99, 121, 152, 155, 166, 179–182, 187, 189, 192–193, 201, 206, 210, 240, 271
Dravidian Model, 272
Dravidian movement, 8, 12, 25, 30, 42, 64, 66, 70–71, 83, 91, 121, 139, 171, 195, 270
Dravidian republic (also Dravida Nadu), 3, 11, 14*n*4, 19, 25, 31–34, 36–37, 41, 48, 61*n*4, 63, 97–100, 106, 214, 222, 241–242, 251, 253–256, 262, 264, 267–268
Dravidianism, 9, 12, 19, 23–25, 37–38, 41–45, 48–50, 57, 70, 72–73, 265, 267, 276*n*5
Dravidian–Tamil, 10, 13–14, 20, 31–32, 43, 54, 65, 134, 163, 182, 245, 250, 253, 258, 265, 268, 271–272, 276*n*2
Dühring, Eugene, 81
Duara, Prasenjit, 15*n*7, 126
  Rescuing History from Nation, 41

elections, 5, 35, 37, 61*n*4, 86, 89–90, 94, 121, 179, 185, 187, 190–191, 194, 197–198, 199, 209, 213–215, 232, 237, 239, 241–242, 246–252, 254–256, 264–267, 269, 272–273, 275
  as event and history, 242–245
  local body/municipal, 195, 240

electoral pledge (for DMK endorsement in 1952), 251–252
elite, 11, 25, 36–37, 77, 89, 138, 212, 217, 227, 250, 252, 257, 273–274
  cultural, 264
  formations, 8
  language of, 218–221
  Maratha, 111
  nationalist, 3–4, 10, 21
  non-Brahmin, 35–36, 57, 180, 263
  political formations, 262
  power, 7, 100, 246, 263
  -sponsored nationalist project, 72
Ellis, F. W., 21, 38*n*4, 44
emancipation, 9, 12, 262, 264, 267
empty signifier, 7, 20, 22, 50–53, 55–56, 60–61, 63, 66, 74, 90, 100, 120–121, 241, 258, 268
Engels, Friedrich, 80–81
Era.Chezhian, 185–186, 189

faciality machine, 110
Feuerbach, Ludwig, 81
Fichte, Johann Gottlieb, 42, 56
fiction, arrival of, 160–161
form of content, 7, 12, 37–38, 115, 122*n*7, 250, 252, 264–265, 271
form of expression, 7, 12, 37–38, 115, 122*n*7, 250, 252, 264–265, 271
formations of the political, 8, 10, 13, 15*n*12, *n*13, 20, 89, 110, 178, 258, 260, 263, 266, 268, 271–272
funds/fundraising, 3–4, 106, 121, 186, 190–191, 193, 198, 204, 207–211, 246–247, 252, 254, 274
  lack of funds, 190, 246

Galanter, Marc
  compensatory discrimination, 270

Gandhi, Indira, 184, 255–256, 266
Emergency Rule of, 267
lost in Raebareli in 1977, 242
Gandhi, M. K., 3–4, 39*n*8, 90, 92, 95, 120, 122*n*8, 124, 180, 192, 221–222, 241, 261–262
civil disobedience movement, 36
Harijan Sevak (journal), 223
Hind Swaraj, 25, 52, 120
Wardha Scheme, 209
war of positions against colonial government, 96
Gandhi, Sonia, 56
Ganesan, L., 232, 237
Ganesan, V. C. (also Sivaji Ganesan), 109–110
Ganesha (godhead), 128, 202
Geertz, Clifford, 67–69
Ginsberg, Carlo, 141
Giri, V. V., 92
God, 29, 53, 65, 67–69, 73–75, 77, 79–82, 83*n*7, 112–113, 115, 127–130, 133, 135–136, 142, 144–148, 150–152, 154, 210, 247, 259, 275*n*1
"Godiva" (poem), 139
Goenka, Ramnath, 251
Gopal, Pa., 200
Govindasamy, A., 252
Gramsci, Antonio (Gramscian), 54–55, 122*n*8
concept of hegemony, 90
war of maneuver and position, distinction between, 120
grassroots, 164, 181–182, 185–186, 191, 228, 252, 254, 264
activism, 163
mobilization, 14, 23, 89–90, 95, 177–178, 194, 245, 249, 262
organization, 13
politics, 194–200, 250
Guha, Ranajit
adbhuta, use of, 160
Gurusamy, Kuthoosi, 145

Habermas, Jurgen, 161
Hanuman, 127, 133
Hardt, Michael, 12, 15*n*10
hegemony, 23, 50, 58, 82, 90, 93, 120, 218
Aryan–Brahmin, 63, 150, 220
Brahmin/Brahminic, 3–4, 13, 22, 25, 31, 35, 37, 48–49, 55, 57, 66, 72, 83, 95–96, 98–99, 108–109, 112, 121, 139, 201, 262–263
casteist, 3, 13, 22, 36, 45, 53, 61, 72, 88, 107, 201, 262
Hindu, 46
Herder, Johann Gottfried, 42
Hindi, 3, 5, 13–14, 22, 44–48, 57, 96, 121, 126, 130, 134, 139, 160, 180, 203, 212, 214–218, 220–223, 227–230, 235, 237, 238*n*3, 254–255, 266
anti-Hindi agitation, 14, 32–33, 36, 52–53, 72, 74–75, 123, 230–234, 256, 276*n*2
extremists, 224–226
imperialism, 210
Hindi against India: Meaning of the DMK, 46
Hindi imposition, 13, 48, 53, 228–229, 235, 266
Hindi Prachar Sabha, 204–205, 207, 210
Hindu law, 26–27
Hindu Mahasabha, 25–26, 28*n*11, 31, 46, 180, 201
Hindu transcendence, 262
Hindustani, 22, 220, 222–224, 226
Hiranya, 142, 145–146, 149, 208. *See also* Iraniyan
Hitler, Adolf, 47, 78
Homer, 160
hypergood, 67, 78–80

Ilamvazhuthi, 192
Ilanchezhian, Ma., 189
Ilango, N. S., 189
Ilaṭciya Varalāṟu (*The History of the Political Goal*), 25, 31, 34–35, 38, 53
Imayam, 274–275
immanence, 7, 13, 73, 80, 82–83, 127, 183, 243, 258–268, 270–272
immanent, 7, 12, 129–130, 259–260. *See also* Immanence
Indian National Congress (Congress Party), 3–6, 9–11, 13, 15*n*9, 22, 25, 31–38, 39*n*13, 44, 46, 48–49, 59–61, 61*n*1, 68, 80, 86, 90, 92, 95–99, 107, 110, 112, 120, 124, 128, 134, 137, 140*n*3, 159, 179–182, 184, 189, 191–192, 194–195, 197, 201–202, 204, 206–207, 209–210, 212, 214–215, 220–223, 225, 227–231, 233, 241, 243–246, 251–256, 261–264, 266–267, 270, 272
Indian Union Muslim League, 6, 256
internal frontier, 7, 20, 22, 30, 38, 50–54, 61, 63, 66, 88, 90, 99–100, 120–121, 154, 157, 241, 258, 268
intimate enemy, 157
Iraṇiyaṉ, 144–150, 157
Irraniya Dasan, 208
Is India a Nation? (pamphlet), 106
Israel, 124
Iyer, Alladi Krishnaswamy, 221, 225
Iyer, Vanchi, 261–262

Jains, Jainism, 73, 129
Jan Sangh, 46–47, 227, 267, 269
Jeevanantham or Jīvāṉantam, Pā (also Jeeva), 80–81, 83, 96–97, 241
Jinnah, Mohammed Ali, 36, 39*n*12, 261
Josh, Bhagwan, 11, 15*n*9, 90–91, 96, 101*n*1
Joshi, Sashi, 11, 15*n*9, 90–91, 96, 101*n*1
justice effect, 259–260, 265, 271
Justice Party (also known as South Indian Liberal Federation), 1, 9, 12, 14*n*2, 22, 33, 35–37, 45, 49, 53, 57, 66, 71, 83*n*5, 91, 179–182, 200*n*4, 201, 262, 270

Ka. Appadurai, 100, 205
Kakithap Poo (play), 246
Kalapriya, T. K., 164, 173
Kalasi workers, 197–198
Kalki (journal), 153
Kallakudi struggle, 210–211
Kalyanasundaram, Kanchi, 189
Kalyanasundaram, V., 179–180, 189
Kamaraj, K., 5, 34, 84*n*11, 122, 158*n*3, 194, 202, 229–231, 252–256, 262, 266–267
Kamban Kazhagam, 188
Kamban, 105, 123, 126, 130–134, 136–140, 150–152, 160, 188
Kamparacam, 123, 137–139, 150
*Kamparām*āyaṇam or *Irāmavatāram*, 123, 126–127, 129–136, 138–139, 150, 152, 160
Kanchi (journal), 74
Kannada, 22, 54, 56, 160, 230, 271
Kannadasan, 198, 207, 211–212
Kannan, R., 36–37, 122*n*1, *n*3, *n*6, 166, 252
Kannappar, 35
Karunanidhi, M., 4, 43, 69, 82, 83*n*2, 86, 94, 105–106, 110, 121, 153, 160, 164–165, 168–169, 171, 185–186, 188–189, 193–194, 206–208, 210–215, 228, 246–247, 249, 252–255, 266–267, 274
Kierkegaard, Søren, 67
King George V, 261
"K" plan, 256
Kriplani, J. B., 6

Krishnamachari, T. T., 225
Krishnamurthy, Kalki, 107, 126, 153, 165
Krishnan, N. S., 193
Kshatriya, 107–108, 111, 114–117, 119
Kudi Arasu (journal), 106, 122*n*2
Kulakalvi Thittam or Modified Scheme of Elementary Education, 153, 210
Kundrathur firing, 207

Laclau, Ernesto, 7, 11, 19–20, 30, 38*n*2, 50–58, 88–89, 120, 258
Lefort, Claude, 259–260
left populism, 7, 83, 87–91, 95, 100, 241
Lingayat, 244
Lohia, Ram Manohar, 46
Lord Murugan (godhead), 128
Love of Dust (novel), 274

Macpherson, C. B., 89
Madras School of Orientalism, 21, 38*n*4, 44
Mathiazhagan, K. A., 24, 185, 189, 195, 211
Mahabali, 142
Mahabharata, 142, 145, 188
Mahalingam, Pollachi N., 272
Maintenance of Internal Security Act (MISA), 184
Maithili, 219–220, 238*n*3
Majeed, A., 252
Malai Mani (newspaper), 24, 190
Malaikkaḷḷaṉ (novel), 159–160
Malayalam, Malayalee, 22, 54, 56, 160
Mandal Commission, 124
Maniammai, 2
Manickam, S. Needhi, 190, 197
Manimagudam (play), 121
Manimozhiar, Kanchi, 185
Manoharan, 189
Manram (journal), 100, 192
Maratha, 46, 107, 111–112, 117–119, 121, 129, 169, 195
Marshall, John, 133
Marx, Karl, 54, 80–81, 91, 93
medai Tamil, 58–61
Minh, Ho Chi, 190
mlecchas, 143
modernity or modernization, 67–69, 73–74, 183, 260
  of caste, 64–65
  colonial, 261, 263
  defined, 63
  impinging, 68
  political, 9, 66–67
  Tamil, 107, 130, 161–162, 259
Moghuls, 112, 120, 195
Mohan Ram
  Hindi against India: The Meaning of the DMK, 46
Mookaji, 153–154
Moonje, B. S., 25–26, 180
moral allegiance or affinity, 64, 74–80
Mouffe, Chantal, 85, 87–90
Mudaliar, C. Nadeasa, 35
Mudaliar, Chidambaranatha T. K. (T. K. C.), 126
Mudaliars, 162, 166–167, 179, 182
Mudiyarasan, 188
Müller, Max, 133
Munshi, K. M., 226
Munshi–Ayyangar formula, 226
Murasoli (journal), 153, 165, 169, 193, 255
Murdoch, Iris, 74
Murugan, Durai, 232
Muslims, 32, 112, 125, 135, 140*n*3, 197, 247, 256, 261–262, 270
Muthu, Sathiyavani, 192, 196
Mysindia (journal), 85

Nadars, 51, 72, 253
Naicker, Manickavel, 162, 179, 251
Naickers, 162, 179, 251
Naidu, Varadharajulu, 25–26, 179
Nanda, Gulzarilal, 230

Nandan, 259–260
Nandy, Ashis, 157
Nangavaram farmers struggle, 213
Narasimha (godhead), 145–146, 158*n*2
Narayanan, Jayaprakash, 6
Narayanasamy, D. V., 109
Natarajan (of anti-Hindi imposition struggle), 222
Natarajan, N. V., 185–186, 189, 211, 222
nationalism, 54, 56, 83*n*4, 218, 264
  anti-colonial, 95, 99, 260
  bilingual, 222
  civil, 68, 70–71
  Congress, 262
  cultural, 269
  ethno-, 249
  Hindi, 46
  Hindu, 26, 31, 46, 98–99, 269
  Indian, 7, 28, 31, 36, 38*n*5, 41, 46, 95, 99, 111–112, 163, 254, 262, 269
  linguistic, Tamil, 41–43, 48–49, 56, 62*n*8, 64, 68, 72, 254, 269, 271
  pan-Indian, 10, 24–25
  and populism, difference between, 51
  romantic, 68–70
nationalization of banks, 255
Nedunchezhian, Era., 4, 185, 189, 193–194, 209, 211, 213, 252
Neelamegam, K. K., 190, 206
Negri, Antonio, 12, 15*n*10
Nehru, Jawaharlal, 4, 6, 32, 34, 92, 98, 125, 133, 140*n*4, 154, 210, 212–216, 223–224, 227–229, 241, 253–257
Nenjukku Needhi, 206
neo-Shaivism, neo-Shaivite, Naveener Shaivite, 44–45, 52, 57, 61*n*6, 62*n*7, 63–64, 71, 82
  as template of regionalism, 65–67
new sociality, 177, 182–185, 189, 192, 263–264
nodumalan, 100
non-Brahmin, 7, 10, 20–27, 32, 35–36, 43–45, 49–58, 61, 63, 65–67, 71–72, 82, 88, 90, 99–100, 107, 112–113, 116, 121, 144, 154, 156–157, 162–163, 171, 179–182, 184, 191, 220–222, 241, 249, 253, 257–258, 262–264, 268, 270, 274

"Onre Kulam, Oruvane Thevan" (Singular is the race, Singular the Lord), 66–67, 69, 82
Ōr Iravu (play), 107

Pā. Nā. Vuṭaṉ Patiṉāṟu Āṇṭukaḷ (memoirs), 194
Paige, Nicholas. D., 160–162
Pakistan, 32–34, 36–37, 43, 98, 220, 256
Palanichamy, Pethampalayam, 2, 190
Palestine, 124
Pallar (also Devendra Kula Vellalar), 194
Palti, Elias Jose, 258–259, 265
Panathottam (pamphlet), 91, 210
Panchama, 112, 261
Panchamar Mahajana Sabha, 261
Pandian, M. S. S., 14*n*3, 38*n*5, 49, 57, 61*n*5, 62*n*8, 71, 122*n*4, 168, 222, 270
Pannan ("Kāviyap Pāvalar" Paṇṇaṉ), 163–164, 194–200, 204–205, 227, 247, 250, 252, 271
Panneerselvam, A. T., 37
Pantulu, Tanguturi Prakasam, 92
Parasakthi (film), 110, 121, 168
Parsi, 93, 98
Parthasarathy, Indira, 161, 173*n*2
partition, 33, 43, 87, 209, 223–224
Passions of the Tongue (PoT), 38, 40–41
patru, 38
Periya Purāṇam, 123, 129, 132–136, 152

Periyar, 1–5, 14*n*2, 22–25, 31–32, 35–37, 39*n*12, 43, 45, 49, 52–53, 57, 60, 61*n*5, 64, 66, 67, 69, 71–73, 81–82, 83*n*5, 85, 91, 96–98, 101*n*3, 106, 109–110, 121, 122*n*1, 127–129, 134, 144–145, 166, 179–182, 188, 192–195, 201–202, 206, 222, 229, 240–242, 253, 261–263, 266, 268, 270, 276*n*3
Persia/Persian, 142, 169, 220, 223–224
Perumal, S. A., 121
Pillai, Manonmaniam Sundaram, 65, 71, 83*n*3, 133
Pillai, Nallasamy, 71
Pirakirutivātam, 127, 263
plebs, plebeian, 7, 20, 30, 58, 89, 181–182, 257, 268
political society, 11, 89, 219, 276*n*6
"Ponnakaram" (short story), 154–157
Ponniyin Selvan (novel), 165
Populus, 20, 30, 38*n*2, 50, 51–52, 54–55, 58, 61*n*3
Prahalada, 145–146, 149
Praja Socialist Party, 6, 256
Prasad, Rajendra, 223–225
primordial sentiment, 68–72
pseudo-factual, 160–161
public sphere, 182
    linguistic, 217, 219–221
    vernacular, 218
Pudumaipithan, 154–157, 158*n*4
Puranas or Puranic, 13, 21, 28–29, 82, 128, 141–146, 149, 152, 154, 156, 188
Purohit, Vinayak, 46,
Puthaiyal (novel), 165, 169–172

Radhakrishnan, Sarvapalli, 227
Ragavaiangar, Mu., 28
Raja of Ettayapuram, 134
Rajadurai, S. V., 14*n*2, 101*n*3, 192
Rajagopalachari, C. (also Rajaji), 5, 57, 86, 96, 107, 126, 153, 180, 201, 221–222
Rajamannar, 26
Rajangam, Gudalur, 235, 247
Rajendran, M. (martyr, anti-Hindi agitation), 231
Ram Janmabhoomi, 124
Rama, Subbiah, 188, 208, 211, 250
Ramachandran, M. G., 160, 267
Ramalingam, Namakkal, 40, 61*n*1, 62*n*9, 159, 162, 173*n*1
Ramamurthy, P., 5, 15*n*6, 91, 94, 266
Raman, V. P., 186, 254
Ramanathan, J. N., 35
Ramanuja (Vaishnavite philosopher), 65, 83*n*2, 127, 273
Ramanujan, A. K., 39*n*10, 84*n*10, 124
Ramasamy, Coimbatore Agricultural college student, 237
Ramasamy, E. V., 109, 127, 145, 179–180, 188, 190. *See also* Periyar
Ramasamy, K. R., 190
Ramasamy, Sumathi, 38, 40–41, 69, 228
Ramayana, 105, 123–129, 132–133, 135, 137, 142, 153–154, 188
Rameswaram, 125
Ranade, 261
Ranga, N. G., 251
Ranganathan, self-immolator, 231
Raṅkōṉ Rātā (Rangoon Radha) (novel), 165, 171–172
rasa, *rasābhāsa*, 137–138, 140
Rashtriya Swayamsevek Sangh (RSS), 46, 124, 128
Ravana, 125–126, 128, 133–134, 142, 150–152, 243
Ravichandran, M. N., 231–232
regional/regionalism, 9, 99, 124, 223
    autonomy, 34
    distinction, 257
    governments, 14*n*4, 239

Hinduism, 65, 70–72
identity, 8
interests, 98
political formations, 269
variation, 247, 249
reservation, 101*n*2, 203, 274
communal, 56, 179, 262, 270
in educational institutions and Union government services, 124
Richman, Paula, 124
Rousseau, Jean-Jacques, 82, 160, 189
Ryerson, Charles, 64–65, 67–72, 82

samanyargal, commoners, 10
Sambamurti, Bulusu, 159, 162
Sampath, E. V. K., 4, 61*n*4, 99, 185–186, 189, 193–194, 197, 200*n*11, 210–212, 214, 227, 252, 254
Sanghata Socialist Party, 6, 256
Sanskrit, 21, 26–30, 36, 39*n*11, 44, 49, 53, 57, 65, 70, 108, 125, 127, 130, 133–134, 137, 141, 143, 208, 220–222, 225–227
Santhanam, K., 224–225
Sarkar, Jadunath, 107–109, 111, 122*n*2
satyagraha, 95, 120
Savarkar, V. D., 25–26, 180
Schmitt, Carl, 7, 259–260, 264, 266
Seenivasan, P., 231
self-immolation, 41, 45, 74–75, 177, 228, 230
Self-Respect Movement, 1, 9, 12, 14*n*2, 22, 33, 35–36, 45, 57, 66, 71, 80, 123, 129, 145, 180, 182, 188, 201, 221, 262, 270
Senguntha Mudaliars, 182
Sethu Samudram Canal Project, 126
Sethupillai, R. P., 132–134, 150
Shaiva Siddhanta, 44, 61*n*6, 67, 75, 82
Shaivism, 36, 62*n*6, 65, 69, 71, 129, 135, 220
Shankar Ram, 273–274
Shanmugam Chettiar, R. K., 180
Shanmugam, P. U., 190
Shanmugam, T. K., 106, 122*n*1
Shanmugasundaram, A. P., 158*n*4, 272
Shastri, Lal Bahadur, 229, 233, 256
Shivaji (Maratha emperor), 107–109, 111–121, 150
Shukla, Ravi Shankar, 224
Siddha tradition, 83
Siegel, James, 59–60
Singaravelar, 85
Singh, Naraynan (also Udumalai Narayanan and Pa. Na. Udumalai), 163, 194, 200, 204
Singh, Tej (also Desingu Rajan), 194
Singh, V. P., 124
Sitrarasu, C. P., 187, 189
Sivalingam (self-immolator), 230
sovereign/sovereignty, 6–7, 12, 15*n*10, 19, 31–35, 37, 43, 47, 52, 108, 111–112, 114–120, 150–151, 192, 215, 218–219, 256, 259–261, 275*n*1
axis, 51, 262, 264, 267, 271
becoming, 7, 113
Hindu, 109
fragmented, 72
nation-state, 12, 38, 181
popular, 7, 15*n*11, 88–90, 92, 94, 268, 276*n*6
Soviet Russia, 81
Spratt, Philip, 85–87, 89, 96, 101*n*1
Sri Lanka, 11, 92, 125–126, 170
Stalin, Josef, 94–95
Stalin, Muthuvelar Karunanidhi, 95
subaltern/subalternity/subaltern aspiration, 3, 37, 61*n*3, 72, 105, 162, 165, 181, 276
aspirations, 264
audience, 173
energy, 14, 57, 75, 89, 181, 212
politics of, 218–221
positions, 263

uprisings, 234
Subramaniam, C., 233, 272
Subramanian, K. N., 126
Subramanian, Narendra, 178, 257*n*3, 258, 267, 269–271
Subramanian, T. V., 35
Subramanya Mudaliar, V. P., 133
Sudra (also Shudra), 26–27, 29–32, 51, 108–109, 111–117, 119, 156
Suyamariyathai–Samatharmam, 96
Swami Vivekananda, 29, 221
Swarajya (journal), 86
Swatantra Party, 5–6, 48, 86, 94, 254–256, 264–267
synecdoche, synecdochic, 54, 56, 63, 72, 241

Tagore, Rabindranath, 130, 221–222
Tamil, 3, 8–10, 19–20, 22, 27–30, 37–38, 39*n*11, 41, 54–55, 58, 61*n*5, *n*6, 63, 66, 71, 73, 79, 83, 91–92, 100, 105–107, 109–110, 121, 122*n*3, 125–126, 128–139, 144–145, 147, 150, 153, 157*n*1, 159–165, 173*n*2, *n*4, 179, 181–182, 194–195, 199, 202, 210, 217, 220–222, 230, 237, 238*n*6, 241, 243, 252–253, 258, 265, 268–269, 272–274
devotion, 42–46, 48–49, 74
as empty signifier, 50–53, 90
language, 13, 15*n*8, 20, 23, 31, 40, 56, 68–69, 188, 228
nation, 42–43
nationalism, 48, 62*n*8, 64, 68, 72, 271
nationalists, 11, 56, 63
performing, 58–61
purists, 36
Shaivism, 36, 57
Tamil Desiya Katchi (Tamil Nationalist Party), 61*n*4, 99
Tamil Eelam, 12
Tamil Nadu, 3–4, 6, 8–9, 11, 14*n*4, 19–21, 25–26, 30–34, 40–41, 43–44, 46, 48–51, 53–54, 56, 58, 61*n*1, *n*6, 63, 65–66, 68–70, 72–75, 80, 83, 83*n*3, 85–87, 89, 91–92, 95–96, 98–99, 107, 109, 127–129, 135–136, 141, 143, 150, 153, 156, 162, 166–167, 169, 178, 194, 202, 206, 212, 217–218, 220–221, 226–227, 229–233, 235, 237, 241, 245, 247–252, 254–256, 257*n*4, 258–259, 261–262, 264, 266–271
Tamil Socialist Forum, 24
Tamil Thai, 44, 66
Tamizhan (journal), 261
Tandon, Purushottam Das, 224
Taylor, Charles, 63–64, 67, 73–83, 83*n*1, 84*n*9, 177
Telugu, 22, 54, 56, 159–160, 230, 253, 271
Tennyson, Alfred Lord, 139
Thalamuthu, 222
Thapar, Romila, 143–144
The Lord of Justice Fainted! (*Nītitēvaṉ Mayakkam*) (play), 137, 150–153
Theni assault, 234
Thennarasu, S. S., 165
Thenral (journal), 198
thinai, 28–29, 39*n*10
Thirukkural Kazhagam, 188
Thirukkural Thenappan, 188
Thirunavukkarasu, 39*n*14, 273–274
Thiruvalluvar, 129–131, 190
Thoothukudi conspiracy case, 211
three-front struggle, 203, 209–213
Tī Paravaṭṭum (Let the Fire Spread), 123, 129
Tirukkuṟaḷ, 129, 131, 188
Tirumantiram, 67, 81–82
Tirumular, 67

Toilers party, 251–252
Tolkāppiyam, 28
Tolstoy, 190
tradition, great tradition, little tradition, 65, 70, 73
transcendental (also transcendence), 7, 82, 114, 116, 177, 182–183, 275
transcendental immanence, 82
Trautman, Thomas R., 38*n*4, 44
Tulsi Das, 126
Turner, Victor, 65

Union of States, 239
universal adult franchise, 9, 11, 31, 64, 89–90, 179, 221, 240, 257
Urdu, 220–223

Vaishnavism, 65, 126, 129, 135
Vaitheespara, Ravi, 61–62*n*6, 64, 71–72
Valmiki, 123, 125, 127–128, 133, 153
Vanan, P., 185
Vandaiyar, Poondi, 251
Varna system/Varna dharma, 29, 50, 117, 143, 270
Vasan, S. S., 128, 164
Vedas, 28–29, 108, 142–143, 146
Vēlaikkāri (film), 107
Vellala, 44, 51, 57, 72, 82
  Shaivites, 53, 71, 156, 164
Venkatachalapathy, A. R., 71, 200*n*5, 219
Venkatraman, M. R., 274
Vethanaik Kural (play), 207
Viduthalai (newspaper), 32, 106
Vietnam, 77
  self-immolation of Buddhist monks in, 228
Villalan, Thillai, 164, 207
Vishnu (godhead, also Perumal), 126–127, 130, 136, 142, 145–146, 149, 154, 272

Wakankar, Milind, 124, 140*n*1, 276*n*1
war of maneuver, 96, 120
war of positions, 96, 120–121, 122*n*8
"We Tamils" movement of Adithanar (political organization), 43
Wilkie, Wendel, 38, 76
Workers and Peasants Party (WPP), 85, 95